Money over Mastery, Family over Freedom

STUDIES IN EARLY AMERICAN ECONOMY AND SOCIETY
FROM THE LIBRARY COMPANY OF PHILADELPHIA

Cathy Matson, *Series Editor*

Money over Mastery, Family over Freedom

Slavery in the Antebellum Upper South

Calvin Schermerhorn

The Johns Hopkins University Press
Baltimore

© 2011 The Johns Hopkins University Press
All rights reserved. Published 2011
Printed in the United States of America on acid-free paper
9 8 7 6 5 4 3 2 1

The Johns Hopkins University Press
2715 North Charles Street
Baltimore, Maryland 21218-4363
www.press.jhu.edu

Library of Congress Cataloging-in-Publication Data

Schermerhorn, Calvin, 1975–
    Money over mastery, family over freedom : slavery in the antebellum upper
South / Calvin Schermerhorn.
        p.   cm. — (Studies in early American economy and society)
    Includes bibliographical references and index.
    ISBN-13: 978-1-4214-0035-8 (hardcover : alk. paper)
    ISBN-13: 978-1-4214-0036-5 (pbk. : alk. paper)
    ISBN-10: 1-4214-0035-9 (hardcover : alk. paper)
    ISBN-10: 1-4214-0036-7 (pbk. : alk. paper)
    1. Slavery—Chesapeake Bay Region (Md. and Va.)—History—19th century.
2. Slavery—Economic aspects—Chesapeake Bay Region (Md. and Va.)—
History—19th century. 3. Slaves—Family relationships—Chesapeake Bay
Region (Md. and Va.)—History—19th century. 4. Slave trade—Chesapeake
Bay Region (Md. and Va.)—History—19th century. 5. Slave trade—Southern
States—History—19th century. 6. African American families—Chesapeake Bay
Region (Md. and Va.)—Social conditions—History—19th century. 7. Plantation
life—Chesapeake Bay Region (Md. and Va.)—History—19th century. I. Title.
    E445.M3S45 2011
    975.5'1803—dc22   2010046799

A catalog record for this book is available from the British Library.

*Special discounts are available for bulk purchases of this book. For more information,
please contact Special Sales at 410-516-6936 or specialsales@press.jhu.edu.*

The Johns Hopkins University Press uses environmentally friendly book
materials, including recycled text paper that is composed of at least 30 percent
post-consumer waste, whenever possible. All of our book papers are acid-free,
and our jackets and covers are printed on paper with recycled content.

Contents

Series Editor's Foreword

*I*n this new title in Studies in Early American Economy and Society, a collaborative enterprise between the Johns Hopkins University Press and the Library Company of Philadelphia's Program in Early American Economy and Society (PEAES), Calvin Schermerhorn explores North America's oldest reproducing slave society. *Money over Mastery, Family over Freedom: Slavery in the Antebellum Upper South* explores how slave families in the region coped with the brutal reality of sale and forced migration into the developing cotton and sugar regions in the South and Southwest.

Having been part of an economic culture that for generations had incorporated the skilled and agricultural labor of slaves into both plantation development *and* wage-paying enterprises, slaves in the Chesapeake and coastal North Carolina were familiar with nonplantation markets as well as the power of masters to command their labor at will, on and off plantations. In post-Revolutionary America, slaves continued to play a crucial role in the booming interregional and international markets for cotton and sugar. However, slaves rarely were able to take control over their individual or collective economic destinies, and when Chesapeake planters began to sell large numbers of their slaves into the great maws of "King Cotton" and sugar production, they made manifest their power in slaves' lives. Schermerhorn finds that when they were sent into the breach of forced migrations, slaves struggled mightily to protect vulnerable kin from sales that tore families apart by using the very market that sought to separate them.

Slaves could do so by various means. Most importantly, Schermerhorn argues, rather than resist outright the system of slavery, many slaves grasped at opportunities to preserve and expand "families." Great numbers of slave families incorporated nonblood kin, which provided a shelter against forced sales for myriad individuals. Slaves also cultivated networks of patrons and informal allies who could help keep kin out of slave markets. Female slaves became wives and companions to slave traders to shield themselves and their kin from innumerable brutalities. Slaves of all occupational backgrounds accumulated small property, rented relatives, or purchased family members with credit in order to prevent forced separations.

Time after time, slaves who were confronted with the unthinkable departure of loved ones used various strategies to preserve family under slavery. As Schermerhorn reveals, slaves consistently chose to muster resources to protect family rather than to flee toward individual freedom. Slave families in the Chesapeake forged relationships, sometimes fleeting ones, with slaveholders, slave traders, employers, and sympathetic white people in cash and wage economies, which amounted to their making strategic decisions to compromise with the slave market in order to preserve families, as defined and shaped by slaves, from the horrors of forced separations. As a result, slaves' own agency in the revitalization of the Chesapeake and coastal North Carolina during the early republic years, which served the interests of masters and internal improvers, became a source of strength and means of endurance for slave families.

Schermerhorn's meticulously researched and intelligently argued study is admirably suited to the ongoing efforts of PEAES to reach across scholarly disciplines and methodologies and to promote discussion of the early American economy in the broadest terms possible.

Cathy Matson
Professor of History, University of Delaware
Director, Program in Early American Economy and Society,
Library Company of Philadelphia

Money over Mastery, Family over Freedom

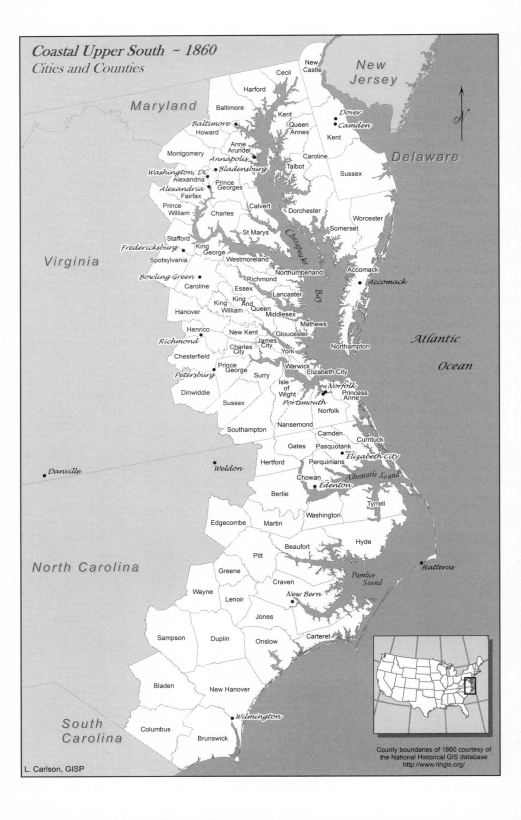

Coastal Upper South ~ 1860
Cities and Counties

New Jersey

Maryland

Delaware

Virginia

Atlantic
Ocean

North Carolina

South
Carolina

L. Carlson, GISP

County boundaries of 1860 courtesy of
the National Historical GIS database
http://www.nhgis.org/

Prologue

merican slavery was an intricate dance between forced labor and the forces of modernity. This book explores the redevelopment of the coastal region of the upper South from the turn of the nineteenth century to the beginning of the Civil War through the lives of the enslaved people who built it. The enslaved men and women whose life dramas populate the following pages were put to work building the future of the region and with it the future of slavery. The men, women, and children enslaved in the early American republic participated in one of the largest forced migrations in modern history, one that supplied the workforce that underwrote agricultural revolutions in the lower south of an expanding continental empire. In the Chesapeake and coastal North Carolina, new employments for enslaved people in growing urban areas and in transportation trades held out opportunities for them to develop strategies to keep vulnerable family members out of the coffles into which their friends and relatives regularly disappeared. With tragic irony, enslaved people sought to use the changing market that was responsible for slavery's new commercial vitality to defend themselves from market-made separations. Cotton and sugar exports may have been the engine of the U.S. slave trade and responsible for much of its economic might, but the enslaved people left behind in all that commerce and commotion—the subjects whose ordeals are represented here—were absorbed into a dynamic, adaptive, and commercial landscape where staple crop agriculture was increasingly losing out to alternative means of making slavery pay.[1] From the point of view of the enslaved, changes in the American landscape looked very different than for slaveholders at the intersection of an expanding political nation and a far-flung network of customers hungry for slave-produced commodities. For the enslaved, any conception of bondage involving paternalistic ties between slaveholders and slaves crumbled under the weight of the reality that slaveholders broke up families for profit, not merely in the abstract, but literally. Instead of cotton or sugar, their children, sisters, and brothers were prime commodities. Consequently, their primary endeavor was to construct networks to protect families in the middle of one of the most destructive and sustained devaluations of kin and affinal bonds in the history of the modern world. For seventy years in the antebellum South, enslavers used the success of African American families and their reproduction as the fuel for a pair of modernization processes. They moved and sold enslaved people, especially young men and women, to the cotton and sugar frontiers, where enslavers, many of them members of white Maryland, Virginia, and North Carolina families, were creating an astonishingly dynamic zone of agricultural commodity production. At the same time, in the upper South itself, enslavers were modernizing what at the turn of the nineteenth century had been a superannuated plantation society. They were turning it into a diversified modern economy of varied commodity production, processing, transportation, and commerce. At the heart of those processes were African American families who struggled against the odds, using local economic transformations to keep loved ones from being bound away to the punishing fields of snowy lint and woody cane.

⌇⌇⌇

By the early decades of the nineteenth century, the old tobacco-producing region that had once been a model for British and French North American colonial development was exporting people in addition to plants. Because the new lands in the southwest were part of one political nation whose government outlawed international slave immigration in 1808, upper South slave owners thereafter held a legal monopoly on supplying bound labor to a growing plantation system that relied on it. On lands that once had produced the bulk of the region's tobacco exports, enslaved people cultivated grains and foodstuffs, which required less labor. Those who came of age after the American Revolution began to see their children put to work in a variety of occupations, which scattered individuals within the region. Slaves were increasingly the backbone of the commercial processing and transportation trades—they played, for example, a critical role in the construction of railroads south of the Potomac River. Enslaved women performed the domestic drudgery for the town and urban middle classes and gave birth to the next generation of the enslaved.[2]

Plantations were made for slaves, not slaves for plantations. Increased local mobility meant that to an enslaved person there was little enduring distinction between slavery as an urban or rural phenomenon or between agricultural and nonagricultural slavery. Boys and girls hired to work in a city alongside their mothers might return to a farm, for instance, when they reached an age at which their agricultural work would become profitable to the slaveholder. Children put to work in fields or pastures at six or seven, about the time they learned to follow directions, might end up processing tobacco, constructing ships, or plying trade routes on wagons or canal boats in adulthood. Conversely, a skilled tobacco or dockworker could be sold south on reaching adulthood to toil in the cotton or sugar fields of the lower South. A dispute among owners, or the death of one, might precipitate a move from city to country or vice versa. In the antebellum redevelopment of the Chesapeake and coastal North Carolina, even farm workers who never left the county of their birth could expect to be hired out to perform nonfarm labor such as canal or railroad construction and maintenance. Those circumstances were the incremental results of broad changes in the landscape.[3]

At the turn of the nineteenth century, some Tidewater grandees complained that their holdings in slave families were making them poor. Growing black families supposedly cost them money in food, shelter, and clothing. A generation and a half later, there were few such complaints. By the 1830s, Chesapeake merchants and processors of goods became large slaveholders (or renters), and slaves not needed on farms were put to work in factories. African American families paid the price. Enslaved families not separated through the slave trade felt the strain of family separation when loved ones disappeared to cities to manipulate the tobacco and other raw commodities their ancestors had once grown.[4]

Geographically, the coastal upper South comprised the plain east of the fall line from the Delaware Bay southward to the mouth of the Cape Fear River. The terrain connected through common experiences of the enslaved supported local natural diversity. The forested coastal flatlands of Delaware sat atop sandy soil. As in other parts of the Chesapeake, seventeenth- and eighteenth-century settlers carved the land up into plantations and rotated fields rather than crops. By the time of the Revolution, tobacco cultivation waned as Delawareans diversified agriculture. An early nineteenth-century observer wrote that wheat "grows here in such perfection as not only to be particularly sought by the manufacturers of flour throughout the union, but also to be distinguished and preferred for its superior qualities in foreign markets." Delawareans also grew barley, buckwheat, corn, flax, oats, potatoes, and rye. They raised sheep for wool and, like wheat flour, the linsey-woolsey that slave women spun from wool and flax in the southern part of the state reached out-of-state markets.[5]

In neighboring Maryland, the seasons were "well marked but not severe." Besides black and white oak, beech, walnut, and chestnut, forests abounded in hickory, white ash, yellow locust, and often-towering tulip poplars. Bald cypress, with its stalagmite knees, thrust up through shallow swamps, and tall grasses radiated upward from marshy banks. Where the forest broke on fields, honeysuckles bloomed in summer, and locals had to beware of the poison ivy that grew up promiscuously side by side with benign vines like Virginia creeper. Brambles of blackberries and raspberries also flourished.[6] Sometimes the natural landscape could be cozening. "Several old logs and stumps imposed upon me, and got themselves taken for wild beasts," Frederick Douglass remembered of the eastern Maryland woodlands he encountered as a child. "I could see their legs, eyes, and ears, or I could see something like eyes, legs, and ears, till I got close enough to them to see that the eyes were knots, washed white with rain, and the legs were broken limbs, and the ears, only ears owing to the point from which they were seen." In the bright of day, the landscape could be magnificent.[7]

The Chesapeake Bay, the world's largest natural estuary, was part of an interconnected series of waterways along its forty-six hundred miles of tidal shoreline in Maryland and Virginia. The "great shellfish bay," or "great waters," as the Algonquin peoples had known the Chesapeake, had formed some twelve thousand years before when a great ice sheet melted flooding the Susquehanna River Valley. By the nineteenth century, the shimmering waters were a panorama of human activity. Douglass recalled from the "lofty banks of that noble bay" that its "broad bosom was ever white with sails from every quarter of the habitable globe."[8] Douglass surveyed the northern reaches of the bay from his Eastern Shore vantage point. There, with its sandy beds of oysters, clams, and blue crabs, the bay was narrow and shallow except for the spot where the ancient Susquehanna had cut a deep central channel. Striped bass and sturgeon were among the denizens of those deeper, colder waters. Douglass's assessments of inland waterways suggest a less salutary environment. "Decay and ruin," characterized the Choptank River region, he remembered, and from that river, locals caught an "abundance of shad and herring, and plenty of ague and fever."[9]

The Virginia Tidewater, south of the Maryland Chesapeake, was composed of a "broad belt of undulating and river-gashed plain" bordering the eastern seaboard of Virginia to North Carolina. The lower stretches of those rivers were "great estuaries" of fish and shellfish, which drained into that broader, deeper section of the Chesapeake Bay. The lower Chesapeake was fed by several rivers flowing east from the Blue Ridge Mountains, including the Potomac, the Rappahannock, the York, and the James. Waters on the western shore were less saline than the eastern shores of the bay, and home to a greater abundance of marine life as a result. That landscape influenced the human environment by providing abundant avenues for transportation and with it commerce, especially in the deepwater ports of Baltimore and in the bay's southern reaches.[10]

Like Maryland's climate, that of the Virginia Chesapeake was seasonal and mild, lacking the more severe winters to the north and the "debilitating summer heat" of lands to the south. The growing season lasted about 200 days, and the land saw sunshine about 258 days of the year. The farther south one traveled the more pine woods appeared among the oaks, ashes, and other hardwoods. In spring, abundant redbuds and dogwoods bloomed in clusters. As fields gave way to brackish marshlands and swamps, marsh grass appeared in waves of green.[11] The enslaved recalled the tributaries of the Chesapeake and eastern North Carolina as blessed with an abundance of fish in season. The Roanoke River "was shallow and the bed rocky," recalled Virginia native Henry Goings. "During the month of August the slaves would frequently be put to fishing with nets. Rock fish were as fine in size as they were abundant in quantity. I have seen some specimens weighing from sixty to seventy pounds."[12]

Coastal North Carolina shared some of the Virginia Tidewater's characteristic geography, including a flat, forested plain giving way to stretches of swampy coastline, varying from thirty to eighty miles wide between the coast and the fall line, where the rivers were no longer navigable to oceangoing vessels. But North Carolina's coastal terrain was less hospitable to overland transport than the Chesapeake and included swampy no-man's-lands into which hundreds, if not thousands, of slaves disappeared in the first half of the nineteenth century. The northern reaches of North Carolina's archipelago of wetlands formed the Great Dismal Swamp, which spanned the border of Virginia and North Carolina. It had a particular reputation for sheltering fugitive slaves. Harriet Beecher Stowe set her third novel there and used its distinctive geography as a stage on which Dred, the title character patterned on Nat Turner, preached revolution from comparative safety. Nearby, "multitudes of slaves" worked out of sight of their employers making barrel staves or shingles from the cypress, cedars, and other trees that were useful in shipbuilding and in manufacturing naval stores.[13] To the south, swamps called pocosins or dismals occupied areas between rivers and sounds. There travelers encountered a variety of snakes and the occasional alligator. To the east of that maze of swamps and sounds were barrier islands, later known as the Outer Banks, of sand dunes, some only a foot or two above tide level and at some places about one hundred feet. Between those sand dune banks and the swampy coast a connected series of ship-navigable sounds, including Albemarle (which bordered the colonial capital of Edenton) and Pamlico, connected an intercoastal waterway spanning the state's 320 miles of coastline. As Stowe's characterizations suggest, local economies varied according to the landscape, but the lives of the enslaved were connected through family and friends, which in turn linked neighborhood to neighborhood and county to county.[14]

In the maze of swamps, rivers, bays, and backwaters of the Carolina coast, enslaved people were able to form maroon communities. After a 1788 robbery of a Wilmington merchant, authorities discovered that there "appeared to have been a long camp or asylum for runaway negroes" along a creek that flowed into the Cape Fear River.[15] The runaways managed to relieve the merchant of "a hogshead of tobacco, a hogshead of molasses, and two barrels of beef," a crime for which a man named Peter, who had absented himself from his owner, was later tried and executed.[16] The diversified economy, coastal locations, and proximity to navigable water gave enslaved people great mobility, and in later generations, coastal North Carolina slaveholders would deploy slaves in riverine and maritime trades extensively.[17]

Until the Revolution, tobacco cultivation had been the mainstay of the Chesapeake and coastal North Carolina colonies. Whether they directed its planting and enjoyed its profits or suffered under the summer sun cultivating it, nearly everyone in the colonial Chesapeake agreed that "tobacco is our meat, drinke, cloathing and monie." The rise of tobacco processing in the early nineteenth century as tobacco cultivation declined was one part of a diversification of slave labor that stratified the ranks of enslaved people's occupations, giving skilled slaves some chance at defending family relations and making it increasingly unlikely that less skilled slaves could do the same. The enslaved people who manipulated tobacco in nineteenth-century factories held in their hands one means of property accumulation and along with it the chance to keep slave traders' hands off their loved ones. Their world bore scant resemblance to that of their ancestors who had cultivated tobacco along the banks of rivers and estuaries of the seventeenth- and especially eighteenth-century Chesapeake and coastal North Carolina.[18]

The story of slave labor in the coastal upper South began with tobacco cultivation and the Atlantic markets that sustained staple crop production. Chesapeake tobacco cultivators remade the landscape in the seventeenth and eighteenth centuries, driving bound laborers to hack fields out of forests. By the mid-eighteenth century, the architects of a tobacco kingdom had created a highly stratified and self-reproducing society augmented by newcomers from Europe, Africa, and the Caribbean. Beginning in the seventeenth century, European demand for the "sot weed" sustained the development of the lands surrounding the bay and Carolina sounds. Indentured servants and later African slaves grew the crop, and the planters, shippers, merchants, and middlemen who took it to market relied on tobacco as cash, paying their taxes with it and demanding it as payment when citizens ran afoul of the law.[19]

Colonial coastal North Carolina planters cultivated tobacco but not to the extent of their Chesapeake neighbors. From the middle of the eighteenth century to the eve of the American Revolution, North Carolina showed "extremely low density patterns of its black population, by far the lowest in the South," which was the result of "relatively late settlement" and an "immature slave economy, with its diversified production of tobacco, lumber products, naval stores, grains, and provisions." Men outnumbered women by "about one-third during the last fifteen years of the colonial period," and North Carolina slaveholders bought tens of thousands of Africans in the twenty years before the American Revolution. Fewer African American families formed as a result, compared to in the Chesapeake. The enslaved produced goods that were as often consumed or resold in other colonies as in North Carolina. Half of its tobacco and foodstuffs, including corn and livestock, for instance, was transported overland to other colonies for sale. English planters aggrandized coastal lands and built large plantations, but the coastal geography, including forbidding shoals along the barrier islands, made the commercial centers of Norfolk, Virginia, and Charles Town, South Carolina, more attractive to slavers and merchants. Following the Revolution, large planters like Josiah Collins of Washington County, North Carolina, continued to import slaves directly from Africa, and the southern city of Wilmington, on the Cape Fear River, became an important entrepôt for tobacco and other exports.[20]

Although the colonial tobacco regime was punishing to workers, the Chesapeake was the womb of the African diaspora in eighteenth-century British North America. Since the late seventeenth century, Chesapeake slaveholders had bought men and women from Atlantic slavers in roughly equal proportions (not because of their foresight but because African slaving strategies furnished males and females in roughly equal proportions during critical moments in the formation of the Chesapeake tobacco complex). After the 1720s, the enslaved population increased through natural reproduction. When Tidewater planters shifted from tobacco cultivation requiring gangs of laborers to mixed grain and fruit agriculture in the upland Piedmont in the last quarter of the eighteenth century, they needed fewer laborers from among the rapidly reproducing enslaved population. These enslaved workers were members of American families deeply imbued with the religion and culture they helped to make.[21]

By the first decades of the nineteenth century, enslaved families in the Chesapeake had roots often several generations deep. Douglass's African-descended ancestors had lived on Maryland's Eastern Shore since the first decade of the eighteenth century. His great-great-grandfather Baly had arrived in Talbot County, on the Eastern Shore of Maryland, by 1701. By the late eighteenth century, branches of those families were large and growing. Douglass's grandmother Betsey, born in 1774, had her first child at sixteen in 1790 and her last at age forty-six, in 1820. Douglass, born Frederick Augustus Washington Bailey in 1818, was the fifth generation of Baileys to have lived there. Although Douglass recalled interacting with "slaves there who had been brought from the coast of Africa" to Maryland as children, importations of enslaved people from Africa and the Caribbean declined as new generations of enslaved Americans came of age, despite a surge in imports in the last decade before the United States curtailed the foreign trade. In the latter half of the eighteenth century, however, African American families in the Chesapeake were being disrupted by planter migration to the Piedmont. There the distance was often too great for family members to maintain regular contact.[22]

Perhaps because they achieved social reproduction independently by the middle of the eighteenth century, British North Americans began to see themselves increasingly as a culture of independence.[23] By the time of the American Revolution, Chesapeake slaveholders prided themselves on having constructed a society ordered through white deference and black servitude. Scholars looking back on that history have viewed putative class antagonisms as having been dissolved in ostensible racial solidarity. Ambitious middling and even landless whites could imagine their sons' slaveholding futures and identified more with inclinations to limit citizenship—to make more citizen-slaveholders—than to open it up and extend a political franchise to those lacking property. Although Virginia became a hotbed of radicalism during the Revolution, and Virginians were instrumental in weaving a language of political liberty and equality into the cause for independence, the founding ideals did not cause slaveholders to stumble over their financial ambitions.[24]

Their slave-supported social order survived the Revolution, though a few Virginia slaveholders agonized over whether and how to emancipate their slaves. But by the conclusion of the American War of Independence even Virginia Quakers, who had independent religious reasons for opposing slavery, could not quite free themselves from slave ownership. Despite railing at the Atlantic slave trade, the Pleasants family of the upper James River in Virginia, for example, practiced only selective manumission. Echoing a popular view of the relationship between the international slave trade and North American slavery, Robert Pleasants of Goochland County wrote to fellow Quaker Robert Pemberton of Philadelphia that "if success should attend the unabated endeavours which are using in Gt Britain & France, for abolishing the odious traffic to Africa, the evil root of Slavery will be extirpated, and of course the poisonous branch must gradually decay." Pleasants was not merely a passive advocate for abolition. Declaring that "freedom is the natural right of all mankind and that no Law Moral or divine has given me a right to or property in the persons of any of my fellow creatures," Pleasants freed twenty-seven enslaved boys and girls in November 1781. Also motivated by "Natural Right of all mankind," Mary Pleasants of the same county set free "five Negroes," young and old, on the Fourth of July in 1781. Yet the Pleasants family could not let go of slavery completely. They unburdened themselves of the young and very old but were silent on the manumission of slaves of working age. The twenty-seven enslaved boys and girls and five elderly and very young slaves had fathers and mothers, sons and daughters, siblings and cousins still in bondage, whose work carried the Pleasants family fortunes. Despite their Revolutionary ferment and momentary break with custom and economic calculation, the Pleasants family, like nearly all other Virginia planters, quickly resumed slaving, advertising for the sale of slaves in 1800 and receiving proceeds from slave sales by the 1820s. Slaving seems to have been a component of the national soul or, as historian David Brion Davis contends, in a similar register, "racial exploitation and racial conflict have been part of the DNA of American culture."[25]

Although planters complained of soil exhaustion, tobacco cultivators in the Chesapeake shifted their production away from a colonial staple crop economy to one that better supported their evolving interests as independent market actors in an expanding commercial republic. Natural increases in the enslaved population and a "mania for western emigration" to the southwest created a seeming surplus of enslaved laborers by the time the Caribbean sugar complex expanded to the North American continent during the Haitian Revolution. Meanwhile, planters working to profit from cotton cultivation, which was labor-intensive, looked to the Chesapeake for a supply of captive workers. Unlike in the southern interior, cotton did not grow particularly well in the Chesapeake, but to slaveholders' ways of thinking slaves did. From old American families they selected the young and able, fit and fertile, for sale and transport out of the Chesapeake and coastal North Carolina.[26] The forced migration that began in earnest in the final decade of the eighteenth century was not quite a "Second Middle Passage," but the descendents of Africans landed on the shores of British North America could look on the ports cities of the upper South as not unlike Bonny, Calabar, and other slaving ports in the Bight of Biafra. Cities with names evoking an English colonial past—

Annapolis, Baltimore, Norfolk, and Richmond—became entrepôts of a great American forced migration.[27]

By the end of the first decade of the nineteenth century, Virginians and North Carolinians especially were reasserting control over the people they claimed to own. Racial boundaries were also hardening, even if the population of people with both European and African ancestors was expanding. There were enough enslaved people whose light skin tones revealed European or Native American ancestry that those without evident European antecedents were noteworthy. Virginia native John Brown recalled, as a child, meeting his Igbo grandfather "when he came to visit my mother." Compared to most enslaved people, Brown recalled, "he was very black."[28] The unions between slaveholders and enslaved women, consensual or not, produced a significant number of enslaved migrants who embodied a multiethnic American society and were shipped in large numbers out of the Chesapeake and coastal North Carolina. That "landscape of sexual violence" was mapped on the social geography of the antebellum South.[29]

The likelihood of family separation increased following the War of 1812. In each decade between 1820 and 1860, slaves' forced migration from the Virginia Tidewater, for instance, hovered at above 20 percent of the enslaved population and peaked at about 30 percent in the 1830s. The sheer volume and prevalence of the trade meant that enslaved people had to prepare to lose a family member every decade. Assuming that extended kin networks averaged fifty people, every family in the area might lose ten members in half a generation. That environment influenced how those who avoided sale and removal gathered and allocated resources.[30]

Forced migration was incipient and multigenerational, and it terrified those susceptible to it. On the plantation on which Douglass first became conscious of slavery of as institution, he recalled that "scarcely a month passed without the sale of one or more" of his fellow bondspeople to slave traders. Curiously, "there was no apparent diminution in the number of [the owner's] human stock: the home plantation merely groaned at a removal of the young increase, or human crop, then proceeded as lively as ever."[31] Douglass noticed a key aspect of that process. Slaveholders sold off those they deemed surplus yet did not utterly destroy families. By reforming family ties and reproducing, enslaved people increased their numbers, and sometimes at a rapid pace, in the face of regular removals. American law and custom made children born of an enslaved mother slaves themselves, which put slaveholders in the position of being able to profit from enslaved women's fertility. The transformation of slavery in the Chesapeake took place in the shadow of a market in which enslaved people lost relatives in every generation. Slaveholders in Douglass's native Talbot County removed (or, less often, manumitted) enslaved people in large proportions between 1790 and 1860. (Manumitted slaves in Maryland made up a steadily increasing percentage of the population, and many free people of African descent in Maryland migrated voluntarily from states with more punitive antiblack laws.)[32] Between 1800 and 1810, 25 percent of Talbot County's slave population disappeared (this percentage includes those sold, those who migrated with owners, and those manumitted). By the 1810s, 32 percent had disappeared. And by the 1820s, when Douglass made his observations, 43 percent had disappeared. The demographic trend continued until the eve of the Civil War, with Talbot County slaveholders selling off or otherwise disposing of 36 percent of the slave population in the 1830s, which was the height of the slave trade and U.S. domestic migration. In the 1840s another 14 percent disappeared, and another 33 percent disappeared when the slave trade surged again in the 1850s. Yet for all that human disruption—sales, removals, and shattered families—the slave population fell from 4,777 counted in 1790 (36.5 percent of the county's population) to 3,725 slaves in 1860 (just over 25 percent in absolute numbers). That was not atypical in the Chesapeake.[33]

Reproduction, as Douglass suggested, sustained the population even during a prolonged catastrophe for African American families. Each generation faced the commerce in people Douglass witnessed, and Talbot County was hardly peculiar in the old tobacco-producing regions of the Maryland and Virginia Chesapeake. In anticipation of such enforced separations, Virginia native Henry "Box" Brown's mother took her son "upon her knee and, pointing to the forest trees which were then being stripped of their foliage by the winds of autumn, would say to me, my son, as yonder leaves are stripped from off the trees of the forest, so are the children of the slaves swept away from them by the hands of cruel tyrants."[34]

As the nation expanded and slaveholders' demand for young American slaves rose, enforced separations began to have adverse effects on enslaved families' ability to reproduce. In the 1830s, the peak decade of forced migration, the natural growth rate among slaves fell to 24.0 percent after having steadily risen between the 1790s and the 1820s. That rate is a stark measure of the family disruption brought about by forced migration, even though it was still high by historical standards, and thus slaveholders were easily able to replenish their stock of saleable property. Fewer children were born to parents whose marriages and unions were increasingly susceptible to termination through dislocation. Fewer children survived in extended families ravished by slaving that removed the most able caregivers. In the 1840s, the natural increase of the slave population rose to 26.5 percent as long-distance forced migration slackened, but in the 1850s, the natural rate of reproduction decreased to 23.4 percent as the interstate slave trade surged ahead again. In the antebellum decades in which American slaveholders developed a fully articulated ethos of domestic slavery, and apologists mounted a full-throated defense of the institution as they imagined it, the domestic lives of slaves themselves suffered, as measured in their reproductive successes.[35]

As a consequence of forced migration, the geographic center of slavery in the United States began to move to the south and west, from Petersburg, Virginia, in 1800 to the western border of Georgia by 1860.[36] Americans separated young, able enslaved people from their families, forcing them to shoulder the new labor burdens, and left behind the very young, the aged, and the infirm. As that process transformed the landscape and political economy of the Tennessee and Mississippi river valleys, its effects rippled through slave quarters back in Virginia, Maryland, and the Carolinas. Madison Jefferson recalled the fear of separation that haunted him as a child: "We have a dread constantly on our minds," the Virginia native recalled, "for we don't know how long master may keep us, nor into whose hands we may fall."[37] As Americans hurried to supply cotton to expanding world markets, wave upon wave of enforced migrants were scattered across the Cumberland Plateau, marched down the crest of the Appalachian Piedmont, or sailed around the Florida peninsula to Mobile, Natchez, or New Orleans. They often entered lands newly vacated by Creeks, Choctaws, Chickasaws, Cherokees, and Seminoles, who were driven west on another terrible American forced migration. With each passing season, enslaved people had ever greater cause to worry that they or their children might be the next to go. "The categories of the trade," argues Michael Tadman, "were almost custom-built to maximize forcible separations." Hiring at a distance was one among many causes of forced separation, but the most enduring was the interstate slave trade and slaveholder migration. When southwestern migration beyond the Appalachians increased substantially in the first two decades of the nineteenth century, enslaved people migrated with owners.[38]

That migration was hardly a family venture, and African American families bore the costs of owners' poor planning or bad luck. Since enslaved people tended to marry partners whose owners were not their own, migration within one plantation "household" did not merely transplant enslaved families. Tidewater Virginia native Henry Goings recalled that his master became infected with the "Western Fever" of his neighbors around 1820. The move from eastern North Carolina to middle Tennessee with a coffle of "460 slaves, including old and young" split up enslaved families. Forced migration, he wrote, "involves not merely the dissolution of life long friendship, but it severs the most sacred ties of domestic relationship. Not only is the child separated from the parent, but not unfrequently the husband is separated from the wife." Successful planters like Goings's owner aggrandized large estates and demanded increasing numbers of people to carve up forests, lay down long furrows, and plant cotton in the soil. "A bankruptcy, a death, or a removal" could "produce a score or two of involuntary divorces."[39]

The location of that recentering of the enslaved population became synonymous with the very activity of slave trading. Charles Ball remembered the "*Georgia trader*" who bought and "kidnapped" him from his native Maryland in the first decade of the nineteenth century. Two decades later, Douglass recalled the specter of the "Georgia trader" who haunted the farms of his first owner's employer. "Without a moment's warning," Douglass recalled, loved ones were "snatched away, and forever sundered" from family. A visitor to Baltimore in 1846 happened upon "a perfect riddle" of "a sign," which read simply, "Hope H. Slatter, from Clinton, Georgia." An inquiry solved the riddle: the Georgian's establishment was a slave detention and trading operation off a major city thoroughfare. Just advertising his home state was signal enough to potential buyers and sellers. Even during the Civil War, "a Georgia man came and bought my brother," Harriet Tubman recalled, adding that quick work by family and friends kept the trader from his purchase.[40]

Rather than being domesticated, slavery was increasingly commercialized, and each new commercial technology presented new challenges and perils for the enslaved. At the beginning of the nineteenth century, the large natural estuary at the center was the hub of a riverine transportation network that made nearly every corner of that area accessible to another. As the decades rolled on, the region got louder, more urban, and more interconnected. The

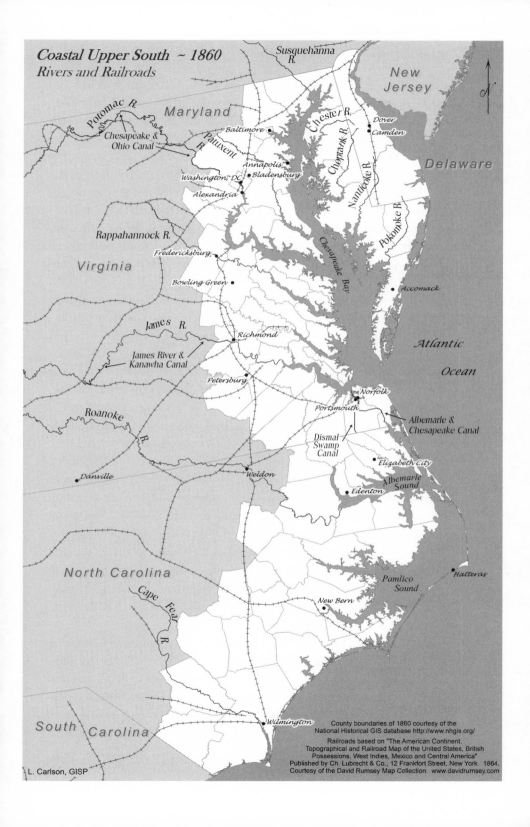

Coastal Upper South ~ 1860
Rivers and Railroads

Susquehanna R.

New Jersey

Potomac R.

Maryland

Chesapeake & Ohio Canal

Patuxent R.

Baltimore

Chester R.

Choptank R.

Dover
Camden

Delaware

Nanticoke R.

Annapolis
Washington, DC *Bladensburg*
Alexandria

Pokomoke R.

Rappahannock R.

Virginia

Fredericksburg

Chesapeake Bay

Bowling Green

Accomack

Atlantic

Ocean

James R.

Richmond

James River & Kanawha Canal

Petersburg

Norfolk
Portsmouth

Albemarle & Chesapeake Canal

Roanoke

Dismal Swamp Canal

Elizabeth City

R.

Danville

Weldon

Albemarle Sound

Edenton

North Carolina

Pamlico Sound

Hatteras

Cape Fear

New Bern

R.

South Carolina

Wilmington

County boundaries of 1860 courtesy of the
National Historical GIS database http://www.nhgis.org/

Railroads based on "The American Continent,
Topographical and Railroad Map of the United States, British
Possessions, West Indies, Mexico and Central America"
Published by Ch. Lubrecht & Co., 12 Frankfort Street, New York. 1864.
Courtesy of the David Rumsey Map Collection. www.davidrumsey.com

L. Carlson, GISP

building of railroads and canals and advances in technology such as the tele-graph sped commerce and communications among urban hubs of Baltimore, Washington, D.C., Richmond, Norfolk, and Wilmington, and from there back into to the hinterland. Urban areas in the region intensified commercial de-velopment by processing commodities such as tobacco, flour, and iron using slave labor. Internal improvements and the transportation revolution in the Chesapeake relied heavily on slave labor as well. Enslaved people dug canals, mined coal, drove wagons, piloted boats, and constructed railroads. Enslaved people's relative lack of social, civic, and economic resources left them in-tensely reliant on one another, which in the context of multigenerational families gave rise to an intense family-anchored spirit of solidarity and mu-tual support.[41]

The modernization of slavery threatened those very bonds that motivated them and on which they depended for psychic survival. Enslaved people's market-centered activities augmented and imbued slave "culture" with im-portant dimension, showing it to be a historical process rather than ances-tral inheritance. The market, which was neither entirely separate from nor arrayed against the broader dynamics of life in the nineteenth-century South, infused enslaved people's culture. Nor were the values and assumptions of the enslaved necessarily at odds with the market. Even on the auction block, enslaved people influenced their sales and took some measure of control back from the people who bought and sold them. The chapters that follow offer a view of what enslaved people did or could do—rather than a description of the conditions to which they merely reacted—before finding themselves on the auction block, at which time it was usually too late to defend blood kin. They won local status but had no portable rights. When the slave trade ex-panded in the cotton boom of the 1810s, intensified again in the 1830s, and surged in the 1850s along with railroad track, the enslaved in the upper South faced more immediate threats to their security than had their grandparents, who lived before Americans conquered the tyranny of distance with steam power and the telegraph.[42]

The market created a few precious opportunities in the course of destroying what did not fit its categories, including families. Commercial intensification gave enslaved people an increasing variety of opportunities to avoid sale and removal, even if it raised the stakes of contests over loved ones. Enslaved peo-ple responded to each new slaveholder strategy to make slavery pay by seizing whatever opportunities they could find to work against the commercial centrifuge in which they increasingly found themselves. They formed networks of patrons and allies, establishing connections with people they encountered in their work growing the crops, navigating the canals, riding the rails, staffing the factories and homes of the coastal upper South. Through networks, the enslaved made use of the material resources they cobbled together, including money, since enslaved people risked being cheated with impunity if they attempted to make contracts to buy or rent loved ones on their own.

Combined with the invisible hand of the market were the visible hands of slave owners, slave traders, and employers, who exposed enslaved people to new markets. The enslaved in turn tried to use those new markets to keep their families together. This was not a process unique to the coastal upper South. Enslaved people elsewhere in the nineteenth-century United States sought to use the market to keep family members from being bound away, but this book investigates how enslaved people used market-based strategies to keep their families together in a place in which historians have explored seventeenth- and eighteenth-century interconnections rather than nineteenth-century commonalities. Recent literature on the slave trade and migration has refocused attention on the differences among slaveholding regions of the United States in the nineteenth century and on the interdependence that complementary regional slaveholding interests cemented. This book looks back at the homelands of the many forced migrants whose history is well told, to the places in which plantation slavery first took hold in British North America.[43]

The transformation did not portend an end to slavery, and despite the numbers of Chesapeake and eastern North Carolina natives forced south, many remained on the eve of the Civil War. By 1860, the census recorded 182,368 slaves in the Virginia Chesapeake's thirty-six counties, just over 41 percent of the population there. Census takers counted 3,185 slaves residing in Washington, D.C., or 4.2 percent of the district's population. There were 81,062 slaves in the Maryland Chesapeake, or 14.6 percent of the population and 1,798 slaves in Delaware, totaling a scant 1.6 percent of that state's population. The census recorded 239,203 people in eastern North Carolina's twenty-seven counties in 1860, including 102,906 slaves or 43 percent of the population. Despite seventy years of slave sales out of state, a total of 380,277 slaves counted in those regions in 1860 made up 27 percent of a total population of just above 1.4 million souls.[44]

The nineteenth-century Chesapeake was at once the oldest site of Anglophone North American slavery and in many respects also the future of the

institution. By the late antebellum decades enslaved people could be seen everywhere laboring in the lower regions of the Chesapeake, a spectacle rivaled
only by the ubiquity of enslaved people marching on roads, riding the rails,
or boarding slaving vessels as property being taken south. Slavery seemed to
be attenuating in the upper reaches of the Chesapeake, but the chances that
an enslaved person would lose a relative to sale were nevertheless increasing.
Seth Rockman argues that because enslaved people's "bodies did not just perform labor, but also stored capital as a highly fungible form of property," slavery was no less viable in the upper Chesapeake on the eve of civil war. Even in
Baltimore, the Chesapeake city with the lowest proportion of enslaved versus
free people of African descent, "the market could serve to entrench slavery as
readily as to undermine it." That was because "distant purchasers on the cotton frontier gave Baltimore slaveholders a powerful incentive to hold firmly
to slavery even after it had been supplanted by other sources of labor."[45] Frederick Douglass knew that, and so did those who claimed the wages he earned
as a skilled self-hired slave. To an enslaved person, a society with slaves was
still a slave society, in which he or she could be bound away at the whim of
an owner. As Edward L. Ayers contends, slavery was slavery right up to the
border and "shaped everything it touched." Maryland and Virginia were no
exceptions. Only in the three counties that composed the state of Delaware
did laws routinely protect enslaved people from being sold out of state, and
the small minority of citizens who were Delaware slave owners clamored for
the lifting of those restrictions during the antebellum period.[46]

    In Atlantic-wide markets, slaveholders and others who deployed slave la-
bor and reaped the profits were not the sole economic and political actors.
Enslaved people constituted the all-but-invisible labor lynchpin of that hemisphere-wide commercial system, but they had some stake in it as well. Slave
hiring and the slave trade were two of three components of a larger, integrated market that reallocated human resources, the third component being
brokered by enslaved people. As enslaved people's implication in the national
political economy deepened, they seized opportunities to use the market for
their own ends. Although scholars have emphasized enslaved families' versa-
tility, they strove to keep family members out of the slave market rather than
to accept their loss as a consequence of forces beyond their control.[47]

    In contests with slaveholders, and when and where they could, most en-
slaved people chose family over freedom. Slaveholders, in turn, chose money
over mastery. As the modernity of slavery worked remorselessly through an

intensifying market hungry for the bodies and labor of slaves, enslaved people sought to defend blood kin from the worst aspects of the market by participating in it. In the pages that follow, I survey how they built networks that allocated resources to defend family ties while they were put to work rebuilding the coastal upper South, replacing its plantation past with its commercially diverse future.

CHAPTER 1

Networkers

o I went out trusting in the Lord," wrote Solomon Bayley of his family's trials, "but I should soon have fainted in mind, if it had not been for the encouragement I met with, both from God and man." That was how the enslaved cooper framed networking. On Virginia's Eastern Shore in the 1790s, he had begun a family of his own after his father and siblings were sold away by a slaveholder who lived across the Chesapeake Bay. He planned to go to court in Delaware, as had his father and siblings, to sue that man for his freedom. Delaware was hearing pleas from slaves like himself who had been taken across state lines against anti-slave-trade laws. But any precipitous action, such as an escape attempt or contact with a lawyer, might leave his wife, Thamar, and his daughter, Margaret, without him, if he were sold in retaliation. Courts were not the sole option. Methodists were then sowing seeds of a new faith, and Thamar's owner was among the converted. Circuit riders were appearing regularly, preaching the good news, and residents saw the work of the Holy Spirit in the spiritual increase that followed. Bayley had been born again too, and he would reach out to fellow Methodists in hopes that they would protect his family from separation. The gospel preaching to which Bayley and so many of his neighbors responded emphasized sin and the urgency of salvation. Many were also moved by antislavery appeals. Bayley worshiped side-by-side with whites on the same spiritual basis, but Thamar's owner clung to his financial interest in human property.[1]

As Bayley and so many others enslaved in the early American republic discovered, God was in the details of their everyday experiences and associations. Slavery was transforming from an institution bounded by plantations and focused on staple crop production into a slave market society in which the enslaved were tied to nearly all available human and material resources. The enslaved were networkers as well as workers. Rather than rely primarily on a network of family, slaves like Bayley integrated themselves into webs of strategic associations and accessed those resources through them. They made strategic plans based on local circumstances and calculations. The coastal upper South of the nineteenth century was rich in human and material resources, but slaves' ability to procure status, security, goods, information, and allies was only as good as the network they cultivated and in which they participated.[2]

The Bayley family had been established on the Delmarva Peninsula since the seventeenth century, yet the local knowledge they had accumulated over the generations did not prepare them for the ordeals they faced in the 1780s and 1790s. Solomon Bayley was born a slave in Delaware about 1770. He had "a religious character, remarkably humble, patient of wrong, poor as to worldly possessions, but rich in faith and in many other christian virtues." "A self-taught penman," he would through his writings relate a succession of strategies he used to cultivate and maintain a network to protect his family. The Kent County native was moved to the Eastern Shore of Virginia by the 1790s, around the time Delaware enacted manumission laws designed to prevent such removals. His ancestors had been Americans for at least three generations, and not long after his removal to Virginia, he had married and was helping raise the fifth generation of American Bayleys.[3]

Like Frederick Douglass's ancestral Bailey family on Maryland's Eastern Shore, the enslaved Bayleys of Delaware and the Virginia Eastern Shore could recall ancestors stolen from Africa. Bayley remembered his great-grandmother as a "Guinea Woman," born around 1679, who survived the Middle Passage, arriving in the Chesapeake around 1690. She became the mother of fifteen children while serving a Virginia family remembered for their abuse. When the owners died, she recalled the "great distress and dispersion" as the property in people was divided among heirs and sold off to meet the financial obligations of the deceased. Some of her descendents were removed to Delaware, including the ancestors of Solomon's father, Abner Bayley.[4]

Networking was a way in which enslaved people like Bayley sought to order their world, and they did so through strategic ties and sets of exchanges. It was a political activity as well as a strategy for survival, and it reveals how the enslaved viewed the world in which they were bought and sold and pushed and pulled about. In contrast to relationships ordered along axes of difference or conflict such as that between slaves and slaveholders, networks allowed slaves to reorder their environment so as to make available human and material resources as well as information under severely constraining circumstances. Exchanges were not usually equitable, and there was little margin for error in dealing with citizens and slaveholders. But associations with patrons or allies could help to mitigate violence, improve working conditions, and establish status. As those associations grew, the potential advantages multiplied, though at any time the precise extent or potential of the network was unknowable, as were its pitfalls and unintended consequences.[5]

Such strategies were bound up with enslaved people's agency, but agency, as Susan E. O'Donovan contends, does not mean winning.[6] In the 1780s, when Solomon Bayley was a young man, the Bayley family, led by his father Abner, was among the first to attempt to contest their enslavement in Delaware courts, seeking to take advantage of the state's suddenly imposed restrictions on out-of-state sales. For petitioning the court, they paid a high price; their Virginia owner disposed of them.[7] Without warning, Bayley recalled, "we soon were all sold and scattered very wide apart."[8] The Bayleys' enforced separation was a terrible lesson in the power of slaveholders and the impunity with which they acted. "My father and mother they pretended to set free," Bayley explained, "to stop a trial in court, and after they had been free about eleven months, they came upon them unawares." The captors arrived at the Bayleys' lodgings one winter night. Mrs. Bayley fled through a back door, compelled to leave her infant behind.[9] The men who invaded the Bayley home carried off Abner, a brother, and a sister, leaving a crying infant to fend for itself. The Bayleys never got to say farewell, but on the night they were abducted, "some friend" rescued the infant, Bayley recalled, "and carried it to mother; then mother took her son about eleven months old, and travelled near a hundred miles from the State of Virginia to Dover in Kent

County, State of Delaware; and from thence to New Jersey." Solomon Bayley was able to visit her just once over the subsequent eighteen years. He was not with his mother and father on the winter's night they were separated. Bayley reported that after being abducted, members of his family, "were taken in the night, and carried to Long Island, one of the West India Islands." Long Island, about two hundred miles to the southeast of the Florida peninsula, was over a thousand miles by sea from Virginia. The planter who bought them eventually sent word back, which was the way the family learned of their fate. Instead of growing grain and flax for American slaveholders on the Delmarva Peninsula, Abner, Abner Jr., and Margaret Bayley would cultivate cotton for British slaveholders in the Bahamas.[10]

Bayley recruited coreligionists into his network to help protect his family from such a separation. He did so as a brother in the faith, offering and receiving fellowship and prayers and, perhaps as importantly, receiving instruction in reading and writing. In 1797, Thamar fell out with her owner, and he tried to sell her and their daughter to a slave trader. The owner's young daughter "broke out and cried in such a distressing manner, for my little daughter," Bayley wrote, that the deal collapsed. The scene "caused him to recant at that time; but he made two more attempts, but was misput most providentially." Thamar and his daughter were safe, at least for the moment. A generation later, slaveholders would work to prevent children of slave owners from developing such affections. Maryland native Leonard Black found that out when he was hired out to a family whose child was taught to abuse him. His mistress "had a son about ten years old," he recalled, and "she used to make him beat me and spit in my face. Here I was, a poor slave boy, without father or mother to take my part."[11] The attempted sale put strains on the Bayley family. "At the same time" as his wife's attempted sale, Bayley recalled, "her master and I were both on one class-paper, which made it very trying to me, to keep up true love and unity between him and me, in the sight of God" (a class paper was the record of members of a Methodist congregation). That was an understatement. Receiving the gospel, taking communion, and singing hymns with his wife's owner tested Bayley's piety. Bayley's agency is clear in his forbearance, worshiping week to week, month to month, and year to year with a man actively attempting to break up his family. Bayley could mark the man's voice and spot him from his shadow, and he knew his stench, too.[12]

Whether Bayley realized it, his timing in using the church strategically was propitious. The Methodist Church was by the last decade of the eigh-

teenth century responding to slaveholders' appeals and abandoning its antislavery imperatives. As far as slaveholders were concerned, too many people
like Bayley were using Methodist connections as he had done. An enslaved
man named Jem ran away from his Annapolis owner in December 1797. The
slaveholder advertised that he "is, or pretends to be, of the society of Methodists—he constantly attended the meetings, and at times exhorted himself,"
despite having "great hesitation in his speech" when addressing the owner.
The twenty-eight year-old, he suspected, had altered a pass to go to Baltimore,
and "has been used to waiting, to taking care of horses and driving a carriage,
is something of a gardener, carpenter and bricklayer."[13] Jem was resourceful,
possessed a variety of skills, and also had a church full of potential allies and
tutors. In 1780, antislavery bishop Francis Asbury had won passage of a statement requiring preachers to educate slaves and also to attempt to persuade
their owners to manumit them. Four years later, the Methodist *Discipline* directed slaveholders to free their slaves within two years of joining the church
or else be denied Holy Communion. Some southern converts submitted to
such injunctions, but by the spring of 1785 in Virginia, Methodists had raised
"a resounding furor" against the rules. Methodists' numbers had expanded
rapidly; they doubled between 1780 and 1785 and grew from fifteen thousand in 1784 to fifty-eight thousand members by 1790. In the wake of mass
appeals, a seemingly indefatigable clergy, and a flood of converts, Methodist
leaders were winning church members much more rapidly than they were
able to build the church as an institution.[14]

To institutionalize its victories in gaining converts, southern Methodists
softened early positions against slaveholding. Decrying markets for slave labor
in the 1790s, Bishop Asbury confided to his journal, "My spirit was grieved at
the conduct of some Methodists, that hire out slaves at public places to the
highest bidder, to cut skin, and starve them."[15] By the close of the decade and
after thousands of miles of circuit riding, he had appraised many men like
Thamar Bayley's owner. "I am brought to conclude," he prophesied in 1798,
"that slavery will exist in Virginia perhaps for ages; there is not a sufficient
sense of religion nor of liberty to destroy it." Asbury's Methodism was push-
ing uncomfortably against the growing market for slave labor.[16]

Aware that slaveholders who were unreceptive to the Methodist gospel owing to the instructions in the *Discipline* might not proselytize slaves, preachers
deemphasized manumission as a condition of church membership. If slaveholders were turned away from the church, they reasoned, neither slavehold-

ers nor their slaves would receive the saving good news. Souls, after all, were more precious than bodies. White Methodists were moving away from the spirit of brotherhood that had energized early African American Methodists, but "black preachers adopted their own version of Methodist faith." Richard Allen, a former Delaware slave, for instance, led an exodus from the church among African American Methodists in Philadelphia in the 1790s and established the African Methodist Episcopal Church in 1816.[17]

Bayley did not exit his congregation, and it would not have been to his family's immediate benefit to have done so. Forming ties within an interracial church meant gaining access to possible assistors among people who did not share a class interest and to their resources, even if, as Bayley understood well, there were other congregants who harbored deep-seated racial prejudices. It is impossible to map the shape of Bayley's network, but the practical benefits of worshiping with whites and slaveholders are clear. So long as his wife's owner was his coreligionist, Bayley would have some mechanism by which to counter the master's plans to sell off his wife and child. The man seemed to be moved by the sentiments of the congregation, or at least he was shamed by them. For his part, Bayley did not view the church merely instrumentally. He was a believer. Of his conversion, he wrote, "In the 26th year of my age, I was favored to find repentance for sins past; then an inquiry rose which was sure the way to heaven; then to follow Christ appeared to be the only sure way." His narrative is an intensely self-searching spiritual autobiography, punctuated by fervent prayers and pious praise. "And when I came to think that the yoke was off my neck," he reflected years later, "and how it was taken off, I was made to wonder, and to admire, and to adore the order of kind providence, which assisted me in all the way." Providence complemented the everyday occurrences of human divinity. With the church relinquishing its antislavery principles, however, Bayley's efforts to recruit church members to protect his family were becoming more urgent.[18]

After Bayley made it known to his congregation that he wanted to buy his wife's freedom, another female member of his wife's owner's family spoke up. Following some deliberation, the wife of Thamar's owner asked that Bayley be allowed to have his wife, at which point the owner "gave up with a whining tone, and said 'He may have her.'" Thamar's owner was not yet persuaded that his soul would be improved by giving a wife to her husband but knew that his finances would be improved by selling her to him. Bayley would initially rent his wife and child until he had enough money to buy them outright. Thamar and Margaret had a price in the market, which the husband would have to pay. In the interim, Bayley arranged to pay a hiring fee for Thamar so that the two could live together.[19]

Membership in the church gave Bayley some leverage against his wife's owner that helped him in his efforts to prevent her owner from selling her and cheating him, but he had to rely on his moneymaking skills if he was to preserve his family's integrity. The slave market advanced more quickly than antislavery Methodism attenuated. Bayley's owner, who had so abruptly split his family up, had also sent him to be apprenticed as a cooper, a trade Bayley had mastered, despite his hesitance at fashioning barrels to hold whiskey and other spirits. By the time Thamar's troubles began, Bayley was hiring his own time from that absentee owner, which meant that he could keep the profits he made from coopering over and above that self-hiring fee. He paid his owner for the privilege of working where he pleased, and the owner did not seem to mind where Bayley worked so long as he paid promptly. After paying his owner the agreed-on money, his surplus earnings would now go to paying Thamar's owner for her hire. To keep his family together, he was paying two masters. Were he free, surplus earnings would go to buying or renting land, educating his child, or building his own business, which reveals how the "chattel principle" of slavery affected Bayley's productive resources. To pay a man to rent his wife and child, Bayley set off in search of new employments and the cash he could generate through them. Bayley did not reveal how much extra money he earned or how he earned it, but after a year, he paid his wife's owner "his money for her hire."[20]

A year into the arrangement, Thamar's owner decided he was not wringing enough cash out of Bayley. Did it gall him that Thamar was enjoying a domestic arrangement after crossing him and that his pious black coreligionist was doing so well? The day Bayley paid him the yearly hiring fee was also a church meeting day, and Bayley reported that "some friends there who saw me pay the money, said to me, 'you had better buy your wife at once.'" Well-timed information could be more valuable than cash to a husband who could not seek legal recourse for broken contracts. Thamar's owner had not succeeded in punishing her for the falling out years before, but in the face of the congregation he again surrendered to popular sentiment, declaring, "I want him to buy her." For her manumission, Bayley was to give him $100 above her annual hiring fee. To attempt to ensure that he would not renege, Bayley asked that the deal be written down. The master complied.[21]

Over the next few years, Bayley worked to remit money for his wife's freedom, but he also sought additional protections to secure the integrity of his family. He was a shrewd observer, and a church surrendering its antislavery principles could offer few guarantees against the caprice of a slaveholder. His family was also growing, which compounded the urgency. Sometime between 1797 and 1800, Solomon and Thamar had a son, Spence. Thamar would give birth to a second daughter, Leah, in 1802 or 1803. Any increase in the family while Thamar was still enslaved posed a problem for the young couple since the children were property of their mother's owner.

Bayley did not yet have money enough to purchase Thamar outright, so as an interim tactic, he sought to have their marriage legally recognized in 1798. There was more than one reason for doing so. He reported growing "uneasy about my wife and me living together without being married; and while I was studying how to bring it about, a tradition arose in the methodist church, to turn out all free members, that lived together as man and wife without being married." Bayley went to the preacher with his intention to have their marriage legalized. He had doubts about securing recognition for two slaves' marriage in Virginia, since the commonwealth did not protect them, but the preacher reassured him, saying "it is easy driving when we are willing." The preacher then asked Thamar's master publicly if he had any objections to the arrangement. Bayley recalled that "her master, answered, 'they may be married, and welcome, for what I care:' then said the preacher, 'you can just give him an instrument to the clerk of the court, and he can get a licence and be married, and finish your business afterwards.'" The master "then wrote to the same effect," Bayley recalled, "and I went and got a licence, and we were married according to law." Remarkably, the commonwealth granted two slaves a marriage license on December 28, 1798. At this time, Bayley paid another year's rent for his wife, plus whatever extra monies he had saved toward her purchase. The Bayleys' troubles were not at an end, but they were at least closer to being rid of slaveholders meddling in their family affairs.[22]

The Bayleys' religious ties were instrumental in preserving their family so long, but their family integrity was far from secure. After Delaware passed laws in the 1790s directing that any slave transported beyond state lines was automatically freed, slaveholders whose property was in jeopardy scrambled to sell their slaves beyond the reach of Delaware's laws. Unlike their counterparts in New York in the 1820s, Delaware slaveholders lacked advance notice of the legislature's passing extensive restrictions. New York's gradual emancipation, granting most slaves freedom by July 4, 1827, gave slaveholders a timeframe in which to sell off slaves before they could be manumitted, as had Pennsylvania's.[23] About half of New York slaves met that fate, being sold down the river to the cotton South.[24] With the example of his father and siblings etched into his consciousness, Bayley initially avoided taking his case to Delaware court. In 1799, two years after Delaware passed additional restrictions on slave sales out of state, Bayley's owner decided to sell him. That was the catalyst for his pursuing the strategy that had resulted in his father and his brothers and sisters being captured and sold. Bayley was aware, he later wrote, that "the laws of Delaware did say, that slaves carried out of that state should be free; whereupon I moved to recover my freedom." He hired lawyers and showed up at the Sussex County, Delaware, courthouse on two subsequent court days to sue for freedom.[25]

Delaware was then hearing petitions from runaway slaves. A 1798 case in Sussex County involved Cager, who was born a slave in Delaware and transported out of state before the manumission laws were passed. Cager ran away from his mistress in Snow Hill, Maryland, and when his mistress's husband came to claim him, he hired a lawyer and petitioned for his freedom in Delaware's court of common pleas. In reaching a verdict of manumission, the court found that the defendant had violated Maryland's laws forbidding the importation of slaves. Whatever the jurisprudential peculiarities of the Cager case, the fact that Delaware was hearing pleas from fugitive slaves motivated plaintiffs like Bayley.[26]

Before his case could be heard, however, Bayley's Virginia owner seized him. Bayley's court case had been carried over six weeks to the next session of the court, during which time he returned to work in Virginia. "But two days before the court was to sit," Bayley wrote, "I was taken up and put on board of a vessel out of Hunting Creek, bound to Richmond, on the western shore of Virginia, and there put into Richmond jail, and irons were put on me; and I was brought very low." Out of Hunting Creek, in Accomack County, Virginia, Bayley sailed down the Chesapeake Bay, through Hampton Roads, and up the James River to Richmond, a distance of about 150 miles. Eastern Shore Methodists could not help him in Richmond, but Bayley was not without resources. His owner appeared and offered him his freedom if he would quit his freedom suit and pay or promise to pay £40 (about $133 in contemporary dollars). With the financial burdens he was carrying to buy his wife, he refused. His honesty about his financial situation failed to mollify the owner.

After a period of anxiety and confusion, Bayley "was taken out of jail, and put into one of the back country waggons, to go toward the going down of the sun."[27]

At that point he joined the trickle of slaves forced to migrate west in the 1790s across the Cumberland Plateau or down the crest of the Blue Ridge Mountains, where they would toil on the cotton frontier in Tennessee, Kentucky, the Carolinas, or Georgia. It would be another quarter century before Bayley's recollections emerged in print, and by that time, his experiences would be shared by hundreds of thousands of enslaved people taken from loved ones along similar paths. "Now consider, how great my distress must have been," he asked a correspondent many years later, "being carried from my wife and children, and from my natural place, and from my chance for freedom." Removed from his network in the neighborhood and church, he lost the hard-earned status of a cooper who could meet his obligations and as a Methodist class member. Slave traders turned him from a father and husband into a saleable worker. To buyers in the market the condition of his family and soul mattered less than that of his limbs and back and how many pounds of cotton those bones, muscles, and sinews could grow and glean from a distant field.[28]

In erasing his history and robbing him of his status, his owner deprived Bayley of a critical part of his personhood. Those human connections that networking tended to increase were the raw materials of most enslaved people's identity. Bayley was not an individual actor. He saw himself fundamentally as a Christian, husband, and father, and distance threatened to strain and sever the human constituents of that identity. To most Americans of the early nineteenth century, not just slaves, personhood was the sum of the roles one lived (not played) in one's social contexts, a rather different notion of self than the twenty-first century liberal construction emphasizing individual rights and the agency implied by those rights.[29] Moreover, civil rights were guaranteed to citizens, but most Americans were not citizens, including married women, children, nonnaturalized foreigners, Native Americans and other nonwhites, felons, the severely mentally ill, and in many states adult white men without real property. Relational personhood and a lack of civil rights left Bayley and people like him immensely dependent on his family ties, church community, and neighborhood bonds. In creating status without civil protections, the enslaved were much like eighteenth-century American female market participants, whose identities "were relational rather than fixed, able to adapt to the changing settings they found themselves in," according to Ellen Hartigan-O'Connor.[30] Seeing slaves as networkers reveals the historical constructions of family, personhood, the market, and the multigenerational forced migration during which so many thousands were "stolen" from their families and deposited on the frontier of a rapidly expanding political nation.[31] Looking at enslaved people as networkers also responds to challenges historians have posed with regard to conceptions of agency and how enslaved people went about in the shadows of a market to protect their bodies and those of friends and relatives.[32] When Bayley spied an opportunity to escape his captors, recover his family, and reestablish network ties, he took it.

Bayley soon discovered that the men who carried him off to the west were not well organized or efficient. Had Bayley been sold in the Richmond slave market of the 1840s or 1850s, he would have been chained head to foot in a coffle or else crammed into a railroad car and spirited beyond the western horizon under close guard. Later traffickers in slaves would not suffer men to ride in wagons, loosely bound. In the future, wagons would be reserved for children and sometimes pregnant women. Usually, armed men on horseback would accompany large coffles to keep watch, which was one advantage slaveholders got from using slave traders that they couldn't get if they transported slaves themselves. At the close of the eighteenth century, there were few passable roads or canals to the west, no steamboats, and no railroads. Three days into the trek, Bayley leaped out of the wagon and hid in the undergrowth by the side of a road.[33]

The slave traders raised an alarm. While his captors searched for him, Bayley listened to their conversations. They sent dogs after him; he fled. By the evening, a violent summer thunderstorm put a halt to the search when the dogs lost his trail. His troubles were not over. Bayley made his way east through fields and woods but soon came down with dysentery, "which came on so bad," he recalled, "I thought I must die; but I obtained great favour, and kept on my feet, and so I got down to Richmond; but had liked to have been twice taken, for twice I was pursued by dogs." Despite the dysentery, dogs, and difficult terrain, Bayley avoided recapture, and in Richmond he got directions to Petersburg, where he hid out for nearly three weeks before meeting another fugitive, "a poor distressed coloured man," who had, like him, been transported across the Chesapeake Bay for sale.[34]

Bayley and the man had both planned to return to Delaware to sue for their freedom. Like Bayley's, the man's owner was an absentee living across the bay in Virginia, and the fugitive had been transported to the western shore to be sold. Also like Bayley, he wound up in Petersburg after escaping from his captors. Bayley and his new comrade commandeered a vessel and sailed back down the James River to the Chesapeake Bay. Somehow avoiding scrutiny of whites they encountered after leaving Petersburg, they crossed the bay and landed in Nandua, Virginia, in Accomack County. Bayley was nearly home.

Their homecoming was not a joyful one, however. From Nandua, they trudged north about fifteen miles to Hunting Creek, from where Bayley's owner had shipped him to Richmond. "We found both our wives," Bayley recalled, "but we found little or no satisfaction, for we were hunted like partridges on the mountains." Like the biblical David persecuted by Saul, Bayley and his friend got no respite from their pursuers. Their owners had missed them and sent word back to their homes that the two had escaped. (Bayley's escape somehow voided his sale.) Slavers' networks were both expansive and effective. Bayley and his fellow fugitive dodged the local whites who sought bounties for their recapture.[35]

Bayley's friend was determined not to leave his family before saving up enough money to press his case in Delaware. The man decided to earn money where he could. He found work on a boat harvesting clams along the bay's sandy shallows. The man knew that if his owner showed up, he would be bound away again, but he refused to abandon his plans. That was a tragic miscalculation. One day some local whites spotted him working, likely operating tongs along clam beds near the shoreline. "He was said to tell" his would-be captors, Bayley reported, "that he had rather die than to be taken and carried away from his wife again: and it was said, they went down into the cabin and drank, and then came up on deck and seized him, and in the scuffle he slipped out of their hands, and jumped over-board, and tried to swim to an island that was not far off." Emboldened by alcohol, the pursuers resolved not to let him go. "They got out the tow boat," Bayley continued, "and went after him, and when they overtook him, he would dive to escape, and still he tried to reach the island: but they watched their opportunity as he rose, when they struck him with the loom of the oar, and knocked his brains out, and he died." Bayley decided not to risk meeting a similar fate and thought it best to return to Delaware should his owner return to the Delmarva Peninsula to recapture him.[36]

Despite his friend's grisly end and his initial failure, Bayley did not give up. He decided to again seek the help of Delaware authorities. After conferring with his wife, Bayley made the 120-mile journey north toward Dover, traveling at night, again hunted in the woods, and reaching his family's erstwhile hometown of Camden in late July, 1799. It was not too long before his owner showed up and confronted him.[37] Bayley later wrote that "upon first sight he asked me what I was a going to do?" and "how did I think I was a going to get free, by running and dodging about in that manner?" Bayley replied that since he had "suffered a great deal, and seen a great deal of trouble, I think you might let me go for little or nothing." Like his wife's owner, that man would not let him go merely for his troubles, declaring, "I wont do that, but I will give you the same chance I gave you before I sent you away; give me forty pounds bond and security, and you may be free." Bayley did not agree immediately. "I work hard at nights to get a little money to fee my lawyers," he insisted, "and if it had been right for me to be free, I ought to have been free without so much trouble." The owner would not be persuaded through argument, "but finally he sold me my time for eighty dollars and I dropped the lawsuit," Bayley recalled. The owner was satisfied that his slave would hold up his end of the bargain and consented to let him again hire his own time. "I went to work," Bayley recalled, "and worked it out in a shorter time than he gave me, and then I was free from man." At length, Bayley disposed of his owner's financial interest in him, but Thamar, daughter Margaret, and son Spence were still enslaved in Virginia.[38]

Bayley set himself to work in animal husbandry, and through hard work and astute use of his business skills, he soon rose to a supervisory position on the farm of an employer. He then found higher-paying work in Delaware, though that had the drawback that he would have to be apart from Thamar and the children. He was also back at work networking. Bayley was on a farm near the state capital, Dover, when he met a former Delaware governor, perhaps Daniel Rogers, a Sussex County miller, owner of fourteen slaves, and then-speaker of the state senate. Bayley engaged the governor in conversation, "believing it to be his duty to speak to him on the great responsibility of the station in which he was placed." Rather than taking offense at being importuned by a slave, the "Governor was so well pleased with his communication," that he "promoted" Bayley "to the oversight of one of his farms, admitting him as a joint sharer with himself in the profits."[39]

The slave, working off his freedom, went into business with the former governor of a slave state. His new employer provided the implements, and Bayley hired workers and directed the operation of the farm. The work was arduous, but Bayley demonstrated a talent for direction. "This mode of farming," Bayley's editor remarked, "which requires great confidence on one side, and skill and industry on the other, was not uncommon at the time." Bayley also took work as an overseer at a saw mill. He reported visiting his mother in New Jersey in the early months of 1800 and giving her his earnings, which he estimated to be "seventeen or eighteen dollars." Rogers died in 1806, and Bayley subsequently hired himself out in Camden, Delaware, for an unspecified amount of time. The distance between Camden, Delaware, and Accomack County, Virginia, was about one hundred miles overland, which meant that Bayley maintained only intermittent contact with his wife and children, visiting at Christmastime as was customary or whenever work permitted.[40]

Bayley's strategy to protect his family by having a slave marriage recognized was put to the test soon after Leah was born. He had paid his wife's owner $63 and owed $40 more when his wife's owner confronted him, saying that he "would take her away" with all the money he had received for her freedom. Bayley had receipts for the money but no bill of sale for her. Leah was born free according to the deal Bayley had negotiated with the owner. Nevertheless, selling the child with her mother would profit him substantially. Market demand and prices were then rising beyond what he had bargained with Bayley for, and buyers wanted fertile women as well as female workers. Bayley reported that "he said he 'would have the negroes or money.'"[41]

At that point, Bayley went to court again in Virginia and pressed his right as a husband. He did not say who brought suit for him, but it may have been a preacher or member of his erstwhile congregation. A sympathetic judge heard a plea in Bayley's behalf and decided "that her master could not get her, nor any more money." Leah's freedom was recognized as well. That was more than Bayley had asked. His strategy to protect his family by having their marriage legalized had worked. He did not take the judge's assurances to heart, however, and paid Thamar's owner the balance of her purchase price as quickly as he could. "With great difficulty," Bayley recalled, "I got him to fix the business; when done, then I paid him, and then she was manumitted free, and I desired rest." He had also paid a little over $100 for Margaret. Thamar's freedom came on the eve of Virginia's 1806 passage of strict antimanumission laws, which would have required her to leave the state. In Accomack County the law was not enforced so long as those manumitted did not displease local citizens.[42]

Whites bringing suits against citizens in behalf of slaves was not usually an approach that succeeded. An enslaved man named Michael had an enter-prising strategy similar to Bayley's, but he had a paucity of allies and a cor-respondingly weaker network. In St. Mary's County, Maryland, to the north-west across the Chesapeake Bay from Accomack County, Virginia, Michael worked to buy his freedom after contracting with his owner Edward Fenwick in 1825. Fenwick promised Michael his freedom should he earn the amount of his purchase price and repay it with interest. Fenwick had no intention of freeing his slave, and Michael was left enslaved after holding up his end of the bargain, having paid cash for his freedom. By the time Michael's employer Charles Gardiner made the complaint, in 1833, Michael had remitted eight years' wages, likely earned growing tobacco and corn.[43]

After taking Michael's money, Fenwick refused to honor his contract and, in court, "denies that he is under any moral or legal obligation to give a deed of manumission to the said negro Michael." Fenwick admitted that he had intended to trick his slave, testifying that he had "entered into these several obligations with the negro Michael in order to excite an ambition in him to exert himself the more to pay your respondent the large sum of money your respondant [*sic*] had purchased him for, and to secure negro Michael's fidelity and obedience as a servant." Gardiner and Michael may have found Fenwick's admission of duplicity refreshing, but it could not have been satisfying. By holding out Michael's freedom as an incentive to be a pliant worker, he had used a market-based ploy to maximize Michael's wage-earning potential. De-spite Gardiner's actions, that Maryland court refused to recognize a contract between a citizen, Fenwick, and his property, Michael. Gardiner's attempt to right Fenwick's wrong was valiant, but it did nothing to get Michael's money back. It is unclear what options Michael was left with, but the Bayleys and their patrons had secured Thamar from sale.[44]

Despite the Bayley's networking successes, their family's troubles with slaveholders were still not over. Following Thamar's manumission, the fam-ily moved to Camden, Delaware, took up tenant farming, and raised their two daughters, Leah and Margaret. Spence was still enslaved, but his parents seemed to have tolerated it while he was relatively close by. That changed when in 1813 Spence's owner died and he was to be sold along with the other estate property. Bayley recalled that his son was "appraised at the death of his master at four hundred dollars." The father was not sanguine about the pos-sibility of raising that amount of money. Spence was nine months old when his father had been sent to Richmond and bound away in a wagon. He was now about thirteen, and prices and demand had risen dramatically. Recalling the "fit of distress" he went through to secure Thamar's freedom, the father anticipated going through "another fit," which, owing to the prices slaves were being sold for, would "seem like double trouble." Friends and neighbors nevertheless encouraged him to buy Spence, and Bayley agreed to try.[45]

Despite having left Virginia years before, Bayley was still recognized as a pious and upstanding Methodist and father back in Accomack County. On the day of the appointed sale, Bayley gathered with the rest of the spectators, citizens, and others who arrived in Drummond, Accomack's county seat, for court day. Court days in Virginia and other states were gatherings of people who had business before the county court, for representatives to return from the capital and politick and for residents to meet and talk—and drink—with neighbors. One white Virginian remembered court day as "a day of bustle and business." On the "roads diverging from the town," would come "horsemen and footmen . . . moving, helter skelter, to a single point of attraction. Justices and jurymen—counsellors and clients—planters and pettifoggers—constables and cake-women—farmers and felons—horse drovers and horse-jockies, all rushing onward." For most free residents, it was a social event, and merchants and vendors capitalized on it as well. The court usually convened every six weeks, and court days might include a jury trial and sometimes the spectacle of a public flogging, slave sale, or even a hanging.[46]

Appealing to patrons in the neighborhood and church, the Bayleys were able to preserve a father's claim to his son over the slaveholder's demand for money, even though that meant the Bayley family would have to devote their resources to paying back a loan. Before the sale, Bayley offered the executor of Spence's late owner's estate $250. He refused. Spence would bring $400 on the market and there were slave traders from across the bay that would pay it. The slave trade had changed since Bayley was tied up in a wagon and carried west. The slave trade was now carried on largely by opportunistic business-men whose primary occupations lay elsewhere. There were not yet the large auction houses and professional traders of a generation later, but demand was strong despite the United States being at war. After Bayley surveyed the situation, he turned to a justice of the peace, from whom he extracted the promise that if Spence were auctioned off to him he would not resell him or take him away. Bayley recalled that at the appointed time, "the crier made a noise in the court yard, before the court house door, and said, 'a likely young negro fellow for sale,' and then asked for a bid." The father started at $200, a sum that he was sure he could raise. Slave traders offered more. Bayley bid as much as he could afford, but it was not enough. The justice of the peace offered $357 but no more. The Bayleys' local patrons had their limits.[47]

The market seemed poised to gobble up Spence when some others acquainted with Bayley appeared in the crowd. Three "great men," including two young gentlemen and a "very rich" Methodist preacher stepped forward. The two gentlemen "were acquainted with me," he explained, adding that God had "touch[ed] their hearts, with such a sense of sympathy and pity towards my case, that they could not endure." Whether by divine intervention or the strength of Bayley's old ties, "the dear young neighbour man" said, "I had rather give twenty dollars out of my own pocket, than Solomon should not get him, but if Solomon will bid once more, I will give him four dollars." Bayley's piety and reputation for honesty helped turn the sale to his favor. Bayley hurriedly arranged a loan with the patrons. Witnessing the last-minute maneuvering, another gentleman halted the bidding, saying "There, let the old man have him, he is his son, he wants him, he can get security." The auctioneer kept the price offered by Bayley's allies "till the switch went down," at which time Spence "was knocked off to me at three hundred and sixty dollars and a shilling." Bayley recalled, "I went to sign the bond; then three of my securities agreed upon the spot, to make me up twenty dollars at the day of payment."[48] The market had lost to the prestige of a former slave's patrons.

The men kept Spence out of the coffles of traders who were prepared to offer more money for him by daring the auctioneer to defy their honor as gentlemen and community leaders. The estate of Spence's former owner would have to settle for less than the slave's market value. The patrons were moved by empathy for Bayley and his son rather than an abstract principle. They recognized the former slave as a coreligionist, client, community member, and as a father. He had prayed and worshiped with them, had worked among them, and had cultivated ties that survived despite his having moved away. Did they recall a time when Bayley did some odd work they appreciated or did they admire his resourcefulness in dealing with Thamar's former owner? Whatever they thought of him, Bayley's allies were no abolitionists, and his maneuvering did not threaten the system from which Spence was saved.

Like so many other members of families half in and half out of slavery, Thamar and Solomon Bayley exhausted their family's savings and borrowed against future income to buy or rent relatives. Freedom became a pressing concern when owners threatened to exercise their property rights in members of the Bayley family to effect forced separations. Bayley had been able to shame his wife's owner into foregoing selling her away and make a contract to sell her to him owing to the fact that they were members of the same church. Through a sympathetic minister and a compliant judge, he had managed to legalize a slave marriage and claim the rights of a husband against a refractory owner. His civic inequality was not tantamount to "civic exclusion," because he used his ties to outwit competitors. From Petersburg, he had escaped the western shore of Virginia and its slave market with an ally who had also been sold because he threatened to press his case in Delaware courts. None of that would have mattered without his ability to accumulate cash and secure the confidence of creditors. After meeting his owner's demands back in Delaware, Bayley was able to cultivate a business relationship with a former governor, which allowed him to purchase his own freedom and give some limited economic assistance to his fugitive mother. The shock of his father, brother, and sister's sudden removal to the Bahamas became the inspiration for the defensive tactics he and Thamar developed to protect their family, which coalesced in his multifaceted strategies as an enslaved networker.[49]

Thamar and Solomon Bayley and their three children, Spence, Leah, and Margaret, were all finally free by 1813 (although, sadly, Spence died soon after he'd been freed), after over a dozen years of trials, during which time they had drained all their savings and secured all the credit they could to buy their freedom. Before entrepreneurship expanded with the market, Americans tended to avoid debt, which was culturally engrained as profligacy and folly. Whether he shared that value or not, incurring debt was the best option Bayley had, and he would be back on succeeding court days to pay principal and interest on his son's mortgage.[50] In part to pay debts, the Bayleys apprenticed Leah and Margaret to domestic work and encouraged them to learn to read. Bayley especially valued the ability to read and reported that Margaret took "delight to read the Bible, and ask the meaning of certain texts of Scripture." He groaned that Leah possessed an "inclination to vanity and idleness" until she was bound out to an "industrious mistress, to learn to work and to have schooling."[51] Once introduced to a culture of reading, however, "she seemed to possess as great a deadness to the world," her father remembered, "as any young woman I ever observed: she seemed not ashamed to read in any company, white or coloured; and she read to the sick with intense desire, which appeared from her weeping, and solid manner of behaviour." Deadness to the world was a high compliment from her father. It seems she learned Solomon

Bayley's renegade ways as well, if she ignored the color line when reading. Having a father who had not been afraid, as a slave, to good-naturedly engage the governor of Delaware in a conversation about his duties to the people—and come away with a business partnership—gave the daughters a compelling example of character. But they too, like their brother died young, in the summer of 1824 after a short, undiagnosed illness. Leah was twenty-one and Margaret was in her mid-twenties. Thamar and Solomon Bayley survived their children and were living in Camden, near Dover, Delaware by the mid-1820s, when Bayley wrote his autobiography; later they emigrated to West Africa.[52]

The Bayleys' tactics were contingent on the human and material resources in the local environment. They were also historically conditioned. Bayley's strategies of using a neighboring state's laws and the church were novel when he executed them in the 1790s. By the 1810s, at least, the Methodist Church in Virginia was in full retreat on the issue of slaves' ecclesiastical equality with slaveholders. Delaware's liberal manumission laws also circumscribed African American civil rights. Most Delaware voters seemed to abhor African Americans as much as they did slavery. By 1825, argues Patience Essah, "whether free or slave, blacks were forbidden from being within half a mile of the polling stations on election day."[53] Partly as a result of the high number of manumissions in the state, Delaware passed strict black codes restricting African Americans' civil liberties, commerce, and access to education. Free blacks were invited to move elsewhere. Even the criminal codes instituted harsher and more publicly humiliating punishments for nonwhites.[54] In the wake of eroding civil rights protections for people of color, the coastal plains of the first state became a haunt of kidnappers who sold their African American captives into the slave trade.

Enslaved people never conceded to owners the right to sell them or their relatives. Kidnapping African Americans was the moral equivalent of the slave trade, and though the numbers kidnapped did not rival those transported in the legal trade, it was common enough to send terror rippling through African American neighborhoods. Incidents of kidnapping in Delaware also showed the importance of networking. Cultivating allies and patrons was critical not only for members of families in slavery but also for those whose African ancestry marked them potential slaves. Like many other states, Delaware denied free people of color the right to testify against whites in court, which exposed them to victimization although the interstate slave trade was illegal there.[55] It took some victims years to recover their freedom, and others never returned.

Physical violence and the trauma of separation were regular components of the legal slave trade, and from the point of view of the victims of kidnapping there was little difference between the two. Aaron Cooper spent three years toiling away on a Mississippi cotton plantation before an Adams County, Mississippi, court decided that he was in fact a victim of kidnapping and not a slave. Cooper and his wife, Hetty, were free African Americans living in Kent County, Delaware, with their three daughters, Elizabeth, Abigail, and Susan. One night in early May 1811, shortly after the Coopers had retired to bed, they were awakened by a knock at the door. As Cooper unlatched it, five armed white men stormed in, seized him, and tied his arms with rope, while his wife and children looked on. Bayley would have shuddered at the description of that modus operandi. From Cooper's home in Duck Creek Hundred, the captors took him twenty miles to the west, into Maryland, and sold him at Dixon's Tavern (now Sudlersville). (By the 1820s, slave traders' agents would be stationed at strategic places in outlying counties, often taverns, where slaveholders could trade slaves for cash conveniently.) Cooper's family raised an alarm, and as news of the kidnapping spread, local men who knew or heard of Cooper joined together to rescue him.[56]

Like Bayley, Cooper had status in his neighborhood, even if he lacked most civil rights. He may have found allies in slaveholders, who were also interested in arresting kidnappers since they stood to lose property in slaves stolen and sold away. Cooper's allies pursued his captors but missed him at Dixon's Tavern by one day. They convinced Maryland judges in Dorchester and Queen Anne counties to issue warrants to apprehend Cooper. Meanwhile, the kidnappers moved him down the Delmarva Peninsula some fifty miles to New Market (now East New Market), where he was confined aboard a ship bound for Norfolk, Virginia. The ship sailed before the rescue party could head it off. Cooper landed in Natchez, Mississippi. In Adams County, on the cotton frontier, he cultivated a new set of allies and eventually enlisted the help of a lawyer who made his argument in court. Cooper was forced to work for three years in a strange land before the territory of Mississippi decided he was a free man and ordered his return, along with monetary compensation for his wrongful enslavement. By 1820, Cooper was back with his family in Camden, Delaware, farming, and a new son had joined the family.[57]

Kidnappers hatched elaborate schemes, sometimes involving victims' ostensible friends and neighbors, exploiting local cleavages and undermining locals' networks. The flat terrain of the Delmarva Peninsula that allowed slaves to visit family and friends and engage in various occupations was also advantageous to kidnappers. The thirty-mile long Nanticoke River, which flows southwest into the Chesapeake Bay, was a major transportation artery between southern Delaware and the Maryland Chesapeake. It was also prime hunting grounds for kidnappers, who stole children to be sold in the lower South. Children were more compliant and easier to smuggle than men like Cooper. They were common enough in the legal slave trade that it was possible for them to be passed off as having been legally traded. In the summer of 1817, a slave trader got hold of two of Stephen Dredden's sons after summoning him to court in Laurel, Sussex County, Delaware, on a false warrant. Dredden, a free African American, later claimed that the kidnappers had enlisted the help of his neighbor, a white woman named Sarah Moore, who persuaded Mrs. Dredden to accompany her husband to court and offered to watch their five children in their absence. The neighborly gesture was a ruse to get the parents out of the way. After persuading the two boys, eleven-year-old Sampson and his seven-year-old brother Jonathan to help her gather firewood, Moore ambushed them in the woods and turned them over to kidnappers who hid them until dark. The men then sold them to a known slave trader. Moore offered no explanation for her actions, instead advising the Dreddens, "Don't grieve about your children, it is not worth while, you will never see them any more." By the time the plot was uncovered, the boys had reportedly been resold to slave traders in Maryland and shipped to southern slave markets. The grieving parents took their case to the newspapers in hopes of stopping the trader before they reached New Orleans, but it was too late to rescue Sampson and Jonathan.[58]

Such acts of betrayal and predation illustrate that networkers needed to be wary of whom they allied with and befriended. The terror that accompanied fears of kidnapping (legal or not) contributed to a culture of hypervigilance that pervaded the slave South. Recognized today as a reaction to trauma and a component of post-traumatic stress disorder, hypervigilance was a natural reaction to the suspicion, well founded in the Dreddens' case, that even neighbors could be harboring plans to spirit off children or loved ones. They needed to be vigilant, too, of whites who served as slave patrollers, lawmen, and overseers. When the enslaved formed networks, they were not cultivating bonds of trust so much as strategic alliances that were extremely fragile and based on mutual exchanges of goods, information, and other forms of social capital. When networkers dealt with anyone it was like sitting down at a gambling table with the deck loaded against them, and often they were forced to bet everything.[59]

Charles Ball's ordeals were similar to Aaron Cooper's except that his owners had legal title to his body. With surprise and anger the Bayleys, Coopers, and Dreddens would have found familiar, the Maryland native described the sale in 1805 that separated him from his pregnant wife and children in Calvert County as a kidnapping.[60] Born in 1781, he had grown up in southern Maryland, worked in agriculture, and had been entrusted with driving wagons of tobacco to market unsupervised.[61] Ball had traveled widely over his southern Maryland terrain and underwent a practical education in networking. When one owner decided he was not needed for agricultural work, the man hired him out to the Washington, D.C., Navy Yard, where he worked as a cook aboard the USS *Congress*, a 1,250-ton thirty-six-gun frigate and one of the flagships of the U.S. Navy. Then about twenty years old, Ball reported that he "strove by all means to please the officers and gentlemen who came on board," and received clothing and money for his services. On Sundays off, he "generally went up into the city to see the new and splendid buildings." Thomas Jefferson had recently moved into the new executive mansion, and his allies largely replaced Federalists in Congress. Surveying the new national capital, Ball "often walked as far as Georgetown," he recalled, "and made many new acquaintances amongst the slaves, and frequently saw large numbers of people of my colour chained together in long trains, and driven off towards the south." Among his acquaintances was a black man who encouraged him to flee to Philadelphia, but before the plan could be executed, his owner retrieved him and took him back to Calvert County, Maryland. Ball had been sold to another man unbeknownst to his owner, and a dispute over who owned Ball ensued.[62]

Settling back in southern Maryland, he married a woman named Judah, and they began to raise a family. Ball grew tobacco and corn while his putative owners took each other to court over who actually owned him. Judah worked as a domestic servant in the house of a wealthy family, where she gathered knowledge on the goings-on of Maryland society. The couple welcomed two more children into the world. Court wrangles at an end, Ball became the property of a man named Ballard, whom, he reported, was "sullen and crabbed in his temper, and always prone to find fault with my conduct—no matter how hard I had laboured, or how careful I was to fulfil all his orders, and obey his most unreasonable commands." Ballard deprived him of the quantities of food and quality of clothing to which he had been accustomed.[63]

Ball chafed under Ballard's restrictions on his movements, and after repeated protests over living conditions Ballard decided to dispose of him. There was cash to be had for an able young worker. One day he ordered Ball to drive to a store he owned. There at breakfast, Ball saw Ballard talking with a stranger, after which five men arrived and assaulted him. "This man came up to me," he recalled, "and, seizing me by the collar, shook me violently, saying I was his property, and must go with him to Georgia." The events of that morning were ominous. "At the sound of these words," he recalled, "the thoughts of my wife and children rushed across my mind, and my heart died away within me." He was to leave immediately and asked "if I could not be allowed to go to see my wife and children, or if this could not be permitted, if they might not have leave to come to see me; but was told that I would be able to get another wife in Georgia."[64]

Judah and their young children were not the sole anchors he had to his home, and he was not the first of his family to be bound away in chains. Like Bayley, Ball could recall members from several generations of his African American family being bought and sold, including his grandfather "old Ben," who was brought from Africa and "sold as a slave in Calvert county, in Maryland, about the year 1730." When Ball was four years old, in 1785, the man who owned his family died, and the family was sold apart from one another according to the owner's will. His brothers and sisters disappeared into the hands of Carolina slave traders, and his mother was sold away from his father and handed over to a Georgia slaveholder. Ball's father "never recovered from the effects of the shock which this sudden and overwhelming ruin of his family gave him. He had formerly been of a gay social temper," but afterward, "I never heard him laugh heartily, or sing a song." Ball also reported that his father "became gloomy and morose in his temper, to all but me; and spent nearly all his leisure time with my grandfather, who claimed kindred with some royal family in Africa, and had been a great warrior in his native country." Though enslaved, the Ball family did not act like slaves. Because of his intractability, Ball's father's owner had decided to sell him, too. Before the Georgia buyer could capture him, however, the grandfather "gave him a bottle of cider and a small bag of parched corn, and then praying to the God of his native country to protect his son, enjoined him to fly from the destruction which awaited him." Ball never saw his father again and guessed he had made good an escape to Philadelphia. His grandfather, he recalled, "was the only person left in Maryland, with whom I could claim kindred."[65]

And so Ball commenced, in the first decade of the nineteenth century, the long forced march through Virginia and North Carolina into the cotton country of South Carolina and Georgia, following his mother and siblings. As he was marched overland, bound and wearing an iron collar, he made an intricate mental map of the terrain over which he walked. Chained to other Chesapeake natives, Ball recalled crossing the Patuxent River on the way out of his native Calvert County, then crossing the Potomac into Virginia, then the Rappahannock, Mattaponi, North Anna, South Anna, James, and Roanoke, and finally the Yadkin in North Carolina. It was only at that point that the slave trader felt it safe to remove Ball's iron restraints.[66] On his journey south, he noticed the landscape change from seemingly exhausted old tobacco lands in the Virginia Tidewater to the cotton country where his labor was in demand.[67] Ball's mental cartography reflects the slow pace at which he traveled. "By repeatedly naming the rivers that we came to, and in the order which we had reached them," he recalled, "I was able at my arrival in Georgia, to repeat the name of every considerable stream from the Potomac to the Savannah, and to tell at what ferries we had crossed them." After crossing the Catawba River and reaching a stopping place outside Columbia, South Carolina, a prospective buyer offered $400 for him, which the man claimed was twice the going rate for "Guinea" slaves—newly landed Africans—offered for sale in Charleston.[68]

Ball was sold in Columbia, South Carolina, following a court day feast to celebrate the Fourth of July. Citizens had much to celebrate. Jefferson, now in his second term, had doubled the size of the country with the Louisiana Purchase two years before, and the United States was in a period of "unparalleled prosperity."[69] Amid his countrymen's celebrations, Ball attempted to enlist allies and develop a strategy that would allow him to return to his wife and family, exchanging information with other enslaved people. After he was sold, he met another enslaved man, who "was the chief hostler in the stable of this tavern," where Ball's new owner was lodging, and "who was born and brought up in the Northern Neck of Virginia, on the banks of the Potomac, and within a few miles of my native place." The two talked fondly of home and of how to get to Philadelphia, to where the man planned to seek refuge. Ball credited him with assisting in his escape, years later, by confirming the best route back to Maryland from his native part of Virginia. The man advised him to flee in late summer when a person "could live well on roasting ears, as long as the corn was in the milk; and afterwards, on parched corn, as long as the grain remained in the field." The man wanted to know from Ball how to get to Philadelphia, but Ball confessed that although he knew generally how to get there from Maryland, he "was not able to give him any very definite instructions."[70]

As in Maryland, Ball had a considerable amount of geographic mobility in South Carolina. He quickly mastered the human geography of his new surroundings as well. "At the time I first went to Carolina," Ball recalled, "there were a great many African slaves in the country, and they continued to come in for several years afterwards. I became intimately acquainted with some of these men."[71] The slave population of the lower South, in contrast to that of his home in the Chesapeake, included many newly arrived captives who had survived the Middle Passage.[72] The United States did not outlaw the foreign importation of slaves until 1808, and there was a heavy demand for captives of the Atlantic slave trade in the lower South. Between 1803 and 1807 United States vessels participating in the transatlantic trade transported about one in seven captives across the Atlantic. Most of those Africans ended up in places other than the United States, but between independence in 1783 and the legal ban on international slaving to the United States in 1808, southern planters bought more than fifty-five thousand Africans, some shipped from as far away as Mozambique. South Carolina newspapers were filled with advertisements for their sales.[73]

Ball strove to learn from his fellow bondspeople and forge new ties. He recalled being "joined by the man who prayed five times a day; and at the going down of the sun, he stopped and prayed aloud in our hearing, in a language I did not understand." Ball added to his geographic knowledge, learning from his Muslim fellow captive of "the confines of a country, which had no trees, nor grass upon it; and that in some places, no water was to be found for several days' journey. That this barren country was, nevertheless, inhabited by a race of men, who had many camels and goats, and some horses."[74] Those connections sustained him, and he rose through the ranks of agricultural workers, not the least because he was effective at politicking, communicating, and adapting to the new environment. He learned how to grow cotton, how to tend, and how to harvest it. That redounded to the owner's benefit as well, and by the year he escaped Ball was "entrusted with the entire superintendence of the plantation," as black drivers often were.[75]

All the time that he searched for a way to escape those surroundings he was incorporating within his network anyone who might provide useful information. A year after his master died in a duel, he learned of the death of his mistress during childbirth "from the mouth of a black man, who was the travelling servant of the eldest son of my old master."[76] Well aware that a change of owner might mean a return to the violence he had endured on the long march south, he finalized plans for an escape. The mistress had died in May 1809, but Ball bided his time until August when the corn ripening in the fields would serve as available food for his journey northward. "My heart yearned for my wife and children," he recalled, "from whom I had now been separated more than four years." Their memory propelled him to take a step that would have severe repercussions were he caught. "My purpose was fixed," he recalled, "and now nothing could shake it. I only waited for a proper season of the year to commence my toilsome and dangerous journey." He told no one and bid goodbye only to a dog, a longtime companion named Trueman.[77]

Ball then lit out, using densely wooded areas as cover and his memory as a guide. He slogged back along the route he had trodden years before, traveling at night to avoid detection. He arrived in Columbia, South Carolina, where he "recognized the jail," he later testified, "and the tavern in which I had lodged on the night after I was sold," which "discovery made me feel almost at home, with my wife and children."[78] Characteristically, he noticed "that every thing on this plantation was nearly as it was when I left it."[79] Using navigational techniques he had learned, perhaps from his fellow bondspeople, from fishing in the Chesapeake, or from days aboard the *Congress*, he steered by the stars.[80] "Keeping the north-star on my left hand for three nights," he strove "to get as far east as the road leading from Columbia to Richmond, in Virginia."[81] Hampered by clouds at night and "parties of patrollers," he nevertheless set about traveling the 450 miles between Columbia, South Carolina, and his home in Calvert County, Maryland, along the streams yet against the current of the interstate slave trade that had brought him south.[82]

Along the way, he met others on a similar journey, including a former domestic laborer from Delaware he described as a "dark mulatto, small and slender in person, and lame in one leg." The man had sustained an injury in his flight from a South Carolina planter into whose possession he had fallen. Ball paused to learn the man's story. (In another age, with his acute ear for detail, interest in humanity, and political instincts, he might have been a Studs Terkel, a Claude Lévi-Strauss, or a Bill Clinton.) His fellow fugitive's Delaware owner had agreed to free him at age twenty-five, a promise that died along with the owner. The deceased's executor hired him out in Wilmington. The employer sold him to a man who transported him to Baltimore and then re-sold him to another trader, who then took him to the cotton country of South Carolina and sold him again.[83] Ball could sympathize. The man had toiled three years before escaping. He been on the run three weeks, and "becoming fatigued by travelling, he had stopped here and made this shelter of boughs and bark of trees." There was no place a fugitive could stop for medical care. In the first year of the James Madison administration, the Underground Railroad was no more a reality than its coal and iron namesake. Local slaves were unlikely to welcome strangers. The Delawarean, Ball recalled, "had been well bred, and possessed good manners and fine address." His leg may have pained him, but he was not hurting for supplies. The man "had an old skillet, more than a bushel of potatoes, and several fowls, all of which he said he had pur-loined from the plantations in the neighbourhood." Alarmed that the elabo-rate camp would give the fugitive away, Ball cautioned him to quit the place and travel solely at night. After a sustaining meal, Ball left the man's company and continued on his journey.[84]

Ball's cautiousness attenuated as he approached home. So did his luck. Af-ter crossing the Mattaponi River, north of Richmond, Virginia, he began trav-eling near a main road and was discovered by armed slave patrollers. He flew. They shot. He fell, and his captors descended on him. "One of my eyes was almost beaten out," he recalled, "and the blood was running from my mouth, nose and ears." Writhing with pain, he was lodged in a jail in Bowling Green in Caroline County, Virginia, about seventy miles from home.[85] After a doctor was summoned to "examine my legs, and extract the shot from my wounds," Ball languished for thirty-nine days while the authorities cast about for some-one who claimed to own him. When escapees like Ball were captured, local authorities routinely searched for owners who would pay the cost of the fugi-tive's maintenance and, often, a reward on top of that. The jailor of Norfolk, Virginia, advertised for twenty-four year-old Charles Brown in 1819. Brown claimed that he was a free man kidnapped from Philadelphia. The jailor gave a description (including that his "right eye" was "half out") and requested that the "owner, if any, is requested to come forward, and act agreeable to law or I shall."[86] Another similar ad directed the owner of yet another fugitive Charles, jailed in Washington County, Maryland, in 1814, "to release him, otherwise he will be sold agreeably to law."[87] Ball refused to divulge details of his story, which risked him being sold by local authorities as unclaimed property. One morning, after he failed to receive breakfast, he began to beat on the cell door to get the jailor's attention and in doing so discovered that a portion of the oak-floored brick cell was a "hollow shell" of "rotten wood." That night, Ball broke out of jail, made for the Potomac River, crossed over it in a small boat, and then crossed the Patuxent River the next day. He was finally home.[88]

Like the legendary Odysseus, Ball returned from several years' captivity, enduring hardships, cultivating alliances, and outwitting enemies to a wife and children who scarcely recognized him. Arriving late at night at Judah's cabin, he hesitated. "I at length rapped lightly on the door, and was immediately asked, in the well-known voice of my wife, 'Who is there?' —I replied 'Charles.'" His wife opened the door, "slowly," and said, "Who is this that speaks so much like my husband?" Ball entered, but "it was some time before I could convince her, that I was really her husband, returned from Georgia." In the darkness, Judah then called their children, Ball remembered, "but they had forgotten me."[89] She "gather[ed] all three of her children in her arms, thrust them into my lap, as I sat in the corner." As the apparition of her husband became real, she "clapped her hands, laughed, and cried by turns; and in her ecstasy forgot to give me any supper," Ball remembered, "until I at length told her that I was hungry." Pondering his situation, Ball was chagrined at the "idea that I was utterly unable to afford protection and safeguard to my own family, and was myself even more helpless than they." He recalled being "tormented [in] my bosom with alternate throbs of affection and fear, until the dawn broke in the east, and summoned me to decide upon my future conduct." He resolved not be forced away from them again, but the means of accomplishing that would be some risky alliances.[90]

Ball set about rebuilding a network to help accomplish his goal. He first turned to his wife's owners, an unlikely choice except that he needed a patron or at least cooperation from local whites. Building alliances with other African Americans was not an immediately pressing concern. Though better able to trust his black neighbors, he needed more tangible protections than they could provide. Ball realized that "everybody must know that I was a runaway slave" in that county but gambled that he could use his wife's owners strategically. "When morning came," Ball recalled, "I went to the great house, and showed myself to my wife's master and mistress who treated me with great kindness, and gave me a good breakfast." Ball ingratiated himself to the slaveholders. "In the course of conversation," he recalled, they seemed to forget their class interests. The wife's master "first advised me to conceal myself, but soon afterwards told me to go to work in the neighbourhood for wages."[91]

An international calamity in the form of War of 1812 broke upon Ball's world and forced a change in his strategy. He was working as a fisherman in late 1813 when British warships appeared off the Calvert County coast. The British Navy blockaded the Chesapeake in an effort to choke off trade and stop the Americans' ability to wage war. They also took advantage of the fact that thousands of enslaved people with knowledge of the area might join them and rise up against their masters. British troops destroyed the seines and sheds that Ball and his colleagues used in their fishery and along with it components of Ball's network. Every croaker, spot, rockfish, or bluefish that Ball gathered in his nets were resources that propelled the plan he had adopted to protect his family forward, as he salted, smoked, or cured fish to eat or to sell to others and formed alliances with other fisherman and customers. Seine fishing also lent him geographic mobility because it required a boat.[92]

The British upset the Ball family's dynamic equilibrium and the ties or bonds they used to maintain their status. As they summoned African Americans to leave their masters, British marines "burned the house of a planter," Ball recalled, stole "several cattle, that were found in his fields," and "carried off more than twenty slaves, which were never again restored to their owner."[93] The owner attempted to ransom his slaves but was denied. "These were the first black people whom I had known to desert to the British," Ball commented, "although the practice was afterwards so common." The United States had declared war on Britain the previous year after France and Great Britain each outlawed U.S. trade to the other and in the process captured U.S. ships, sailors, and the cargoes they transported. The war against Britain was broadening in the west, as future presidents William Henry Harrison and Andrew Jackson led armies against ostensible British allies, including Red Stick Muskogee-Creeks and Shawnees, exacting large land concessions from those they defeated. In the Chesapeake, the British ravaged the countryside and recruited thousands of slaves to join them.[94]

When an opportunity arrived for Ball to run away to the British Navy, he refused. At a glance, Ball's refusal is counterintuitive. The United States was a rapidly expanding empire for slavery, Louisiana being the latest state to join the Union, in 1812. Ball had already been brutalized, bound, removed from his family and then driven to work on cotton plantations. Another misfortune might have landed him in the New Orleans slave market. British commanders issued specific appeals to African Americans to rise up against their owners and promised freedom and resettlement not just to the men but to their families. As long as Judah and their children were nearby and unable or unwilling to escape with him, however, fleeing to the British was a risky strategy. His patrons, including his wife's owner and his employers, were United States citizens. The ties that bound him and his family to a network of allies, patrons, information, and resources were stronger than the putative strength of British freedom purchased at the price of dissolving that network. In conventional terms, he was no revolutionary against slavery and had tolerated and even allied with slaveholders in order to be near his family and make a living in the neighborhood he had known all his life.

Ball was better placed than most African Americans in his neighborhood, who willingly accepted deracination for liberty. Some four thousand slaves fled to the British in the Chesapeake during 1813 and 1814. "Black people deserted from their masters and mistresses, and escaped to the British fleet. None of these people were ever regained by their owners," Ball reported, "as the British naval officers treated them as free people, and placed them on the footing of military deserters."[95] The British did more than that. They incorporated willing African American men into a fighting force called the "Colonial Marines," based on Tangier Island on the eastern side of the bay. Preparing to invade Maryland and Washington, D.C., Vice Admiral Sir Alexander Cochrane, who "utterly detested the Americans," contended that African American troops would terrify the American forces and claimed that if they were "properly armed and backed with 20,000 British troops, Mr. Maddison [sic] will be hurled from his throne."[96]

Dethroning an American president was a more ambitious plan than that which enslaved Virginia revolutionaries had hatched a dozen years earlier. In the spring and summer of 1800, Gabriel, an enslaved blacksmith hiring his time in Richmond, had organized a broad and diverse network of rebellious slaves and free people (including some whites) and planned to hurl then-governor James Madison from office in a violent campaign to capture Virginia's capital, take vengeance on merchants and magistrates, and force an end to slavery.[97] James Sidbury argues that they did not act according to prevailing legal categories of race but as people in contingent circumstances, as husbands, Christians, and black Virginians. In Gabriel's day, as in Ball's, people of African descent did not act with one accord but as members of families, as part of a circle of friends, and constituents of neighborhoods.[98]

Gabriel and his would-be revolutionaries also fashioned their own understanding of the legacy of the American Revolution and the not-yet-complete St. Domingue revolution that would establish the independent republic of Haiti.[99] After a violent August thunderstorm postponed Gabriel's rebellion, the network unraveled as the plot was made public. Gabriel and many others were captured and tried. Several conspirators, including Gabriel, were hanged. Some conspirators were sold out of state. Two years later, a waterman not unlike Ball planned another armed rebellion in Halifax, Virginia. Inspired by Gabriel, Sancho's rebellion also failed, and Virginia legislators passed a raft of repressive laws against people of African descent.[100] That insurrection plot had spread as far east as Norfolk. In late 1813 and 1814, the British were directing a much larger slave rebellion, which they scarcely needed to drum up support for. The memory of Gabriel and Sancho was likely alive among those who joined the British. Just north of Norfolk, near Lynnhaven Bay, Virginia, white patrollers discovered a band of fugitive slaves encamped together awaiting the British in October 1813.[101] Those African Americans almost certainly would have recalled Gabriel or Sancho as they scanned the horizon for tall masts of British warships. They likely whispered words concerning the Haitian Revolution, too.[102]

Neither Ball nor Bayley seem to have been animated by such ideas, which shows that contingent circumstances worked against a historical drama of slavery as class struggle.[103] Ball did not have one chance to escape but several. Each time, he acted as a father, as a husband, and as someone with a stake in the status quo, even though agents of that status quo had kidnapped and brutalized him. His family's choice was the least-bad option for them. Others chose differently, according to their own circumstances and calculations, and "welcomed the invaders." A former slave of Caleb Jones of St. Mary's County, Maryland, fled to the British in August, 1813, then returned to his former home with British troops. While his new allies looted the plantation, Jones "spent the night verbally tormenting his former master," armed with pistols and a sword. Panicked citizens responded to such incidents by demanding legislation curtailing schooling for African Americans and forbidding slaves to travel from their owners' properties. Whites moved to secure small craft slaves might use to flee.[104]

Determined to preserve slavery and reassert control over slave property, they also intensified violence against African Americans. Virginia already compensated owners for slaves executed by the state (as it had Gabriel's owner). Those payments doubled between 1812 and 1813 and then rose again 20 percent in 1814. The white patrollers who discovered the Lynnhaven Bay encampment shot first, killing and wounding several. Still, slaves made off for the British in large numbers. On one occasion, a wealthy Maryland slave-holder Ball worked for lost over one hundred slaves in a single night. The next morning, Ball recalled, he "arose, and went to call his hands to the field, he found only empty cabins in the quarter, with a single man remaining, to tell what had become of his fellows."[105]

The man who remained was in a position much like Ball. He "had a wife and several children on an adjoining estate, and as he could not take his family with him, on account of the rigid guard that was kept over them, he refused to go himself."[106] Although it is unlikely that Judah and their children were held captive by her owner, such ugly impediments were not necessary. Those who fled to the British took risks as refugees, and formerly enslaved Americans could find themselves left without any means of provision; such was the fate of Boston King, who fled slavery in South Carolina during the American Revolution, and ended up nearly starving in Nova Scotia. In 1814, as in 1781, the British were more interested in punishing American enemies than in liberating African American allies. Like Thamar and Solomon Bayley, Boston King and his wife, Violet, made their way to the coast of West Africa after their ordeals of liberation. Relocating to Nova Scotia, Bermuda, or the West Indies was not a step Ball was prepared to take just then.[107]

As the British invasion of the Chesapeake advanced, Ball adjusted his calculations. Networking involved gathering information as well as allies, and it also meant adapting quickly to new contingencies. Ostensibly acting in behalf of his Calvert County patrons, he took part in an attempt to persuade runaways to return. Posing as the servant of a "young gentleman," he boarded a seventy-four-gun British warship, where, he recalled, "the whole of the run-aways were on board . . . lounging about on the main deck, or leaning against the sides of the ship's bulwarks." That description does not betray much sympathy for the defectors. Ever the networker, however, he "went amongst them, and talked to them a long time, on the subject of returning home; but found that their heads were full of notions of liberty and happiness in some of the West India islands."[108] The British officers promised passage to Trinidad and encouraged Ball to join his fellow bondspeople. He tactfully declined, claiming that he was already free and had plans to rent land to farm. He was not allowed to leave the British ship, which was by then sailing to Tangier Island, from where the British were staging an invasion of Maryland and the national capital. Ball "endeavour[ed] to procure some means of conveying both" him and the white man that had accompanied him "back again to Calvert."[109]

His hosts refused, but he had little problem making friends aboard the British ship. "I amused myself by talking to the sailors," Ball recalled, "and giving them an account of the way in which I had passed my life on the tobacco and cotton plantations; in return for which, the seamen gave many long stories of their adventures at sea, and of the battles they had been engaged in." Being black became an advantage, and Ball networked even as he was held against his will as the ship made for Virginia's Eastern Shore. "I lived well whilst on board this ship," Ball remembered, "as they allowed me to share in a mess. In compensation for their civility, I gave them many useful instructions in the art of taking fish in the Bay." He made himself an asset to the British but refused to report fleeing American prisoners he witnessed escaping "out of the port-holes" of the ship to which he had been confined.[110] When he made his way back to the western shore, however, he took sides.

Ball joined U.S. forces fighting the British, both because he viewed British depredations as "atrocities" and also because he thought it was strategically savvy, providing him with a lever he could used to protect his family. Ball was familiar with navy culture from his service on the *Congress* and could cook for sailors. When "Commodore Barney came into the Patuxent with his flotilla," Ball recalled, "I enlisted on board one of his barges, and was employed sometimes in the capacity of a seaman, and sometimes as cook of the barge."[111] Commodore Joshua Barney's operation became an opportunity for Ball to augment his network in concert with his sponsors once his seines and fishery were gone and he had refused British assistance. Ball's local knowledge was as good as anyone's under Barney's command, and the fifty-four year-old Revolutionary War veteran and privateer found a military asset in a slave. In 1813, President Madison had directed Barney to initiate a defense of the Chesapeake, and he responded with a plan to counter superior British naval strength by harassing ships with boats.[112] Barney's flotilla included "lateen-rigged and oared gunboats," which were nimble and effective in the shallow waters of the bay.[113]

The commodore's operation made good use of Ball's skills, and he joined at a critical time. "I had been on board, only a few days," he recalled, "when the British fleet entered the Patuxent, and forced our flotilla high up the river." In June 1814, Barney's boats sought refuge in St. Leonard Creek. That was no far-flung adventure for Ball since the creek was an estuary of the Patuxent River in his native Calvert County. As a fisherman, he knew it well. "I was present when the flotilla was blown up, and assisted in the performance of that operation upon the barge that I was in," Ball recalled. Barney's forces scuttled their boats, and superior British forces converged on Benedict, in Charles County, burning that port town before heading north to Prince George's County.[114]

Ball followed his comrades, gambling that faithful service would lead to legal freedom and an opportunity to return to Calvert County and his family permanently. "I marched with the troops of Barney, from Benedict to Bladensburg," following the British, "and travelled nearly the whole of the distance, through heavy forests of timber, or numerous and dense cedar thickets." He recalled thinking that the U.S. commanders ought to have used the woods strategically, as he had done when escaping from Georgia. He contended that if General William Winder had attacked the British in the heavily forested area of "the lower part of Prince George county," then "not a man of them would ever have reached Bladensburg." That was overstating the situation, but nobody asked an African American volunteer for military advice. Again, however, Ball knew the terrain, having driven tobacco wagons there. After taking active part in the battle, he retreated along with the rest of the army. The United States lost the Battle of Bladensburg, even with the four hundred sailors from Barney's flotilla, and the British marched on Washington, D.C., sacking the city in August 1814. Some of the African Americans who had fled to the British took part in burning the city, including the seventy-five man "Colonial Marines" composed of former slaves that was formed at Tangier Island.[115]

Ball's siding with the United States launched his independence from his southern Maryland sponsors, even as he fought for a slaveholding republic. He joined the army "after the sack of Washington," in 1814, "and assisted in the defense of Baltimore, as a free black man," he reported.[116] He did not disclose where Judah and his children were during his military adventures. Did the movement of armies hold allure for a man in his early thirties? Regular rations of food and spirits and pay (even poor pay) were benefits as well.[117] Ball shared in the U.S. victory, if victory it was, and took his freedom as a reward for service. For six years following the war, Ball "worked in various places in Maryland, as a free man; sometimes in Baltimore, sometimes in Annapolis, and frequently in Washington," saving up $350.[118]

His self-designation as "a free man" indicates that he was no longer dependent on his old southern Maryland network and could plausibly go about in the postwar world of the upper Chesapeake with a badge of honor for having served the American cause. Judah died in 1816, and following that, Ball reported, "I was not often in Calvert county."[119] He bought a twelve-acre farm near Baltimore, in about 1820, "upon which I erected a small house, and became a farmer on my own account, and upon my own property." Ball shifted his focus to animal husbandry and market gardening. "I purchased a yoke of oxen and two cows, and became a regular attendant of the Baltimore market," he recalled, "where I sold the products of my own farm and dairy." There was no bright line between slaves' participation in informal economies and Ball's participation in a formal economy. The distinction was less important in the upper South than it was in the lower South in part because of market diversification and business networks that connected formal to informal market actors.[120] Saving the proceeds of his enterprise, he recalled, "I brought my little farm into very good culture, and had increased my stock of cattle to four cows and several younger animals." Out of his new customers Ball recruited potential allies, including a white tavern keeper, whom he "supplied with vegetables from my garden." He met and married a woman named Lucy and "now lived very happily," with "an abundance of all the necessaries of life around me." In the next several years, Lucy gave birth to four children. They also forged ties within their African American neighborhood. "I now looked forward to an old age of comfort, if not of ease," Ball recalled, "but I was soon to be awakened from this dream."[121]

Ghosts from his past returned to haunt him and terrorize his family. At nearly fifty years old, in 1830, Ball was plowing one day when three men showed up and arrested and beat him. Then they took him to Baltimore. He did not say where Lucy and the children were just then, but he did not get to say goodbye or ask that they send for help. Shut up in the "city jail," he recalled, "with several other black people," Ball learned that they "had lately been purchased by a trader from Georgia." City jails served as collection points for the enslaved who had been captured or who were being offered for sale. Sites of confinement were also some of the freest places for conversation and gathering intelligence. Few jails were segregated, either by gender or race. That was no comfort to Ball, for whom events were unfolding according to an alarmingly familiar pattern.[122]

His apprehension and puzzlement at the situation soon dissolved into despair and disgust. A man with "thin and gray" hair appeared and asked if Ball recognized him. Ball did not, initially. When Ball had last seen him over twenty years before in Georgia "had black, bushy hair." He then knew his captor as the younger brother of his late mistress. "I now saw the extent of my misfortune," Ball recalled. He lacked the money to ransom himself, and after two weeks in jail, "strongly ironed," he, along with the others, was taken by his captors out of Maryland, "chained together, handcuffed in pairs." It was a familiar tableau. Marched out of Baltimore in the direction of the national capital Ball passed through Blandensburg. There, "sixteen years before," he recalled, "I had fought in the ranks of the army, of the United States, in defense of the liberty and independence of that which I then regarded as my country." Ball's editor did not publish his gloss on the unintended consequences of fighting for the American side from the perspective of the coffle. "The thought now struck me," he averred, "that if I had deserted that day, and gone over to the enemies of the United States, how different would my situation at this moment have been." The strategy that served to protect Ball, Judah, and their children in 1813–14 had devastating consequences for his new family in 1830.[123]

By the 1830s, the domestic slave trade was intensifying. Ball, kidnapped, bound, humiliated, and forced to play the biddable chattel once again, trudged through Washington, D.C., past the architectural symbols of a republic he fought to defend. Fellow War of 1812 veteran Andrew Jackson then occupied the White House. Ball's coffle made its way down the well-trodden paths of the interstate slave trade, to Milledgeville, Georgia, "near which the man who had kidnapped me, resided." When Ball was first marched to Georgia, the lands surrounding Milledgeville were being evacuated by the Muscogee-Creek Indians, and it was not yet the capital of the state. By 1830, it was a thriving southern metropolis, home to Greek-revival mansions and buildings of state as well as the new Georgia penitentiary. Ball was not impressed, recalling instead the sparseness of the human environment: "I was now a slave among entire strangers, and had no friend to give me the consolation of kind words, such as I had formerly" in Georgia. On his second passage to the lower South he met no newly arrived Africans.[124]

Initially, Ball's struggles to escape were futile, though he went about gathering what human resources he could. He sought the assistance of a lawyer and attempted to sue his captor in court, but the man who kidnapped him in Maryland ordered Ball beaten senseless. Then he forged a bill of sale. When Ball's day arrived, the court legalized his kidnapping when it ruled that he must prove his freedom (though he had no legal right to challenge a white man) and presumed him a slave. A color line had also hardened since he had fled the lower South. Ball returned to the man's cotton plantation, where he was locked in a cabin at night to prevent escape, stinted of food, and beaten regularly in retaliation for his having sought a legal remedy for his enslavement. On Sundays, he was supervised by "an old African" and allowed to work marginal land for his own use. On a dark night in September, however, one of his captors neglected to secure the lock on his cabin, and Ball once again escaped. "Twenty years had wrought no change in favour of the fugitive," Ball discovered as he made his way out of the vicinity of Milledgeville and northward, keeping to densely wooded areas to avoid detection. A party of patrollers discovered him, beat him, and returned him to the owner, who promptly sold him for $580. Whether slave patrols were more effective or he lacked the nimbleness of a young man, he did not say.[125]

Ball soon escaped from that man's plantation and made his way to Savannah, Georgia, where he hired himself out transporting cotton from wagons to docks in the hopes of gaining passage aboard a ship. On the docks, he began once again to gather human and material resources to use in his plans to return to Lucy and his children. Ball befriended an African American sailor who, he learned, was a family man from New York. "Free sailors appeared as angels of liberty to some slaves," argues W. Jeffrey Bolster, and that black sailor—among whom 90 percent were northerners—was no exception.[126] Ball told him his story and asked his help, but the sailor reported he had strict orders "not to let any of the negroes of Savannah come on board." The sailor did give him some clues as to how to stow away, however, until the ship reached its destination in Philadelphia. "In my situation there was nothing too hazardous to undertake," Ball recalled, and after getting work loading the ship—and taking the opportunity to survey its architecture—he boarded, the sailor promising not to report it if he did. Ball had bought provisions with his wages and had arranged a small apartment between some cotton bales. He later remembered feeling great trepidation as the ship weighed anchor, sailed out into open waters, and past Cape Hatteras, North Carolina, on the northward voyage. After landing in port, Ball managed to talk his way onto land "with much difficulty" after he was discovered "on board a ship that lay alongside of that in which I had come a passenger" (not initially making land, he fled to another ship in the harbor in the desperate hope that onboard he would not be recognized as a fugitive from Georgia).[127]

Not sure where he had landed, Ball cast about for anyone who might help. He asked a black man he met on a darkened street if he was in Philadelphia. The interlocutor laughed "loudly" but gave no other response. Then Ball happened on a man "with drab clothes on," who gave him "a civil answer," that he had indeed landed in Philadelphia. The man was an African American Quaker who took him in, fed him, gave him a new set of clothes, "not more than half worn," Ball recalled with a measure of gratitude, and also "money to buy a hat and some muslin for a couple of shirts." His new benefactor "seemed a little incredulous" at the fantastic story Ball unfolded of his having escaped twice from slavery in Georgia but from then on was "a kind friend" to him. Ball's story was no more fantastic than that of Olaudah Equiano or Venture Smith generations before, but he did not insist on being believed. After a few weeks in Philadelphia, Ball returned to Maryland to gather Lucy and their children, sell the farm, and return to Pennsylvania and his hard-gotten release from bondage.[128]

At the close of his second American odyssey, Ball came home to find "his triumph enveloped in tragedy."[129] "Lucy and the children have all been stolen away," Ball recalled an African American neighbor saying to him immediately on his return. Like Ball, they were kidnapped and taken along the routes of the interstate slave trade to the land of cotton. Thunderstruck, Ball found out that they had disappeared in a similar manner to himself, abducted by white men and sold "in Baltimore to a slave-dealer from the south," according to the neighbor, herself a former slave who befriended Lucy and stayed with her and the children following Ball's abduction.[130]

Lucy's network had failed. A few weeks after he had been kidnapped, and "before Lucy had so far recovered from the terror produced by that event," Ball found out, she and her friend were awakened by a rapping at the door one night. A voice that seemed to be a woman's bid them to open it, but when she did several white men with blackened faces rushed in, closed the door against any escape, bound Lucy with rope, and "dragged out" the children hiding in bed. The men had taken care to disguise their identity and blend in to an African American neighborhood, where the presence of a gang of white men would raise an alarm. The neighbor was also bound tightly while her friend and her children were brutalized and then abducted. She languished undiscovered another full day and night before her release. "This intelligence almost deprived me of life," Ball reported. He departed Maryland for Pennsylvania immediately, without investigating further. After all, his Georgia owner sought him as a fugitive, and his friend the tavern keeper had shown him a "handbill . . . in which a hundred and fifty dollars reward was offered for my apprehension." Four years later, Ball published his ordeals. Neither Lucy nor their children returned.[131]

The Bayley and Ball families witnessed a small part of a hemisphere-wide movement of enslaved laborers, which changed the contours of the African diaspora in the nineteenth century and made the southern United States the most robust, dynamic, and profitable slave society in the Atlantic world by 1850. Those geopolitical and macroeconomic developments came about incrementally through the epochal theft of loved ones from families like Bayley's and Ball's. Through that everyday violence, legal or illegal, the United States slave market expanded and intensified in the nineteenth century at the same time that the Atlantic slave market was closing, albeit slowly. When the United States outlawed international slave trading to its shores, the Chesapeake became the headwaters of a great national forced migration that spanned half a continent. That process was the sum of thousands upon thousands of incidents such as that which transpired in the Bayley and Ball households.

The interconnection between broad historical processes and the everyday ordeals of the Bayley and Ball families is what Edward L. Ayers calls the "deep contingency of history."[132] Each kidnapping, sale, or separation was embedded in the development of the market for slaves and the goods they produced, in a manner similar to activities among people more identifiable as market actors, including planters, merchants, legislators, and mariners. Such a view suggests the human costs of the market expansion that is usually seen in abstract terms of cotton prices, internal improvement projects, tariffs, and ships at sail. In the first decade of the nineteenth century, Ball's labor was already part of a slave market that stretched up the Eastern Seaboard to New York, across the North Atlantic to the European trading centers of Lisbon, Liverpool, and London, and down to the inland slaving frontiers of West and West Central Africa. The transatlantic slave trade would supply some 3,466,000 slaves, including French and Portuguese "contract laborers," between 1801 and 1900 to a plantation complex stretching from Rio de Janeiro to the Chesapeake. The great age of abolition dawning by the time Bayley was put in a cart in Richmond and Ball was taken down the Eastern Seaboard was a time in which some 31 percent of all those taken across the Atlantic, from 1450 to 1900, would embark. At the same time, the geographic center of Atlantic slavery was moving north from the Caribbean Sea, from the punishing canebrakes of the Brazilian and Caribbean sugar complex, to the Black Belt of mainland North America. As the flow of captives across the Atlantic slowed, the march of coffles between the upper and lower South of the United States advanced. The terror of separation suffered by Igbo, Akan, Mende, Wolof, or Kongolese families was replicated in the African Americans who were sold away from their families in Maryland, Virginia, and North Carolina. One difference between those Africans landed in the Caribbean or Latin America and those landed in the United States was that forced migrants to the former replaced populations that did not sustain themselves. In the United States, they were captured by their countrymen and joined other Americans in a slave population that was forming families and multiplying. When Ball first arrived in the lower South, he was surrounded by newly arrived Africans. By the time he returned, there were scarcely any African-born slaves. Their children were instead in chains.[133]

Thamar and Solomon Bayley witnessed a crosscurrent of all that mobility. They became émigrés in Liberia in 1828, sailing to Monrovia with just over one hundred other African Americans in late 1827. With their children gone, they had little reason to stay in Delaware. Their piety informed their mission, and after the ordeals of buying a family out of slavery, they followed their faith and sense of separation from the world in which they had suffered the scattering of kin, forced to flee slave traders' confinements and bled dry by slaveholders. Solomon managed to visit Haiti before they moved, and they considered moving to Sierra Leone. In the early 1830s, he sent back to Delaware *A Brief Account of the Colony of Liberia*. He visited the United States in 1833 but returned to Africa as a missionary and preacher. There, the Bayleys formed a new network as citizens of an emerging expatriate community.

There, too, Thamar died of "old age" in 1835 and Solomon followed in 1839, of the same cause.[134]

Far from being strangers and afraid in a world they never made, the Balls and Bayleys of the upper South were network actors working in behalf of the constituents of their identity, their families and loved ones. Only when Thamar and Solomon Bayley lost their children did they leave the slave South. Ball fled back to Maryland and possible reenslavement twice rather than forego bonds with wives, children, and—not inconsequently—his personhood as husband and father. In the next chapter we see others who had similar experiences and met challenges by forging their own strategic ties following the War of 1812, as market intensification (or the "market revolution") worked to strengthen ties among market actors and at the same time placed additional burdens on enslaved families. As the coastal upper South became more interconnected owing to steam travel and the construction of canals, the enslaved who plied arteries of riverine commerce, piloted boats, or worked on docks found new ways to network and acquire through their ties information and resources to defend their own families.[135]

CHAPTER 2

Watermen

*O*n ships, boats, docks, canals, and waterways, enslaved people participated in the upper South's commercial redevelopment. The market whose sinews they in part constituted made possible the resources they sought, yet the same process of market intensification exposed more and more enslaved people to traumatic family separations. That was an irony of nineteenth-century American slavery and perhaps its tragedy as well. Modern political economies such as the United States and its trading partners around the globe saw increased demand for products that architects of the system put slaves to work producing. Whether Europeans or Americans bought cotton clothes, tobacco twists, sugar crystals, or coffee beans, their money found its way into the pockets of those who wrung the raw materials—and some of the finished products—from the sweat of the brow of enslaved African Americans. But enslaved people too stood within that system of cash and trade. Markets were made of people. As slaves in the coastal upper South of the United States piloted boats, ferried goods, packed, sailed, or constructed ships, they formed ties with coworkers, customers, employers, and other market actors. They drew resources from maritime contacts in commerce and reallocated them, using them to maintain family ties, often working overtime and out of sight of owners and overseers. Slaves like Moses Grandy moved many of the goods and people that knitted together a revitalized political economy in the coastal regions of the upper South after 1814.[1]

The circumstances under which Grandy lost his family members were connected to increasing demands for enslaved laborers in locations distant from his natal neighborhood in a swampy northeastern corner of North Carolina. Yet the means by which he accumulated resources to gather them up again also sprang from commercial intensification that integrated Grandy's immediate environment into an Atlantic and global market. By the time Grandy published his autobiography in 1843 the formerly enslaved boatman witnessed four generations of his family separated by sale. When he was young, Grandy recalled that his father "was often sold through the failure of his successive owners," until he was removed beyond reach of communication, and "four sisters and four brothers" had likewise been sold away. In desperation, Grandy's mother hid him in the woods. She could not protect him, however, from being taken from her and hired out to a succession of abusive masters as a child.[2] Tough early working conditions eventually gave way to work aboard canal boats in the first decade of the nineteenth century, on which Grandy learned the arts of riverine navigation. By his twenties, he was piloting boats and managing men. In swamps of solemn cypress, their knobby knees pointing up at the Spanish moss hanging from ponderous limbs, Grandy supervised other enslaved workers loading boats with timber and other goods. On the canal system that connected the Albemarle Sound with Virginia's James River trading complex, he guided boats to market and brought back goods and profits to his masters.[3]

From the docks, boats, and brackish waters of coastal North Carolina, Grandy witnessed the slave trade intensify in tandem with the market for the goods he hauled. Neither was an abstraction. Piloting a boat on the Dismal Swamp Canal, he looked up one Friday in response to a woman shouting his name to see a coffle of slaves marching away from home, led by two men he knew. He recognized his wife in the drove of people bound together and walking. She was tied up in a wagon. "She cried out to me, 'I am gone,'" Grandy recalled. With considerable "consternation," he then approached one of the slavers, asking, "for God's sake, have you bought my wife?" The man said that he had and matter-of-factly reported that "she had done nothing, but that her master wanted money." Such excuses rang in the ears and broke the hearts of generations of enslaved husbands and wives, fathers and mothers, sons and daughters. When Grandy advanced, the man he identified as Mr. Rogerson drew a pistol, warning him to come no closer to his property. "I asked for leave to shake hands with her," Grandy recalled, "which he refused, but said I might stand at a distance and talk with her." The captors seemed unmoved at a husband and wife so affected. By the time Grandy rid himself of bondage and traveled to England to tell that story some forty years later, six of his children, "three boys and three girls," had been "sold to New Orleans."[4]

Grandy had resources, but they were insufficient buy his wife. After learning that her owner was not using sale as punishment, Grandy tried to bargain with the buyer. Rogerson refused. "My heart was so full, that I could say very little. I asked leave to give her a dram," he reported. Grandy received permission only to empty his pockets and hand his few coins to Rogerson's partner, who conveyed them to Grandy's wife. There had been no warning or cause to formulate a strategy to forestall sale. They had been married eight months, and the owner had betrayed no plans to dispose of her. "She was well, and seemed likely to be so," Grandy recalled, hinting that she was pregnant, and "we were nicely getting together our little necessaries." He had left her the night before at the house of her owner, Enoch Sawyer. The next day, Grandy recalled, "I was at work as usual with the boats." It is impossible to know how Grandy felt and what passed through his mind as the wagon carrying his wife lumbered out of sight, amid the evergreen shrubs and smells of the waterfront. She was likely bound for Norfolk, Virginia, and an American slave ship. Grandy never heard from her again, though he recalled, "I loved her as I loved my life."[5]

Enslaved people were likely to have more than one person claim to own them in their lifetime. Grandy was owned separately by six men, and despite his being at the top of a hierarchy of skilled and self-hired slave laborers, four of his owners sold him as an adult. His first wife was sold, and Enoch Sawyer threatened him with the sale of his second and also sold several of his children. Michael Tadman contends that "forcible separation probably destroyed about one in three of all first marriages for Upper South slaves." Grandy's first owner sold at least one of his brothers when he was a small child, had sold his father before Grandy got to know him, and bequeathed Grandy to his son. After the first master died, Grandy was hired out at age eight to perform a variety of tasks to earn income for his second master, James Grandy, who was also his age and with whom he played. Mastering his riverine trade during the

War of 1812, Grandy transported goods from Norfolk to Elizabeth City so that they could be shipped out of the Ocracoke Inlet during the British blockade of the Chesapeake. In that line he earned the confidence and a measure of respect from potential patrons.[6]

Though enslaved, Grandy was well-placed enough in his small corner of the Atlantic commercial system to in time pry members of his family from the vicelike grips of their American owners. So did other enslaved workers in maritime trades who worked for cash or property and also for sponsors and citizens whose resources and recognition conferred "status without rights," Laura F. Edwards's provocative formulation. But slaves like Grandy faced a double bind of participating—however unintentionally—in the same commercialization that was dispersing their children in the hope of securing the means to avoid the sale and removal of loved ones. They competed in a market that prized skilled and able workers. Grandy's struggles and small triumphs came in the aftermath of the War of 1812, when trade between North Carolina's Albemarle and Pamlico sounds and Virginia was flourishing.[7] That enslaved businessmen like Grandy were conducting commerce on interstate waterways was tacitly recognized by a Virginia law enacted in the first decade of the nineteenth century, which threatened arrest and whipping for any "waterman of colour" who was found "strolling from his boat above the banks of the river." Enslaved watermen's independent commerce was something the architects of the system discouraged.[8]

In similar contexts other enslaved maritime workers were also able to use their skills in maritime trades to their advantage. Frederick Douglass, Abel Ferebee, and Peter Robinson were three of them. During the 1830s, Douglass was put to work in Baltimore shipyards, and from his Fell's Point neighborhood he witnessed the workings of the slave market into which many of his relatives disappeared. His lucrative maritime employments gave his master good reason not to sell him, and the geography of antebellum Baltimore presented opportunities to learn and grow, the streets and churches of the city serving as informal schoolyards and schoolhouses. He reached out to a patchwork of substitute caregivers as well. Along the docks of antebellum Elizabeth City, North Carolina, Abel Ferebee's maritime work saved his family from permanent separation. In the 1850s, on the same waterfront as Moses Grandy had worked, Ferebee managed to save his wife from transport after a fight with her owner led to her sale. Meanwhile, Peter Robinson's savvy operation of a steam tugboat in the harbor of Wilmington, North Carolina, launched a network that took him to California in search of resources to free his family. Over successive generations, Grandy, Douglass, Ferebee, and Robinson worked within the economic culture of American slavery seeking ways to protect against the family devastation it brought about. Their local environments were points on a far-flung Atlantic network, the reaches of which they could scarcely imagine.[9]

The Atlantic cotton trade was the engine of the American domestic slave trade, and with each ship's cargo that left New Orleans, Savannah, or Wilmington, loaded with southern products, producers in the southern interior demanded more slaves from upper South owners. By the time Moses Grandy was bidding farewell to family members who were being taken away in the 1810s and 1820s, the agricultural revolution in the lower South's cotton and sugar economies was creating a large and increasing demand for slaves like them. That process, in turn, was driven by increasing demand for American staple crops abroad. Liverpool merchants and Birmingham manufacturers transformed American raw cotton into textiles, and that transatlantic commerce propelled collateral industries such as shipping, banking, and insurance. Between 1800 and 1825, half of New York's exports were southern products. The U.S. government supported and protected the cotton trade and textile industry and as a consequence the slave trade. More cotton leaving southern ports meant more bound workers taken from upper South families.[10] Charles Ball had observed that process in its infancy.

Whether carried on by "Georgiamen" or migrating slaveholders, by the 1830s the domestic slave trade dwarfed the Atlantic trade to British North America that had brought the African ancestors of Moses Grandy, Frederick Douglass, and Abel Ferebee to the shores of eastern North America in the seventeenth and eighteenth centuries. As Ball had witnessed, there was overlap between the forced migration of captives from Africa to North America and the United States domestic slave trade. But nearly three times as many enslaved people were bound across state lines in seventy years, between the founding of the republic and the outbreak of civil war, than had arrived on the shores of British North America and the United States in the two hundred years before 1820.[11]

Numbers of human beings moved in that commerce merely suggest the intensity of the commerce and scale of its human misery. The Atlantic trade from Africa, the Caribbean, Gulf of Mexico, and Latin America had furnished slaveholders in British North America and the young United States some

361,100 slaves over nearly two centuries, between the second decade of the seventeenth century and the end of the first decade of the nineteenth century. In comparison, about 175,000 people were transported across state lines between 1790 and 1820. Some 155,000 enslaved people went after them in the 1820s, and 285,000 enslaved men, women, and children were forcibly taken across state lines in the decade of the 1830s. About 184,000 would follow in the 1840s, and 251,000 more would go after them in the 1850s. Like Grandy in the 1800s, 1810s, and 1820s, Douglass in the 1820s and 1830s, and Ferebee and Robinson in the 1850s, one generation bid farewell to members of the next who would themselves be bidding farewell one day. In 1790, census takers counted some 3.9 million people in the United States, of whom they counted over 690,000—18 percent—as slaves. By the time of disunion in 1860–61, the United States contained within its borders over 3.9 million slaves in a nation of over 31.4 million people. Over 12 percent of the U.S. population was enslaved in 1860, and their bodies had a higher cash value than that of any single species of property other than land.[12]

The U.S. government guided and supported the domestic slave trade by embracing the diffusion of slavery for three and a half decades, argues Edward E. Baptist, between the first legislation for the Northwest and Southwest territories and the first major political conflict over slavery extension in the Missouri crisis of 1819–21. When Moses Grandy was born in 1786, North Carolina claimed the territory north of South Carolina and south of Virginia west to the Mississippi River. The United States incubated the slave trade by permitting slavery in the Southwest Territory, ceded from North Carolina in 1790, while it banned slavery in the Northwest Territory. It supported the slave market, too, permitting, for example, state and national banks to sponsor slave purchases by selling bonds to finance cotton production. The federal government left it to states to regulate the domestic slave trade and, according to David L. Lightner, "no act of Congress ever attempted to ban the slave trade." The demand for slaves on the cotton and sugar frontiers gave lower South planters and upper South slaveholders' complementary interests in the slave market as sellers and buyers, though by 1850 even portions of the cotton South were net exporters of the enslaved. As Steven Deyle argues, "The domestic trade was not simply a consequence" of the "market revolution." Instead, he contends, it was "a central component in propelling it."[13]

As the sons and daughters of old African American families were sold into that commercial stream, slavers erased their identities, effaced their history, and turned them into labor components of the commercial empire American citizens relentlessly expanded in the first several decades of the nineteenth century.[14] When it came to selling slaves, according to Tadman, "the business of striking the right bargain was the question at issue, and against that consideration the integrity of the family took the lowest of priorities."[15] With a heavy heart, Moses Grandy would agree. As the southwestern portion of the nineteenth-century American empire expanded, it drew ever more human resources into the market for slave-produced products. The slave trade accelerated in the 1810s, especially after 1815 when American cotton and sugar planters pushed into territories newly claimed from France (and coerced from Native Americans) and after the United States concluded its war with Britain and completed land cessions from Indian nations. The cotton boom of the 1810s further integrated the young United States into an Atlantic and even a global trading system. The trade decreased after the panic of 1819 and subsequent economic slowdown but surged ahead in the "flush times" of the mid-1830s, again driven by production of staple crops in part financed first by the Bank of the United States and then by "pet banks." For several years after the panic of 1837, the process again lagged, but it did not lag much since by this time it was being underwritten rather efficiently by state banks. It began to boom again in the 1850s, this time with the help of advances in communications and transportation technologies.[16]

Perhaps perversely, what the market took away with one invisible hand it held out with another. Hired slaves in the seaboard upper South like Grandy participated in what Dylan C. Penningroth terms an "economy of time" in which they strove to work for extra wages or earn profits above what slaveholders received in hiring contracts for their labor. Flexible hiring arrangements, especially among semiskilled, skilled slaves or those working in urban centers, allowed some to work "overtime" or pay a flat fee for their hire and therefore keep some proceeds of their work. At the opening of her narrative, North Carolina native Harriet Jacobs mentions her enslaved father's remunerative carpentry work in the maritime town of Edenton, his independent hiring arrangements, and the reasons why he plied that trade. "His strongest wish was to buy his children," Jacobs recalled many years after his death, "but, though he several times offered his hard earnings for that purpose, he never succeeded." Like Grandy, Elijah Jacobs saw generations of his family separated and sold off. He knew the high stakes of his inability to protect his children. "Being, as he was then considered, the best house-carpenter in or near the town," Elijah Jacobs's son John recalled, "he was not put to field-work" but instead given "the privilege of working out, and paying his owner monthly." When his first owner died, and he fell into the hands of a man who had other plans for him, Jacobs's privilege of hiring his own time was "now denied him." His son recalled that "this added another link to his galling chain—sent another arrow to his bleeding heart. My father," wrote John S. Jacobs, "who had an intensely acute feeling of the wrongs of slavery, sank into a state of mental dejection, which, combined with bodily illness, occasioned his death when I was eleven years of age." Were the owner more lenient and the vicissitudes of the market more favorable, Jacobs's son might not have fallen victim to his daughter's tormentor James Norcom and Harriet Jacobs might not have spent seven years secreted in a garret after bearing one white man's children to avoid being sexually victimized by another (a strategy explored in the following chapter).[17]

To enslaved boatmen and porters, transportation trades offered practical instruction in business and the opportunity to use commercial ties to their own advantage.[18] Some were trained as boys or young men, and Melvin Patrick Ely argues that "some of the Afro-Virginian boatmen of the early nineteenth century" may "have learned their job from grandfathers or even fathers, who had worked as watermen in riverine societies of West Africa."[19] Educated in the arts of riverine commerce, Moses Grandy's skills eventually came to match his ambitions to preserve those family ties he could defend and to collect those scattered about the South. By the 1810s, Grandy was hauling goods on the twenty-two mile Dismal Swamp Canal that connected the ports of Elizabeth City and Norfolk. He was among an elite group of enslaved boatmen whose commercial activities gave them more mobility than those plying other trades at the time, sailors excepted. The canal itself was one of the largest public works projects in the South. George Washington had first surveyed the Great Dismal Swamp for Virginia with an eye to building a canal in 1763.[20] In 1792 the Dismal Swamp Canal Company advertised that it was "desirous of purchasing a number of good Slaves," provided that they were "not over 30 years of age, nor adicted [sic] to running away," and indicated that "a liberal price will be paid in cash." Construction commenced the following year. Initially, it was "a tedious meandering canal system designed to maximize the use of existing rivers and creeks." Built and maintained by slave labor, the canal "developed over a period of time before 1830," and though it gave business to Elizabeth City, it took it away from established port cities like Elijah Jacobs's Edenton. But it was not until the 1850s that technology permitted an efficient canal system to be completed. Nevertheless, even in its inefficient form, the canal gave eastern North Carolina direct access to the deeper and more accessible Virginia ports of Norfolk and Portsmouth. The slave-built canal incorporated eastern North Carolina into Chesapeake trading centers; it represented an incremental step toward commercially integrating the South and the nation. As on nearly all major commercial river routes south of the Potomac River, enslaved boatmen like Grandy transported goods, occasionally trading on their own accounts and sometimes assisting fugitive slaves. As the market expanded, so did slaves' paths of communication.[21]

Until the railroads and telegraphs eclipsed them in the 1840s, canals and the natural water routes they served were the primary arteries of commerce and information, which to the enslaved gave the Chesapeake and coastal North Carolina properties not dissimilar to the Internet two centuries later.[22] Navigable rivers flowed into bays and estuaries, and the enslaved people who worked in riverine and maritime trades were conduits of news and information, which they carried back and forth from port to port. With them, word passed from person to person, radiating inland and back out again from localities and trading posts where black boatmen, porters, sailors, and draymen congregated at the behest of, yet usually out of sight of, their masters and mistresses. Information was in turn diffused by family members, and kinship ties were maintained often at a distance through these information conduits.[23] Grandy conveyed word of happenings in Norfolk along with the goods he transported to Elizabeth City and back as far south as Ocracoke, a range of 150 miles, and relayed messages to and from more distant geographic locations. That was the grapevine telegraph before the telegraph was invented.[24]

The advantages, especially sailors' geographic mobility, conferred on those slaves who worked in riverine and maritime trades did not go unnoticed. Grandy's brother Benjamin was an enslaved mariner who worked on vessels plying the Atlantic trade. Owners worried, not without reason, that African American sailors were potential carriers of a contagion of liberty and sought to limit the exposure of local African Americans to them. The nautical knowledge of "black jacks" jarred masters, as it gave black sailors a special identity and importance. While a young man, Grandy witnessed Benjamin kidnapped and nailed to the floor one night for fear that he would use his knowledge of the seas to escape before his owner had disposed of him. Benjamin had just "returned from the West Indies, where he had been two years with his master's vessel," Grandy recalled. Hoping to be reunited with his brother, Grandy asked for and received permission to visit him. "While I was sitting with his wife and him," Grandy recounted, his wife's owner interrupted and asked him to carry some water into a storeroom. Benjamin complied. "While I was waiting for him and wondering at his being so long away," Grandy reported, "I heard the heavy blows of a hammer: after a little while I was alarmed, and went to see what was going on." What happened next was "the usual treatment under such circumstances." Grandy recalled, "I looked into the store, and saw my brother lying on his back on the floor, and Mr. Williams, who had bought him, driving staples over his wrists and ankles; an iron bar was afterwards put across his breast, which was also held down by staples." Benjamin had "done nothing amiss," according to the man who was nailing him to the floor, but he had been sold because "his master had failed," and Benjamin's sale would help pay the debts. His brother and wife could do nothing as he "lay in that state all that night." On the "next day he was taken to jail," Grandy recalled, "and I never saw him again."[25]

A seaman with knowledge of navigation and access to passage to the West Indies, Benjamin might well have escaped if he had learned of his impending sale and had not been immobilized. Runaway ads from early nineteenth-century North Carolina reflect that resourcefulness. A typical runaway ad in 1817 warned, "All masters of vessels and others are cautioned against harbouring, employing or carrying" off a fugitive named Jacob. The man in question was thought to attempt "to make his escape to the North in some vessel." Fugitives could blend in with other African American sailors. Ships' masters always wanted labor, and many crews were majority or all black, composed of free men and hired slaves. In 1814, an Edenton, North Carolina, slaveholder sought George, a thirty-seven year-old enslaved cobbler, and Joseph, a twenty-five year-old nail cutter, who had "followed the sea for some time past." The owner suspected that a maritime network offered the pair safe harbor. Joseph's "connexions live in the neighborhood of Capt. James Hathaway," the owner complained. Joseph "commonly wears ear rings, and is a very likely smart fellow . . . and has no doubt procured a free pass" for the purpose of escaping to the North. The earrings were fashionable sailors' jewelry and the "connexions" were erstwhile shipmates, friends, or family. The owner suspected he faced a conspiracy and not merely the desperate attempts of two men. Perhaps Captain Hathaway felt compassion for one or both men, but as the owner of eighteen slaves in 1810, Hathaway could not have been a conductor on a prototypical underground railroad.²⁶

Moses Grandy's bid for freedom was not simply an individual attempt to throw off his shackles. It was part of a strategic plan to prevent the sale of loved ones using the cash he earned. His strategy supports Penningroth's contention that "property was at the heart of African Americans' ideas about family." The key to Grandy's success was finding partners who were willing to let him allocate his resources to his own ends. In agricultural areas, enslaved people might expect to farm small plots of land on their own, as Charles Ball had done in Georgia. Some slaveholders went further. Former slave Henry Goings recalled speech a Tennessee slaveholder reportedly gave to his slaves. He gave them permission to "have coal kilns," in which to smelt metal, "and any Saturday night for a small share in the profits, I would let you take my waggon and horses and haul it to some blacksmith." He allowed them to cultivate a "patch" of land "and raise some sweet potatoes or water melons," agreeing to "go shares with any" of the enslaved. The owner promised to "furnish the land"; they could "do the work on Saturday nights" when there was moonlight. In sum, he stated, "there's a thousand ways in which you can make all the pocket money you need." In the antebellum Chesapeake and coastal North Carolina, that kind of informal economy was centered on cash or trade goods such as grain, timber products, or even oysters. In the tobacco-producing Piedmont, slaveholders gave slaves a stake in the market by allowing them to grow and trade tobacco on their own accounts.²⁷

Grandy set his plan to protect his family in motion by making an agreement, at the suggestion of a merchant, Charles Grice, with his owner James Grandy to buy his freedom for $600. Grice was the mainstay of Grandy's network and his principal employer. Brother-in-law of Grandy's owner, Grice was a shipbuilder and master of trading schooners that shipped coffee and other commodities from the Caribbean to the Chesapeake, North Carolina, Philadelphia, and New York. All his coffee and some of his wheat were produced using slave labor. Sometime magistrate in Elizabeth City, Grice owned the boats on which Grandy worked and, in 1810, twenty-eight slaves. When his daughter Susan married local merchant William Rogerson in 1829 (perhaps a member of the man's family who hauled off Grandy's first wife), a newspaper referred to him as "Charles Grice, Esq." In their business arrangement, Grandy partnered with Grice, taking on "shares" of the gross income for freight. Grice took half of the revenue off the top and Grandy used the rest to hire and provision his crew, keeping what remained as profit.[28]

The successful partnership between an international merchant and a slave was anomalous but not illogical. Grice had a lot of confidence in Grandy, so it made sense to have Grandy manage his boats and to rely on him to keep his own accounts. Grandy was in turn hiring his time from his owner. The enslaved man could not write and probably could not read, but his numerical literacy complemented his shrewd business skills. He quickly built social capital in the form of the trust of Grice's Norfolk customers and with it status based on his reputation for honesty and efficiency. In the canal boat trade, Grandy was quickly able to earn and remit money to his master for his freedom. Grice held up his end of the bargain, but the owner did not. "When I made him the last payment of the 600 dollars for my freedom," Grandy recalled, "he tore up all the receipts." Cheated of his money by a man who had been a childhood playmate, Grandy was beside himself.[29]

There was little anyone could do since Grandy had no legal standing as a party to a contract, despite his status as a business partner of a leading citizen. To embarrass his brother-in-law, Grice sued James Grandy for violating a contract. Grandy later reported that Elizabeth City residents were upset at the wrong done to a man they knew as "Captain Grandy," and supported the action. Grice's partner in the suit, William T. Muse, was a "Pasquotank land speculator who owned slaves and over 20,000 acres of swamp forest." He was a native of Westmoreland County, Virginia, who settled in Elizabeth City and served as clerk of the County Court of Pleas and Quarter Sessions between 1798 and 1823. It is unlikely that they viewed Grandy as a bondsman suffering slavery's dehumanizing effects. In suing Grandy's owner, they were not self-consciously striking a blow at the institution in which they were heavily invested as slave owners and shippers of slave-produced goods. The putative defendant, James Grandy, was a younger man who owned fewer slaves. The court refused to recognize a slave as a party to any contract, but by suing a slaveholder in behalf of a slave, Grice and Muse questioned James Grandy's honor. James Grandy was not shamed enough to give Moses his freedom or his $600 back.[30]

James Grandy took the next opportunity to dispose of his slave, and it seemed that like-minded men were lining up to squeeze money out of Moses.

James sold him to a "Mr. Trewitt," a businessman who had received word of Grandy's impending sale.[31] Trewitt had appraised Grandy in Norfolk and rushed to buy him when word of the scandal reached him. Knowing that Grandy's allies in business had made trouble for his erstwhile owner, Trewitt isolated Grandy from his old employers and customers. Grandy would no longer work on contract for Grice or hire his own time. Trewitt forbade Grandy to work on any boats but his own and curbed his profit-making abilities by controlling the terms on which he did business. Grandy did not like the restrictions, but he was still earning money. Impressed by Grandy's desire for freedom and inspired no doubt by his former owner's duplicity, Trewitt made him the same manumission deal: if Grandy could come up with another $600, he would be freed.

Trewitt's promise turned out to be as hollow as his canal boats. "Just when I had completed the payment," Grandy reported, Trewitt "failed." Without Grandy's knowledge, Trewitt had mortgaged him to his erstwhile sponsor Muse to finance an unsuccessful trading venture in the Caribbean. Having laid up $1200 and paid for his freedom twice, he was now the property of Muse. Grandy was unaware of his mortgage or Trewitt's failure in business until he delivered a letter to his new owner informing Muse that the man who bore it was now his property. Trewitt sent Grandy with that letter as he was going on his way to visit his second wife on Christmas. Trewitt cravenly paid Grandy $2 to deliver it, along with a shipment of goods to a customer on Newbegun Creek in Pasquotank County. Grandy did not recover the $600 he paid Trewitt after losing the $600 he had paid James Grandy. But for the fact that husband and wife could spend it together, that Christmas was not joyful for the Grandy family.[32]

Down $1200 and now forfeited to Muse, Grandy's trials were far from over. His reputation for being able to pay large sums of money to whoever owned him attracted the attention of another planter he knew all too well. Enoch Sawyer of Camden County had sold his first wife and now owned Grandy's second wife. After learning that Grandy was on the market, he refused to let him see his wife unless the slave agreed to help tug along his ship of fortune. Muse agreed to sell Grandy to Sawyer, perhaps at Grandy's request. Sawyer had demonstrated both cruelty and intransigence. As an ally, Muse may have sued James Grandy to embarrass him, but there was little he could do to move Sawyer, a merchant and planter of his own wealth and standing.

Sawyer was nothing if not consistent in his esteem for profits above slaves' sentiments. Grandy had been Sawyer's victim before, as a child abused in his employ. Then, Sawyer taught him an early practical lesson in slavery by starving him and leaving him exposed in cold weather. Sawyer was rising in the propertied classes when he bought Grandy. He owned "two plantations, ten slaves, a schooner, eight lots . . . in Elizabeth City, and approximately 10,000 acres of swamp forest in Camden and Pasquotank Counties." By 1820, he owned thirty-four slaves. Sawyer was also a trustee of the University of North Carolina and brother of Congressman Lemuel Sawyer. He was active in Republican Party politics and probably as a consequence was confirmed as collector of the customs and inspector of the revenue for the district and port of Elizabeth City shortly after President James Monroe's second inauguration in 1821. He also served as collector for the port of Camden from 1791 until his death in 1827.[33]

Like Trewitt, Sawyer worked to limit Grandy's commercial ties, even if he had nothing to fear from Charles Grice or Will Muse. Like Trewitt, Sawyer forbade Grandy to hire his own time. He could, however, return to the transportation business and start earning money again. Sawyer made Grandy foreman of his boats and hired assistants for him. Grandy began lightering shingles out of the Dismal Swamp, likely on the White Oak Spring Canal, in which Sawyer had invested. Lumber works were large employers of slaves, and eastern North Carolina was a major timber producer.[34] With little exaggeration, Harriet Beecher Stowe later dramatized Dismal Swamp timbering concerns in which "multitudes of slaves hired from surrounding proprietors" lived "in a situation of comparative freedom, being only obliged to make a certain number of staves or shingles within a stipulated time, and being furnished with very comfortable provision." They had "extensive camps in the swamp" and lived there "for months at a time" in "rude cabins."[35] In that line, Grandy recalled, "I got into a fair way of buying myself again." Soon, however, Sawyer too failed in business. He sold off eighteen slaves, his property near the Dismal Swamp, including two plantations, and put Grandy to work in his remaining fields, where he could scarcely accumulate resources. He thereby undermined Grandy's attempts to extricate his family from the owner's grip, which by then included his children as well.[36]

Having few local allies made Grandy more vulnerable to abuse. Sawyer ran his plantations like factories in the fields. The overseer regimenting ditching work "stood with his watch in his hand," Grandy reported, and "when he said 'rise,' we had to rise and go to work." Grandy protested such industrial discipline. After repeated requests to be let go from field work, Sawyer relented. He too wanted the money Grandy could earn. Grandy offered to arrange for a patron to put up the $650 Sawyer now wanted for him, but the owner consented only after Grandy received an endorsement from a canal overseer who he believed would not just rubber-stamp his slave, as he was known for his brutality toward slaves and contempt for people of African descent. That was in 1827. Grandy was forty-one years old.

Sawyer was not convinced that Grandy could raise the sum quickly, but his slave jumped at the chance. Grandy immediately rented a horse and rode fifty miles—a journey that took him into Virginia—and called on Edward Minor, with whom he had "done much business" in the past. Minor received him enthusiastically.[37] Minor lived on the road to Norfolk and was probably not the first potential patron Grandy planned to visit. Stopping for rest, Grandy explained to his erstwhile customer that he was going to "Norfolk, to get some of the merchants to let me have money to buy myself." Minor reminded Grandy that he had promised to help purchase his freedom should he get the opportunity. The Minor family had "strong antislavery beliefs," argues David Cecelski, but just as likely they had cultivated a respect for Grandy, as had Muse and Grice, by doing business with him. Mrs. Minor "rejoiced to hear" that Grandy and her husband had struck a deal for his manumission. Minor invited Grandy to board his horse at a nearby tavern, telling him that he "need go no farther" since Minor had "plenty of old rusty dollars," promising that "no man shall put his hand on your collar again to say you are a slave."[38]

Minor, who held no slaves, bought Grandy and let him set up his own business and arrange his own lodgings. Sawyer died the same year, in March 1827, which made it even more urgent for Grandy to work quickly. His wife was bequeathed to one of Sawyer's Virginia heirs. Sawyer's executors also distributed the Grandys' children to heirs or else sold them. While he worked on Dismal Swamp canal boats, during which time he spent one year on Lake Drummond recovering from "severe rheumatism," Grandy lived in a flimsy tent exposed to the elements and wild animals. He repaid the $650 Minor gave Sawyer for him by 1830. Grandy received manumission papers, which all told had cost him $1,850. Using his network of patrons and allies, he had finally gained his freedom. The year following his manumission, in response to the Nat Turner rebellion, North Carolina made such arrangements illegal.[39]

After being manumitted, Grandy commenced a struggle to collect members of his scattered family, an endeavor that would occupy him for the rest of his life. Under North Carolina law, any freed slave was obliged to leave the state within a year after manumission. He worked in Providence, Rhode Island, for two months before returning to his wife. But in North Carolina, "fear of a slave uprising grew into hysteria," argues Cecelski, and the violent and frenzied responses "led to a broad exodus of the free black population, particularly the more successful tradesmen." The legislature severely limited African Americans' liberties, including their freedom of association and movement, which meant that the sun seemed to be setting on the day black watermen could move about unsupervised. Grandy took to the sea, working on packet ships between Elizabeth City and northern ports, yet soon returned to New England. Initially, he was a stevedore, but he was soon working aboard ships that voyaged to the Caribbean and across the Atlantic. Making his home in Boston, he set about buying his wife from Sawyer's heirs. Seafaring was dangerous and the pay was hard earned, but it was one of the few areas of the U.S. economy in which African Americans enjoyed rough equality with whites. Grandy kept his object in front of him. "My entire savings up to the period of my return from this voyage amounted to 300 dollars," he reported. "I sent it to Virginia, and bought my wife. She came to me at Boston. I dared not go myself to fetch her," he recalled, "lest I should be again deprived of my liberty, as often happens to free coloured people."[40]

By 1840, his herculean efforts generated success, but most of his family was still scattered. In his fifty-fourth year, Grandy was living with his wife in Boston and had bought his eldest son and three grandsons. He had also been able to locate a daughter who lived near Norfolk, Virginia, whose master wanted $500 for her—$500 he did not then have. At least she had been found, unlike his three sons and three daughters who had been shipped to New Orleans, perhaps to pay Sawyer's debts. After he had purchased his eldest son and sent him to Boston, Grandy was able to arrange for a business ally to buy his sister, only to have the purchase nullified when it turned out that the owner had secretly mortgaged her, as Trewitt had done with him, and then failed. The new owner beat her repeatedly and sold her to Georgia, away from her two children, Grandy's nephews. Grandy located daughter Catherine, who was sold three times after leaving Virginia. She worked in cotton and sugarcane fields before being bought to take care of a mistress suffering from tuberculosis. After the mistress died, Catherine worked on Mississippi steamboats selling fruit to buy her freedom. Catherine afterward found her sister, Charlotte, working in sugarcane fields in Mississippi. Catherine and Charlotte struck a deal to buy Charlotte's freedom, using local arteries of riverine commerce. Both of them sold fruit and other small items and worked on Mississippi steamboats to raise the money. While away from her family, Charlotte's husband died, and Charlotte's owner—after freeing her for the sum of $1,200—demanded $2,400 more, or $600 each for of her four children. That was a sum she did not have. Even as members of the Grandy family reassembled, the newest generation was being scattered beyond reach. Grandy publicized his plight and sold his narrative in the hopes of bringing in enough royalties to buy them. "There are thus no lasting family ties to bind relations together," he lamented in 1843, "not even the nearest, and this aggravates their distress when they are sold from each other." The fifty-seven year-old former slave concluded, "I have little hope of finding my four children again." He did not say how he located family or name the agents he used to transact business back in Virginia and North Carolina. Grandy died before the decade was out.[41]

The Grandy family's ordeals show how precarious market-based networks were, even for the most well placed of the enslaved. If born free (and white), Grandy might have risen by talent and have become a successful businessman like Grice or Muse, sent his sons to college, and bought property. Perhaps like Sawyer he might have been a trustee of the University of North Carolina or a U.S. representative like his penultimate owner's brother. Instead, he spent his life's fortune buying relatives scattered about the South. His failures at the hands of James Grandy, Trewitt, and Sawyer illustrate how slaves' market participation usually benefited slaveholders and employers more than slaves and what bargains with whites entailed for people without rights. The unsuccessful lawsuit against James Grandy shows the limits of commercial patronage. Grandy's persistence is a testament to how much he valued both his own independence and the integrity of his family. His efforts took him on voyages to Great Britain, New Orleans, and the Mediterranean. In the end, Grandy sold the story of his struggles in England to buy his children. The pounds and dollars that resulted in manumission were drops in a sea of capital that flowed back across the Atlantic, capital that in part went to slavers who separated more families, and so on for another generation.

While he was enslaved, Grandy's strategy depended on flexible hiring arrangements, but for the enslaved, hiring was more perilous than advantageous. Hiring exposed workers to the market's risks and costs and disrupted family life because year-long or seasonal labor contracts between owners and employers usually separated workers from families. Hiring was the local complement to the long-distance slave trade. Grandy's stake in temporary work such as hauling shingles also enforced discipline that tended to forestall rebellion. Slaves were unlikely to run off if they were busy piling up resources to put toward manumission and family maintenance. Flexible working arrangements such as hiring also boosted productivity by efficiently reallocating slave labor to those who lacked the means to buy slaves.

The psychic and spiritual costs of separation from spouses and other family members are impossible to calculate, and those costs do not figure in the toll the bargains slaves made with owners and employers took on them. In antebellum Maryland, where slaves could expect to be hired more than they could expect to be sold, Barbara Fields argues, "even when manageable distance and agreeable owners and employers allowed regular visits, the result was hardly what a free person would have considered a genuine family life."[42] Children, deprived of nutrition, love, and instruction, bore the costs when mothers or other caregivers were hired away from them. "Frequently, before the child has reached its twelfth month," recalled Frederick Douglass, "its mother is taken from it, and hired out on some farm a considerable distance off, and the child is placed under the care of an old woman, too old for field labor." Douglass indicted the motives of slaveholders, contending that the arrangements were meant "to hinder the development of the child's affection toward its mother, and to blunt and destroy the natural affection of the mother for the child," which was "the inevitable result." The bitterness with which Douglass recalled the family effects of hiring—his mother had been subject to the conditions he described—suggest the ramifications of slave hiring on affective bonds and effective parenting. In the shadows of these powerful images lies the fact that enslaved people could and did use hiring strategically.[43]

Enslaved people outwitted laws and customs in the way they used the market, yet they were simply trying to do what so many Americans in the early republic strove to do: make money. They were often no less resourceful. Virginia slaves amassed property, for example, by selling stolen grain and harvesting oysters for the market in their free time. Penningroth argues that "strands in slaves' social networks reached out to fellow slaves, white neighbors, and shopkeepers"; all of them "participated in the informal economy, and their participation turned something that legally was nonsense into something that most southerners simply took for granted."[44] The participation of the enslaved in commerce upset some citizens, who petitioned legislatures and authorities attempted to curb these activities. Slaveholders largely acquiesced in their slaves' commerce, however, so long as their individual interests were not threatened and slaves' attention to their small enterprises tended to shift it away from serious plans for rebellion. Some owners were perpetually in debt to their slaves as customers who bought on credit. The savvier slave-holders knew in the nineteenth century what industrialists formalized as industrial psychology in the twentieth century. They gave slaves a stake in the market that would undercut nascent class interests and stifle organized dissent. Faced with the trade-offs between joining other discontented workers and protesting working conditions or redoubling efforts to earn extra money, demonstrate loyalty, and cultivate a network of allies, Moses Grandy or Elijah Jacobs would not risk losing another relative to forced removal for the sake of organizing with other slaves. Perversely, the market sliced through whatever solidarity existed within a neighborhood or "community."[45]

Frederick Douglass, eloquent abolitionist, and perhaps the most effective civil rights leader of his age, underwent a practical education in slavery. An important component of his early struggles was his strategic use of his environment in Baltimore and on his native Eastern Shore of Maryland in the 1820s and 1830s. Baltimore's human resources complemented the maritime industries that thrived there. Douglass's upbringing on the streets and docks of Baltimore was characterized by violence and abuse, yet he managed to form ties with enough caregivers, teachers, and supporters to tap into necessary resources for his development. Dislocations from family strained and severed many ties, but the bonds he built with substitute caregivers, educators, and other allies gave way to his participation in remunerative wage labor. As a school-aged boy, he traded biscuits for lessons and a few coins for a spelling book and oratorical primer. As a young man, he learned a maritime trade that led to self-hire and unsupervised mobility around Baltimore. He was shuttled across the Chesapeake Bay, not needed for field work on the Eastern Shore but too profitable as a maritime worker in Baltimore to sell into the interstate trade.

As the son of a white man who refused to recognize him and a mother who was hired at a distance and the grandson of a grandmother who was denied access to him after age six, he had few blood relatives to nurture and care for him. Unlike Bayley, Ball, and Grandy, family did not anchor his world. At least nine close relatives were sold during his childhood in Maryland. His cousin Betty and his aunt Maryann, for instance, were sold in 1825, the same year he saw his mother for the last time. He recalled that Baltimore traders sent "agents . . . into every town and county in Maryland, announcing their arrival through the papers, and on flaming hand-bills, headed, 'cash for negroes.'" (By 1815 Austin Woolfolk, who would quickly become Baltimore's most notorious slave trader, was indeed advertising "CASH FOR NEGROES" in a Baltimore newspaper.) The professionalization of the slave trade was underway.[46] Dislocations did not end there. In 1826, both his mother and his first owner died. At the age of eight, he was sent across the bay, having been selected by his second owner's wife to be a caretaker of her brother-in law's infant son in Baltimore.[47]

Douglass entered a maritime and commercial city whose resources were concealed within a formidable physical environment. After landing, he made his way with a new master to a new home on Aliceanna Street, just a block from commercial wharves and a short walk from the shipbuilding district of Fell's Point. The many new smells would have been at once exotic and familiar: fish and tar along the waterfront, horse and hog manure in the streets, and smoke from kitchens frying food for the urban workforce. The sounds of work were everywhere: shouts of sailors at the docks and foremen in the yards, the clatter of horse-drawn carts and carriages, and hoofbeats on the brick streets. Douglass found himself "walled in on all sides by towering brick buildings," in a bustling city in which the "hard brick pavements under my feet . . . almost raised blisters, by their very heat, for it was in the height of summer." He had received a pair of trousers for the journey but no shoes. In the second largest U.S. city, the human environment was just as imposing; "with troops of hostile boys ready to pounce upon me at every street corner," he recalled, "with new and strange objects glaring upon me at every step, and with startling sounds reaching my ears from all directions," the total effect was initially disorienting. His Eastern Shore home seemed "more desirable" just then. "My country eyes and ears were confused and bewildered here; but the boys were my chief trouble. They chased me, and called me '*Eastern Shore man,'* till really I almost wished myself back on the Eastern Shore." But initial bewilderment gave way to resourcefulness.[48]

Reaching out to people in his environment, Douglass soon began to take advantage of the situation in which he found himself. The new owner's brother Hugh Auld was in the shipbuilding business, and his absence from home during workdays gave Douglass the chance to learn to read from Sophia Auld, mother to the infant for whom he helped to care. When Auld found out, he refused to allow Douglass's reading lessons to continue. His new master's prohibition on his mistress's attempts to instruct him inspired him to reach out to the neighborhood schoolchildren who had initially taunted him.[49] For the first time in memory he was well fed, and he used the biscuits in the Auld's larder for tuition.

For Douglass, learning was inseparable from networking. He used pocket money he earned to buy books, tangible property that also proved to be good investments. In 1830, at twelve years old, he strolled into Knight's bookshop on Thames Street, and with fifty cents he had earned running errands—wages he was obliged to surrender to his master—Douglass bought a copy of *The Columbian Orator*. Twenty-five years later, he recalled, "Fortunately, or unfortunately, about this time in my life, I had enough money to buy what was then a very popular school book." What he failed to mention was the self-discipline it took to accumulate fifty cents and the audacity it took for a slave to walk into a neighborhood shop in order to purchase a book whose title page read, "Cato cultivated ELOQUENCE as a necessary means for defending THE RIGHTS OF THE PEOPLE, and for enforcing good Counsels." He also acquired a copy of *Webster's Spelling Book* and stole enough time to learn how to master both, with the help of hungry neighborhood schoolchildren.[50]

Douglass's love of learning led him to seek out other teachers, and he attended a Sabbath school at the Dallas Street Baptist Church, just north of his home, rising to instructor at fourteen. By 1830, the city and its environs had a sizeable African American population, over 10,500 enslaved people and nearly 18,000 free people of color in a county of 120,000.[51] Douglass's geographic mobility enabled him to form friendships with a religious mentor, Charles Lawson. "I could teach him *'the letter,'*" Douglass recalled of the African American drayman and lay preacher, "but he could teach me *'the spirit';* and high, refreshing times we had together, in singing, praying and glorifying God."[52] Waldo E. Martin Jr. contends that Douglass's relationship with

Lawson "gave him a much-needed father figure and role model," someone who could nurture the young man and affirm him. His network of allies was fragile, however, and Lawson's fellowship was short lived.[53]

The events that took him away from Baltimore and back to the Eastern Shore for three years, where he was hired out, show just how tenuous his ties were and yet how assiduously he recruited allies. In 1833, at fifteen, he was sent to work in St. Michael's, Maryland, a fishing village on the Chesapeake Bay. The cause was a disagreement between Thomas Auld, his Eastern Shore owner, and Hugh Auld, his Baltimore master, over whether Hugh would take Douglass's crippled cousin Henny Bailey. He refused, and so Douglass was sent back across the bay. Back in his native Talbot County, Douglass took the lessons he learned in Baltimore and sought connections with other young black men. He organized a Sunday school, which he designed to teach literacy in preparation for escape to the North. His efforts were quickly suppressed, an armed gang breaking up his meeting one Sunday. Unlike Grandy, who cultivated many white connections, Douglass sought to train up black rebels. "One of this pious crew told me," he recalled, "that as for my part, I wanted to be another Nat Turner." Douglass did not record whether he disputed that.[54]

For his efforts at organizing a school, Douglass was turned over to Edward Covey, self-styled "negro breaker," who rented the labor of enslaved people deemed by their owners to need to be taught obedience through violence and deprivation. There, cut off from friends and allies, his city clothing worn out and his rations cut desperately thin, Covey worked him "steadily up to the point" of his "powers of endurance," liberally applying a cow-skin whip. Douglass suffered from overwork, collapsing from heat exhaustion during the August harvest when he was sixteen.

But even in the ensuing fight with his employer that sparked his determination to escape north, he enlisted new allies. After running away from the employer, Douglass took refuge in the house of an enslaved man, Sandy, whom he described as a "genuine African." In the confrontation with Covey that followed, he did not face his employer alone. When another hired slave, Bill, found Douglass fighting the man to whom he had been sent to be "broken," Covey directed him to restrain his adversary, to which Bill responded, "My master hired me here to work, and not to help you whip Frederick." Neither Bill nor Douglass had been "broken," partly as a consequence of their alliance. Covey did not punish Douglass further. If word of the fight got out, his reputation as a hard driver would suffer. Following his year with Covey,

Douglass was hired out again, this time to Talbot County farmer William Freeland. He again reached out to other young men in the neighborhood and organized another Sunday school, which—like the first one—was actually an academy of rebellion. After he was caught, jailed, and threatened with sale out of state, Thomas Auld sent him back to Baltimore to learn a remunerative trade. Promise of profits from Baltimore work outweighed slave traders' ready money.[55]

Despite his agitation, Douglass's owners decided not to sell him and instead turned him into a cash machine in Baltimore's maritime industry. Slave traders were always in the market, which was skyrocketing in the mid 1830s, and time seemed to be on the side of Douglass's owners. Prices peaked for men in their late teens and early twenties, and in 1836, slave prices were as high as they had ever been (and would ever be, at least in terms of average prices for "prime field hands" in neighboring Virginia). Douglass was just eighteen, and any self-interested rational market actor would expect prices to rise farther at the same time that Douglass became worth more money. The young man had his own uses for his time in Baltimore. Like the fictional Ishmael's whaling ship, Douglass's Baltimore shipyards were his Yale College and his Harvard. After being severely beaten by white journeymen in William Gardner's shipyard, Douglass's master Hugh Auld put him to work in another owned by Asa Price. "There," Douglass recalled, "I was immediately set to calking, and very soon learned the art of using my mallet and irons." Caulkers sealed joints in the hulls of ships, making them watertight. It was an important part of construction, and he must have been very good at it because otherwise it was not likely that he, a slave with a history of subverting authority, would have been left to it. After a year of work, Douglass recalled that he "was able to command the highest wages given to the most experienced calkers. I was now of some importance to my master."[56]

His wages were considerable. Douglass remitted his pay, "from six to seven dollars per week" and "sometimes . . . nine dollars per week: my wages were a dollar and a half a day." Working six days a week, he would earn $9 or up to $450 a year if he worked all but two weeks at Christmas. His "importance" was rapidly growing. Like Grandy, Douglass was rising swiftly on account of his skill and ingenuity. Once he had mastered his trade, Douglass wrote, "I sought my own employment, made my own contracts, and collected the money which I earned," market behavior emblematic of capitalistic social relations. "My pathway became much more smooth than before; my condition was now much more comfortable."[57] Though obliged to turn over his wages to his master, he was able to spend a considerable amount of time outside of work and Auld's supervision. He also worked as a domestic servant, found debating partners in the East Baltimore Mental Improvement Society, of which he was the only enslaved member, and met his future wife, Anna Murray. But there was an irony to his paid work.[58]

The shipyards in which he worked were mainly turning out vessels for the coastal North American and Atlantic trade, much of which was in cotton and other slave-produced goods. Those shipyards in Douglass's Fell's Point neighborhood were hives of activity. In 1832, for instance, Price's shipbuilders, where he would work after returning to Baltimore after working for Covey and Freeland, completed "a brig two hundred and forty tons." Meanwhile at Durgin and Bailey's shipyard "two large brigs" were under construction. "At Robb & Donaldson's a brig two hundred and fifty tons" was being built, and at Duncan and Beacham's shipbuilders, workers were building vessels of five hundred tons each. At Gardner's shipyard, where Douglass would be brutally assaulted by journeymen caulkers angry over having to compete with African Americans for work, workers were also building a five-hundred-ton vessel. A "large ship" was under construction at Kennard's; a "large schooner" was being built at Miles's shipyard; a "schooner" at Stevens's; "a ship" at Culey's; and at Skinner's shipyards a "beautiful steamboat 'Patrick Henry'" was then "receiving her machinery." Also at Skinner's, "on the stocks in a great state of forwardness" workers were constructing "a steamboat which bids fair to rival anything of the kind on the Chesapeake." Finally, a "noble ship 'Medora'" owned by Luke Tiernan and Sons, bound for the Liverpool trade, "was launched from P. Beacham's yard" in August of 1832. That vessel would transport cotton from U.S. ports to England.[59]

Douglass's work in the local labor market also contributed to the Atlantic trade in slaves. Among the many vessels Douglass sealed were the hulls of slave ships. Douglass assisted in the building of the *Delorez*, the *Eagle*, and the *Teayer* at Price's shipyard in Baltimore. All three coastal trading vessels would head to the international slave trade in the Caribbean and South America after being refitted with iron restraints for the captive Africans. The enslaved caulker did not comment on whether he noticed that the ballast tanks were constructed to carry fresh water rather than salt water.[60]

Amid the social chaos of having several members of his family sold out of state and the upheavals of being sent from place to place at the whims of his owners and their family members, Douglass entered adulthood as fully formed and socially literate as any white person he came across in Maryland. He faced severe challenges, not the least of which was workplace violence and a master who was hostile to his efforts at self-improvement. He gleaned news, information, and even wisdom from his surroundings, reading newspapers and sacred texts. His cash wages complemented the social capital he accumulated as a clandestine participant in civic organizations such as the East Baltimore Mental Improvement Society. Those, in turn, broadened to affective connections such as that with Anna Murray. Unlike former associations, such as with Charles Lawson and the Dallas Street Baptists, that he made before his return to the Eastern Shore and Covey, the alliances he formed in late 1830s Baltimore provided him with social ties with the potential to last. Were Douglass forty-one, as Grandy was when he finally broke free of his owner's grasp, and not twenty when he boarded railroad cars bound for the North in 1838, Douglass might have used his resources and resourcefulness to protect family members from enforced separations. The actions of his owners and those who owned his family stripped him of all of his close family members, which cut blood ties that would have anchored him to the land of his birth.[61]

Douglass honed skills in a market that paid his master well for them. His earnings were much higher than the average Baltimore worker in a city where the almshouse was choked with the desperate in winter and many free workers were merely scraping by. Though Douglass competed with "free" workers, his work was more remunerative than that of most of Baltimore's workforce, illustrating that in purely economic terms there was no bright line between free and slave labor, despite the persistence of the distinction in antebellum political ideology. There was no sharp distinction between white and black labor in Baltimore either, and employers routinely stifled white workingmen's initiatives to draw one. Douglass faced exclusion from the caulking business only when he reached New Bedford, Massachusetts, where no master was standing behind him ready to steal his wages. In antebellum Baltimore, even "free labor" was often free solely in a theoretical sense.[62]

Markets were not guarantors of the equality of parties to labor agreements, and the prevailing free labor ideology ignored the actual conditions in which most antebellum workers eked out a meager living. Seth Rockman argues that free laborers suffered when they did not meet employers as equal parties to labor contracts in which they were legally and ideologically equivalent.

Nonenslaved children, women, the ill, and disabled, unskilled, or utterly impoverished workers were legally free workers, though all had serious market disabilities. Children and women in the free labor market did not receive living or "family wages," even for more valuable work, because employers assumed they were dependent upon a male breadwinner. Among the desperate and destitute, the necessity of generating income, however desultory, created a wage market that was often below subsistence levels.[63]

Labor market realities partially explain why Douglass was subject to violence at the hands of white workers. Even among adult males, unskilled, sick, physically disabled, and even foreign workers had trouble earning a living in the Chesapeake's free labor market. Union organizing, protective labor legislation, and health and safety regimes were in their infancy. So was poor relief. Social insurance, compensation for disability, and unemployment payments were unheard of. The prevailing ideology of work was that people were poor owing to individual moral failings and that the laboring classes were fundamentally lazy. "Celebrating the capacity of an impartial market to dole out material rewards," Rockman argues, "the advocates of American economic development rarely paused to explore the consequences of transforming labor into an undifferentiated commodity. . . . In the ensuing scramble, those selling their labor like bread and meat would find it increasingly difficult to afford either, while their spent bodies revealed the voraciousness with which the market could consume them." The blood Douglass's attackers spilled in an antebellum shipyard illustrates the resulting discontents.[64]

Abel Ferebee's family trials show the market could consume the income of a skilled maritime worker, even as he used it as a lever to keep family from being scattered about at the whims of slaveholders. Ferebee worked in Elizabeth City, a generation after Grandy plied the sounds and canals of northeastern North Carolina. It had also been two decades since the panicked responses to Nat Turner's rebellion and David Walker's *Appeal . . . to the Coloured Citizens of the World* had led to tightened restrictions on African American watermen. Ferebee worked out of sight of his owner, who lived thirty miles away in Currituck County. Elijah Jacobs failed and Moses Grandy only partially succeeded in making the market work to cement family ties, but Ferebee had more luck, although there were the unintended consequences that usually accompanied such arrangements. As in so many cases of enslaved family separation, a single incident inflamed smoldering animosities, which resulted in one member's sale and removal.

On a Tidewater morning in the late 1850s, Chloe angered her mistress, Sally Whitehurst. The mistress confronted her slave in the kitchen of her Currituck County farmhouse and attempted to hit her, in response to which, Chloe's son recalled, Chloe said, "If you strike me, it will be the dearest lick you ever struck." The mistress's son Peter then confronted her. "Chloe," her son recalled the man saying, "if you don't let me whip you for saucing your mistress, I'll shoot you." Chloe's son London reported that she responded by "opening her bosom" and exclaiming, "Shoot; that's the only way you can whip me." Peter took the bait and attacked her with a "cowhide" whip. Chloe counterattacked. "She cut it in two with a butcher knife," London Ferebee recalled, after which "they then gathered each other and my mother threw him, and as he fell the gun discharged." The shot missed. "She put one knee in his breast," Ferebee recalled, and the other "on one arm" and then "wrested the gun from his hand and struck him over the head with the breech, wounding him badly, so that he called for help." Chloe was shortly "removed by some of his men." By embarking on that course of action she seemed likely to be bound away to labor on some distant cotton field. Sale as punishment for disobedience was the cornerstone of the domestication of slavery in the nineteenth century, since a few earnest threatening words could accomplish what a branding rod or iron collar had accomplished the century before. "That morning," Ferebee recalled, "he sold her to a speculator" from neighboring Camden County.[65]

For most enslaved women who rose up against a master or mistress, that would have been the last their loved ones heard of them. Chloe was poised to enter the stream of Atlantic commerce that would, if she were taken to the cotton South, connect her field work to the Manchester or Massachusetts manufacturer, London or New York banker, Portsmouth or Philadelphia shipper, and Liverpool or New Orleans factor. But Chloe managed to prevent that. She thought quickly and told the slave trader that her husband, Abel Ferebee, might be able to arrange for her purchase. By the end of the day, Chloe's husband's master, Enoch Ferebee, had bought her for $1,100, even though Enoch lived in Sally and Peter Whitehurst's neighborhood. Buying a rebellious slave punished for an attack on a white man was not something designed to promote good will between white neighbors. There was, however, an overriding financial incentive.[66]

Abel Ferebee could pay for his wife and child. He could not buy them out-right, but he could pay the owner a retainer or fee that would allow them to be reunited. An enslaved shipbuilder, Ferebee was hiring his time from his owner and working at the Burgess and Martin shipyard on what was Shipyard Street (now Pearl Street) in Elizabeth City. After paying Enoch Ferebee a flat hiring fee each year, Abel kept whatever he earned on top of that. W. F. Martin and his partner were constructing vessels for trade with the West Indies, which connected Elizabeth City to a broader economy. The North Carolina interior had abundant lumber supplies and an able workforce. Ferebee was in a position not unlike that of Douglass in Baltimore two decades earlier, except that he had a family to protect. The arrangement gave Ferebee some financial stake in his employment, just as similar arrangements had done for Grandy and Douglass. It gave him an incentive to be a more efficient worker and some hope of improving his situation.

By the 1850s, Elizabeth City, the point of entry to the Dismal Swamp Canal system, was suffering a fate similar to that of other eastern North Carolina ports: the railroad from Portsmouth, Virginia, to Weldon, North Carolina, which had opened in the 1830s, was siphoning off Roanoke River trade that before had passed through the Albemarle Sound on its way to the deep water ports of the lower James River in Virginia. In the late 1850s, Virginia constructed the Albemarle-Chesapeake Canal from Albemarle Sound to Norfolk, twenty-five miles above Elizabeth City, which diverted freight traffic from the old Dismal Swamp Canal. "The large trade that now centers in Elizabeth City from the hundreds of vessels that yearly pass through the Dismal Swamp Canal," a local editor warned in 1859, "will be, in large measure, carried to other places." Grandy's economic niche had largely closed, but Ferebee was able to plug his talents into a maritime trade serving a larger market and earn money enough to pay his owner and provide for a family.[67]

In doing so, Abel Ferebee chose the immediate defense of his family over whatever promise of freedom his lucrative maritime trade made possible. Ferebee's choice is better described as that between family or not-family rather than between family or freedom. For most of the enslaved, freedom was not on the table in negotiations with slaveholders.[68] Abel secured his wife's purchase price by agreeing to remain a pliant worker and to contribute whatever extra cash he earned to the maintenance of his family, which his owner no doubt found financially appealing, although it's also possible that in the swiftness of the transaction, Enoch Ferebee bought Chloe before finding out the cause of her sale. The nuclear family was thus reunited through the slave trade, the trader making the calculation that the Ferebee family's ties were worth more than the price of a rebellious slave on the open market.

Like so many slaveholders in the upper South, Enoch Ferebee was hiring Abel out at a distance and bidding him to work unsupervised in exchange for a yearly rent. But this was not necessarily a permanent situation, especially given that in the 1850s, slave prices were rising faster than they had in a generation. Furthermore, even if market fluctuations in Enoch's part of the South meant slaves were being hired to perform an increasing variety of work, that did not mean they were getting any closer to freedom. Abel's family unity probably came at a price high enough that he could not expect to buy his freedom or that of his family any time soon. As slave prices rose, so did the amount Abel would have to pay for manumission. North Carolina's restrictions on free blacks were still in effect, if not as rigorously enforced as they had been when passed, but freedom for one member of the family obliged her or him to leave the state. Virginia passed a voluntary enslavement statute in 1856 to remedy that requirement. Maryland followed suit in 1860. Slavery may have enervated the creativity of southern planters, but employers of slaves were caught up in capitalist calculations.[69]

In a sea of perils, successes for the enslaved Ferebee family worked more like bilge pumps than safe harbors. Abel Ferebee's emergency dealings worked imperfectly. Chloe and Abel enjoyed the last of their twenty-two years of marriage near each other, but the new owner bound out Chloe and Abel's oldest son London as soon as he was able to learn a maritime trade. London Ferebee later recalled the harshness of his new master and saw his mother only twice again before her death. He nevertheless learned seamanship and navigation from his father. Husbands like Abel Ferebee were reunited with wives like Chloe, but sons like London were lost to the hiring market as a consequence.[70]

Though the Ferebees managed to salvage some components of a nuclear family in the ordeal, enslaved families tended not to form according to a regular structure. Strategies like the Ferebee and Grandy's more often failed to support family cohesion. Building a flexible family structure was a secondary strategy, and most enslaved people lived with a mix of distant and close relatives along with nonblood relations such as adopted children. The stability of enslaved families partially depended on the solvency and longevity of owners, whose financial probity and health could provide the means of keeping families together, if only temporarily. Careers of slaveholders such as John Cowper Cohoon of Nansemond County, Virginia (today the city of Suffolk) reveal how large slaveholders' livelihoods could influence the lives of the enslaved. Herbert Gutman contends that Cohoon initiated a cycle of "family destruction," around 1835 when the young and aspiring planter assembled slaves to work his lands. The initial destruction of families in that assemblage was followed by "construction," when Cohoon became "a planter who allowed slave families to 'stabilize' in order to nourish and enlarge that enterprise." When owners like Cohoon failed in business or died, slaves faced forced separation, since wills divided property among heirs.[71] Perhaps an ironic epitaph to Grandy's struggles is that today "Moses Grandy Trail" (Virginia route 165 in Chesapeake) takes visitors to the "Cahoon Plantation" golf course. Moreover, Ferebees intermarried with Grandys by the emancipation generation, showing the proximity of Abel Ferebee, Moses Grandy, and their extended families.[72]

Where there were few strategies the enslaved could use to save blood kin from sale, enslaved families engrafted parts of families to replace trees' severed limbs. For example, on Somerset Place Plantation in Washington County, North Carolina, enslaved people faced with an unusually high rate of mortality and with the loss of heads of families to sale formed a variety of family structures, based on local contingencies. Wayne K. Durrill contends that the enslaved families of Somerset Place Plantation "did not centre their working lives around extended families, marriage by strict rules of exogamy, or an exchange of resources among organized kindreds. . . . Instead, they formed many households—nuclear, stem, extended." Not conforming to a sociological model of mutual exchange and adaptation, Durrill argues, "the social life of slaves was subordinated to the production needs of planters supplying cotton to a world market."[73] The trials of another family from coastal North Carolina contextualizes the perils even the most well placed enslaved family faced.

The Robinson family's ordeals show how broad a slave's network could be and how quickly it could vanish. They reveal slaves' extraordinary geographic mobility and simultaneous resourcefulness. Rosy and Peter Robinson were members of "the Madagascar tribe," their son William Robinson wrote, in which "father was prince." That was unusual but not unique since the Atlantic slave trade to the United States had slowed but not stopped in the antebellum period, and other Madagascar-descended American slaves lived in the coastal upper South.[74] Political leaders were captured and sold into the Atlantic slave trade by rivals. In his new surroundings, Peter Robinson became an "engineer and a skilled mechanic" in Wilmington, North Carolina, operating a steam tugboat for his owner in an area that "fairly teemed with steamers" in the 1850s.[75] That busy port on the Cape Fear River linked the interior of south-eastern North Carolina with markets for its turpentine and timber products. By 1850, fourteen of Wilmington's thirty-four manufactories were distilling turpentine, which sealed the wooden hulls of ships. Slaves' participation in the local economy is suggested by the diversity of work they performed. Wilmington slave owners took out insurance policies on the lives of workers, including an engineer, steam sawmill workers, coopers, masons, a mason's ap-prentice, maritime cooks, stewards, waiters, millers, distillers, domestic cooks, house servants, turpentine workers, bricklayers, carpenters, a "Book and shoe maker," and two slaves working as "Penman." In addition to products from the Cape Fear region, the port shipped cotton from the southern interior and imported molasses and other goods from farther south.[76]

From his tugboat, Robinson surveyed all that traffic and commerce and even derived a small living from it. Over his fifteen-year career he received many "tips," his son William remembered "by being courteous and always on the alert for ships heaving" or drifting with the bow into the wind. The owner consequently "received pay for the towage," and Robinson, through "con-stant contact with white men, received money in many other ways." Other employments on the docks included sewing up sacks of peanuts, for which the laborer received one and a half cents per bag. African American women, working on their own initiative, gathered molasses from barrels left in the sun after being unloaded from ships arriving from New Orleans. The heat caused molasses to escape through the chimes, and they would scoop it by hand into pails and sell it to poor whites. Through their remunerative work, the Robinsons integrated themselves into a network that could confer advantages to family and members of their neighborhood in a corner of the South where nearly half the population was enslaved and more than half were nonwhite.[77] "As association breeds assimilation," his son explained, "so my father learned the art of making and saving money until he had accumulated about eleven hundred dollars."[78]

Robinson also gathered wealth in people. In addition to goods, Peter Rob-inson was an important conduit of information for African Americans in his neighborhood. "Father was almost a prophet among my people," William Robinson recalled, "because he secured all the news through his Quaker friends, and other white men that were friendly to him, with whom he came in contact. Then he would tell it to our people." Prophets were not predictors of the future so much as they were intermediaries with the ability to interpret the divine. Robinson mediated the outside world to those who lacked his mobility and associations and consequently made allies among the enslaved.[79]

Transmitting news and information that would not likely appear in the *Wilmington Daily Herald* or *Wilmington Journal*, Peter Robinson also formed strategic associations with black maritime workers and other Wilmington residents. Two Quakers who owned oyster sloops were Robinson's owner's frequent customers. They were also active in the Underground Railroad. Robinson sought to cultivate that network as well. Towing the sloops out to sea gave the Quakers and Robinson "an opportunity to lay and devise plans for getting many into Canada," his son recalled. Robinson assisted slaves in his neighborhood, and he himself planned to move his own large family beyond the reach of slaveholders by first buying himself and then setting up in Canada. Once established, his friends would send wife Rosy and his children, including son William, after him.[80]

Robinson's success in recruiting allies through his work is partly the result of what sociologists have termed the "strength of weak ties."[81] His alliances with his owner's customers, people with whom he putatively shared little, was a first step in gathering resources not available through the strong ties of his family, church, or neighborhood. Those strong ties were the constituents of his identity, but he was able to draw in far-flung resources through men with whom he shared weak ties—those with whom he could converse on board his owner's tug. He could not expect to form public friendships or any but clandestine alliances with them. Although sociologists who work with concepts of weak versus strong ties construe network actors as autonomous individuals, the proposition that enslaved people used weak ties to their advantage does not imply that their personhood conformed to twentieth or twenty-first-century conceptions of liberal individualism.[82] Robinson was first and foremost a father and husband, and he used his weak ties to protect those relationships that mattered most rather than to accrue benefits as an individual.

Perhaps through the weak ties he formed with his Quaker acquaintances or other customers of his owner's tugboat, Robinson hit on a strategy that could allow him to quickly put into action a plan that would first give him legal freedom and second allow him to accomplish the escape of his large family. He would strike out to California, the El Dorado of the American West, and work for the high wages that even African Americans could earn in gold country. Although it is unclear how, Robinson was able to map out how to get there and then to beat the odds against failure by overcoming the obstacles that stood in his way: the uncertainties of distance, the threats to his health, the vicissitudes of local and distant labor markets, and the fact that he had to rely on the slaveholder whose word would seal or break any deal. By sea, California was farther away from North Carolina, even by way of New York, than Madagascar was from the Atlantic coast of North America. Robinson may have viewed his geographic location as a point on a globe far from home rather than as the place of his enslavement that he was tied to. There were distinct perils in that outlook, but other captured African nobles, such as Abd al-Rahman Ibrahima bin Sori, had a similarly broad geographic understanding of the world of slavery they inhabited.[83]

Without knowing the extent of Robinson's plans, his owner reluctantly agreed to take $1,150 for his slave's manumission: $450 down with installments to follow. He also required Robinson to pay interest on his purchase price and train his replacement at the tug. By agreeing to sponsor Robinson's independent production, his owner became the lynchpin of his network. Since the owner also held Robinson's large family in bondage, he had a surety that Robinson would pay the balance, which he began to do after joining a surveying crew in California. For Robinson, that surety was the very obstacle to family integrity he was seeking to remove.[84]

California gold country was attracting hundreds of thousands of anxious migrants in the 1850s, and North Carolinians were as susceptible to as anyone to "gold fever."[85] (Robinson wisely chose to work in an enterprise other than mining.)[86] Moreover, wages were much higher in the "gold-enriched economy," and African American steamboat porters could earn $150 a month, an unheard-of wage back east.[87] Robinson's travel to California to earn cash shows how slaves' networks expanded along with the United States. When Grandy saw his first wife disappear in a wagon, the site that would become San Francisco was largely sand dunes occupied by Ohlone-speaking Indians and a Spanish mission. When Douglass was working in Baltimore, it was a small Mexican seaport village. By the time Robinson formulated his plans, it was the newest state's swaggering boomtown and the gateway to gold country. Robinson likely obtained passage first to New York on one of the schooners or other sailing ships that regularly transported goods and passengers to and from Wilmington.[88] From there, he steamed to California in the late 1850s, probably on a Pacific or U.S. Mail Steamship Company ship traveling between New York and Panama, and then went overland on the Panama Railroad, boarding a ship to San Francisco on the Pacific side of the isthmus.[89] His son left few details of his travels, but Robinson likely worked on those steamships in order to gain passage. Without using a post office or the telegraph, Robinson was also able to get news back to his family by word of mouth, the "news" traveling "clear from California to North Carolina," likely through other African American sailors.[90]

Robinson took a big gamble by straying so far from his familiar environment. His family must have paid a price too. How many mornings did Rosy or one of their twelve children go to the Wilmington docks to scan the horizon for the New York packet or to enquire from other black sailors news from California? How many sleepless nights did they spend wondering when or whether Robinson would return from so far away? Care of children fell squarely upon Rosy's shoulders. During the holidays, Robinson returned from California, likely with big stories and small gifts—and with $350 cash, which he turned over to the owner. And then he departed again.

When Robinson was on his way back to Wilmington to visit his family the following year, he fell into a trap. His owner sent a slave trader to capture him at a transport location, likely New York City. The owner pocketed his freedom payments and the proceeds of his sale, just as Grandy's owner and many other owners had done. Did Robinson's work on the Underground Railroad come to light? If so, it would have conjured memories of subversive activities among slaves in the past. It had been nearly thirty years since Jacob Cowan, a man owned by the same Cowan family who owned the Robinsons, had been discovered distributing two hundred copies of David Walker's inflammatory *Appeal* in Wilmington and beyond. Maybe the owner simply got greedy. The Robinson family heard no reason for his sale. The slaveholder took advantage of a network of slave traders and the legal latitude to cheat Robinson with impunity. Robinson would have been easy to find. He was due to return to his family, possessed a certificate of permission from the owner, and he was probably working on a steam vessel. New York was no safe haven, as Frederick Douglass recalled of his own sojourn there twenty years before: "There were hired men on the lookout for fugitives from slavery, and who, for a few dollars, would betray me into the hands of the slave-catchers."[91]

When next Rosy and their children saw him, he was in chains. "We saw him pulling his whiskers," his son recalled, which was "a mark of deep sorrow with him." He had been shackled constantly for fourteen days in transit to his native North Carolina, and the manacles had left his "flesh . . . swollen so it made it almost impossible to unlock them." Robinson's Wilmington friends suffered as well. A few nights after Robinson was sold, local whites threatened one of the Quaker agents of the Underground Railroad who helped him, and that man soon disappeared and was "never . . . heard from" again. His family suspected murder.[92] Robinson's network had collapsed, and his family lost him to the market for his body.

As maritime workers, Moses Grandy, Frederick Douglass, Abel Ferebee, and Peter Robinson all confronted the market directly, using its tools to their putative advantage. Their local opportunities, decisions, and strategies were influenced by broader social, economic, and political processes they could hardly glimpse. None knew the full ramifications of their work or the precise geopolitical reasons their relatives were scattered to the west, but they knew intimately the costs of those processes and the stakes for which they worked in, through, and against the market. When Moses Grandy looked up from his canal boat in the first decade of the nineteenth century to see his wife bound to a coffle of slaves marching to market, he could not know exactly why they were being separated. By the time he was a grandfather telling his story to British abolitionists, however, Grandy had witnessed the devastating social effects of the population shifts those coffles embodied. The burgeoning maritime industries of the Chesapeake and coastal North Carolina gave each, in his own time and in his own way, opportunities to keep blood kin out of coffles, collect them when scattered, or else protect themselves from sale and removal. Each effort, however, must have felt like rowing against the tide. Grandy expended all of his resources to free himself and collect his family, one by one, and by the end of his life slavery was as deeply entrenched as ever. His life's resources went into the pockets of slaveholders who were happy to cheat him and sell his children. As he and Ferebee found out, earning money was secondary to cementing patronage ties with a trustworthy free agent, whether Edward Minor or Enoch Ferebee. Douglass escaped but lost so many of his relatives in the slave trade that coffles appeared as apparitions. "In the deep, still darkness of midnight, I have been often aroused by the dead, heavy footsteps and the piteous cries of the chained gangs that passed our door," he recalled to an abolitionist audience.[93] Networks and the resource accumulation they permitted were complementary components of enslaved people's strategies to make the market work for them. But slaveholders' financial interests were the submerged shoals on which the best strategy could founder. Peter Robinson perhaps knew that best of all.

CHAPTER 3

Domestics

*C*ontemporary defenders of slavery characterized it as a domestic institution framed by bonds of reciprocal duty and even affection. In 1850, George Fitzhugh termed Virginia slavery "a joint concern, in which the slave consumes more than the master, of the coarse products, and is far happier, because although the concern may fail, he is always sure of a support; he is only transferred to another master to participate in the profits of another concern."[1] Fitzhugh's imagined world of domestic slavery hits a snag when one scrutinizes these transfers in the real world. Absent in his characterization, and perhaps intentionally so, was that in a slave market society, bonds of affection and duty were constantly threatened by the market. Those without the ability to generate cash as a counterstrategy to being "transferred," especially children and women, sought and exchanged human resources instead. They did not have the remunerative skills that kept Frederick Douglass in shipyards and Moses Grandy on canal boats rather than in fields of cotton. Enslaved domestic workers looked for alternative strategies to earning money for use in dealings with slaveholders. Their trials featured contests of wits using interpersonal skills and sentiment, and sometimes sexuality, within a local and intensely personal set of circumstances. They recruited allies to act on their behalf in public roles, but instead of canals, dockyards, or farms, their sites of strategy were kitchens and parlors, where they built social capital, relied on family members and neighbors, and forged emotional ties, all of which time and again exposed Fitzhugh's brand of slaveholding paternalism as obfuscation. Yet the market did not stop at the front gate of slaveholders' households. Some enslaved domestic workers used the market as part of contingent, evolving, and often desperate strategies to reunite with family members or prevent further dislocations of themselves or kin.

At eleven years old, William Robinson saw his father cultivate a broad network that suddenly vanished when his owner sold him. "He shook my hands and kissed me good bye through the iron bars," Robinson recalled of his father, bound in a slave trader's coffle set to depart Wilmington. "Then three sisters and two brothers climbed upon the wheel and bade him good bye."[2] They would never see him again.

The Robinson family's woes did not end with the father's disappearance and along with it plans to free their family. The owner died the same year he sold Peter Robinson, about 1858, and the Robinsons fell to a violent and iniquitous son, who employed Rosy as his cook and William as his manservant. Robinson found himself regularly serving at his owner's gambling table. Following a breakfast dispute over biscuits, in which the new owner assaulted Rosy, William struck him with an ax handle, an action prompted by the memory of his missing father. The child ran off and fell in with a band of local fugitive slaves who were moving about the countryside helping other runaways and "foraging" for food and other provisions at night. Robinson was caught a few weeks later in a raid in which he witnessed a slave shot and killed at the behest of the young man's owner, who also happened to be his father, from whom he had escaped. Robinson was returned to town and whipped severely. His family had been punished as well. "When I arrived home I found that my mother, one brother and one sister that were with her when I left, had been sold to negro traders" and that three brothers who had been sold to a brother of his owner "were also sold away, and no one could tell me anything about their whereabouts. Of course my master wouldn't tell me." Then he too was sold.[3]

Like his father, William Robinson responded to adversity by seeking allies who could provide information and protection. Unlike his father, William had no marketable skill or property to barter with whites, no tangibles other than his head, body, and limbs. Confined in a local slave trader's pen, he began by investigating the whereabouts of his family. Three of his siblings were sold from Wilmington, at least two of whom, "it was said," "were taken to Georgia." Inside the slave market, Robinson learned what he could about his relatives, plugging into the grapevine telegraph. After three weeks, Robinson was chained into a coffle of 350 slaves and marched to the Richmond slave market, 250 miles to the north, for sale. The slave market in Virginia's capital was then the largest in the upper South. The coffle traveled over sixteen hours a day on foot, over several days, picking up more members along the way. Robinson recalled that "when we reached Richmond about ten o'clock the fourth night, there were about four hundred and fifty of us, footsore, hungry and broken-hearted."[4]

Like Frederick Douglass's Baltimore, the city of Richmond was a forbidding place for the young William Robinson. In the 1850s, a visitor wrote, "Richmond, at a glance from adjacent high ground, through a dull cloud of bituminous smoke, upon a lowering winter's day, has a very picturesque appearance." It was the biggest city Robinson had seen and, counting the surrounding county, contained four times the population as his native Wilmington and New Hanover County.[5] "It is somewhat similarly situated upon and among some considerable hills," Frederick Law Olmsted wrote, "but the moment it is examined at all in detail, there is but one spot, in the whole picture, upon which the eye is at all attracted to rest. This is the Capitol, an imposing Grecian edifice, standing alone, and finely placed on open and elevated ground, in the center of the town."[6] Crossing Mayo's Bridge over the James River, Robinson marched straight toward that august white building with its classical pediment and columns. The slave market was practically in its shadow.

Robinson entered that maze of commerce, which "was a perpetual business every day in the year," he wrote, with little exaggeration, "and the prices were quoted on the bulletin and in the papers the same as our stock and wheat are quoted today." The slave trader who consigned him to auction was M. M. Lee, a Kentuckian in his late thirties whose slaving operation was on Franklin Street, a few blocks southeast of the capitol. There, Robinson and other coffle members "were taken to Lee's negro traders' auction pen, which was a very large brick structure with a high brick wall all around it." Despite there being a "very large hall ran through the center," he recalled, "no furniture," was available to the inmates, "not even a chair to sit upon." In that "pen," he wrote, "the handcuffs were taken off for the first time since we left home." He counted between "three or four hundred" captives present on arrival. "Many found relatives. One woman found her husband who had been sold from her three or four years before." Robinson "was not so fortunate as to find any of my people." He would not give up looking. In the meantime, rest was imperative, even if ground was cold.[7]

Early the next morning, in preparation for the day's auction, Lee's deputies commenced the elaborate ritual of making people into products. After being roused, the enslaved were led through a "back door" in order "to wash," Robinson recalled. There were "three or four pumps in the yard," near which were "long troughs" that an attendant filled so that the captives "would wash our faces and hands." In order to bring the highest prices, slaves needed to appear clean. At breakfast, Lee's "cooks handed out our tin pans with cabbage, or beans and corn bread, without knife, fork or spoon." Some knew the ritual well. "Many having been sold before," Robinson recalled, "and knowing how they would fare, carried such things with them." Following breakfast the gathering was "ordered into a long hall, where we found wire cards, such as are used for wool, flax or hemp" and then "ordered to comb our hair with them." "When we started" that morning, he remembered, "we had on our best clothes, which consisted of a pair of hemp pants and cotton shirt. . . . The women, and sometimes the men, wore red cotton bandanas on their heads," although "most of us were barefoot." Slaves were often encouraged to take personal effects, including clothing, and they were directed to don the best of what they had brought. Following the costuming, the group was "ordered into a little ten by twelve room" and entered it "ten or twelve at once."[8]

Readying people for the auction block also involved degradation, especially for girls and women. "There were five or six young ladies in the gang I went in with," Robinson recalled. "The traders, forgetting the sacredness of their own mothers and sisters, paid no respect to us, but compelled each one of us to undress, so as to see if we were sound and healthy." One woman named Fannie Woods, Robinson recalled, "pleaded to be exempt from this exposure. They gave her to understand that they would have her hit one hundred lashes if she did not get her clothes off at once." She steadfastly "refused, and when they tried to take them off' by force, fought them until they finally let her alone." Following the "humiliating ordeal of examination," Robinson and his fellow captives were ordered "into the auction room," which measured "about forty by sixty feet, with benches around the sides, where we were permitted to sit until our turn came to get on the auction block." Members of the public assembled to appraise the human property and act as consumers.[9]

Robinson witnessed a startling manifestation of an emerging American consumer culture. The slave market into which Solomon Bayley had landed sixty years before had changed beyond recognition. Antebellum slave traders, Walter Johnson argues, packaged slaves as consumer goods for sale, which in turn reflected the demands of an emerging middle class of slaveholders and those who aspired to their status. Slaves reflected who buyers imagined themselves to be, even confirming the buyers' whiteness. The market, which exhibited a regularity of sales that prefigured retailing of a later age, opened nearly every day and operated with railroad efficiency. Robinson recalled that auctions began "about nine o'clock each day and lasted until noon," and then resumed "again at one o'clock and continued until five p. m." Customers abounded. "At these sales we could find the best people of the South buying and selling." Some buyers were slaveholders who had traveled hundreds of miles in order to cut out the middle man or have first pick of those newly on the market. Others were neighborhood slave traders who resold slaves they bought cheaply. Many were there to buy the vulnerable for sexual exploitation. Robinson recalled, "When I got on the block, the first bid was one hundred and fifty dollars. It went up to seven hundred, when the bidding ceased." Those who offered him up had not finished shaping his sale. "The negro trader went to the auctioneer and told him that I came from the Madagascar tribe and that my father was an engineer and a skilled mechanic." That must have chilled William. Had Peter Robinson stood on the same spot, facing much the same audience? William did not say. Once his history was explained, "the bidding became brief." Robinson's ancestry was not quite enough to meet his seller's expectations. The auctioneer warranted Robinson's market legitimacy, saying he was "right and title guaranteed," meaning he was not kidnapped or stolen property. The man then "slapped" Robinson "on the head," and "continued by saying 'he's sound as a silver dollar.'" That was enough to bring the desired result. "I was knocked off at eleven hundred and fifty dollars."[10]

The new owner was one of the aspiring, a "poor man in East Virginia," who agreed to pay "four hundred and fifty dollars cash" and give "a mortgage on his sixty acres of land, his stock and everything he owned, including one colored girl," Robinson reported, "whom he had bought four years before."

Perhaps in the auction's excitement, he had bought beyond his means. Taking (or issuing) a mortgage on the buyer's property, Lee acted as a banker as well as a slave trader. Somewhat like durable goods dealers generations later, he extended credit to a buyer unable to pay in full, collecting interest on a loan paid back in installments. If the buyer defaulted, he could foreclose on the mortgaged property. The man who bought Robinson had reasons why he was willing to incur such a debt. Upward mobility meant scrambling up the social ladder on the backs of slaves. He bought eleven-year-old Robinson as a present for a young child and hinted at plans to use him to produce offspring with the teenaged slave woman, whom Robinson discovered had been abused and disfigured by the owner.[11] After arriving at the man's farm, Robinson decided in short order not to stay.

He struck out in order to return to Lee and the slave market of Richmond. "It may seem strange to the reader that I would go back to this place of human misery," he wrote, but he explained that he "had learned from older men and women" that if a slave had been sold to a poor owner, he or she had an excellent chance of rescinding the sale. He had appraised the owner and found a weakness.[12] Robinson fled to Richmond, falling in with two more fugitives who were returning for the same reason. The party was discovered by slave patrollers and returned to Lee's compound in chains. One fugitive was the property of a wealthy man, and he was returned. Lee agreed to resell Robinson, giving the excuse that the buyer "was behind anyhow." His second payment on the mortgage for Robinson's purchase was overdue.[13]

Lee had a better reason to rescind the sale. The Tennessee owner of Robinson's mother had been to see him about buying her son. His mother had passed through the Richmond slave market before him, and she had used the grapevine telegraph in the slave market to send word back to Richmond concerning her son. Lee calculated that the value of selling Robinson to that man was greater than returning him to the erstwhile buyer (and pursuing payments that were not forthcoming). It also permitted Lee the slave trader to be Lee the family unifier. After Lee's wife Mariah directed he be washed and fed, the slave trader kept him on as an assistant. "I cleaned the office and was errand boy," Robinson recalled. After four or five weeks, Robinson's mother's new owner arrived and bought him. His strategy had worked, at least for the time being. Robinson arrived at his new owner's Tennessee farm to find his mother and three siblings. The happy reunion gave way to even more joy. "On account of the agitation of the slave question," Robinson recalled, likely alluding to John Brown's raid, the new owner temporarily removed them to Wilmington, North Carolina, where his brother had a farm and where they "found another brother and sister, making mother and six children together again."[14] (His father and the other six were still missing.) The Tennessee owner's brother bought Robinson but promised him he could visit his mother every two or three months back in Tennessee. Robinson then ran across a brother of his second owner, a shipping merchant, who said it "was a shame that his father had allowed my father to be sold away, [and] that he was going to buy us all back and get us together again."[15] The twelve-year-old's luck seemed really to be turning, and he consented to be sold again, since the merchant promised to buy his mother and brothers back as well. That did not happen, but Robinson became the merchant's manservant and driver, and, he recalled, "I had become almost a prophet among my people, because I would get the news from the white people, and in the day would tell it to the slaves in the fields and cabins."[16] The memory of his father guided him as he established his neighborhood status and sense of self worth. Eventually, Robinson would find his mother again amid the flames of civil war and then lose her in its smoke.[17]

Robinson used the emotional appeal of a son separated from his mother as a domestic strategy in the slave market. Perhaps without knowing the full ramifications, he appealed in making his case to M. M. Lee and subsequent owners in Tennessee and North Carolina to a paternalist slaveholding narrative that had become fully articulated because its antithesis, the very business Lee was in, had become institutionalized. "Historians have tended to cast their analyses of these turbulent times in terms of ideology," argues Phillip D. Troutman. "But the ideology of domesticity was about nothing if not emotions." Emotion and sentiment were essential parts of the consumer theater Lee put on daily in his slave auctions and also of the slaveholding paternalism Fitzhugh sold to his readers. Buyers imagined themselves as the able stewards of dependent people, if not the kind masters of sentimental fiction that by the 1850s was so popular. How else could they buy and sell individual African Americans so obviously ripped from their own families? When Robinson returned from his Virginia owner seeking succor from a slave trader, he cast auctioneer M. M. Lee in the role of slaveholding paternalist and goaded him into playing it. "Sentiment was no doubt manipulative language," Troutman contends. Lee played his part flawlessly and, not inconsequently, was well paid for it. Without cash to barter, Robinson contested the outcome of his capture and sales using emotional language. He fell victim to a Wilmington slaveholder's seductive use of the same narrative when he consented to become the property of a man who promised to reunite his family.[18] The strategy of contesting slaveholders' behavior by appeals to emotion and sentiment was a risky one. It was a critical component of the tactics of people caught in domestic slavery networking used to secure allies, people who were at a distinct disadvantage compared to enslaved workers like Bayley, Douglass, and Grandy who had tangible resources they could use to mitigate their precarious position in the slave market.

Domestic workers' networks of protection were forged across lines of color and class, gender and generations, and framed in terms of sentiment. Enslaved women workers in antebellum Richmond arrived, like William Robinson, to find a landscape of perils and also some advantages concealed within it. While the commercial fortunes of cities like Edenton and Elizabeth City declined in the antebellum decades, Richmond's rose. The resulting diversification of enslaved people's employments meant that some enslaved women could hire their own time and, at hiring time, could, like their skilled male counterparts, bargain for working conditions. The dynamism of the urban Chesapeake slave labor market did not signal an attenuation of the "chattel principle," since any enslaved person who sought to subvert an owner's plans in the hiring market could end up on the slave market.[19] Even George Fitzhugh participated in undermining the paternalist ideology he had a hand in crafting. In the 1840s he sent several slaves, including "a girl" named Caroline to be hired out in Richmond in behalf of his law partner, John Thornton, of Caroline County, Virginia.[20]

The importance of forming webs of protection is most evident in situations in which enslaved people found themselves without one. An enslaved young woman Susan, probably not more than about fifteen or sixteen, was hired out in Richmond in 1847, about sixty miles from her King George County home. In an attempt to return to her husband, she pretended to be ill and unable to work. Feigning illness to protest working conditions was not uncommon, but Susan misjudged the ramifications of withdrawing her labor. Instead of playing the role of protector, her master ordered a slave trader to "sell Susan the first opportunity whatever you can get for her, as she is making so many complaints." Declaring that her behavior was "all pretentions & false representations," made "with the hope of returning to King George to live with her husband which she will never do," he reiterated that "you will please sell her at once." He added, "I really think that Susan is sound for I never heard any thing to the contrary before I carried her to Richmond." Two weeks later, Susan was sold to another slave trader for $575. The incident shows the perils an enslaved person like Susan faced when attempting to return to her family or protest working conditions without allies. For the supposed crime of feigning illness to return to her husband, she was sold and unlikely to return. Gambling with a strategy like Robinson's had produced the opposite emotion—anger—than that which she sought. When word reached her husband and King George County neighborhood, it must have been chilling.[21]

Hiring usually meant dislocations, which could give rise to desperate strategies. In 1840, one King William County, Virginia, slaveholder, the husband of one of Patrick Henry's granddaughters, decided to teach a recalcitrant slave a lesson. He was fed up with a woman named Aggy based on "nothing that is criminal but a continual disregard to my orders," he wrote, instructing a Richmond agent "to hire her out for 3 or 4 months—and if negroes rise I will then sell her." When Aggy became pregnant some months later, the slaveholder refused to let her return home to her family, instructing the agent "to contract with some physician to attend her" through her pregnancy. He notified the agent, however, that her baby would "not stay with her longer than the first good weather in the winter or Spring." Once Aggy had finished nursing the infant, in other words, it would be taken away from her. Aggy's pregnancy may have been the result of a relationship with a prospective ally or the result of sexual abuse. Perhaps Aggy fell in love and married; the circumstances were not disclosed. Like Susan, she found herself without a network that could shelter her from an owner who refused to adhere to a paternalist script.[22]

Forming a romantic alliance for protection almost always meant risking adverse consequences should the arrangement unravel. Sentiment was an unreliable strategy. For most of the 1830s, an enslaved woman Eliza lived as a concubine with owner Elisha Berry of Prince George's County, Maryland.[23] Because of the affair, Berry became estranged from his wife, Deborah, and daughter and lived instead with Eliza and her young son, Randall, housing her in her own dwelling and even assigning her house servants. A few years into the arrangement, she bore him a daughter, Emily. It is unclear where on a continuum of consent and refusal the arrangement lay. Annette Gordon-Reed argues that "enslaved women practically and legally could not refuse consent." The relationship cost Berry rapport with his family, but it would cost Eliza a great deal more.[24]

In 1841, Berry's jealous daughter got control over Eliza. One day Berry's son-in-law appeared while Berry was away and informed Eliza that she was to be emancipated that day.[25] Berry had promised only to free her children, so the news that was to be emancipated as well must have come as a pleasant surprise. With understandable optimism, then, Eliza put on a silk dress and gold earrings, dressed Emily in finery as well, and accompanied her master's son-in-law to neighboring Washington, D.C., where she expected to receive manumission papers. By the end of the day, however, she was united with her son in a slave trader's jail, where she and Emily found out that the freedom paper was actually a bill of sale.[26] There they met New York native Solomon Northup, who had been kidnapped in the days following William Henry Harrison's presidential inauguration. By steamboat and railroad, they were taken to Richmond's slave market. They were later loaded on a ship in Richmond bound for New Orleans. In the New Orleans slave market, after mother and son were hospitalized with smallpox, Randall was sold away from Eliza and then she was sold away from her daughter Emily. Ignoring the mother's pleas, the New Orleans trader decided to keep seven-year-old Emily as an investment since the daughter of a white man and a light-skinned woman could be offered as an enslaved sex worker when she reached her teen years, if not before.[27] Eliza was too distraught to do much work. "Having become useless in the cotton-field," Northup later reported, "she was bartered for a trifle."[28] Having lost Berry as an ally, she eventually lost everything. "Grief had gnawed remorselessly at her heart," Northup went on, "until her strength was gone."[29] Eliza died grieving for her children.

Enslaved women seeking to avoid the victimization to which Eliza was subject manipulated human ties that might keep them out of the slave market. That was domestic slaves' version of networking. Allying with other African American women, they cemented bonds of trust and cooperation, but in a city like Richmond they also sought allies at work.[30] Slaveholders hiring out domestic workers sometimes consented to self-hiring arrangements, similar to the "living out" arrangements favored by some factory owners in antebellum Richmond, leaving it to slaves to find employers with whom they were compatible. A Fredericksburg owner sent a young woman to Richmond in the early 1850s with instructions to an agent "to hire out Patty for me for another year, getting her as good a home as you can. Let her select a place for herself if you can do so without serious objection." He made the pretense of valuing Patty's satisfaction with an employer, which he hoped would not conflict with his financial interests. "I wish to sell the girl to someone who . . . would likely prove a good master. I have told her to look out herself if she could find a permanent master."[31] Between Christmas and the first two weeks of the New Year, many enslaved people plied the streets and intersections seeking employment on the terms they—and their owners—found most favorable. It was a strange hiring fair.

Women like Patty bargained for wages and conditions alongside men, gambling that in agreeing to year-long hiring contracts between employers and owners they might avoid the slave market for at least that year. More immediate were enslaved women's concerns that they not find themselves isolated and subject to abuse. A foreign visitor to Richmond in the late 1850s found the city "literally swarming with negroes, who were standing in crowds at the corners of the streets in different parts of the town." He encountered a coachman who reported "he was not quite healthy, and would not be worth more than 700 dollars" in the slave market. The man nevertheless had "a slip of paper on which was written, 'Isaac, for hire, apply to Mr. —, 140 dollars per annum.'" The visitor witnessed an enslaved woman making arrangements with a prospective employer, a market gardener. "The price that her owner had put on her services was not objected to by him," the visitor reported, but the woman refused to do gardening in addition to house work. After taking an "hour's walk in another part of the town," he returned and "met the two at the old bargain." On inquiring what the difficulty was, he "learned that she was pleading for other privileges—her friends and favourites must also be allowed to visit her."[32] The two eventually took the discussions into the house of the would-be employer, but the incident shows that enslaved women could be shrewd hiring agents, submitting the prospective employer to an interview, evaluating his intentions, and making sure they would not be cut off from allies.

A white Georgian happening on the Richmond self-hiring market in the 1850s was horrified. Unlike the "amused" foreigner, he witnessed a future in which slaves would have bargained away their bondage. The Georgian wrote that the first few days of hiring time were the "most woeful" days "of the year!" He saw enslaved people "promenading the streets decked in their finest clothes . . . hail[ing]," the "advent" of hiring time, "with heartfelt pleasure." The observer decried the apparent freedom labor markets provided and suggested that enslaved people were hoodwinking prospective employers, who "swapped the devil for the witch" at hiring time. Instead of owners allocating labor to employers, they were deputing that duty to the enslaved. Did the Georgian imagine city blocks in Augusta or Savannah crowded with self-hired slaves in the fullness of time?[33] Virginia slaveholders tolerated their slaves bargaining for their own working conditions since they would still profit from the contracts, and employers showed more concern with cheap pliable labor than in implementing a labor regime of white over black. Whether he saw them in the apparent disorder, he was also witnessing innovations in slavery. Arrangements like those in Richmond might have been forerunners of slave labor markets in other southern cities.[34]

Avoiding permanent dislocations often meant forming domestic alliances that went beyond manipulating emotion or sentiment for short-term advantages. In that register, Corinna Hinton used her sexuality as a defense by becoming the domestic partner of Richmond "Negro trader" Silas Omohundro. Her story shows the full ramifications of the strategic use of sentiment. Omohundro had been trading slaves for over two decades by the time their paths crossed in the 1840s.[35] Initially, the enslaved woman may have simply caught the eye of the slave trader, owner of a private jail, and sometime slave hiring agent.[36] Omohundro was a habitué of auctions like the one in which William Robinson was sold. When Hinton attracted his (perhaps unwanted) attention, she began networking in a desperate attempt to keep from being sold away from a place where she could gather allies and a patron. The relationship she formed with Omohundro was profoundly asymmetrical with regard to power and what each received in the exchange. Hinton was about twenty, without a protector, and enslaved. Omohundro was twenty years her senior, a businessman of long standing in Richmond and his native Fluvanna County, Virginia, and a citizen. Hinton's historical situation mirrored that of William Wells Brown's fictional Clotel, an enslaved woman who found herself disposed of in the Richmond slave market, though she looked to the world like a white woman.[37] Even George Fitzhugh was forced to admit that "to defend and justify mere negro slavery, is to give up expressly the whole cause of the South—for mulattoes, quadroons, and men with as white skins as any of us, may legally be, and in fact are, held in slavery in every State of the South."[38]

The auction rooms of the Richmond slave market were sites of sexual exploitation. Steven Deyle argues that "southern slave traders were notorious for raping the young enslaved women under their control."[39] A member of a slave trading business based in Alexandria, Virginia, suggested in 1834 that the firm sponsor a "whore house" in New Orleans so that slaves sent there, including an "old lady and Susan could soon pay for themselves" by running it.[40] In addition to supplying laborers to lower South buyers, that firm trafficked in enslaved sex workers such as "*fair maid* Martha" in 1832 and "fancy maid Alice" offered for $800 in Natchez in 1833.[41] Whether in Alexandria, New Orleans, or Richmond, there were no authorities to which enslaved rape victims could appeal. Richmond levied a tax on auctioneers and slave jailers beginning in the 1840s but made no effort to regulate the slave trade until 1860.[42] Omohundro sold enslaved women in the sex trade, and Hinton perhaps encountered him through that segment of the market. Slave traders regularly called their victims "fancy maids," a euphemism that usually indicated enslaved women of both European and African descent. Buyers paid prices that often exceeded what they would pay for male agricultural slaves in their prime working years. A visitor to the slave auctions of Baltimore, Alexandria, Fredericksburg, and Richmond in the 1830s reported that "mulattoes are not so much valued for field hands" and consequently, "they are purchased for domestics, and the females to be sold for prostitutes." There was a kernel of truth in that overstatement. Women like Hinton were sold for exploitation in the sex trade by men who had a keen sense of their customer's sexual proclivities, nourished perhaps in their own slave quarters or those of fathers, uncles, or brothers.[43] Omohundro and his brother Robert recorded buying female slaves Maria Johnson and Willy in the winter of 1859 for prices approaching what an adult male field worker would fetch. Omohundro labeled both "fancy" in account records. He published suggestive descriptions, referring to them as "mulatto," "light mulatto," and "second-class and yellow" women. That was in 1860, indicating that Omohundro continued to participate in the market for sex slaves after he began his public relationship with Hinton.[44]

Hinton used the momentum of events she could not control to her own spontaneous, evolving advantages. At first, she may have been simply the favorite concubine of a slave trader who specialized in the enslaved sex trade. When it seemed that Hinton was about to be hit by the market, she seized the market to deflect the force of the blow. Such market kung fu involved some awful calculations, not least choosing between making a grab for temporary personal security versus putting others in the same vulnerable position beyond reach of their relatives. What she formed to gain some security was not a plan or well-developed strategy; rather what she did was seize on an opportunity. Hinton used the "weapons of the weak," though with the ironic twist of reinforcing her weakness, settling into the position of a slave trader's domestic partner.[45]

Hinton publicly acted as Omohundro's wife and agent doing business with local merchants, and so unlike Eliza, who depended entirely on her owner's good will and had nothing to do with his affairs, she was able to build status or social capital and to recruit allies besides Omohundro. Hinton became responsible for buying provisions for the slaves themselves. In 1855, for instance, Omohundro gave her nearly $600 to buy "Negro clothing" for slaves awaiting sale in his jails. Hinton's job meant keeping accounts with local merchants and making sure that deliveries of food and fuel made it to the slave trader's compound. In accumulating personal wealth, including presents of gold jewelry, a diamond ring, and cash, she acquired material goods in addition to allies.[46] The details of their relationship are unclear, but Omohundro introduced her as his wife on visits to Pennsylvania in the late 1850s.[47] With the birth of each of their five children, her network became increasingly a family network.[48]

Hinton's choices stand as testament to the trade-offs inherent in a slave market society. To preserve herself from further exploitation, she was ready to sacrifice more remote considerations and instead seize immediate gains and build on them incrementally by running Omohundro's boarding house, bearing his children, and cooperating in his business. Her choices were the ephemeral trade-offs made by someone at a distinct disadvantage, not the result of a conflict between an abstract principle such as slave solidarity and immediate practical goal such as self-preservation. Hinton's strategy was not hypocritical, because the idea of slave solidarity or a slave community born out of the shared experience of slavery was not a part of her horizon of understanding.[49]

A slave in law, Hinton was anything but an enslaved woman according to her local status. The situation in which Hinton found herself enslaved reveals dual conceptions of the state, "one in which law was an abstraction," argues Laura F. Edwards, "and the other in which the rule of law was realized through concrete relations within the community." The two "coexisted in the post-Revolutionary South." Hinton was connected to Silas Omohundro by more than the arrangement they both recognized as a marriage. Their children were not subject to the deprivation and violence to which other enslaved children were subject. Omohundro was an indulgent father. On occasion, he gave his children a dollar to "go see the Balloon" outside Richmond; on others, pine-apples and circus tickets.[50] Growing up amid coffles of chained and miserable human beings entering and leaving their father's compound, the children may not have internalized the legal similarities between themselves and the chattel slaves their father bought and sold, the profits of which sales bought them fine clothing and other trappings of middle-class childhood. (Some he sent to school in Pennsylvania.) Alternatively, year in and year out in close proximity to Omohundro's business may have been too much for Hinton. Following the Civil War, Littleton Omohundro, his son by a previous marriage, observed in a suit he filed against his father's estate that his father "had been building a house in Ohio for his wife (or reputed wife) and children, who resided there and where he was in the habit of visiting them till the rebellion broke out."[51]

When Corinna and the five children she had with Omohundro were freed by stipulation of his will upon his death in 1864, her public transformation was invisible even if the heavy legal burden was lifting. Troutman argues that she had "access to large amounts of cash" by the time of her husband's death, and he willed most of his property to her.[52] In that will he testified that she "has always been a kind, faithful, and dutiful woman to me, and an affectionate mother and will continue to be so." "Corinna Omohundro," the name by which he identified her in his will, and their five children had all remained legally enslaved while Silas lived, which caused the trouble Corinna encountered following his death. When she sued to collect her inheritance, which included property in Philadelphia and Lancaster County, Pennsylvania, she found out that a critical segment of her network was not legally recognized. The will was proved but her marriage was not. Omohundro had not freed her before marrying her, and consequently the marriage had no legal standing, even after 1865. Had Omohundro freed Corinna or her children, they would have been obliged to leave Virginia or face reenslavement. As long as he held them in bondage he could control and protect them.[53]

That power dissolved on his death, and without clear instructions that his family was to be manumitted, they might have landed in the slave market. Omohundro could not but have been cognizant of the fact that the same laws that gave him legal title to the many human beings whom he bought and sold also posed significant difficulties for his flesh and blood offspring. After making sure so many other people were denied any rights, Corinna was denied those Omohundro claimed for her as a wife and mother to his children.

After Silas's death Corinna married again, this time Nathaniel Davidson, a white coal merchant from New Hampshire. As in 1860, Corinna Davidson and her children were recorded in the 1870 census as "white."[54]

Corinna's open complicity in Omohundro's business presents an apparent interpretive dilemma of whether to view her on her own terms, as a woman who put the interests of her blood kin ahead of her identity as a slave, or as someone who was complicit in the most destructive form of antebellum commerce. Viewed in terms of the institution of slavery, Corinna's activities in behalf of Omohundro's business contributed—in a small way—to its strength and vitality, over against the interests of slaves. By clothing other enslaved people for auction, she packaged them as highly valuable consumer goods for would-be buyers, on whom she also waited at Omohundro's boarding house. Viewed in terms of her own concern for her blood kin and for herself, Corinna's concerns seem understandable. In each enslaved human being she clothed or fed, she could comprehend the horrors that might befall her own children should the unforeseeable happen and she became the property of someone other than Silas Omohundro.[55]

Corinna Hinton was not alone in attaching herself to a patron who was also a slave trader. In her Shockoe Bottom neighborhood, Mary F. Lumpkin, who lived across "Lumpkin's Alley" from Hinton, had made a similar set of choices. By 1854, twenty-one- or twenty-two-year-old Mary, herself enslaved, was living as a wife of Robert Lumpkin. The couple had five children together. She had stumbled on the same strategy for self-preservation that her neighbor had, to ally herself with someone she met in the market. Lumpkin had run a slave jail since the 1840s. Its conditions, according to one witness, were appalling. When the famous fugitive Anthony Burns was returned to Virginia from Boston in 1854, he was detained in Lumpkin's cells, occupying a "room only six or eight feet square, in the upper story of the jail, which was accessible only through a trap-door," according to Burns's biographer Charles Emory Stevens. Burns was kept in shackles "during the greater part of his confinement," the pain of which was "excruciating." The iron manacles on his feet "impeded the circulation of his blood . . . and caused his feet to swell enormously." Never unlocked, the "fetters also prevented him from removing his clothing by day or night, and no one came to help him. . . . His room became more foul and noisome than the hovel of a brute; loathsome creeping things multiplied and rioted in the filth." The fare was no better. "His food consisted of a piece of coarse corn-bread and the parings of bacon or putrid meat," which he received once a day. Nor was fresh water provided: "The only means of quenching his thirst was the nauseating contents of a pail that was replenished only once or twice a week." Not surprisingly, he soon "fell seriously ill."[56]

It seems, however, that Mary Lumpkin was not wholly insensitive to the plight of people who landed in her husband's jail. Described as "yellow woman," Mary "manifested her compassion for Burns by giving him a testament and a hymn-book." Had Burns had requested the articles? He was a Baptist preacher when he fled Virginia and could read and write. Mary Lumpkin herself may have taken an interest in the religious lives of those who passed through Robert Lumpkin's dungeon. The First African Baptist Church received for baptism three of Lumpkin's "servants" in March, 1854, including Lucy Henry, Sarah Jackson, and Matilda Smith. Henry and Jackson were excluded from the church two years later for adultery, though Jackson returned to membership in the fall of 1857. The First African Baptist Church also noted the passing of another of Lumpkin's slaves, Mahala Carter, who died in September 1857. Mary Lumpkin was not listed as a member, perhaps because she chose not to identify herself as African American.[57] She was not the only member of the Lumpkin household drawn to the fugitive Burns. Lumpkin kept a black concubine, who like Mary, had calculated that an affective connection with Robert Lumpkin might protect her from sexual violence by another man or else sale. Stevens mentioned that this concubine "also manifested a friendly spirit toward the prisoner" by communicating with him. "The house of Lumpkin was separated from the jail only by the yard," Stevens reported, "and from one of the upper windows the girl contrived to hold conversations with Anthony, whose apartment was directly opposite."[58]

Burns had much to tell. Like so many skilled slave workers in Richmond, Burns had been hiring his own time from his owner and even supervising the hiring of other slaves when he had had enough of slavery and decided to board a ship for Boston. Apprehended under the 1850 Fugitive Slave Act, Burns's case became a cause célèbre for abolitionists, Bostonians incensed at the federalization of slavery, and proslavery activists who supported the divisive law. In May 1854, a gathering of black abolitionists led an assault on the federal courthouse where Burns was held, during which a federal deputy was killed. That June, some fifty thousand New Englanders turned out to protest the court's decision that Burns was a fugitive subject to be returned to his owner. The case attracted so much attention that President Franklin Pierce sent a federal ship to deliver Burns to Virginia. After returning to his native state, he languished in Lumpkin's jail for four months while his owner arranged his sale. Lumpkin's concubine was impressed with Burns. Her "compassion," reported Stevens, "changed into a warmer feeling." Those attentions met with Robert Lumpkin's disapproval, and "[h]e took effectual means to break off the intercourse."[59]

Neither Mary Lumpkin nor the woman her husband kept for sexual entertainment could have been oblivious to the kind of commerce that took place within Lumpkin's compound or what it portended for their own families. While Burns was being held, he heard "a woman entreating and sobbing, and [sounds] of a man addressing to her commands mingled with oaths." Straining to investigate, Burns "beheld a slave woman stark naked in the presence of two men," one who was there to buy her, the other an attendant. Stevens reported that the "overseer had compelled the woman to disrobe in order that the purchaser might see for himself whether she was well formed and sound in body." The women who befriended Burns had probably been subject to the same humiliation and threat of sale. Lumpkin had made his fortune in the slave trade and was inured to such spectacles. Perhaps it was a cruel irony for Lumpkin, then, that his daughters were legally his property and could be transferred to his heirs should he die or become insolvent. Fearing that the same debasing treatment Burns witnessed might befall their children, Lumpkin sent two of his daughters by Mary to school in Massachusetts. Later, like Omohundro, Lumpkin sent them to live in Pennsylvania. He was worried, reported a witness, that a "financial contingency might arise when these, his own beautiful daughters, might be sold into slavery to pay his debts."[60]

Unlike Omohundro, Lumpkin lived to see emancipation come to Richmond in the form of the Union Army. Just after Richmond fell in April 1865, he attempted to evacuate his slave property—some fifty men, women, and children, shackled together and weeping—but before he could reach the railroad depot, he was forced to free them. He died the following year, leaving all his real estate to Mary. She did not stay in Virginia. She later ran a restaurant in Louisiana with one of her daughters and died in New Richmond, Ohio, in 1905, at seventy-two.[61]

The role of "fancy maid" assigned to many enslaved women gave way to enduring domestic partnerships when they endeared themselves to slave traders who initially treated them as objects of sexual exploitation. At first blush, slave traders acted with a perversity approaching the classic definition of chutzpah: they saved women from the slave market even though they themselves were offering them as objects of sexual exploitation. But slave traders were not immune from the inconsistencies in their own narratives. In the highly articulated Richmond market, Mary Lumpkin or Corinna Hinton could appeal to slave traders using the categories that they had imposed on them, as "fancy maids." Women and girls had always been susceptible to sexual exploitation, whether in Solomon Bayley's day or Silas Omohundro's, but a slave market that denominated the enslaved according to categories of consumer goods also gave Lumpkin and Hinton roles and scripts that were market identities, which they could manipulate to their own ends. On brighter days, passing for white and introduced as wife of a businessman, their legal status was more a nuisance than an existential reality, yet when Corinna Hinton's domestic partnership dissolved so did the lynchpin of a network that had been many years in the making.[62]

Ann Davis, another enslaved neighbor of Hinton and Lumpkin, allied with a more affluent slaver than did her neighbors. Davis lived as the concubine of a slave "auctioneer" Hector Davis in the 1850s and bore four of his children.[63] When she met him in the 1850s, he was a man on the make. In 1850, Davis owned $3,500 worth real estate. No dependents were listed on his census entry, which was right next to that of Silas Omohundro.[64] The 1850s had seen Davis's fortunes rise considerably. At forty-two-years old, in 1860, Davis held some $20,000 in real estate and $100,000 in personal property, including fifteen slaves counted by the census taker that July, and could be counted a successful member of the fraternity of Richmond slave traders.[65] (In 1860, he appears on the same census page as M. M. Lee.)[66] He also owned Ann Davis, who passed for white.

Like Hinton and Lumpkin, she and their children were safe from sale so long as he lived. Moreover, he had promised that she would receive her freedom and a substantial sum of money upon his death. In his 1859 will Hector Davis wrote, "I give to a servant-woman, Ann, of mine, her freedom, to be removed out of the State, with her four children, [Matilda,] Jannie, Audubon, and Victoria, and after their removal the sum of $20,000, she, Ann, to have the interest on one-fifth of the amount, and the interest of the balance to be expended in raising the said children till they become of age; then the principal to be given them." Davis was careful to assert his ownership of Ann but did not testify to the sentiment that framed Omohundro's will. In 1860, Ann was between twenty-eight and thirty; her son Audubon was eight and daughter Victoria was just two.[67]

In contrast to Corinna Hinton and Mary F. Lumpkin, Ann Davis did not play an obvious role in Davis's antebellum business, but her extraordinary efforts to collect her legacy suggests how invested she was in her role as Davis's domestic partner. Ann Davis could not have been unaware of Hector's line of work. In March 1862 he advertised the sale of "twenty-five likely Negroes" to be sold at his auction rooms, and in October 1863 he advertised "50 likely slaves" to be sold at auction where they lived, on Franklin Street, between Mayo and 15th Street.[68] The man who sold all those people did not survive the war. Davis died in1864 leaving his free nephews and nieces $20,000 and a sister the balance of his "large" estate, consisting of "real property, slaves, bank and other stocks, a small amount of Confederate bonds, . . . some furniture," and debts owed to Davis that totaled just over $91,000. Like Mary Lumpkin's daughters, Ann Davis and her children had already left Richmond for Philadelphia. After the Civil War, Davis returned to collect her inheritance, which was tangled up in court proceedings after the executor moved to settle the estate in November 1865. Davis took the case to the Virginia Supreme Court of Appeals in 1873 and eventually the United States Supreme Court, which in 1876 returned it to Virginia. It is not clear from court records whether she received anything from the estate of the father of her children. Like Corinna Hinton Omohundro Davidson, Davis's marriage to Hector had not been legal. In 1880, she was living with her son Audubon, a journalist in Philadelphia, who served on the editorial staff of the Philadelphia *Daily News*. By then, the son of a slave trader was married and had a young son, Hector, and an infant daughter, Matilda, named after his sister. Audubon's choosing to name his son "Hector" is intriguing. Was he aware of his father's business or that he was born his slave? Regardless, his naming choices suggest familial love and close bonds that endured the war and relocation. More of Ann's family moved in together in later years. Her son shared a house with her daughter Victoria, a domestic servant, and a boarder. Audubon died in 1885. By 1900, Ann was living with Victoria, by then a saleswoman in a department store in Philadelphia and a sister, Virginia Savage, perhaps also a former slave.[69]

It is difficult not to see Ann Davis as in some profound way betraying other enslaved people. Analyses in which slaves were inimitable adversaries of slave traders are premised on realities the enslaved faced every day. But both proslavery apologists like Fitzhugh, who argued that slavery was a benign organic institution, and abolitionists, who drew sharp lines of difference between slaves and slaveholders, obscured a more complicated historical reality. They neglected the subtleties of a system that diabolically played divide and conquer—a system that was more pernicious in its shades of gray than in the black and white of contemporary characterizations. Abolitionists like Wilmington, North Carolina, native David Walker made class-like characterizations of slavery, arguing that enslaved people shared a universe of interest over against those who enslaved them. That was both plausible and a necessary step in characterizing U.S. slavery as an institution susceptible to abolition through broad-based moral reform. Abolitionists needed angels and demons. Slaves had to deal with the devils they knew lest they be sold to the devils they did not. Ann Davis's choices therefore defy contemporary abolitionist narratives in which slaves shared a common interest.[70]

Walker was not the first to suggest that slaves were participating in a corporate struggle. The prime target of his invective was the first southerner to articulate the idea of such a historical drama. In Thomas Jefferson's view, African-descended slaves as members of a wronged race of human beings shared an interest in seeking revenge on their captors. In his *Notes on the State of Virginia*, Jefferson conceived of enslaved people as having a protonational consciousness as Africans. Were slavery to end, in his view, former slaves would punish the beneficiaries of a system of bondage that had stolen their ancestors and driven them to labor in the Americas. Confusing slavery with race, Jefferson nevertheless affirmed the humanity of the enslaved even though he castigated the intelligence, art, emotions, and achievements of African-descended people. Walker's response to Jefferson's racist indictment of enslaved African Americans was to plead the humanity of all people, and yet he borrowed the premises Jefferson had used and then stood them on their head. African Americans indeed shared a corporate interest, in Walker's view, but it was more deeply historical: it was as the ancient Israelites of the Book of Exodus facing Egypt under the Pharaoh.[71]

There was no room within Walker's world-historical narrative for women like Ann Davis. Walker excoriated a woman who helped a slave trader after his coffle had been overtaken by rebellious slaves in Kentucky. In the summer of 1829, members of a coffle of about sixty "of all ages and sexes" were being marched from their homes in Maryland to the Mississippi River on their way to the lower South slave market. The men were shackled but women and children were not. Several men surreptitiously filed through their chains and at an opportune moment, sprung on their three captors, killing two and injuring the leader. The rebels seized a significant quantity of cash and then fled, after which the surviving trader begged the aid of a female slave. She helped him onto his horse. One of the men from the coffle pursued the trader on foot with a pistol, but when the wounded man made it within sight of a plantation house his pursuer gave up the chase. Local whites mobilized, recapturing the fugitives.[72]

Walker let loose righteous anger. "The actions of this deceitful and ignorant coloured woman," he thundered, "in saving the life of a desperate wretch, whose avaricious and cruel object was to drive her, and her companions in miseries, through the country like cattle, to make his fortune on their carcasses, are but too much like that of thousands of our brethren in these states." Walker lost his patience over any enslaved person who trucked with slavers, though he acknowledged that there were many like her. Heaping bitterness on scorn, he continued, "if any thing is whispered by one, which has any allusion to the melioration of their dreadful condition, they run and tell tyrants, that they may be enabled to keep them the longer in wretchedness and miseries."[73] Though strangely true with regard to Hinton, Lumpkin, and Davis, that characterization missed the point of those women's contingent circumstances. Walker appealed to his fellow African Americans to adopt the "the spirit of man" and bind together to rise up against slaveholders. "Had you not rather be killed," he implored readers, "than to be a slave to a tyrant, who takes the life of your mother, wife, and dear little children?" There was no space for accommodations with slaveholders. What angered him the most was the "servile deceit" and "gross ignorance" of enslaved Judases who undermined the supposed interest of the slave community. Walker's polemic was compelling. Abolitionist William Lloyd Garrison endorsed it by covering Walker's arguments in the *Liberator*, and his premises influenced abolitionist thinking and later historical interpretations of the peculiar institution. Walker's rhetoric also inflamed white southerners. Reports of African American watermen like Moses Grandy distributing copies of the *Appeal* up and down coastal North Carolina, from Wilmington to New Bern and Elizabeth City, sent them into a panic. (A slave owned by the same family that owned Peter Robinson was found with two hundred copies; was he related to the Robinsons?) Walker's writings reached far and wide, but the realities faced by so many of the enslaved, realities Walker and Garrison looked past in their noble work, lies in its shadows.[74]

Walker's was an ironic contrast. It was also stellar rhetoric. He and other abolitionists accented a classlike view of slavery in order to characterize an institution susceptible to legal termination. Published one year before Nat Turner's Southampton County, Virginia, rebellion, Walker's call to arms reflected the urgency of the struggles of the enslaved. Slavers were tearing families apart at such an alarming rate that armed revolt seemed to be the best way to respond. If, like the biblical Israelites' bondage, American slavery had been allowed to continue through its appointed time until it were willed to be removed, Walker and other prophets of emancipation would have been correct to impute to the institution a divine plan ending with woe to the enslavers. But although he appealed to the enslaved and other African Americans as people united in oppression and as a people who ought to be united in liberating themselves, he overlooked the realities of the situations slaves found themselves in, situations that transcended the civic distinction. Had Walker been able to look over the horizon and into the 1830s, he would have seen a decade in which three people were marched out of the Chesapeake for every two who had gone before in the 1820s. He would have seen the largest slave state, Virginia, lose slaves in absolute numbers, despite high rates of reproduction, for the first time in its history. After copies of Walker's *Appeal* appeared in North Carolina and the Nat Turner rebellion erupted in southern Virginia, slaveholders relied more and more on forced separations to control the slave population, even as southern citizens intensified violence and terror against all people of African descent. Slaveholders seemed to brook no compromise with the people they held in bondage, instead selling off those who seemed most likely to revolt and sending them to distant lands, where a new wave of insurrections broke out in subsequent years. In the intensifying market that dispersed all those people, opportunities arose, as Americans sought to domesticate slavery, for women like Ann Davis. Walker might have added another chapter to his *Appeal* if he had lived to witness the kinds of networks some enslaved women constructed in antebellum Richmond and beyond.[75]

In the wake of Walker's *Appeal* and Nat Turner's rebellion, yet far from the urban slave auctions of her upper South home, Harriet Jacobs struggled against an abusive owner by using every human tie she could forge and every scrap of fortitude she could muster. Her extraordinary trials and escape from James Norcom of Edenton, North Carolina, is one of the most celebrated contests in the history of antebellum American slavery. Yet beyond her heroism lay a supple and resilient network of human and material resources, similar to Corinna Hinton, Mary Lumpkin, and Ann Davis's, which crossed lines of race, class, and gender. Unlike those women, Jacobs attempted to escape sexual abuse and exploitation in slavery rather than to reinforce it, but she used sentiment and affection in strikingly similar ways.[76] The network that Jacobs and her allies constructed was protean and ephemeral, and its reach extended and retracted in response to local contingencies. It involved calculations in a face-to-face community of neighbors, mostly African American and mostly enslaved, which together formed the backbone of a body of allies. Yet in Jacobs's Edenton, allies sometimes became adversaries, and no one in Jacobs's network knew its full scope, the extent of the resources it could furnish, or its precise limitations.

Jacobs was born in 1813, and her struggles began in earnest at age fifteen when she attracted the attention of a suitor. Her biographer Jean Fagan Yellin argues that she "was in love with a free-born black carpenter who wanted to purchase and marry her." Norcom forbade the union, threatening: "If I ever know of your speaking to him, I will cowhide you both; and if I catch him lurking about my premises, I will shoot him as soon as I would a dog."[77] That owner was not simply forbidding Jacobs from forming an alliance. Jealous of her affections, he was isolating a victim. Jacobs recalled, "The war of my life had begun; and though one of God's most powerless creatures, I resolved never to be conquered."[78]

By herself, Jacobs was powerless. Her parents had both died and she was the legal property of a young daughter of the Norcom family, living under the same roof as the town physician bent on dominating her. She had no civil or political rights, and her physical strength scarcely matched that of her tormentors James and Maria Norcom (the wife of her master blamed the victim and consequently took part in her abuse). But Jacobs was resourceful and extraordinarily resilient. Faced with an environment in which "sex and violence seemed to clog the very air," Jacobs turned to Samuel Tredwell Sawyer, the scion of a wealthy and politically prominent family, for help.[79]

Jacobs's initial relationship with him was scarcely the result of a strategy or well-considered plan. It was rather, like Corinna Hinton's first attachment to

Silas Omohundro, the product of a spontaneous and evolving set of everyday trade-offs made by someone with serious disadvantages. "His relationship with Norcom's slave girl was typical of men of his time, place, and class," argues Yellin. "He left no record" of their "liaison," she continues, "but perhaps a psychologist with a historical bent could speculate concerning his thoughts and feelings." Her emotional and physical connection to Sawyer carried substantial risks, not least to her physical safety and spiritual and psychological development. The power difference between the two was even more asymmetrical than that between Hinton and Omohundro. Jacobs was fifteen, and Sawyer was twenty-eight. He was an aspiring local representative expected to marry a woman of his family's class. But by entering into a sexual and emotional relationship with Sawyer, Jacobs became a potential beneficiary of the resources Sawyer and his family possessed. She also gained the self-esteem that came from his attentions and affections. "Is it possible that they shared some version of love?" asks Yellin. At the very least, James Norcom could not menace Sawyer the way he had Jacobs's erstwhile suitor.[80]

Jacobs's alliance with Sawyer protected her from sexual violence in the short term, but as their bond strengthened, it began to have far-reaching unintended consequences. Norcom's sexual abuse paused when she became pregnant with Sawyer's child, though his psychological abuse did not. Jacobs endured a terrifying pregnancy, and she gave birth to a premature but otherwise healthy baby, Joseph, named after an uncle who had disappeared into a slave trader's coffle and later escaped from New Orleans. After Joseph arrived, Jacobs's "relationship with Sawyer continued as before," contends Yellin. Jacobs's resolve to thwart Norcom's will deepened, but the owner bided his time, threatening Jacobs again with violence and sexual abuse. She returned to Sawyer, against her grandmother's wishes. That resulted in another pregnancy. "The day Norcom noticed her body rounding," Yellin maintains, "he became furious, and dashing out of the house, returned with a pair of scissors and cut her hair close, to mark her as a whore." She lived with her grandmother Molly Horniblow through most of the rest of the pregnancy, though Norcom "stopped in at Molly's bakery almost every day, spewing out verbal abuse." After Louisa was born, Horniblow returned the compliment, intercepting him one day and saying, "You ain't got many more years to live, and you'd better be saying your prayers. It will take 'em all, and more too, to wash the dirt off your soul." He left in a froth of anger, but the incident signaled that Horniblow was raising awareness in the town of Norcom's misdeeds. Horniblow won the skirmish, but Norcom's claim to Jacobs's children was his next salvo. Sawyer's children were Norcom's property.[81]

In Jacobs's contests with her owner, even the short-term outcomes were unintended. "My master had power and law on his side; I had a determined will," Jacobs summarized. "There is might in each." Yellin contends that she may have entertained the idea that Sawyer would free her and her family, since a local slaveholder had freed his enslaved teenaged mistress after she bore him two children. Was Jacobs also reading the sentimental fiction, popular in her day, in which gallant men like Sawyer used their social position to defend the defenseless? Sawyer did not ask to marry her, but he did attempt to buy his children and John, Jacobs's brother. Norcom would not sell them. When Jacobs later recalled their affair, she framed it in terms of guilt and sin. She pleaded with her "virtuous reader": "you never exhausted your ingenuity in avoiding the snares, and eluding the power of a hated tyrant; you never shuddered at the sound of his footsteps, and trembled within hearing of his voice. I know I did wrong." She begged forgiveness. "No one can feel it more sensibly than I do. The painful and humiliating memory will haunt me to my dying day. Still, in looking back, calmly, on the events of my life, I feel that the slave woman ought not to be judged by the same standard as others."[82]

The more assiduously Jacobs tried to get away from Norcom, the more he resolved to control her. He made Jacobs another offer. If she would take up as his concubine and break her ties with Sawyer, then he would free her children. Otherwise, he threatened to bind out Joseph to hard labor as soon as he was able and put Louisa to work as a prostitute. "Your boy shall be put to work," Norcom told her, "and he shall soon be sold; and your girl shall be raised for the purpose of selling well." "Dr. Flint," the pseudonym Jacobs used for Norcom in her narrative, was indeed flinty. He knew how slavers created "fancy maids," and the female offspring of a light-skinned slave and a white man would fit that market category. Jacobs refused. Norcom moved her six miles out of Edenton, off to the plantation of his son and future daughter-in-law. Jacobs was isolated but at least she was not subject to Norcom's advances while at the Chowan County plantation.[83] There, she was responsible for household chores such as maintaining fires, running errands, preparing, serving, and cleaning up meals, washing clothes and dishes, scrubbing floors, and emptying and refreshing chamber pots. Missing her family, she often absented herself at night, walking six miles each way to her grandmother and children in Edenton. With the possibility of inclement weather, risk of illness and accidents, and the emotional strains of being separated from loved ones, her burden was all the more considerable.[84]

Isolated and in despair, she ran away in 1835, back to Edenton. There she enlisted the help of her grandmother, who in turn mobilized kin and neighbors. In response to the emergency, they lent their resources to keeping Jacobs hidden. But there were significant obstacles. Jacobs's initial flight was not well planned, thus making it easier for Norcom, who was determined to get her back and punish her for defying him, to find her. He raised an alarm, and mobilized his considerable resources, including the county sheriff, slave patrollers, newspapers, and his own family. Horniblow was careful under the circumstances not to publicly defy Norcom. She was a former slave, and in the wake of David Walker's *Appeal* and the Nat Turner rebellion, locals had harassed her and her house was searched for evidence of possible planned insurrections. To potential allies, white and black, she spread the countervailing narrative that Jacobs was an abused girl rather than a fugitive slave.[85]

The network of protection on which Jacobs relied during those anxious days in 1835 had been decades in the making. Molly Horniblow had laid up resources and forged ties that would assist Jacobs since before the twenty-two year-old fugitive was born. Though legally freed by an industrious father in the late 1770s, Horniblow was reenslaved by 1780, while still a small child, and grew up the property of Elizabeth Horniblow. As a young woman, Molly Horniblow learned how to bake and run a tavern. Elizabeth Horniblow ran a boarding house, which was in business by the 1810s. Molly also forged alliances with enslaved people in the neighborhood, and Horniblow's tavern served as a point of contact for a large enslaved family scattered about the area. When Elizabeth died in 1827, Molly and two relatives, Harriet's brother John and uncle Mark (Molly's son) were offered at public auction to settle the late owner's debts. Estate sales following the death of an owner were all-too-common causes of family separation, and the sale of herself and her family was a contingency that Molly Horniblow had anticipated. Though Elizabeth Horniblow had promised that Molly would be freed on her death, Molly, then in her fifties, was offered for sale at public auction in January 1828 about the same time Jacobs's owner began to sexually harass her.[86]

Horniblow had built a reputation among townspeople for her reliability and her baking. She had long run a business that was the domestic equivalent of Moses Grandy's boating operation. Horniblow had "became an indispensable personage in the household" of her former owner, Jacobs later wrote, "officiating in all capacities, from cook and wet nurse to seamstress." Horniblow's "nice crackers became so famous in the neighborhood that many people were desirous of obtaining them," which is how she began a bake shop, "provided she would clothe herself and her children from the profits." The owners shifted to her the burden of taking care of herself and Jacobs's relatives. "Upon these terms," Jacobs recalled, "after working hard all day for her mistress, she began her midnight bakings" and started her business. "The business proved profitable; and each year she laid by a little, which was saved for a fund to purchase her children." By the time Jacobs was born, Horniblow was also catering to Edenton's maritime workers, including African Americans. She had earned enough cash to buy herself and one of her sons later in the same year she had been auctioned off by her late owner's family, insisting on public sale to shame her late mistress's family and employing straw buyers whom she could trust to manumit her. Horniblow remained near her late owner's tavern, which had sometime been the site of a local escape network for fugitive slaves.[87]

Horniblow's residence on King Street, Edenton, later became the hub of a network that extended as far as New York City. King Street was close to the waterfront and as a consequence was in an advantageous place to attract the business of hungry sailors. Publicly a reliable African American matron, she had also accumulated social capital with black sailors who used her bake shop as a point of contact. Horniblow's decades of catering to townspeople who liked her crackers conferred social prestige, and her years of feeding hungry black sailors out of the same kitchen linked her in to an Atlantic-wide network of news and information not printed in newspapers, the kind that Moses Grandy's brother Benjamin had received and disseminated. Edenton's African and African American sailors had for generations been regular conduits of news and information concerning a black Atlantic beyond the purview of most Edenton residents, and she was able to draw on ties to black sailors and other allies with the resources and mobility to shelter her granddaughter. Horniblow was also the matriarch of a family that included many of Jacobs's relatives, a family that had over the previous two decades lost members to the slave trade and seen others like Jacobs's uncle Joseph make good his escape to the North. The town in which they lived was suffering a decline in fortunes despite having geographic advantages for Jacobs and Molly Horniblow.[88]

Edenton had developed as a port city on the Albemarle Sound. In the first decades of the nineteenth century, Edenton exported herring and other fish, tar, naval stores, and other timber products such as staves to cities like New York and Charleston. By the 1810s the city was on a twice-weekly stage line linking it with Petersburg and Richmond, Virginia.[89] But Harriet Jacobs's hometown was losing its competitive advantage. By the end of the War of 1812, Edenton's commercial shipping was being overtaken by nearby Elizabeth City, thirty miles to the northeast, which the Dismal Swamp Canal connected with port cities on the James River.[90] Moses Grandy's business was expediting that process. The slave-built canal diverted so much business from Edenton that by 1830 the local newspaper lamented that the town was "completely destitute of Marine intelligence." Edenton was nearly eclipsed as a commercial center in the 1840s when the railroad arrived in Weldon, North Carolina, some seventy-five miles to the northwest, and began diverting Roanoke River commerce.[91]

In the first decades of the nineteenth century, however, Edenton's commerce, much of it handled by enslaved seamen, presented opportunities to the enslaved. In 1811, for example, an enslaved man named Frank made an escape from his Edenton owner. The twenty-four year-old man "a tailor by trade," could "beat the drum extremely well, was born on the Island of Guadaloupe, to which place he has lately threatened to go," spoke "French pretty well" and was "a very artful insinuating fellow, particularly when in liquor." The owner was so sure Frank would depart "northward or [to] the West-Indies" that he felt compelled to remind would-be employers of the consequences of aiding him. "All masters of vessels and others," the owner scolded, "I strictly forbid harboring, employing, or carrying said fellow off under the severe penalty of the law–which is Death."[92] Frank may have been exceptional in his geographic, cultural, and linguistic knowledge, but he was not alone. The following year, Jack, a twenty-eight year-old fugitive, also a resident of Edenton, was sought by his owner. Jack was "a nail-cutter and blacksmith by trade" who could "read and write." It was "more than probable," the runaway ad read, that he "forged for himself a free pass." The owner suspected that he was "harbored" in a nearby neighborhood because his father and mother were there.[93] Jacobs's grandmother's enterprise shows a domestic and female side of that cosmopolitan slave culture.

To shelter her granddaughter in an emergency, Horniblow reached out to a white neighbor. At her request, Martha Hoskins Rombough Blount hid Jacobs in the kitchen of her Edenton house and enlisted one of her own slaves to care for the fugitive while keeping the arrangement secret from other slaves in whom she did not have confidence. Blount was distantly related both to Jacobs's tormentor and to Sawyer, the father of Jacobs's children. (This was not the first time a white woman had helped Jacobs: Margaret Horniblow, her first owner, and daughter of Jacobs's grandmother's owner, had instructed her in the arts of sewing, reading, writing, and religious devotion, before her death, on which Jacobs fell to the Norcom family.) Horniblow's cooperation with Blount shows Jacobs's network to be one based on local contingencies and ties cemented by sentiment rather than forged by class interests or social affiliations. As a white slaveholder, Blount acted against her putative racial and class allegiances. But Blount was probably moved to sympathy by the story of abuse Horniblow whispered throughout town. Horniblow lived adjacent to Norcom's office, where he put Jacobs's brother John to work, and just two blocks from Blount. Being strategically located in town, Horniblow was likely also responsible for gossiping—and in turn persuading Norcom—that Jacobs had followed her uncle Joseph to New York.[94]

Without Jacobs's knowledge, the father of her children was broadening her network as well. Sawyer worked through an intermediary to buy his children and her brother, John. After Norcom refused to sell the children to their father, Sawyer paid a slave trader to mask his involvement, taking advantage of the fact that Norcom was in debt. Sawyer mobilized the market to retrieve his children, who took part in public theatrics in order to fool townspeople. "My grandmother was told that the children would be restored to her," Jacobs wrote, "but she was requested to act as if they were really to be sent away." She played her part convincingly, taking the children "a bundle of clothes" for their journey, as was customary. "When she arrived," Jacobs recalled, John was "handcuffed among the gang, and the children in the trader's cart. The scene seemed too much like a reality. She was afraid there might have been some deception or mistake." Horniblow "fainted, and was carried home." John, Joseph, and Louisa were paraded through town in the trader's coffle. Jacobs wrote that Norcom "had the supreme satisfaction of seeing the wagon leave town." She quoted Mrs. Norcom as saying that she hoped "my children were going 'as far as wind and water would carry them.'" Jacobs's uncle Mark "followed the wagon some miles, until they came to an old farm house." John's irons were removed but reluctantly, apparently, as Jacobs heard that the trader appraised him as "a damned clever fellow. I should like to own you myself." Mark took the children and John back to Edenton. Hidden beneath floorboards in a kitchen, Jacobs received news that her children and brother were no longer Norcom's slaves. For John S. Jacobs, the alliance between his sister and Sawyer produced the unintended outcome of his reprieve from slavery at the hands of his sister's abuser. Sawyer had gotten her blood kin clear of Norcom, and afterward he took a less active role in protecting Jacobs. When Norcom learned of the ruse, he was furious. The $1,900 he made on the deal had not mollified him.[95]

As Sawyer's ties to Jacobs's allies attenuated, resources reached through her grandmother accumulated. Though he did not publicly recognize his children, Sawyer had an interest in prying them from Norcom's grasp. He had a bond of affection with them, as he had with their mother, though in 1838 he married Virginia native Lavinia Peyton, a woman of his social class. Sawyer confessed to the affair and the children but lied to his new wife by telling her that "their mother was dead." The new Mrs. Sawyer resolved to raise Joseph and allow her sister to adopt Louisa. The news mortified Jacobs, but Sawyer explained that he considered the children free and, moreover, Norcom was reasserting ownership over them, claiming that as they were the property of his daughter, he had had no right to sell them in the first place. For Jacobs, Sawyer's networking in behalf of their children was, as it were, a wheel in the middle of a wheel. She would spend years working against the ersatz benevolence of her children's father.[96]

In the meantime, Jacobs's uncle Mark put his carpentry skills to work crafting a living space in Horniblow's attic. That room would be Jacobs's place of confinement for the better part of seven years (during which time Sawyer married) and yet would be invisible to the inevitable searches to which Horniblow's house was subject.[97] Local African American seamen became active in her protection when it came time to move her out of Blount's kitchen and before the attic was ready. Entrusted to her care, they disguised her and told her to "put your hands in your pockets, and walk ricketty" like a sailor to evade the nightly slave patrols trolling the landscape for runaways. She was escorted out of town by "an apprentice to my father," she recalled, who "had always borne a good character." Dead many years, Elijah Jacobs's professional associations still worked to secure cooperation in his daughter's safety. At the water's edge, Jacobs's aunt Betty's husband, a sailor whom Jacobs never named, ferried her back and forth from a ship anchored off of Edenton, where she would spend nights, alternating with days in a nearly inaccessible no-man's land called "Snaky Swamp." There she fell ill and was bitten by a snake.[98]

The network based in Horniblow's parlor, cemented by her commercial, neighborhood, and family ties, held together against Norcom's frenzied search for his fugitive domestic worker. Once the attic room was finished, Jacobs arrived at her grandmother's house without the knowledge of either her owner, Sawyer, Blount, or even some relatives who had helped secret her. They "blackened my face with charcoal," Jacobs recalled, and the disguise worked so well that "I passed several people whom I knew. The father of my children came so near that I brushed against his arm; but he had no idea who it was." Edenton was indeed a small place, and its residents were looking for a lighter-complexioned female. Sawyer would turn from ally to an obstacle in Jacobs's network on his departure from Edenton after being elected to the U.S. House of Representatives in 1836 as a Whig candidate.[99]

Jacobs spent the next seven years in the care of her grandmother in the room that her uncle Mark had built. Horniblow left doors unlocked and windows open to divert suspicion. The network that had broadened to include slaveholders and African American sailors began to narrow to her grandmother, uncle, and sometimes the father of her children, who himself was unaware of exactly where Jacobs was hiding. She saw her children play and also observed Norcom, under the impression that she had made an escape to New York, grow older and angrier as he relentlessly pursued her. Jacobs even kept a correspondence with him, posting letters to him, through her uncle Joseph, in New York and beyond to give her claims of escape verisimilitude. Joseph and other relatives who had escaped to the North and Canada became part of her network, even though she had never left Chowan County.[100]

Exceptional in its scope and striking in its efficacy, Jacobs's network of protection was formed out of the bonds of family, affection, and professional associations, but it was framed by regional commercial developments and their local ramifications. Maritime commerce in the former colonial capital of North Carolina had helped Molly Horniblow to succeed in business and buy herself and son Mark out of slavery in time to help their granddaughter and niece. The fact that enslaved tradesmen were able to flourish permitted the influence of Harriet's father Elijah Jacobs to reach beyond the grave to his erstwhile apprentice, who had escorted his daughter out of town in sailor's clothes. Edenton's maritime industry, though in decline, gave enslaved workers wide freedom of movement, so much so that the sight of a strange black sailor staggering about town did not raise serious suspicion in a county with a very small free black population.

The best-known female author of an American slave narrative would not have later dipped her pen in ink were it not for her Edenton network. Had Harriet Jacobs not came of age in the antebellum upper South, in a family that had itself accumulated social and financial capital and seized opportunities held out by a commercial maritime town economy, her exceptional character might well have been all but lost to history—reported solely in Norcom's runaway ads and remembered only in living memory. Networks infused civic space in the antebellum south, even reaching into law courts. Laura F. Edwards has found that enslaved women influenced legal proceedings by maintaining "gossip networks" that diffused perceptions, often about the reputations of whites, into the broader community. That knowledge gained currency as it was repeated first by slaves and then by free people, and reports that female slaves manufactured could become evidence in court cases. Enslaved women therefore could influence legal proceedings even though they were barred from giving testimony. Even slave owners could be enlisted unwittingly in such a network when they spread gossip or repeated it. Through Jacobs's letters posted from the North, Norcom and white Edenton was subject to the same sort of dissimulation in the service of Jacobs's protection. The artful lies Jacobs posted him from his own backyard drew attention away from the Horniblow house and the activities of the men and women of Edenton dedicated to Jacobs's safety.[101]

The town geography, place of Edenton within a broader network of trade, and even the physical surroundings, including the Great Dismal Swamp, were used to her advantage. Town geography permitted communications that allowed Horniblow to arrange for Jacobs's nights aboard ship, through her daughter Betty's husband. Jacobs's network was strong enough to withstand the search Norcom initiated upon her escape as well as his relentless pursuit. People without rights and with comparably few resources gave Jacobs the resources to win her "competition in cunning" with her abuser.[102] Few but Jacobs, her uncle Mark, and her grandmother knew the scope of the network. Some participants were motivated by love and loyalty; others were animated by disgust with her owner. Many did not know they were allied in the same cause. Even a slave trader had unwittingly helped her. Jacobs's network was exceptional, but it illustrates how enslaved women assembled and maintained the means to protect family members using human ties. Such networks formed in villages, towns, ports, railroad crossings, and urban areas. They distinguished enslaved peoples' experiences in those locations from slave life in more rural and isolated regions of South. Jacobs eventually left her attic in 1842 in an effort to recover her children when Sawyer treated Joseph and Louisa as property, by giving them to relatives. Once she recovered Joseph and Louisa, Jacobs would keep close to her family for the rest of her life.[103]

The trials domestic slaves faced, along with the shape and scope of their associations, complicates an idea that there was a slave community forged through common bonds among the enslaved as people of African descent. Allying with slave traders seems a perverse way of preserving family against the odds of being sold away in the slave market. We are left to wonder how Corinna Hinton, Mary Lumpkin, and Ann Davis—and their children—felt about the ramifications of their raising a family and living off the proceeds of the trade that was responsible for removing so many people who, like them, were enslaved. Mary Lumpkin, at least, tried to make amends for abetting slave commerce in "the devil's half acre," as Robert Lumpkin's compound was known. In 1867, Baptist minister Nathaniel Colver described her as a "large, fair-faced freed-woman, nearly white, who said that *she* had a place which she thought I could have" to begin a black seminary. Lumpkin leased the compound, which became a school for African American students and later Virginia Union University—after she had the bars torn from the structure.[104]

Using heuristic categories like "resistance" or "agency" to describe complex and contingent sets of circumstances such as these is a bit like attempting to paint the sunrise over Jacobs's Albemarle Sound or sunset on Mary Lumpkin's Richmond solely with primary colors. The subtle mixing of categories—the oranges and violets of cross-class, cross-racial, and cross-gendered alliances—is left out. There were no a priori categories of interests that represented the hegemony of one set of values or determined a known set of outcomes. Slavery was not a totalizing institution; it was instead situated within the complex geography of local circumstances. The market's severing of community and class ties made networking necessary rather than the attenuation of slavery in the upper South making it possible. In Jacobs's Edenton, slaveholders worked against other slaveholders; slaves against slaves; and judicial officer against other judicial officers. Agency abounded, since no parties to Jacobs's escape displayed a sense of being overawed or paralyzed.[105] It seems clear from their choices and from those of women like Harriet Jacobs, Eliza, and so many other women in the antebellum upper South that it was often imperative for women in domestic service to reach out to people who did not share their gender, ancestry, or status in order to protect themselves and family members from the violence slave markets propagated and the prerogatives that legal status conferred on slaveholders and their allies. The ties they cemented with sentiment and emotion were as fragile as those male slaves forged with cash, yet they reordered slaveholders' ideology of domesticity, using a highly elaborated code in the service of their own contingent, evolving, and often anguished strategies.[106]

$\mathcal{M}akers$

$\mathcal{A}$s modernity moved, slavery moved to match it. As upper South cities grew, slaveholders found new uses for enslaved people in the region's processing industries. A Richmond tobacconist in 1804 advertised that he "WANTS to hire two NEGRO FELLOWS by the year, or month, to be employed in the manufacture of Tobacco, for which he will give good wages" to their owners. Others followed suit. Amid such developments, enslaved people avoided studying the workings of the market at their peril. The slave Lott Cary was caught reading Adam Smith's *Wealth of Nations* in a corner of a Richmond tobacco warehouse sometime in the first decade of the nineteenth century, and while his choice of literature was unusual, it illustrates how enslaved people faced with an intensifying market responded to new uncertainties. Their calculated responses confronted slaveholders.[1]

After the destabilizing effects of the British invasion in the War of 1812 and of the panic of 1819 and its aftermath, slaveholders sought new strategies to make profits. Tobacco producers mitigated their dependence on foreign tobacco manufacturers by having their leaf processed locally. Entrepôt cities such as Richmond and Petersburg became centers for tobacco manufacture rather than ports for its transshipment. Virginia slaves whose ancestors had toiled in tobacco fields would work in tobacco factories. At the same time, planters who had mobilized a labor force to grow tobacco locally now scored greater economic success by selling slaves to distant parts of their expanding nation. Some enslaved people faced a choice between processing commodities or being sold as commodities.

Urban centers were theaters of that drama, featuring factories that intensified production in each generation. In the resulting dissonance of a slave market society that embraced both a consumer culture in slaves and the demands of production for world markets, enslaved people working in tobacco and other processing industries found ways to protect blood kin from the slave trade. They saved cash that was by the 1840s regularly being disbursed to enslaved workers in order to shift the burdens of care to the workers. They faced severe constraints, however, and most saw their best efforts to protect family members fail. The economy of time within which they worked had accelerated along with the pace of industrial production and slave sales. The slave market Solomon Bayley had confronted was transforming into the one in which William Robinson was sold. In counties outlying urban areas, slave traders still appeared on court days to bid on human chattel, but in 1840s Richmond, slave auctions such as R. H. Dickinson's were open six days a week, and scores of buyers, from locals like Silas Omohundro to out-of-state traders and planters, flocked to the sites to bid on the people for sale.[2]

The enslaved worked against all that disruption using market-made advantages. Miles and Martha were hired out in Richmond in the mid-1840s, some sixty miles from their owner in Gloucester County, Virginia. Miles was a skilled mason, hired at $125 per year. From the brick yard in which he and some seventy other slaves worked, Miles witnessed the productive energies of his fellow enslaved workers along Richmond's industrial waterfront. The air was thick with soot from smoke from the Tredegar Iron Works, which was just then shifting to using slave labor. The breeze carried the dense aroma of tobacco—and the sweet notes of sugar and licorice boiled to flavor it—from a dozen factories in the neighborhood, all employing enslaved laborers. Miles heard slave work songs from some corners of those tobacco factories. When the long work day was done, he joined hundreds, perhaps thousands, of other slaves like himself making their way to Shockoe Bottom and other African American neighborhoods, where he and his fellow industrial slaves mixed with the free black population, making their own living arrangements. His wife, Martha, and their two children were hired nearby to keep house for a clerk for $20 a year.[3]

When Martha became pregnant with their third child in 1845, Miles traveled east to Gloucester County to make arrangements to house Martha and their new baby away from her employer. Miles and Martha had likely grown up in that rural Tidewater county, and Miles returned there to bargain with their owner. His situation illustrates the artificiality of a distinction between agricultural and nonagricultural slavery in eastern Virginia. "Where cereals, grains, and truck farming predominated or coexisted with tobacco," Gregg Kimball argues, "masters took advantage of the less labor-intensive or seasonal nature of work by hiring slaves to make cash money," and Richmond "offered an excellent opportunity for hiring." Perhaps above 15 percent of enslaved people in the South as a whole could expect to be hired out at any one time in the late antebellum period. In parts of the upper South that was as much as one third or a half. As Sarah Hughes contends, "hiring made slavery a more profitable institution for owners . . . by making blacks work harder."[4] Temporary owners wrung as much work out of an enslaved person as possible. That "cash money" economy gave the slaves some bargaining power as well. Miles used his earning power successfully in his dealings with Warner T. Taliaferro, his owner, but after securing separate lodgings for his family, their child died as so many babies did. Miles moved Martha and their two children into rented rooms anyway. Another young mother, Mary Ann, moved in with Martha and the children from January to May 1846. Miles had received a travel allowance of $5 to return to Gloucester County to make the arrangements, but the some $31 he paid for the room, food, and fuel was deducted from his hire for 1845, as a loan to be repaid to the slaveholder.[5]

Miles and Martha's housing situation illustrates how enslaved people could use the promise of future income to the slaveholder to defend family ties and, in more abstract terms, it shows the trade-offs slaves made between consumption and investment. By arranging to house Martha and the children at over 150 percent of the value of her annual hire, Miles showed the high value they placed on keeping a family together during a sensitive time after the loss of a child. The owner still profited from her hire, and he gained an advantage over Miles at the same time. By moving his wife and children close by, Miles would be less likely to disappear. That would have made him a more valuable asset to the slaveholder, who would be less likely to sell him or his children as a result. Miles used his earning power to give his wife and children and that of a relative or friend some private space where he could actively participate in family life as a father and a husband.[6]

Slaveholder concurrence displayed more than sentiment. Taliaferro's plantations in Gloucester County could be described as large-scale nurseries by midcentury, containing a large number of small children and few adults. Many parents were off working in urban areas. On his way to and from work, Miles possibly crossed paths with Henry Brown, a native of Louisa County, Virginia, who had been sent to Richmond at fifteen to work processing tobacco. Within sight of coffles of slaves being marched out of what was becoming the largest slave market in the upper South, they both knew the costs of lacking the means to keep their families close by.[7]

When Brown got word that his wife and their child were to be sold in 1844, he used the money he had been saving through overwork in a Richmond tobacco factory to deal with the prospective buyer. Tobacconists typically paid extra for exceeding production quotas, which was usually forty-five pounds per day. That was an innovation over canal companies' paying slaves for diligence in liquor. The opportunity for overwork indicates a labor shortage in the factories, which had to compete with buyers in the cotton South. Factory owners, more concerned with profits than policing people, allowed slaves to capture so much of that premium because it increased production and made pliant workers out of people with no other stake in the process. Moreover, most enslaved tobacco workers were hired rather than owned, so factory owners had even fewer ways to control them.[8]

Brown's place atop a hierarchy of skilled industrial slaves gave him the opportunity to pool resources with a buyer and thereby maintain some connection with his wife and children. The would-be buyer, local saddler Samuel Cottrell, had contacted Brown with the news that Nancy's owner (another saddler, Joseph H. Colquitt) was offering her for sale that day for $650 and that he had only $600 to spare for her purchase.[9] Brown had cause to worry. He and Nancy had been married for eight years and Nancy had been sold three times since then, including once before by Colquitt, whose wife had abused her for doting on her own children instead of her mistress. In desperation, lest Nancy be sold out of state, Henry came up with $50 and secured the promise from Cottrell that if he were able to buy Nancy, Henry would be permitted to house her and their children with him. But Brown did not trust Cottrell. "I thought I would let him have the money," Brown recalled after listening to Cottrell plead that his Christianity would forestall the possibility of his selling Nancy and their child, "not that I had implicit faith in his promise, but that I knew he could purchase her if he wished whether I were to assist him or not, and I thought by thus bringing him under an obligation to me it might at least be somewhat to the advantage of my wife and to me." Brown had no alternative than to risk being cheated. Facing the loss of his family, Brown "gave him the 50 dollars and he went off and bought my wife and children."[10]

Whether Brown realized it, he and Cottrell were in the market at a good time for buyers. Prices for "prime field hands" in Virginia were as low in 1844 as any time since 1832 and about where they were when Solomon Bayley bid for his son Spence in 1813. Had Nancy and the children been offered for sale in the peak year of 1837, Cottrell and Brown might have had to pay more than twice the 1844 average price for them. Relatively low demand and consequent low prices of cotton meant that planters were willing to pay less for slaves. When cotton prices rose after 1844, enslaved workers planning to rent or buy relatives would have to accumulate more resources. In the antebellum period, neither slave nor cotton prices would be so low again.[11]

No sooner had Cottrell gotten a hold of Nancy and the children than he began to impose restrictions. Brown recalled that "that very same day he came to me and told me, that my wife and children were now his property, and that I must hire a house for them and he would allow them to live there if I would furnish them with everything they wanted, and pay him 50 dollars, a year; 'if you dont do this,' he said, 'I will sell her as soon as I can get a buyer for her.'" For his part, Brown "was struck with astonishment to think that this man, in one day, could exhibit himself in two such different characters. A few hours ago filled with expressions of love and kindness, and now a monster tyrant, making light of the most social [of] ties and imposing such terms as he chose on those whom, but a little before, had begged to conform to his will." Still, this backtracking notwithstanding, Brown had fewer constraints than most other enslaved people.[12]

Nancy and Henry Brown consented to the conditions, and to make sure he could meet them, Henry drew on complementary sides of his network, the factory and the church. Henry was his master's most efficient tobacco worker, after all, and occasionally earned $5 a week for exceeding his quota in the tobacco factory, on top of the seventy cents he received each week to feed and house himself. By 1844, the twenty-nine year-old slave had been a tobacconist for fourteen years and was in the unusual position of being owned by the owner of the factory in which he worked. But he used the relationship strategically, demonstrating diligence and expertise at his work despite hardships and harsh overseers. Brown's income from overwork was the lynchpin of the deal he and his wife made with her new owner. Brown called upon a friend, a fellow (free) member of the First African Baptist Church, James C. A. Smith Jr., to rent a house. It was unlikely that Brown could find a white preacher to exert moral authority over Cottrell as Solomon Bayley had done forty years before on the Eastern Shore. Brown was a member of an African American congregation and not optimistic that slaveholders would be swayed by American Christianity.[13] Smith quickly complied and rented a house at $6 per month. To ease their financial burdens, Nancy would take in washing and other work. After making the arrangements with Smith and Nancy's new owner, however, the Browns were no closer to buying their freedom or that of their children.[14]

Though participation in a cash economy has a male cast to it, Nancy's work was also market-focused. She likely earned money through domestic work, and in a city in which thousands of enslaved factory workers were "living out" under a system by which they bought their own food and lodgings, it was natural for Nancy to operate an informal cook shop serving enslaved laborers or to take in occasional lodgers. Like her husband, Nancy's hands also would have been hardened from repetitive manual labor, scrubbing laundry, and cooking. Their house would have smelled of soap, smoke, and damp clothes, and those odors would have been cut through with the aroma of fried bacon and bread or biscuits. In between their small chores, the children would have witnessed hungry workers show up to exchange a few cents for meat and bread after a hard work day manufacturing tobacco, making bricks, or packing ships in an industrial city that thrived on slave labor.

But they would embrace a father who arrived home to their mother and enjoy the company of their mother all day long, without seeing her abused or humiliated. Few other enslaved children in the South had such a home life. That is what Nancy and Henry Brown had accomplished, against the odds of doing so. After settling into the arrangement, paying $6 a month to rent the house and a little over $4 a month to rent Nancy from Cottrell, the Browns found extra money to buy sufficient food and even furnishings, participating in some small way in Richmond's consumer culture. Henry later recalled, "We felt ourselves more comfortable than we had ever been before." Whatever obstacles they faced, be they the likelihood Brown would fall ill or suffer an injury at work or that Cottrell would exercise his legal rights to sell Nancy and their children, Brown could arrive home to the wife he loved and learn what his small children had discovered that day. On Sunday mornings they could depart together for the First African Baptist Church, where they had met and where Henry was "a leading member of the choir."[15]

Henry and Nancy Brown's and Miles and Martha's arrangements illustrate the connections between local contingencies and the broad historical processes that framed them. That Miles and Brown happened to be in a position to bargain for improved lodgings for their wives and children was contingent on their having become skilled workers in an urban industrial setting, which also allowed them to earn income. They were born into propitious as well as perilous conditions for anyone enslaved in the Americas. They came of age after the War of 1812 and in eastern Virginia, where opportunities existed to gain industrial skills and earn some cash. They were also born into conditions that complicated their efforts.

Industrialists in the Chesapeake found a ready supply of workers, and slaveholders found a local outlet for surplus slaves. Instead of toiling away in distant cotton fields, some laborers processed Virginia's tobacco and some worked on its railroads, digging its canals, forging its iron. By hiring out workers wherever and whenever they saw an advantage, slaveholders found new ways to profit from an old institution. Industrial processing work in preindustrial America was arduous and dangerous, and enslaved people had no more rights as workers than they had as slaves. For Brown or Miles, succeeding in such an environment meant learning a skill and making himself difficult to replace with another worker. And there were many more available workers as a result of the Chesapeake's distinctive historical development over the previous century.[16]

The surplus of slaves in the nineteenth-century upper South came partly from the reproductive successes of earlier generations. Living conditions in British North America, unlike those in the Atlantic sugar complex of the Caribbean and South America, favored natural reproduction. Work regimes were less hazardous, and adequate nutrition and medical care were more widely available than anywhere else in the Americas. Self-reproducing slave populations were unintended consequences of the Chesapeake's having been peripheral to a booming eighteenth-century sugar complex whose masters were hungry for male workers to feed a charnel house of plantation production. In the early eighteenth century, Chesapeake planters had bought female slaves in larger proportions than their Caribbean counterparts (primarily because proportions of males and females among Igbo and other captives from the Bight of Biafra were more evenly distributed than elsewhere), and by the middle of the eighteenth century, sex ratios had nearly equalized. As Africans and Afro-Caribbeans (or "Atlantic creoles") became Americans they adjusted to the disease environment and helped to transform the linguistic and social environments in which they raised their children. Planters in the Chesapeake saw populations of people they claimed to own increase through natural reproduction and bought fewer slaves from abroad as a result.[17]

Enslaved families in turn made possible the capitalist revolutions that transformed the early U.S. republic and industrial Britain. The ability of enslaved families to cultivate life in the upper South initially peopled the lower South with slaves, which in turn provided the raw materials for industrial intensification in England and New England. Using London credit, Manchester, England, manufacturers paid Philadelphia and Liverpool shippers, who in turn paid cotton merchants in New Orleans, Natchez, or Vicksburg. After taking their profits, urban merchants paid Georgia, Alabama, Mississippi, or Texas planters. Planters in turn paid steamboat operators and warehouse owners in the entrepôt cities through which their produce passed and then ploughed the revenues back into refreshing their assemblages of enslaved laborers with new arrivals from upper South states. Slave traders based in Virginia or Maryland then reaped their rewards and emptied their coffles in the cotton kingdom. To buyers and traders, it would not matter whether the slaves they bought and sold were the daughters of Moses Grandy or brothers of Frederick Douglass. The profits of the domestic slave trade, plus the ingenuity of African Americans in making compromises to save other family members from the slave market, are what financed the redevelopment of the Chesapeake and coastal North Carolina. Their fertility and commitment to family supported that hemisphere-wide activity. The enslaved whose masters "wanted money" would be the likeliest ones to enter into that complex stream of commerce.[18]

To understand what was at stake for the Browns, Miles and Martha, and their children in keeping their families together, then, we must put historical processes usually understood in abstract terms of initial industrial development and the "market revolution" in the context of African American families in slavery.[19] In that environment of commercial intensification, families in slavery bought (or attempted to buy) into an asset and legacy-based interest in the people to which they were related, engaging in a practice that formerly only the wealthy had. That is, slaves like Miles and Martha or the Browns pooled resources to buy or rent other slaves not for their productive value but, put in economic terms, for consumption, because they were related. The antebellum period, then, saw a shift toward enslaved families as property-holding corporations, even if they lacked civic standing to hold property legally. (That was a distinctive feature of American law; in colonial Brazil, for instance, slaves could own other slaves.) Their strategy of accumulating wealth in people, which had a particularly American aspect, stood in contrast to the political strategies of their African ancestors. The nature of the slave trade tended to work against such strategies, however, since young adult men and women, especially young mothers like Nancy, were most vulnerable to sale. Those in the best place to accumulate property were also the most likely to be sold and thereby have their plans undermined.[20]

Property ownership and commercial activity was integral to African Americans' family life.[21] Property considerations framed Miles and Martha's arrangements, and Henry Brown's property ownership—the $50 he was able to hand over to his wife's buyer—was decisive in maintaining his family's cohesion. (American family life in general became increasingly infused with property concerns as the market intensified, so an emphasis on property was not peculiar to African American families.)[22] Hiring out could afford an enslaved person the opportunity to participate in an informal economy and acquire property. Miles was among 70 workers at his brickyard; Henry Brown worked among 150 African Americans in his factory, 120 of whom were enslaved. In those establishments, owners had little incentive to house their hired workers, so they gave them small cash payments for food and lodgings instead. Moreover, factory owners paid slaves overtime to increase their productivity. Industrialists such as "tobacco manufacturers were employers first, masters second," argues Suzanne Schnittman, so "they spent more time procuring and training" a workforce than they did "cultivating, nurturing, and controlling the private lives" of those workers. Enslaved people were regularly subject to protoindustrial labor psychology, which gave them a stake in the system and a crucial means by which to accumulate property. Buying the freedom of vulnerable loved ones was only one strategy to protect families. Scholars have viewed enslaved people's participation in informal economies as giving them quasi freedom, but the emphasis is somewhat misplaced. In contests with employers and owners, family exceeded freedom in a hierarchy of concerns, though—as Brown discovered—trade-offs were more properly framed in terms of family or no family.[23]

Maintaining family ties through the cash slaves could earn was a distinctive feature of upper South commercial culture, a consequence of the slave hiring in the antebellum period that provided industrialists with a ready supply of labor. Hiring, however, was nothing new. Slaves were hired out at least by the mid-seventeenth century in Virginia, as were other bound laborers. Loren Schweninger contends that by the last quarter of the eighteenth century slave hiring and its customs "had been firmly established for generations." In 1782, for instance, some planters in Henrico County, Virginia, complained that "many Persons have suffr'd their Slaves to go about to hire themselves and pay their Masters for their hire[,] and others under pretense of putting them free set [them] out to live for themselves." The petitioners objected to these innovations on established customs, but the flexibility in hiring made economic sense for slaveholders and employers and also gave nonslaveholding whites a greater stake in the institution. Poor whites did, on occasion, compete for agricultural work but the widespread access to markets for hired slaves tended to dissolve animosity toward the system. White people who could not expect to own a slave in their lifetimes could expect to hire one. Yearly contracts, beginning after New Year's and ending at Christmastime, were standard, but slaves could be hired out on a temporary basis and to perform an increasing variety of tasks. Early processing businesses also experimented with enslaved child labor. A Norfolk firm advertised that it wished "to HIRE on the first day of January, 1816, TWENTY NEGRO BOYS, From 10 to 15 years old, To work in a Tobacco Factory. —Liberal wages will be given and the best usage." Such experiments led to systemic developments. That process in turn made possible the contingent events surrounding the Browns' and Miles and Martha's arrangements in the 1840s, which were not uncommon in a city like Richmond.[24]

Transformations of the tobacco industry in the Chesapeake illustrate how commercial intensification and economic diversification changed the market for slave labor and, in turn, created new opportunities available for people like the Browns. Tobacco production had long been the staple of the Chesapeake market, but by the 1820s men involved in its manufacture, rather than its cultivation, were transforming the commercial landscape. By the first decades of the nineteenth century, tobacco cultivation was no longer the mainstay of agriculture in eastern Virginia, southern Maryland, or the Delmarva Peninsula, as it had been for nearly two centuries before. "Before the Revolution," Jack Temple Kirby argues, "most [agriculturalists] had wisely decided to forsake tobacco culture in favor of grains, both maize and wheat, huge surpluses of which were readily marketed in the Caribbean." Instead of producing tobacco, which their western neighbors increasingly did, Chesapeake Tidewater farmers and planters grew food for the booming slave-based sugar complex of the Caribbean and other foreign markets. In the early decades of the nineteenth century, industrialists began to build factories in urban centers that had once simply shipped the leaf to European manufacturing centers. Demand for newly fashionable plug or chewing tobacco for European and North American markets made entrepôt cities like Norfolk, Richmond, and Petersburg prime locations for tobacco manufacture. The fact that tobacco manufacturers were often veteran planters, frequently with surplus slaves, meant that a ready regime of labor could be deployed to satisfy the growing demand for locally processed tobacco.[25]

The considerable labor once expended in its growing would be available to serve new needs. Tobacco was a difficult crop to grow, and its cultivation was a risky investment. It was an eighteen-month crop, requiring the farmer to plant seedlings under protective cover in winter and then to transplant them to the fields in late April or early May. The crop ripened in late summer, but it was often beset by tobacco worms, which—in an age before chemical pesticides—were difficult to eradicate. Harvest commenced in August, but the leaves needed to be cured and processed. The packed leaves reached market in June, a month after the new crop was transplanted. Having made it that far, the tobacco was inspected and graded. Then it passed through several middlemen—and thousands of miles of ocean—on its way to market. With each inspection and step in the long route to market, the producer paid a fee, duty, or commission. Farmers near emerging port cities thus embraced the alternative to this risky process that a growing transportation infrastructure and the resources to build factories provided.

Processing rather than shipping drew on local resources, especially an available labor pool of enslaved people and proximity to deepwater ports. By the 1810s, the federal government was promoting domestic manufacturers, and some Virginians saw the region's future in them. During the 1828 tariff debates, for instance, Tidewater Virginia congressman William Segar Archer wrote a constituent and planter friend near Petersburg Virginia, that "those who come first in any system of commerce, are the men who make the fortunes. It is theirs to skim the cream leaving the milk to others." "Some of our citizens are affected with such an extraordinary character of public spirit," he continued, ironically, "that they are determined not to partake the benefits of the manufacturing system, because they have not approved of Congress imposing it." Archer winked at his friend when he delivered that advice. If the Tariff of 1828 passed, he counseled, "you ought to go to manufacturing." Conservative Virginians, such as John Taylor of Caroline, had argued against federal protections for extractive and manufacturing interests. Archer contended instead that if the federal government were going to meddle in markets, Virginians' account ledgers, at least, should register the benefits. He was not a voice in the wilderness. A generation later, George Fitzhugh and Edmund Ruffin would advocate for the diversification of Virginia's economy and a revitalization of its cities for similar reasons.[26] None of those politicians or improvers had any intention however, of creating conditions whereby enterprising slaves could also seek to benefit from overwork regimes resulting from manufacturers' economies of scale. The factory world that Miles and Brown inhabited was an unintended consequence of a shift in strategies among Virginia tobacco interests and other capitalists.[27]

Planters who might otherwise ship their leaves overseas for processing suffered fewer fluctuations in world markets and gained a profitable outlet for surplus workers by processing their crop locally. In the early 1820s, Henry Clarke of Lynchburg monitored the markets for his tobacco through correspondence with buyers in Liverpool. He was a medium-sized planter who relied on slave labor to cultivate his leaf. Clarke kept abreast of the markets for his crops in London and Liverpool, but also in Dublin, Hamburg, Antwerp, Rotterdam, Marseilles, Bordeaux, Cadiz, and half a dozen other European cities. Through his Richmond agents, he shipped tobacco to be processed in England, receiving whatever proceeds he could after his agents settled on a price and then deducted the inspection fees, tobacco stamps, freight, primage, portage, cooperage, sampling, dock dues, town dues, interest on freight, and commission.[28]

Clarke's slaves had a lot riding on whether, after all those fees had been paid, the planter cleared a profit. Their families ultimately bore the risks and costs. Slumps in the Rotterdam or Antwerp tobacco markets could have ripple effects elsewhere, or if Dublin, Liverpool, and London merchants decided they wanted Kentucky tobacco instead of James River tobacco, Clarke could see eighteen months' work go up in smoke. That in turn made the difference between whether Clarke might sell or mortgage a portion of his slave property to save his enterprise from failure. Prices for slaves had started rising in the 1820s, after the panic of 1819 and credit crisis had passed, leaving the members of enslaved families Clarke owned especially vulnerable to the planter's financial calculations should tobacco prices fall. Since the most saleable people were also the most likely to have young children, one year's failure could wreck two generations of an enslaved family. Even children, however, could be mortgaged, often without their parents' knowledge, and a planter might try to overwork or hire out enslaved people to salvage profits in a lean year. Members of those families suffered if European markets and layers of middlemen upset the planter's calculations. Such market fluctuations were not new, but those set to work in Clarke's Piedmont Virginia fields could do relatively little to use their owner's commercial affairs to their advantage the way Henry Brown could his. As cultivators, they had everything to lose and little to gain from the market until planters like Clarke applied industrial psychology in the fields when in succeeding decades they gave slaves permission to plant and sell tobacco on their own accounts.[29]

Unlike cultivators, enslaved people working in the warehouses along the Richmond docks at the turn of the nineteenth century found some ways to make markets work for them, before the rise of large-scale processing. Lott Cary, the slave caught reading Smith's *Wealth of Nations*, was sent to Richmond from Charles City County, Virginia, in 1804 to work at the Shockoe tobacco warehouse. Cary had a religious awakening, joined the First Baptist Church in 1807, and learned to read and write. He became skilled at his job and earned trust as an employee, often receiving $5 bills as gratuities. From his small corner of the Atlantic market, he sold waste tobacco on his own account. By 1813 he had purchased his freedom and that of his two children, his wife having passed away in the meantime. Cary continued to speculate in tobacco and draw a not inconsiderable salary, eventually saving enough to emigrate to Liberia, where he founded a church and struggled with diseases, native peoples, slave traders, and church organizations in the United States before dying in an accidental explosion in 1828.[30]

The rise of commercial processing in cities like Richmond gave manufacturers and planters who owned slaves reciprocal interests. "Tobacco planters found themselves in an especially enviable position," argues Schnittman, "when some of the slaves who had cultivated their fields could be rented out to manufacture their leaf." Richmond's tobacco processing industry comprised only a handful of shops, employing fewer than 100 slaves, in the first decade of the nineteenth century. In the decade of the 1820s, fifteen to twenty tobacconists employed between 370 and 480 enslaved workers (between 7 and 9 percent of the Richmond and Henrico County slave population in 1820 and between 6 and 8 percent of the 1830 total). By 1840, some thirty factories employed between 600 and 700 slaves (or 4.5 to just under 5 percent of the total number of slaves in Richmond and the surrounding county). Henry Brown and his coworkers processed one hundred thousand pounds of tobacco a year by the 1840s.[31]

The smaller percentage of enslaved workers in the tobacco industry, despite its growth, indicates that Richmond's commercial landscape was diversifying. Slavery was transforming along with it. Virginia industrialists generally took whatever advantages they could of the available pool of enslaved laborers. Most large industrial firms, with the exception of the Tredegar Iron Works, preferred to board out hired slaves, giving them monies to buy their own food and lodging, rather than to institute regimes of supervision. Some slaves saved their meager allowances and slept in alleys. Others haunted local grog shops and kitchens, and some wagered their monies in games of chance. Industrialists' benign neglect became a source of wealth critical in creating informal economies in cities like Richmond, which gave hired enslaved workers practical instruction in how to manage money.

Such networks of urban slaves by turns competed and cooperated with the free black population in cities like Richmond, and their interactions created a substantial economy unintended by the architects of the system. By the mid-1830s, over three thousand enslaved hired African Americans lived out and enjoyed a "type of quasi-freedom" and at night settled in among the nearly two thousand free African Americans in a city of eighteen thousand. By the mid-1840s, several thousand slave laborers scattered themselves among the free black population, who supplied them with food and lodging in every part of the city. By one calculation, between 40 and 50 percent of Richmond's slaves were hired out in 1860, that is between forty-seven hundred and fifty-nine hundred in a city with a total population of nearly thirty-eight thousand. Thousands of enslaved workers moved from work sites to lodgings and kitchens each evening, transporting news and telling stories, sharing their hopes and unburdening themselves of the stresses and strains of their working lives. Men, women, and children walked together during rush hour from

Richmond's industrial areas to the bottoms and boardinghouses that gathered them in each evening and scattered them again each workday morning. By the 1850s, they competed with immigrant Irish for living space. Many Irish had been recruited to work on the James River and Kanawha Canal and "fled" the project's "horrific working conditions" for Richmond, where they competed with African Americans for the lowest-paying jobs.[32] The Richmond Common Council did eventually outlaw the practice of slaves' boarding out, in 1858, but enforcement was impossible.[33]

Living conditions were often unpleasant, and city officials were keen to publicize incidents of infectious disease supposedly carried by African Americans. In 1832, the Richmond Board of Health traced a cholera outbreak to three fatal cases, all African Americans. One woman, "named Jemima, aged 50 years," was examined by three white doctors and found to have been "intemperate in her habits, of feeble health, living in a dirty, damp cellar" and died after two days' illness. Another victim was a middle-aged enslaved man, also lodging in the city. The third was "a mulatto man named Baylor, aged about 30 years, who lodged at Mr. Barclay's garden," who was "subject to bowel complaint, and weakly constitution." That man died the same day his illness was discovered, after he had been "taken sick at Mr. Barclay's Tobacco Factory." Authorities seemed to associate controlling disease with controlling African Americans, but they would have done better to have addressed the poor health, sanitation, and living conditions associated with antebellum urban industrial practices that resulted in epidemics.[34]

Some upper South cities sought to regulate the practice of slaves doing business on their own accord or taking money for services since state laws forbade the practice. The city of Norfolk, Virginia, sold permits or badges to slaves for a dollar, which gave them license to hire themselves in behalf of owners or contract other agreements. That was recognition of slaves' status as contractors, which partly repealed their civic emasculation. To control slaves, the city endorsed the privileges the market had already granted them. On one summer Thursday in 1850, twenty-five black men were rounded up in Norfolk on suspicion of conducting business without such a license. They were all released, however, after producing their city badges. None of their advantages came lightly.[35]

Work in an antebellum tobacco factory was filthy and physically demanding and characterized by an extensive division of labor. When Brown arrived at dawn on a summer morning to start his fourteen-hour workday, he entered a brick building "about 300 feet in length, and three stories high," which he estimated "afforded room for 200" workers. There were 120 slaves working alongside 30 free African Americans, all of whom returned to the same neighborhoods afterward. The fourteen-hour day was extended to sixteen in the winter, and workers set the pace of production. No machines kept the tempo, only the striving of slaves who sought monies for "overwork" and that of free people who earned wages from the piecework they performed. Frederick Law Olmstead summed up the industrial psychology of the overwork regime when he observed that enslaved tobacco workers "could not be 'driven' to do a fair day's work so easily as they could be stimulated to it by the offer of a bonus for all they would manufacture above a certain number of pounds." Of course, if cash incentives did not spur production, the overseer was always ready with a whip.[36]

Tobacco entered the factory packed in hogsheads and left packaged for consumption. The first task was stemming, or removing the middle rib of the tobacco leaf. According to Brown, that was "performed by women and boys." The leaves were then dried, and according to Brown, "the tobacco was moistened with a liquor made from liquorice and sugar, which gives the tobacco that sweetish taste which renders it not perfectly abhorrent to those who chew it." That was called dipping, and it was often performed by children who kept cool by working "stark naked in their rooms near the drying roofs," according to one historian. Once the leaves were flavored, they were placed on the roofs to be dried again.[37]

When they had dried for a second time, the leaves were moistened again, sometimes with rum or another flavoring, after which the skilled physical work of shaping the plugs or twists began. "After being thus moistened," Brown recalled, "the tobacco was taken by the men and twisted into hands, and pressed into lumps, when it was sent to the machine-house, and pressed into boxes and casks." Both twisting and lump making required considerable manual dexterity, and the lumper or twister—often working in concert with an assistant, usually a child—would have to manipulate twist after twist or lump after lump into a standard shape and then weigh and measure it to ensure it was a uniform size. Then the assistant applied the wrapper (another stemmed tobacco leaf) to the product. "Lump" chewing tobacco was shaped into rectangular prisms then wrapped, while "twists" were rolled, wrapped, then doubled and twisted into compact form. Brown was a twister.

The next step, prizing, required strength and stamina. Prizers, or screw men, working "giant-levered screw presses," forced the flavored twist into the desired shape. (Prizing in cultivation settings meant packing tobacco in hogsheads; the name implies the act of appraising or assessing the money value of the object.) Instead of being packed for shipment to middlemen, as the cured leaf was, the prizers squeezed the product into wooden molds for the consumer, which gave the lump the desired shape and firmness. The lump was then dried somewhat so that it would hold form. "After remaining in what was called the 'sweat-house' about thirty days," Brown explained, the finished product "was shipped for the market" but not before being labeled and packaged, a job usually done by women. The product Brown and others produced was a type of chewing tobacco its customers called "Negro Head"; the brand, which was called "Anchor," was shipped to British and Australian markets. When Brown had arrived in Richmond in 1830, his master William Barret was in partnership with an Englishman named William Gilliat. Gilliat set up the sales side of their business in England. The rising popularity of chewing tobacco on both sides of the Atlantic, plus cheap skilled and semiskilled labor, made both partners quite wealthy. Barret and Gilliat built an industrial company with global reach, which relied near exclusively on the labor of African Americans, most of whom were enslaved. The products that Brown manufactured were in high demand.[38]

By-products of tobacco consumer culture landed seemingly everywhere in antebellum America. When Charles Dickens visited the United States in 1842, he could not help but notice Americans' addiction to tobacco and termed Washington, D.C., "the head-quarters of tobacco-tinctured saliva." "In all the public places of America, this filthy custom is recognised. In the courts of law, the judge has his spittoon, the crier has his, the witness his, and the prisoner his; while the jurymen and spectators are provided for, as so many men who in the course of nature must desire to spit incessantly." He witnessed well-dressed young men on the deck of a steamboat from Washington take out their tobacco boxes before breakfast and to commence chewing. "In less than a quarter of an hour's time," the disgusted Englishman recalled, "these hopeful youths had shed about them on the clean boards, a copious shower of yellow rain; clearing, by that means, a kind of magic circle, within whose limits no intruders dare to come, and which they never failed to refresh and re-refresh before a spot was dry."[39] Henry Brown could have told Dickens that theirs were the first white hands to touch the sot weed, which was seeded, transplanted, weeded, wormed, cropped, picked, stringed, dried, prized, stemmed, flavored, twisted, pressed, packed, and labeled by enslaved African Americans. Their factory conditions would have reminded Dickens of his own childhood factory experience pasting labels onto boot-blacking bottles from dawn until dark in cramped facilities on the reeking industrial waterfront of London's River Thames.[40]

The product Brown processed found its way into the mouths of the most eloquent defenders of American liberty, and tobacco culture influenced the manners of America's ruling classes. Visiting the Capitol, Dickens found it "remarkable" to witness "so many honourable members," of the U.S. Senate, "with swelled faces; and it is scarcely less remarkable," he elaborated, "to discover that the appearance is caused by the quantity of tobacco they contrive to stow within the hollow of the cheek." Dickens expressed that he was "surprised to observe that even steady old chewers of great experience, are not always good marksmen, which," he quipped, "has rather inclined me to doubt the general proficiency with the rifle, of which we have heard so much in England." Senators were not the only poor marksman. "Several gentleman called upon me," Dickens reported, "who, in the course of conversation, frequently missed the spittoon at five paces; and one . . . mistook the closed sash for the open window, at three."[41] Dickens found that the executive branch of government rivaled the legislative in its fondness for plug tobacco. Calling at the White House, he wrote, "indeed all these gentlemen" who were waiting on President John Tyler, a Virginian, "were so very persevering and energetic" in their expectoration, "and bestowed their favours so abundantly upon the carpet, that I take it for granted the Presidential housemaids have high wages."[42]

The historical clues in all that "tobacco-tinctured saliva" led to the market that connected slave-produced goods to the slaves who produced them and took a small share of the proceeds for overwork. Each stain on the White House carpet, on the steamboat, in the Capitol, in the law courts, in the public square, and in the prison was connected to "the Inalienable Right" of those who deployed slave labor "to take the field after *their* Happiness" and to direct—and in the process remake—an institution that had so profitably served the interests of their commercial republic.[43] By the mid-1850s, Virginia tobacconists were deeply invested in markets for enslaved labor. Prices for slaves in the lower South became so high and demand so strong that employers had to pay increasingly high rents to slaveholders for yearly hiring contracts. "The interstate slave trade linked prices everywhere," argues Schnittman, "so industrialists in the Upper South had to pay costs which changed in response to the demands of planters in the Cotton South." When employers added monies paid for overwork and boarding out, enslaved tobacco workers cost more than free white laborers in other industries. Commercial processors could not complain too loudly about that state of affairs. In the 1850s, some profited from selling workers they owned and then renting replacements.[44]

Though costs were high, tobacco processors enjoyed other advantages by using slave labor in factories. The enslaved seemed to be ideal workers. A British engineer summarized a common attitude, remarking that in American manufacturing, slaves "are more *docile*, more constant, and *cheaper*, than freemen, who are often refractory and dissipated; who waste much time by visiting public places, attending musters, elections, &c. which the *operative slave* is not permitted to frequent." Barret and his Richmond colleagues would agree. Freedom and citizenship, while salutary to the strength of the American political system, were not helpful to processors with production demands to meet. In an era before widespread and effective labor unions, individual workers expected employers to recognize their freedoms and permit them to "waste much time" participating in civic events. Enslaved workers were instrumental in hobbling industrial action. When white workers protested skilled slave puddlers and rollers working at the Tredegar Iron Works in 1847, the owner "fired the strikers and filled their positions with slave ironworkers." Richmond processors' reliance on slave labor seems startling because classical economic theorists argued against the compatibility of liberal economics and slavery. Ever since Adam Smith, but particularly since the intensification of British emancipation debates in the 1820s, liberal and neoliberal political economists had argued that slavery was not compatible with a modern economy. Yet the experiences of the enslaved working in antebellum Richmond's factories say otherwise. They arrived and departed at standard times (and they were expected to know what those standard times were), made their own living arrangements, and at hiring time could possibly quit their job. The key to their participation was the small incentives for overwork that substituted for wages paid to free workers. Besides the threat or use of violence, the penalties for stepping out of line could be sale, a powerful motivator as well.[45]

Every new white strategy demanded a new black strategy to counter it. Richmond's industrial slave workers formed networks according to their available resources to meet the emergencies and uncertainties to which the new factory system exposed them. Brown used the market to gather his family, but others used it to protest working conditions. Tobacco worker Jasper Woodson and his network of rebels gathered resources in order to give themselves time away from arduous factory work. Without the means to form a union, spontaneously organized absences were the closest alternative to collective bargaining enslaved people had. Running away, usually for a short time, was one way enslaved people signaled that they had reached a breaking point. Woodson managed to lead an industrial action and somehow avoid the slave market.[46]

Woodson's trials highlight how a skilled slave could avoid sale even after repeated offenses and how the limits of networks were tested. His evasion of the auction block was another unintended outcome of commercial processing. Woodson, held in bondage by the same man who owned Miles and Martha, had been hired to a Virginia tobacconist as early as 1828. In 1841, he ran away from his employer and was sought by the Richmond police. Woodson was known by the authorities because he had previously been caught with twenty-seven pounds of stolen tobacco. He was recaptured but did not keep out of trouble. Woodson was arrested again in 1843. Nevertheless, he avoided prison and the slave market and by 1845 was working for yet another tobacconist. That situation did not work out, and in 1846, he was hired to still another tobacco manufacturer. That year Woodson and four other adult male slaves belonging to the same Tidewater Virginia owner were caught after running away. By 1846, then, Woodson was conspiring with other slaves to absent themselves from the tobacco factories in which they were hired.[47]

Woodson cultivated a network through his industrial employments, and his continued reemployment may be accounted for partly by the fact that he was probably too old to bring much in the slave market. Another more intriguing possibility was that his age made him suitable as a teacher. In antebellum Richmond, contends Midori Takagi, "frequently manufacturers selected older 'seasoned' slave workers to train the younger hands and to monitor the quality of their work." His repeated escape attempts could be tolerated if his value was not the product he manipulated with his hands but the skills he could teach to other workers.[48]

Woodson's unwilling participation in industrial enterprises combined with geographic mobility born of the tobacconist's benign neglect to give him a refuge and some means to protest working conditions without severe punishment. He may have fled repeatedly because he wanted to spend time with friends or close associates who were not family members, perhaps propelled by something approaching Frederick Douglass's sentiments of "ardent friendship" and deep affection he felt for his fellow bondsmen at the Maryland farm of William Freeland a decade before. Of them, Douglass recalled, it was "seldom the lot of mortals to have truer and better friends than were the slaves" with whom he worked and attempted to escape in 1835.[49] Woodson did not escape from Richmond but chose instead to spend time with friends or colleagues, though the records do not exclude the possibility that he stole time away to visit relatives, perhaps a wife, girlfriend, or even a lover of the same sex. Homosexuality among enslaved Americans is understudied, and little direct evidence seems to be available, but Woodson may have formed connections with other homosexual men in one of the few areas in the South in which the enslaved had independent resources and unsupervised mobility enough to maintain such relationships.[50]

Unlike Brown, Woodson may not have had a long-term strategy, but that hardly made his choices less rational. Enslaved factory workers enjoyed no safety protections or social insurance, could expect minimal healthcare, few holidays, and no pension or retirement. After age thirty, he had outlived the average slave. If he could repeatedly run afoul of the rules his owners and employers instituted without the severe consequences to which most enslaved people were subject, Woodson had no compelling reason to submit to industrial discipline. The chief inconvenience he seems to have faced was that each time he was apprehended he had to find another job. While white industrialists coerced Woodson's labor, he exploited his skills in a specialized niche in a way that allowed him to see friends and to take vacations from the unpleasant yet lucrative work. He still earned his master $60 per year as a tobacco manufacturing worker and was among the elite of Richmond's enslaved workers, that is, the 8 to 14 percent of hired slaves who were skilled. He had made himself seemingly indispensable.[51]

Whatever their discontents, reasons, or tastes, enslaved workers like Woodson also participated in a culture of consumption. Perhaps more typical than Woodson's haphazard strikes was the industry of unnamed slaves observed by a Scottish visitor in the 1850s who reported that each skilled tobacco worker "earns for himself from two to five dollars a month, which enables him to obtain something more than the mere necessaries of life."[52] Such workers were mollified by the consumer goods they could buy or the more desirable food and drink they could enjoy with earnings. Another visitor on the eve of the Civil War observed that workers used overtime pay to buy "the finery in which they are be-decked on the Sunday to escort their ebony belles to church." That preference could be viewed as part of a consumer culture that competed with the family security the same money might buy, but joining a church could reinforce or expand networks that could be used in times of need. More typical was the industry of an unnamed slave encountered by a visitor to Richmond in the late 1840s. The tobacco processor was working overtime. The man sometimes earned as much as $10 a week for exceeding his task work and had already earned enough to purchase his wife's freedom and was then working to buy his own. She was perhaps more vulnerable to sale. Slaveholders by and large accepted the possibility of manumission because of the high annual rents they received and the fact that industrial slaves earned wages.[53]

The property enslaved people could gain complemented the networks they cultivated for support. Members of church congregations could serve as resources in emergencies, as Noah Davis of Baltimore discovered. As a young man, Davis had been apprenticed to a Fredericksburg shoemaker. He learned to read through his conversion and call to ministry. Through his trade, he also earned enough money to purchase his own freedom, that of his wife, and two of his seven children by the mid-1850s. He moved from central Virginia to Baltimore, became a minister of the gospel, and even took part in the Missionary Board of the Southern Baptist Convention. When faced with the sale of his eldest daughter, still in Virginia, Davis raised her purchase price of $850 from his Baltimore congregation. When he received word that a Richmond slave trader had gotten a hold of another son, Davis broadened his appeal to other Baltimore churches and arranged a loan whereby his son could work to pay off part of his manumission.[54]

His family's troubles did not end there. In 1856, the owner of his remaining three children died and the entire estate was sold at auction in Fredericksburg. Davis persuaded some friends in Maryland to buy his two sons, who had been hired out in Richmond, but a slave trader bid the price up on his daughter to $990 yet later consented to resell her for $1,100 should her father be able to raise the money. Average prices of "prime field hands" in Virginia had risen 100 percent since 1844, when Cottrell and Brown pooled their resources to buy Nancy and her children. Davis again called upon his allies in the church, who suggested he appeal to a larger constituency. Davis traveled to New England and eventually raised the money from Baptists and abolitionists there. He purchased his daughter, and his two sons returned to Richmond to work toward their freedom. He later published a narrative of his struggles to repay his generous creditors. Davis's exercise in collecting his kin is exceptional, but it illustrates that it was possible for the enterprising to use their connections to social institutions to keep their children from being dispersed in the slave market.[55]

In the case of his two sons, Davis's efforts show how hiring could alleviate family strain under the threat of immediate sale, but in the market slaves got precious few chances. Each would-be seller of his children assessed the likelihood of his being able to raise the money. In the case of his daughter, a slave trader calculated what the bonds between father and daughter might be worth and then raised the price accordingly. He was also worried because of the "money panic" of 1857, which "had partially destroyed my hopes of doing anything to relieve my daughter," he reported. Ups and downs in the broader economy affected the fortunes of those who sought deliver relatives from slavers. Like Bayley four and a half decades before, Davis was not as concerned that his sons remained in slavery as he was that they might be sold and removed beyond reach. Being hired in Richmond meant that at least father and sons could remain in contact. Were they transported to the New Orleans slave market, they would have been scattered and very likely beyond reach of regular communication and hope of return.[56]

Slaveholders used markets for hired slave labors, even skilled workers, for speculation. In April 1860, a Hanover County, Virginia, slaveholder sent his slave Berle to a Richmond trader, instructing the trader to sell him "for the best price" he could get for him "but not for less than 1000$." If the price was not right, Berle's owner ordered the firm to "hir[e] him out in the neighborhood of Richmond until Christmas—& then sell him."[57] Berle's situation suggests the constraints enslaved people labored under in seeking to advance their own economic opportunities. Unless Berle were sold immediately, he had eight months to gather resources and alliances to protect him from sale. Even slaveholders who considered themselves good paternalists gave little consideration where the market might land their slaves. For the owner, hiring was a way to bide time in a market he bet would rise. An Essex County, Virginia, slaveholder wrote another Richmond trader to inform him that he would "send two more likely girls over very soon as I can spare some several" and that he preferred to "*sell* than *hire out*," but, he munificently added, "I w[oul]d like for these negroes to get *good homes* if possible." He would consent to hire them out, in other words, if they could not fetch the prices he desired.[58] Skilled slaves were not safe from removal either. One Wilmington,

North Carolina, slaveholder wrote a large Richmond trader in 1861, "I have a first rate *Black smith* and *wood workman* can you sell him or hire him for me." Two weeks later the trader advertised another group of slaves, among whom were three twisters. Twenty years before, the same trader had offered twenty-seven slaves for sale, among whom were twisters, stemmers, and prizeman, all experienced tobacco workers. Possessing a valuable skill in the Richmond processing economy was no guarantee against sale, especially if the possessor were young.[59]

Consideration of their slaves' sentiments for home and family sometimes temporarily shaded some slaveholders' financial considerations, but the do-mestic strategies that worked for Corinna Hinton, Mary Lumpkin, and Ann Davis took time to develop, time that many of the enslaved thrown on the market did not have. John Taylor Jr. of Caroline County requested that the slaves he sent to Richmond to be hired out receive "a good situation" in 1842. "I do not think so much to get the very *highest* prices for them, from a rigid man," he elaborated, "as good prices from good men." Taylor asked that their employers allow "them time to visit their families." His overriding concern, however, was his speculative interest in selling them. "I do not wish them sold at this time," he wrote, "as negroes are too low they are worth $1000 nicely each." The slaveholder, a son of Tidewater political economist John Taylor of Caroline, would consider the feelings of his slaves for the time be-ing or, in other words, until prices rose to his satisfaction. Other slaveholders simply dismissed concerns about family as so much bother.[60]

After Elizabeth Keckley's father was sold away from her and her mother in Prince Edward County, Virginia, in 1833, the "Old Mistress" soon tired of the grieving wife's despair over her loss. "Stop your nonsense," Keckley reported her as saying, "there is no necessity for you putting on airs. Your husband is not the only slave that has been sold from his family, and you are not the only one that has had to part. There are plenty more men about here, and if you want a husband so badly, stop your crying and go and find another." Not only did Elizabeth Keckley lose her father, but she would soon find herself in North Carolina, then St. Louis. Alliances with sympathetic slaveholders were no less vulnerable to being undermined. The possibility of family separations, not just of husbands from wives but mothers from children distressed Miles and Martha and the Browns. They were willing to make concessions to slave-holders and other whites, and they did not revolt because even with serious disadvantages, the fragile network they constructed was protecting them. The market gave them opportunities to defend their families, even if it meant that someone else's wife, mother, sister, or daughter would be bound away in slave traders' coffles instead. That was the grim logic of the market in which Henry and Nancy Brown made their calculations.[61]

What became of Miles and Martha is not clear, but Henry and Nancy Brown soon found out how precarious their dealings were. About four years into their living arrangement, on what Brown described as "one pleasant morning, in the month of August, 1848, when my wife and children, and myself, were sitting at table, about to eat our breakfast," Cottrell appeared at their door and demanded a large amount of money. Nancy's owner had already added new conditions to the Browns' living arrangements, including requiring that Brown pay him in advance of when her yearly hiring fee had been due and that Nancy take in his washing for free, a task made onerous by her then being pregnant with their fourth child. To this latest demand, Brown responded, "You know I have no money to spare, because it takes nearly all that I make for myself, to pay my wife's hire, the rent of my house, my own ties to my master, and to keep ourselves in meat and clothes; and if at any time, I have made anything more than that, I have paid it to you in advance, and what more can I do?" The slaveholder simply sniffed, "I want money, and money I will have" and stormed off.[62]

The encounter sent chills through the household, and the Browns began to dread the manner in which Cottrell would convert them into cash. "My poor wife burst into tears," Brown reported, "and said perhaps he will sell one of our little children, and our hearts were so full that neither of us could eat any breakfast, and after mutually embracing each other, as it might be our last meeting." There was little Brown could do but march off to work. There were neither protective labor legislation nor family emergency provisions of which slaves could take advantage. Brown was anguished, and he walked heavily among "many other slaves," who were "hastening in the . . . direction" of the industrial section along the James River where he worked. Word traveled quickly to Barret's factory on the north side of Main Street between 23rd and 24th streets of the fate of Brown's family.[63] "I had not been many hours at my work," he recalled, "when I was informed that my wife and children were taken from their home, sent to the auction mart and sold, and then lay in prison ready to start away the next day for North Carolina with the man who had purchased them." Brown was beside himself with the thought of his family in a jail—possibly Silas Omohundro's or Robert Lumpkin's. The Richmond slave market, with its maze of auction houses and jails, was just blocks from Barret's office. Cottrell had sold Nancy and the three children there for $1,050 and left the jailer instructions to take Brown into custody should he show up. The $600 the owner made on the deal was partly the result of Nancy and Henry Brown's reproductive successes: their three children and the fourth on the way brought him a $400 profit over what he had paid for her in 1844. The slave market had also smiled on the seller. The average price of "prime field hands" in Virginia had risen 30 percent in four years. Cottrell had already received $200 for her hire from her husband. Beyond that, Nancy had likely washed clean the clothes he wore to the slave market that morning.[64]

Brown traveled to his master's office on the northeast corner of Cary and 14th streets, near the slave auction houses and jails and implored him to rescue his family.[65] Barret refused on grounds that the man who sold his wife was a "gentleman," and Barret professed that he was "afraid to meddle with his business." Brown dispatched a courier with some money to give to his wife. The courier was briefly detained, suspected of being the husband but later released. Brown went back to Barret twice again that day, but his owner remained unmoved. The grieving husband then asked two "young gentlemen" with whom he was acquainted what they could do, to which they wryly remarked that they "did not deal in slaves." Brown's network was failing him. Meanwhile, he learned that Cottrell had the sheriff remove all of their personal belongings (for which Brown had paid a total of $300) from the house to pay an alleged debt, which was less than $20. Faced with a crisis that was compounding by the hour, Brown managed to borrow that money from his friend and fellow church member James C. A. Smith Jr.—the man who had rented his house for him—and claimed his property from the sheriff. When Brown arrived at home late that night, he ran into his erstwhile ally, who had that day sold his wife and children and then cleaned out his house. In company of two others, Cottrell sarcastically mentioned that he had heard that Brown had been to the sheriff's office. Brown responded: "Yes . . . I have been and got away *my things* but I could not get away *my wife and children* whom you have put beyond my power to redeem." Not satisfied with the havoc he had already caused the Browns, Cottrell gave Brown a "round of abuse" for being so impudent as to sketch his day's work of wrecking a family in the company of friends.[66]

Despite Brown's best plans and abundance of human and material resources, he lost nearly everything when the mainstay of his network turned from ally to adversary. He got no relief from his employer, his erstwhile patron. Barret was not short of cash. That summer, his creditors estimated his worth at over $100,000. Brown's best plans had been undermined by an owner who put ready cash over the family ties of the people he owned. Despite his protestations, Cottrell was in no dire straits either. In September 1848, it was reported that the thirty year-old saddler "stands well, is prud[ent] & with lim[ited] Means" though it was "supp[ose]d" that his father and father-in-law were well disposed to help him in a pinch. Whatever temporary financial difficulties he suffered, Cottrell would prosper and remain a successful Richmond businessman for more than thirty years after selling Nancy and her children.[67] Henry Brown had abided by the rules he thought could ensure his family's security, striving to be a faithful worker and reliable source of income for his wife's owner. Returning one last time to his master the next morning, tears in his eyes, Brown met another refusal. "I could get another wife and so I need not trouble myself about that one," he recalled Barret glibly counseling. "My agony was now complete," he explained as he thought back over twelve years of marriage to Nancy, three young children, and the prospect of another child arriving in the North Carolina swamps fatherless.[68]

Barret gave him leave to say goodbye to Nancy and his children, but only after he had completed his day's work. Arriving at the scene of a coffle of some 350 slaves being readied to march south, he recognized Nancy and their children. "I stood in the midst of many who, like myself, were mourning the loss of friends and relations and had come there to obtain one parting look," he recalled. The adults, including his pregnant wife, were bound with shackles and tied together with rope while the small children rode on wagons. Brown bid goodbye to his wife and recalled his "little child looking towards me and pitifully calling, father! father!"[69]

A slave at the top of a hierarchy of skilled industrial wage earners, Brown had still been unable to keep his family out of the slave market. He had met the obligations into which he entered, working tirelessly in strenuous, repetitive manual labor. Yet the Browns' plans had been undermined in the space of a day because a key member of their network recalculated his strategy and acted with impunity. Like Moses Grandy when he was cheated by James Grandy, there was nothing the Browns could do. The network of associations that conferred status did not amount to legal personhood. Other ties were not strong enough to defy the will of a slaveholder despite Brown's fifteen years of cultivating them. When slave prices were rising to levels not seen for nearly ten years, the market in which the Browns had assembled the means to defend family ties and acquire property in the consumer goods they enjoyed naturally prized Nancy and their children above the hard-won earnings of a slave who made a few dollars a week.[70]

But Henry Brown had not risen so far for want of intelligence or determination, and his network had not completely unraveled. With family gone, Brown had few incentives to remain in Richmond. He decided it was time to leave. His friend Smith introduced him to Samuel Smith, a cobbler specializing in making shoes for enslaved workers—and a slaveholder himself—who became sympathetic to Brown's situation. They also enlisted a shopkeeper whom Brown assured he could repay whatever financial backing the man might provide since northern cities also processed tobacco and he could earn a good wage in that line as a free man. New York City, for instance, was second only to Richmond in the amount of tobacco it processed (and Petersburg, Lynchburg, and Danville, Virginia, rounded out the top five American tobacco manufacturing cities before the Civil War).[71]

At length, Brown came up with a novel way to end his days as a slave. He chose not to respond with violence or self-destruction, though the method of his escape could have killed him easily.[72] On March 29, 1849, his allies packed his sturdy five-foot eight-inch body into a canvas-lined wooden shipping box, three feet long, two feet eight inches deep, and nearly two feet wide. They sealed the container and shipped it by rail and steamboat on the Adams Express to Philadelphia. Brown spent the steamboat journey to the nation's capital on his head inside the box, then knocked senseless when the crate was bumped out of a wagon on its way to the train depot. Mercifully righted, Brown spent the remainder of the time on the rails from the nation's capital to the City of Brotherly Love merely crammed into the shipping crate. For once, the paths of interstate commerce were working in his favor. Samuel Smith had made arrangements for Brown's safe passage, should he survive. After what ended up being a twenty-seven hour journey, Brown was disinterred from the crate. Half-dead, he was resurrected by abolitionists. In Philadelphia he earned the nickname, Henry "Box" Brown, later selling his story to raise money and traveling to Great Britain when the Fugitive Slave Law, which he did his part to inspire, made it too dangerous to stay in the United States. His network, at least, had succeeded in putting him beyond reach of anyone who might chain him in a coffle and march him south.[73]

Brown and his allies took great risks in executing the escape. Virginia sen-

tenced Samuel Smith to four years and six months in the fall of 1849 for helping another slave, Alfred, escape in a similar manner. Brown's audacity inspired imitators, often with ghastly consequences. In 1856, an enslaved man
attempted to ship himself to the North via the express. "When the box was
opened," a report reprinted in a southern newspaper read, "the poor wretch
was found dead, his countenance horribly contorted, and his body drawn
into a knot. It appeared on examination that the box had no air holes."[74]

Since Brown had been unable to use his network successfully to rescue
Nancy and the children from the slave market, Nancy used the strength of
her ties to transfer status from Richmond to her new home. A little over a
month gone, she obtained a letter of dismissal testifying that she was in good
standing and a certificate of membership and good character from the African
Baptist Church. That was not unheard of. The First African Baptist Church
dismissed Archibald Walker Lewis to New Orleans in 1844. Nancy Brown had
been sold to a Methodist minister in North Carolina, and after making the
hard overland journey, she knew that all she could retrieve from her Richmond home was her standing in the church, which she could transfer to a
new church. Like Solomon Bayley's religious ties, her church-based network
proved more durable than Henry's industrial one. Henry and Nancy Brown
and their children were never reunited.[75]

The rise of commercial processing in cities like Richmond was not merely a set
of developments to which the enslaved responded but processes they shaped
and in which they were deeply implicated. Although ties of emotion and
sentiment framed some enslaved people's strategies, slavery was not being
"domesticated" in the commercial processing economy of the antebellum upper South. Enslaved people used a market that far more often frayed kinship
networks, which shows the high stakes of their commercial activity and the
unintended consequences of their market participation. For the Browns, success was measured in months and years of family cohesion while they were
enslaved rather than in terms of freedom and relocation. The market in which
they formulated their strategy created precious few opportunities by destroying what did not fit its categories, including families, which shows the ramifications of capitalism's "creative destruction." Commercial processors had few
qualms about the modern form of slavery they were creating, either. Perhaps
Jasper Woodson knew that before Henry Brown. Enslaved people found ways

to supplement and sometimes defend kinship networks that were otherwise excruciatingly vulnerable to being torn apart by the demands of customers of the interstate slave trade. But had Brown been able to rescue his wife and children from the slave market that August day in 1848, it would not have kept a buyer from purchasing another a young woman to work his fields or keep his house. Instead, another wife, mother, daughter, or sister would bid farewell to her husband, children, parents, or siblings.[76]

CHAPTER 5

Railroaders

The transportation revolution simultaneously transformed an old institution and the new commercial landscape of the antebellum South, changing the lives of enslaved people in the process. Railroads and telegraphs integrated interregional markets and sped communications. As in commercial processing, slaves were the primary workforce for railroad construction projects south of the Potomac River, and they worked to support the roads once they were in operation. The whine of a whistle or scent of smoke from a steam locomotive, the song of a railroad construction gang, or the sight of an approaching train elicited an ambivalent reaction from enslaved Americans. The prospect of being hired to work on a railroad construction gang was met with a mix of exhilaration and trepidation. Railroad workers, who were mostly male, anticipated forming connections with others in a military-like organization, but the work was hazardous, repetitive, and punishing. They could also expect to be separated from loved ones. Children, parents, and spouses of enslaved railroad workers had much to lose were they hired. They might die or disappear into a distant city for a year, be broken on a section gang, or else taken beyond reach permanently. Some Virginia slaves were hired to build railroads in Florida. To all slaves, the railroad was a conveyance to places of no return for the black bodies deposited. Relatives and friends also faced fears that were common among all antebellum railroading families. Mixing in with tens, perhaps hundreds, of strangers he might be taken ill, injured, or return with his spirit dimmed, piety diminished, and habits corrupted. But there was also a strategic aspect to getting into such a line of work.[1]

Railroad development incorporated local ties among the enslaved into the transportation revolution of antebellum America, giving enslaved people advantages they had not had before. Companies employed enslaved laborers to construct new roads, maintain existing tracks, service trains in depots, and ride the rails as fireman, brakeman, porters, and stewards. A few former slaves even served as engineers. As they became indispensable to railroad construction, operation, and maintenance, enslaved people used the railroad to their own ends, gathering human and capital resources and turning labor camps into fraternal organizations and even educational institutions. Roads broadened the reach of enslaved people's networks. Working on the railroad could offer a chance to earn cash, hone a skill, or even learn to read and write. But the architects of the new market created efficiencies that also tended to undermine the advantages enslaved people could take of it. On occasion, railroads paid high prices to own slaves. More often, they paid owners high wages and, like urban manufacturers, some paid cash to slaves as incentives to work. As a consequence of an interregional slave market, railroad contractors in Virginia and North Carolina competed with lower South cotton planters for slave labor, just as their counterparts in the tobacco industry did. Insurance companies helped to rationalize the market for industrial slave labor by insuring the lives of slaves engaged in railroad and other hazardous work, which protected owners financially and limited liabilities of employers. Each incremental step in market integration squeezed more work out of the enslaved and put their families in increasing peril.[2]

Like commercial processing, railroad development in the lower Chesapeake hardly signaled slavery's attenuation. By the late 1830s, locomotives fueled by slave-dug coal chugged into cities such as Richmond and Norfolk on slave-laid tracks, bringing slave-grown corn and tobacco to market. They returned to the hinterland with enslaved people bought with the proceeds. Enslaved porters unloaded the trains, and the slaves sold at market wore slave-forged chains. Transportation technology transformed the slave market. In the 1820s and 1830s, enslaved people bound away to the lower South could expect to be driven in droves, packed onto ships, or floated down rivers. In the 1840s, they were more likely to undertake the forced march on foot over the expanding network of roadways, many the results of state and federal internal improvement initiatives. By the 1850s, enslaved people were increasingly likely to disappear from their families on railroad cars, which were financed in part from the proceeds of slave sales and sponsored by states. The majority were still marched south, footsore and forlorn, but the new technologies, which enabled railroads to reach into new corners of an expanding commercial republic, gave slavers more options and made slavery more versatile. In addition to slaves, iron horses fetched goods that had previously been taken by wagon to riverine entrepôts, which reoriented the commercial geography of the South, creating new hubs of commerce like Lynchburg and Danville, Virginia, while eclipsing colonial-era ports like Edenton, North Carolina, and Port Tobacco, Maryland.

The upper South's industrial future was the future of slavery. Heavy transportation, extraction, and processing would not require a shift away from slave labor. A Virginia advocate for developing coal and related enterprises reported in 1835 that at the Chesterfield "mines, and the rail road connected with them, 7 or 800 persons, about 300 horses and mules, several steam engines and other machinery are employed." Those "persons" working at the outskirts of Richmond were mostly slaves. Enslaved colliers dug the fuel for Virginia's initial industrial development and sent it to Richmond on rails. In assessing who would benefit from an expansion of that kind of large-scale industrial extraction, the advocate contended, "the owners of slaves by the increased hires which they receive" would have a stake in redevelopment along with a large spectrum of collateral suppliers of food and building materials, mechanical and industrial tradesmen, and bankers and other financiers. Tidewater planters could scarcely rail at entrepreneurs for introducing industrial innovations adjacent to the agrarian republic they thought they were building when they stood to make a profit by leasing slaves to coal pits, mines, and ironworks. Small-scale ironworks using slaves had been in operation in eastern Virginia since the eighteenth century. According to the writer, intensive mining operations distributed collateral business far and wide. If the enslaved themselves remained invisible it was because they need not have been pictured.[3]

John Jasper knew well the landscape of slavery hidden within that Virginia booster's vision of industrial redevelopment. Born enslaved in the Virginia Tidewater in 1812, Jasper worked as a domestic servant in Williamsburg before his master decided to hire him out in Richmond, shuttling him back and forth to work in extractive and processing enterprises. In 1826, the fourteen year-old "was hired out in the county of Chesterfield," to a new master, "where he worked for one year in the coal pits, and during this year the first railroad was laid from the coal pits to the city of Richmond." His biographer recorded that "the next year he was brought back to Richmond and hired out to [another man] to work in the factory, then situated on the corner of Sixteenth and Cary streets." That was a tobacco manufacturer. "He worked in this factory about six or seven years," his biographer wrote, "during which time stars fell." A giant meteor shower rained down in mid-November 1833, which was visible throughout much of North America. By that time, Jasper had witnessed the first wave of industrial development in Richmond from the point of view of the laborers who made it possible, wielding a pick and shovel, witnessing other enslaved men cutting timber and laying down tracks, and later manipulating tobacco leaves in a factory in that city.[4]

Jasper's industrial work in antebellum Richmond was one component of a broader vision of Chesapeake industrialists. Internal improvement would rely on the labors of slaves. In 1831, French railroad engineer Claudius Crozet imagined a steam-powered railroad that would "procure an uninterrupted and uniform line of transportation" from city to city, port to port. He predicted it would "cost not more than an ordinary canal, produce more revenue, give greater celerity and momentum to [Virginia's] commerce, facilitate traveling and intercourse, save much useful time to industry; which neither frosts nor droughts can impede, and whose ramifications may so easily be extended in every direction, and even search the tide-water district, so well adapted to it, and infuse into it the life of trade." Enslaved people featured in that vision of Chesapeake redevelopment as well. "Let us picture to ourselves a train coming rapidly down to James river," Crozet continued, "across which is a rail-road viaduct; on this elegant locomotive engine is waiting, which, in one day will carry the whole train to Baltimore, without delay, without unloading; on the other side are negroes, resting on their long poles, inviting the produce to the safe conveyance of their boat, under lock and key, down to Richmond." Enslaved boatmen like Moses Grandy would ferry goods to Richmond on the James River and Kanawha Canal while the locomotive would steam northward to Maryland's queen city. Crozet's ideas were taken up. In 1837, a Richmond slave hiring agent advertised for "fifty Negro Men, to work on the James River & Kanawha Improvement, and the Richmond & Petersburg Rail-road."[5]

Crozet's vision for Virginia accorded with what some Maryland advocates for internal improvement envisioned, but internal improvement north of the Potomac River was to rely on disadvantaged free laborers. A proponent of the Chesapeake and Ohio (C&O) Canal commented in 1829 that "if slaves must still be hired," to build the canal, "let them be hired, as they are on the Rail-road, from the Maryland and not the Virginia masters."[6] Maryland slavehold-ers, in other words, should benefit from state-sponsored canal building, just as Virginia owners did in the Old Dominion. The C&O Canal Company also employed thousands of Irish and free African Americans, who in 1826 were "kept separate from each other, for fear of serious consequences," according to a visitor.[7] Attempting to find an alternative to slave labor, directors of the C&O Canal Company sponsored the immigration of some 500 indentured servants from England in 1829, but those arrivals chafed at the punishing work, low wages, and indignities of bound labor. Many ran off as soon as they landed, and the canal company was left to sue them for breaches of their con-tracts. Barbara Fields argues that the C&O Canal was "an extensive flop that led the state to the verge of bankruptcy and for which Baltimore had never shown any particular enthusiasm." The Baltimore and Ohio Railroad, by con-trast, was a success in part because over 130,000 often-desperate immigrants arrived in Baltimore between 1820 and 1850. For some, work in railroad proj-ects was their gateway to independence, but the Baltimore and Ohio Railroad also drew on an available supply of free but desperate laborers, a pool that was increasing in the late 1820s and early 1830s during the initial stages of railroad development, as operators of the Baltimore almshouse could attest. Slave prices rose between 1829 and 1836, and so Maryland slaveholders were more likely to sell slaves in the market than risk their health and dollar value by hiring them out to work on the canal.[8]

Railroads in Delaware, Maryland, North Carolina, and Virginia received state sponsorship, but interstate slave sales also contributed capital to railroads below the Potomac. Slaves hired to railroads in one generation toiled on projects partly financed by the sales of their parents or grandparents. In 1818, Francis E. Rives of Petersburg partnered with a pair of Prince George County residents, father and son Peyton Mason and Peyton Mason Jr., to form a slave trading firm. That spring, the Masons and Rives marched the first of two droves of slaves from Petersburg to the lower South. The market for slaves was expanding. Mississippi had joined the United States the previous year, and Alabama would follow in 1819. Nearly twenty men, women, and children made the grueling overland journey, a thousand miles to the southwest.[9] The firm emptied its coffles and filled its coffers. In 1818, a healthy young adult male agricultural worker who sold for $800 in Virginia, on average, was worth $850 in Charleston, South Carolina, $950 in Georgia, and $1,050 in New Orleans. In the speculative climate of the late 1810s, with easy credit and high land prices driven largely by a booming cotton market, Rives and his partners reaped substantial profits from sale of twenty-six enslaved Virginians whom they force marched to Alabama in the closing months of 1818. The firm bought Tom Irvins for $600 in the vicinity of Petersburg and sold him for a $500 bond and two expensive shares of Marathon town stock. They sold Bob Brown for $1,000 in Huntsville, half cash, half credit, and made $300. Susan was swapped for a gold watch valued at $140 and a $600 bond due the first of January 1820. Urscilla represented a 100 percent markup over her purchase price, selling for a $1,000 bond. Children Anthony, Jolly, Betsey, and Little Amey—also called Frosty—sold collectively for $3250, cash and bonds, a $1400 gross profit. After 1819, such prices would not return for sixteen years. Like Charles Ball's, their families back in Virginia could only guess what had become of them.[10]

Over a dozen years before the arrival of the railroad, Rives's customers in the lower South faced the choice either to transport slaves from Virginia and Maryland themselves or else rely on slave traders and pay a correspondingly higher price. Americans had not yet conquered the tyranny of distance with steam power, and the Masons and Rives drove enslaved people on narrow post roads, through lands controlled by Indians, in unpredictable weather, into a new disease environment, populated by wild animals and often lawless locals. The enslaved who made that long forced march could scarcely imagine the mode of transportation by which their descendents back in Virginia would travel the same routes.

Rives's career blossomed back in Virginia. The sometime slave trader was elected to the Virginia House of Delegates in 1821, where he served ten years before graduating to the state senate as a pro–Andrew Jackson politician. Having built a small fortune from the slave trade, Rives went into business as a principal of the Petersburg Railroad, which would connect that city to eastern North Carolina. Chartered in 1830 and opened in 1833, the Petersburg Railroad was partly state sponsored. In the early 1830s, the commonwealth chartered the competing Portsmouth and Roanoke Railroad despite Rives's attempts to block the legislation. That road connected Portsmouth to Weldon, North Carolina. Weldon was a strategic point on the landscape, geographically centered between Portsmouth and Raleigh, North Carolina's capital. It was a convenient transshipment point for trade flowing east on the Roanoke River from hinterland producers. Whether owned by Rives or his competitors, the railroad diverted trade from northeastern North Carolina port cities like Harriet Jacobs's Edenton.[11]

Railroads were revolutionary because they could redirect commerce, information, and passengers from river and other water routes overland, even over mountains, with increasing efficiency as the technology improved. Railroads reorganized the market as a result. Before the Petersburg and Portsmouth and Roanoke railroads arrived, a farmer or merchant in southern Virginia or the northern North Carolina Piedmont had to ship goods via expensive overland routes on wagons or else float goods down the Roanoke River, using rafts or bateaux on the shallows and wagons to bypass the rapids, and into the Albemarle Sound. There the goods would be transshipped from Edenton or Elizabeth City or else taken up the Dismal Swamp Canal, often by slaves like Moses Grandy, to Norfolk or Portsmouth.[12] In 1834, a farmer described how goods were transported now that the railroad had arrived: "We ship a hogshead of tobacco or a barrel of flour at Danville," Virginia, and "when it reaches Weldon," some 120 miles to the east, "we pay tolls and commission; it is then carried in a dray to the river below; we then have to pay the cost of transportation to Blakely; it then falls into the hands of the Petersburg railroad company, who transport it to Petersburg."[13] Only one step in this new process by which the farmer got his goods to market in Petersburg involved water, and the total distance that his goods had to travel was reduced by half. Once in operation, the Portsmouth and Roanoke Railroad eliminated two more steps in that process. Writing two decades later, Frederick Law Olmsted observed that "the advantages offered by rail-roads, to the farmers of inland districts, are strikingly shown by the following fact: A gentleman, near Raleigh, who had a quantity of wheat to dispose of, seeing it quoted at high prices, in a paper of Petersburg, Va., and seeing, at the same time, the advertisement of a commission-house there, wrote to the latter, making an offer of it." The following day, "he received a reply, by mail, and by the train a bundle of sacks, in which he immediately forwarded the wheat, and, by the following return mail, received his pay, at the rate of $1 20 a bushel, the top price of the winter." That was twice the local rate.[14] Besides drawing producers closer to market hubs, the emergence of railroads had unintended consequences for enslaved workers: it took opportunities away from enslaved boatmen like Grandy and gave them instead to enslaved railroad workers.

Though advanced by the standards of its time, railroads' physical infrastructure was tenuous and unreliable in the 1830s and 1840s. In the 1830s, rails were fashioned out of wood and spiked to wooden sleepers. Beds of sand or gravel supported them. The first engine on the Baltimore and Ohio Railroad was a horse. The second was "two dogs attached to a car [that] trotted off with six persons." Maritime ingenuity prevailed on the third engine. "A car was fitted with a sail, and though the breeze was gentle, six persons were carried in it at a rapid rate."[15] Former slave Jackson Chesney recalled the conditions of Virginia railroads in the 1830s. "The track consisted of pieces of timber with strap iron spiked down on top of them," he told a biographer. "These spikes would soon come loose, and the ends of the straps would turn up, and were called 'snake-heads.' These snake-heads were sometimes forced up through the cars, and did great damage," he explained. "Snake-heads were as common in early railroading as snags were in early steamboating." Wooden rails decayed quickly. The first locomotives in Virginia were oxen or horses harnessed to cars that looked like stagecoaches. "Scarcely was a trip ever made that some serious accident of some kind did not occur," Chesney recalled of the first steam-powered trains. "Few of these mishaps were fatal to life," he elaborated, "but they generally resulted in crippling the machinery so that horses or oxen, often both, had to be impressed in order to drag the clumsy locomotive and its load to the nearest station for repairs. The brakes were very poor and would not stop the train."[16] The Portsmouth and Roanoke Railroad near Weldon "was composed of wooden rails, with bars of iron spiked to them, and the rails were inserted into transverse sills partly imbedded in the soil."[17] The wooden tracks were laid by slaves, and slaves would replace the wooden rails with iron ones, securing them with spikes fabricated by other slaves toiling in Virginia's ironworks.

Frequent accidents, inefficiencies, smoke, noise, and the financial she-nanigans of companies may have convinced contemporaries that railroads seemed hardly worth the bother to build them, but the technology ploughed ahead anyway. Early braking mechanisms consisted merely of the friction be-tween the wheels and rails on early trains, which was supplemented by hu-man power. "When they came to a station," Chesney recalled, "the engineer opened the safety valve and allowed the steam to escape, two big negroes would seize the end of the train, and hold it, while timbers would be placed across the track in front of the wheels. Both the engineer and the conduc-tor favored a curved track in order that they might look back and see that everything was all right."[18] The enslaved brakemen risked losing limbs or be-ing crushed under the train should anything go awry. Technological advance-ments came quickly, however. The size of engines on the Richmond and Pe-tersburg Railroad (RPRR) nearly doubled in fifteen years. The RPRR put two steam locomotives into service in 1838, the Sheppard and the Phoenix. The Sheppard had two drivers and weighed 18,000 pounds (30,000 when com-bined with its tender, or coal car). The Phoenix had four drivers, weighed 21,000 pounds alone and 33,000 with its tender. Fifteen years later, the RPRR launched the Clover Hill, constructed in J. R. Anderson's Tredegar Iron Works in Richmond. It employed four drivers and weighed 38,000 pounds (65,000 with the tender). The Tredegar Iron Works employed a large slave labor force, and enslaved workers forged iron parts. Over the next few years, locomotives in Virginia got heavier by another third. The Virginia and Tennessee Railroad put into service the Knoxville, built by R. Norris and Son of Philadelphia, in July 1857, which weighed 99,400 pounds with its tender. That locomotive hauled goods and passengers over the Blue Ridge Mountains and south to Bristol, Tennessee, and beyond.[19]

Despite transforming the commercial geography of the region, Chesapeake railroad construction was uneven and corresponded to boom and bust cycles in the broader market. The great economic boom in the middle of the 1830s can be charted in railroad construction, which surged in that decade. From its 13 miles of track in operation by 1830, Maryland's railroads expanded to 213 miles by 1840. Virginia's first railroad was also about 13 miles, from the coal pits in Chesterfield County to the west bank of the James River, opposite Rich-mond. A mule-powered train, which John Jasper rode between the coal pits and the tobacco factory, began service in 1831, delivering slave-mined coal to a rapidly expanding city. By 1840, Virginia had 147 miles of track. Delaware's first railroad, the New Castle and Frenchtown, also opened in 1831. Passengers journeyed its 16.5 miles under horse or mule power from the Delaware to the Elk River in about one hour and thirty-five minutes. By 1840, Delaware had 39 miles of track. The panic of 1837 and subsequent depression meant loss of capital and also of Army engineers who had been critical to the early success of the roads. Engineers were diverted from rail projects in subsequent years, notably during the U.S. war against Mexico. Uneven state sponsorship also contributed to the decline in growth. In the 1840s, construction fell off markedly in the upper Chesapeake. Railroad companies in Delaware and Maryland in the 1840s scarcely laid down a rail. Between 1840 and 1850, Delaware added nothing to track running across the Delmarva Peninsula, which connected Philadelphia and Baltimore. By 1860, however, Delaware's miles of track had more than tripled to 127. Maryland took a similar path in the 1850s, adding only 46 miles of track in the 1840s. By 1860, it had added 127 more miles for a total of 386.[20]

By contrast, Virginia's railroads grew steadily in the antebellum decades. In the 1840s, Virginia's roads expanded from 147 miles to 481. In the 1850s, railroad construction boomed, and by 1860 the Old Dominion had 1,731 miles of track. North Carolina experienced a nearly twentyfold increase in miles of railroad between the year American voters elected the first Whig as president, in 1840, and the year they elected the first Republican, in 1860, rising from 53 to 937 miles as it followed the construction model of its northern neighbor and deployed gangs of slave laborers. Meanwhile, construction of communications infrastructure proceeded apace in the 1840s. By the time Americans elected their last Whig president, in 1848, the telegraph connected Baltimore, Washington, Fredericksburg, and Richmond with Philadelphia, New York, Boston, and St. Louis.[21]

For the enslaved, the bright future envisioned by railroad boosters and customers was perilous to their families. The enslaved men hired to build the Southside Railroad linking Petersburg and points west were keenly aware of the road's potential to whisk off loved ones who had been sold. In the 1850s, a young witness, Fannie Berry, herself a slave in her early teens, recalled that in the mornings the men would "all start acomin' from all d'rections wid dey ax on dey shoulder, an' de mist and de fog be hangin' over de pines, an' de sun jes' breakin' cross de fields." They set to work clearing the forest. Swinging axes, they would sing, "A col' frosty mo'nin',/De niggers mighty good,/Take yo' ax upon yo' shoulder,/Nigger, TALK to de wood." The woods were "jes' ringin'" with that song, she recalled, as the axmen worked, striking at the trunks of trees in unison at "TALK." "Hundreds" would be singing to "mark de blows." The songs were not merely about the work at hand. "Sometime," she recalled, "dey sing like dis: Dis time tomorrow night,/Where will I be?/I'll be gone, gone, gone,/Down to Tennessee." The railroad they built was indeed going to Tennessee, and their relatives who were put on the slave market would disappear on the cars. They themselves were taken far from home in their work: they cut the wood, piled up the ballast, laid the track, and then moved on to the next section, lamenting the speed by which they would find themselves forced from relatives and taken west. The pace of construction was swift. During its initial construction, the Richmond, Fredericksburg, and Potomac Railroad (RFPRR) reached the North Anna River, about twenty-five miles north of Richmond, on February 5, 1836. Service opened ten miles to the north at Ruther Glen on June 15, 1836. Trains ran another ten miles to Milford by September 15 and several more miles to Woodford by October 26. The RFPRR extended service to Hazel Run, another dozen miles, by December 23, and workers had in less than a year—working in all seasons—completed more than half the distance from Richmond to Fredericksburg. Companies like the RFPRR and Southside Railroad contracted to hire local slaves to work on the tracks, and as the line progressed, they returned one set of laborers and hired slaves from the next locality.[22]

The Southside laborers' suspicions were well founded. That railroad began service in 1854, and Berry recalled that "slaves were sold off of blocks," and after they were auctioned "dey were marched down to the train. . . . Dar was a great crying and carrying on mongst the slaves who had been sold. Two or three of dem gals had young babies taking with 'em. . . . As soon as dey got on de train dis ol' new master had train stopped an' made dem poor gal mothers take babies off and laid dem precious things on de groun' and left them behind to live or die." Many mothers and fathers did end up in Tennessee or farther south and west, and their children were left to be raised by those the market did not prize, such as grandparents.[23]

Railroad cars were readymade for the interstate slave trade. Unlike coffles marched on roads, railroads offered traders swift transport and a means of confining slaves. Slave traders would not have to camp so often, expend as much time and energy guarding increasingly fatigued forced migrants, or organize a supply system over treacherous terrain. Unlike ships, which needed to be chartered and whose human cargoes were subject to inspection and taxation, railroads ran on a predetermined schedule, could accommodate last-minute customers, and could haul a single slave or dozens depending on available space. Aaron Marrs argues that the railroads lowered fares to attract the business of slave traders. In 1839, the RFPRR reduced fares by half for African Americans in two "8-wheeled baggage cars," which company records indicated had "a special compartment for Negroes." Equating "Negroes" with "baggage" was unambiguous. They were cargo rather than passengers, and the cars were mobile slave jails. In 1858, the Southside Railroad charged the same rates for slaves and children, and the following year the Virginia and Tennessee Railroad advertised that African Americans over three years would be charged half-priced fares; black riders under three rode free. By 1860, five Virginia railroad companies sought the business of westward-moving slave-holders by offering reduced rates to African American children put on their cars. Those were all one-way tickets.[24]

In the mid-1850s, Virginia native J. H. Banks traveled south and west, after being sold along paths Charles Ball and hundreds of thousands of others had walked in anguish. Unlike Ball, however, Banks could not map the rivers and other terrain he crossed. From railroad cars, the landscape moved too quickly. Banks was sold without knowledge of his nearby parents, strapped to a wagon, and then taken by stagecoach to Richmond from his home west of the Blue Ridge Mountains. He soon found himself in one of an archipelago of slave pens. That "establishment was so constructed," Banks later recalled, "as to hold some two or three hundred." Unlike Ball, who was bought, transported, and sold by a person whose business it was to trade in enslaved people, Banks entered a market rationalized by traders whose customers could visit market hubs themselves to pick over the human stock. "Husbands sold," Banks recalled of the Richmond market, "and their wives and children left for another day's auction; or wives sold one way, and husbands and fathers another, at the same auction." Those people passed through the hands of several traders and their agents before reaching the lower South.[25]

Between Ball's journeys and Banks's, the cotton South had expanded, and transportation advances delivered slaves to the cotton kingdom with striking efficiency. When Ball was first sold, the Chickasaws, Choctaws, Creeks, and Cherokees held most of their ancestral lands stretching westward from central Georgia and North Carolina into the lower Mississippi Valley. By the time

Banks made his journey, entire Indian nations had been forcibly removed and their lands seized and given away or resold to citizens like the Alabaman who bought Banks. When Harriet Jacobs entered her grandmother's Edenton, North Carolina, attic in the mid-1830s, steam-powered locomotives were still a new presence on American rails. Two decades later, railroads made it possible to travel from old cities on the Eastern Seaboard to new outposts of the American continental empire in just days. "Leaving Richmond, Virginia, our course lay through North Carolina, South Carolina, and Georgia, into Alabama, all by rail, till we got to Montgomery," Banks recalled. "At this place we took a steamer and went 110 miles to a small place which I do not recollect." When Ball made his journey to cotton country, there had been no steamers south of the Potomac River. From there, Banks reported, "we went by land some thirty miles," to his new owner's "old farm, where we met as new comers with all his old hands." He observed that "the nearer I got home the harder the aspect of things looked for coloured people. As I passed through Alabama, where-ever I saw coloured people they looked desolate in the extreme. They were poorly clad, and had the appearance of being poorly fed. It is a dense cotton region, and in the hoeing season." He was set to work building railroad track since his new master "had taken a contract to finish three miles of railroad, and his intention was to make use of us upon the road till it was finished, and afterwards to place us on the new cotton farm." Banks found himself put to work alongside "young men who were not more than nineteen or twenty [who] looked like men forty or fifty years old." Relentless cotton and railroad work, in alternate seasons, had robbed the men of their youthful vigor, and in the cotton South, railroad companies competed with local planters for laborers. Railroads had a difficult time recruiting slave labor during the cotton harvest, when planters mobilized every hand. That misery was mirrored in the lands Banks left behind in Virginia.[26]

Banks's generation saw commercial activity intensify and along with it the adversities to which such activity subjected enslaved families. As the velocity of the great American forced migration increased in the 1850s, so did forced migrants' hazards. Trains carried off loved ones whose sales slave traders brokered over telegraph wires. One in eight of the slave purchases Silas Omohundro and his brother R. F. Omohundro recorded in 1857 were transported to the Richmond slave market by rail. A larger proportion probably left by rail since the Omohundro brothers recorded out-of-state buyers from Alabama,

Georgia, Louisiana, Mississippi, North Carolina, South Carolina, and Tennessee in the late 1850s.[27]

Railroads could scarcely carry enslaved people out of the Chesapeake quickly enough for slave traders. When Olmsted rode the distance from Portsmouth to Weldon, he encountered "a trader" who "had ready a company of negroes, intended to be shipped South; but the 'servants' car' being quite full already, they were obliged to be left for another train." Later, preparing to board the train to depart Wilmington, North Carolina, he encountered as many recently purchased slaves being ferried to the wharf near the station as white passengers. "All carried on their shoulders some little baggage," he recalled of the enslaved, "probably all their personal effects, slung in a blanket; and one had a dog, whose safe landing caused him nearly as much anxiety as his own did *his* owner."[28] Enslaved people not only encountered railroads as vehicles that carried them off permanently once they had been sold but also as transport that temporarily took them away from family and friends. In 1853, an Orange, Virginia, slaveholder wrote to a Richmond hiring agent, "I shall send you tomorrow . . . by the Central Rail Road a girl Diana by name—who I wish you to hire out for the balance of the year as well as you can." He added, "I can do nothing with her here—at most I hope to punish her." He did not say why. For Diana, the railroad served to separate her from family and friends, and for the owner, it offered an easy way to dispose of her. If Diana's situation was similar to Harriet Jacobs's, her owner could use the road to disrupt her connections and isolate her. There were plenty of ways to profit from her hire in Richmond, too, where she would face new perils.[29]

Communications technology in the form of telegraphs mediated that commerce at unheard-of speeds. "Neither Alexander the Great nor Benjamin Franklin (America's first postmaster general) two thousand years later knew anything faster than a galloping horse," remarks Daniel Walker Howe, yet by the 1840s, "instant long-distant communication became a practical reality."[30] Railroads, canals, and the telegraph helped to cement ties among local markets and integrate the South into the nation in the 1840s and 1850s. By 1848, the telegraph linked Richmond with New York and, soon after, New Orleans, and almost as soon as the lines were up, slave traders were using the technology to facilitate their business. "Let me know by Telegraph what you think of the boys or girls," wrote a Washington, D.C., slave trader to his colleague in Richmond in 1848, "and how they will sell." The "boys or girls" were enslaved children the Washington trader had sent via railroad to the Richmond slave market.[31]

Railroads and telegraphs challenged the defensive strategies enslaved people used, which were grounded in face-to-face communications. For many generations, information had traveled through enslaved people's communications networks at an extraordinary speed. "The spread of intelligence of all kinds among the slaves is remarkable," Olmsted wrote from Virginia in 1853. "A planter told me that he had frequently known of his slaves going twenty miles from home and back during the night, without their being missed at all from work, or known at the time to be off the plantation." "Another told me," Olmsted reported, "that he had been frequently informed by his slaves of occurrences in a town forty miles distant, where he spent part of the year with his family, in advance of the mail, or any means of communication that he could command the use of." Slaveholders' surprise indicates their failure to understand the scope and suppleness of enslaved people's networks. "Also, when in town," Olmsted wrote, "his servants would sometimes give him important news from the plantation, several hours before a messenger dispatched by his overseer arrived." Enslaved people sought to make sure that their version of events reached the owner before an overseer's or an employer's and that other information was shaded to their advantage as well. Those strategies were being undermined. Instant telegraph communications between market hubs, in which enslaved people's futures were decided, beat the quickest enslaved wagoner or the fleetest foot on any farm. It should not be surprising that enslaved people named their clandestine communications network the "grapevine telegraph," in response to the newest communications technology.[32]

The telegraph facilitated efficiencies in the slave market. Slavers telegraphed one another to share news of market conditions, to hatch plans for raising capital, and to broker individual sales. For traders, the telegraph could bring information about cotton and slave prices in distant markets and local conditions such as the weather and the presence of epidemics. The power of that information was decisive in gaining advantages in the market. In 1860, Parr and Farrish, one of the largest slave trading firms in the Virginia Piedmont, telegraphed Betts and Gregory, who were leaders in the Richmond market, breathlessly asking, "Is there any change in the Negro Market—answer immediately."[33] Like a stockbroker demanding an instant quote, the Lynchburg dealer wanted the latest word on the prices for which enslaved people were selling in Richmond and insisted that his colleague compress the results of hundreds, perhaps thousands of individual sales into a compact summary fit for the medium of communication. Such small chunks of information necessarily left out the human costs, which were enveloped in a statement of the health of an abstraction. "Good negroes are scarce and hard to buy" wrote a Washington, D.C., trader in 1847, giving a snapshot of the market as it stood just then.[34]

Communications complemented financial technology, which helped to integrate local economies into the broader market. Telegraphic communications created conditions whereby traders could pool resources and mobilize capital, joining markets hundreds of miles apart. In 1860 a trader telegraphed Richmond from Fredericksburg reporting that a colleague "has gone to Balt[im] o[re] to purchase Negroes," and asked the receiver to "arrange matters so that our drafts on you will be cash there or in Washington City—To the amount of ten thousand (10000) dollars." The Fredericksburg trader asked his Richmond partner to contact banks in Baltimore and Washington, D.C., to ensure that any checks the Baltimore agent wrote would be treated as near to gold coins as was possible. That was the antebellum equivalent of wiring money, without which the several slaves $10,000 would purchase in Baltimore could not be purchased immediately. The Baltimore agent would instead have to delay purchases while sorting out whether the traders' drafts on a Virginia bank would be accepted on par with cash, during which time the slaves might end up being purchased by local traders who could produce the money in the shape of Maryland or Washington, D.C., bank notes. For a telegraph message costing less than a dollar, the traders nearly instantaneously communicated news of their colleagues' itinerary and saved tens, perhaps hundreds of dollars by securing the cooperation of out-of-state banks. The enslaved commodities could then be put on railroad cars and hauled to the Richmond market for resale.[35]

Advancing communications technologies broadened the reach of individual traders, integrating and rationalizing the slave market. A Raleigh-based trader telegraphed his colleague in Richmond in 1856, "I will send you five Negroes tomorrow—drew on you[r credit with a Raleigh bank] yesterday for fifteen hundred dollars. I received your check for six hundred—please pay the [balance]." In that notice, delivered over the 170 miles of wire to the Richmond office of the Washington and New Orleans Telegraph Company, the trader also inquired whether there was "any small pox there" and noted that he had "paid" for an "answer." (Despite availability of the Jenner vaccine, smallpox outbreaks were not uncommon.) In the past, a trader transporting a coffle of slaves from Raleigh to Richmond would at best get a few days' warning if there had been an outbreak of smallpox. With the telegraph, word of smallpox or any other epidemic traveled much more quickly, enabling commerce to be diverted, which—if the market showed any mercy—could save some enslaved people from exposure. It might also raise prices for slaves in local markets that were unaffected, as demand shifted to those areas. In this case the Raleigh trader, satisfied that his chattel would not be exposed to smallpox, sent "one man, one boy, and three girls" along with written instructions as to the terms of their sale. Brokered through the telegraph, they would then arrive on railroad cars.[36]

Increasingly, the slave market stretched beyond physical locations in which interested parties haggled face-to-face over prices and inspected the human goods on display. Quick communications and transportation connected buyers and sellers in cities hundreds of miles apart, allowing the market to become more stratified and, for slavers, abstract. In 1860, Lynchburg, Virginia, trader S. C. Woodroof telegraphed colleagues at Moore and Dawson in Richmond asking, "Have you a number one carpenter [and] if so what is the price[?] [A]nswer by telegraph."[37] Woodroof was in luck since Moore and Dawson had been in touch with a Fredericksburg trader, T. H. Lipscomb, who was offering to sell two such enslaved carpenters. The only hitch was that Lipscomb wanted top dollar for them, "not less than" $3,300 for the pair," he insisted. The Fredericksburg trader had purchased the men from another Virginia trader for $3,000 through a check from Moore and Dawson, but once he learned that there was interest beyond Richmond, he wrote "in answer to your Telegraph" that he raised his price to $3,500 and insured the men's lives in preparation for transport. "If you can sell them for that price Telegraph me immediately and I will send them down by the day train" he replied. Knowing that his colleague and creditor had potential buyers in Lynchburg, the Fredericksburg trader sought to maximize his profit. There was less need to rely on local market prices if slaves could be sold over the wires and sent over the rails. There was little enslaved people could do to thwart or shape sales brokered through the telegraph.[38]

For an antebellum generation of white Americans, railroads symbolized a society racing ahead at an alarming rate, and the great construction projects, sponsored largely by state governments yet built by corporations mainly visible in the gangs of slaves they deployed, were the embodiment of that breakneck speed that elicited their trepidation. George Fitzhugh blamed Europe's ostensible failures on political economists who pushed their theories with "railroad speed and railroad recklessness."[39] Henry David Thoreau worried that American society "lives too fast" and exhorted his readers to "simplify, simplify." "If some have the pleasure of riding on a rail," he admonished, "others have the misfortune to be ridden upon." He had Irish and Yankee workers in mind when he counseled against worker exploitation, but he could have added enslaved African Americans as well. Fearing his countrymen were becoming slaves of new technologies, he put his audience in the predicate, declaring "we do not ride on the railroad; it rides upon us." Few enslaved railroad workers would disagree.[40] Thoreau's friend Ralph Waldo Emerson declared that "slavery is no scholar, no improver; it does not love the whistle of the railroad."[41] But Emerson had not been to Virginia to see for himself. Less agitated commentators recognized what every slave trader and merchant (and most lawmakers) saw as railroads' main contribution: increasing market efficiencies. "Badly as they are managed," Frederick Law Olmsted conceded after visiting the Old Dominion, railroads "must encourage activity and punctuality in the people, besides increasing the value of exports of the country through which they pass, and diminishing the cost of imports by lessening the above-sea freightage expenses."[42] Even southern markets would indeed operate with Yankee efficiency.

Maximizing financial utility, railroad corporations used the strongest, most cost-efficient, and most pliable labor available, mostly enslaved men and boys (although some southern railroads hired women and girls). Hiring slaves in addition to recruiting free labor saved industrial companies start-up costs and the investment in labor itself. While some South Carolina and Georgia roads preferred to buy slaves, Virginia roads tended to rent them, perhaps because cotton South owners would show up and demand back workers needed in the fields. In the lower Chesapeake and North Carolina, slaveholders with a seeming surplus of slaves were ready to furnish bound laborers in abundance.[43]

Virginia and North Carolina railroad companies relied on the work of enslaved people, on the ability to exploit their labor and skills, and on the capital made available for investment by their sale. In Greensville County, Virginia, "the growth of the railroad through the forests and fields, over rivers and ravines, required many laborers," recalled a local historian. "It was the custom to employ slaves from their owners to work on the lines, cutting trees, laying ties and rails, and building bridges." Most "were employed to work in the immediate vicinity of their owner's plantations." Enslaved people's masonry and carpentry skills were needed as well as their brawn. "The bridge over Fountain Creek," near Emporia, "which was originally a railroad bed, has some of the most beautiful stonework in this section of the country and is truly a monument to the strength and skill of the [enslaved] men who built it." Slaves changed the nineteenth-century landscape in constructing railroads as they had transformed the eighteenth-century landscape through building plantations.[44]

Slaves were not necessarily less skilled or less efficient than free workers. They knew the language and, like the men Fannie Berry witnessed working on the Southside Railroad, understood the projects they were involved in building. Immigrant railroaders lacked their store of local knowledge. According to Seth Rockman, by the 1820s, Baltimore city officials found "alarming" the fact that "English parishes and German towns appeared to be emptying their almshouses and disgorging their feeble-minded or disabled inhabitants on American shores." Railroad agents in the lower Chesapeake could look smugly at their upper Chesapeake neighbors' experiments with free labor and the uncertainties they posed. After all, most African Americans could trace their lineages back a century or more and were intimately familiar with the terrain, climate, and weather. In the upper Chesapeake and western Virginia, white immigrants worked alongside or replaced slaves as the former arrived in increasing numbers in the 1840s and 1850s. Some Virginia railroads hired Irish workers in counties where there were few enslaved people and immigrants demanded work. Perhaps for fear of the safety of their slave property, some owners insisted that their slaves not work with whites. An enslaved man, Armistead, was hired out to the RFPRR in 1836 with the proviso that he "was not to work with Irish or dutch [i.e., German] labourers." Perhaps the owner feared violence, but he could also have wanted to keep his slave away from the culture of alcohol that pervaded railroad camps. German workers on a Florida railroad, for instance, "stopped working each day at 10 A.M. and 4 P.M. until each man was supplied with a stein of beer." Antebellum male laborers such as canal workers considered it their right to consume alcohol before and during work.[45]

It was not just enslaved people's knowledge and abilities that railroad companies prized but also their labor, which offered practical and economic advantages to them. The president of the Tennessee and Alabama Railroad Company reportedly "recommended that three hundred slaves be immediately purchased to work on the road," in November 1856, calculating that "the purchase money, interest, insurance and maintenance of a slave will be only about 46 cents per day, or about $115 per year (working days only counted)" and that "[t]he same labor of white men costs [between] two and two and a half dollars per day."[46] The directors of a Georgia railroad reported the "established fact" that "negro labor is perfectly adapted to the construction of works of internal improvement," not only because slaves were pliable but also because—the racist thinking of the day held—blacks were better suited to working in hot climates than whites.[47] Arguing for the utility of slave labor on southern railroads, one New York editor claimed, "in tropical latitudes, or amid that *malaria*, where the negro flourishes and fattens—the free white laborer perishes."[48] Insurance companies disagreed about enslaved people's ability to flourish in "tropical latitudes," but the mistaken belief that African Americans were ideally suited to a malarial southern climate was secondary in importance to their cost effectiveness and lack of rights.[49] Claudius Crozet concurred.

Frustrated at the slow pace of progress on his Blue Ridge Railroad in Virginia in the mid-1850s, Crozet complained that his free hands at the Blue Ridge Tunnel had "returned to work very sparingly: I cannot understand their obstinacy, except by supposing they have been tampered with."[50] Enslaved workers would not be "tampered with" by labor organizers' filling their heads with talk of collective action, theories of justice, or concerns about the effects of dangerous work on family breadwinners. The enslaved could not formally protest conditions or withdraw their labor without threat of summary punishment. The enslaved could not absent themselves on court days, insist on drilling with the militia, or tarry at the polls on election days. Most importantly, they generally cost employers less. It is little wonder that an exasperated Crozet wrote that he regretted "we did not hire Negroes at Christmas."[51]

Hiring slaves entailed short-term costs from the company's point of view. Railroads were always struggling for capital, and in an atmosphere in which it was expected that there would be a great shortage of capital from sponsors such as state governments, plus a lot of corporate debt, hiring made good financial sense at that start-up phase of industrial development. If the rail-road companies owned slaves, as many did, the company's liquidity increased since they could be turned into cash if their labor was not required. Companies used slaves as construction workers and also as assets, buying, selling, and hiring enslaved laborers where and when they thought it in the company's best financial interests.

On the eve of emancipation in 1862, another Virginia railroad engineer perhaps inadvertently signaled how important African American workers were to the success of railroads. "Feeling sure that emancipation on this peninsula is the true policy," he wrote from Eastville, on the Eastern Shore, "I have been casting about for some practical compensation for the immediate loss to the slave holder. This I see in a rail-road connecting Philadelphia with Cherrystone Creek" in Northampton County. The terminus was then in Salis-bury, Maryland, and the engineer envisioned a hundred-mile project linking the Delaware Railroad to a ferry point on the Chesapeake Bay. The key to its success would be forced labor—or hoodwinked labor. "Let the emancipated slaves be compelled as a condition that they should labor on this road a certain time," he recommended, "and if necessary let the contraband now about Fortress Monroe be employed in the same work." Those were refugees fleeing slavery on the Virginia Peninsula across the bay. "Many of these are skillful mechanics," the engineer continued, "and could very well surface & lay the ties and rails. Thus the cost of the R. R. could be reduced to the food for the negroes[,] & wood for bridges over [the Pocomoke River] could be cut from the estates of those absentees now in arms agst. the government." By treating the newly free as corvée labor, the engineer sought to solve a labor shortage problem and to cope with a lack of capital. At the same time he was suggesting cheating former slaves out of wages, however, he was also endorsing their abilities to undertake such a project. Perhaps swindling African Americans whenever possible was standard practice among railroad companies before the war. Whatever the case, the plan went nowhere, and the Eastern Shore of Virginia would not see a railroad until after the Civil War.[52]

By the early 1850s southern railroads were constructing tracks with a full head of steam and enlisting slaves in great numbers to bear the physical burdens. Gangs of enslaved railroad workers formed some of the largest work camps in the South. The Wilmington and Raleigh Railroad had a force of

226 enslaved male workers ages twenty-five to forty-five working in New Hanover County, North Carolina, in August 1850. Some resembled army encampments and produced some of the same effects. In 1851, the Southside Railroad contracted to hire fifteen hundred workers (white and black) and 400 horses for work on the seventy miles of track between Petersburg and Farmville; the following year, the same company hired one thousand workers and 150 horses.[53] Urban manufacturers and processors then had to compete with railroad contractors for their workforce. The construction market for prime males competed with the cotton demand for the same cohorts, which indicates how valuable they were as workers. In turn, women not wanted by railroads would be hired out to agricultural enterprises or else sent to urban areas where domestics were in demand. Enslaved families suffered more dislocations as a result, including from the slave trade. Brenda Stevenson argues that "the loss of slave spouses and family members came to be so great that there is evidence that the last generation of slave families even were threatened with loss of their most resilient familial characteristics—matrifocal structures and supportive extended family and community networks."[54] For enslaved families, localities in Virginia and North Carolina in which the railroad was being constructed looked like war-torn societies: males were away from home, female workers shouldered the burdens of agricultural labor, and older relatives performed domestic and childcare duties. The Virginia and Tennessee Railroad workforce numbering 435 slaves in 1856 was among the biggest assemblage of slaves in Virginia. There was only one plantation larger in 1850 and only five larger in 1860.[55] Some Virginia railroads were in the same slave-holding class as large planters, but in contrast to planters who owned males and females of all ages, Virginia railroads owned or hired males, overwhelmingly men in their twenties and thirties, whose services they procured for "liberal prices."[56] Any enslaved person who found himself in a railroad camp would seriously question the contentions of apologists who argued that slavery was framed by paternalistic sentiments between masters and members of extended enslaved families.[57]

Whether they were sawyers, shovel men, axmen, or cooks, boys and men were thrown in together. They gathered around campfires, shivered in the drafty winter shanties, or swatted away flies in sweltering summer tents. There they would share their stories, hopes, fears, and memories of home. Their dislocations were temporary—they hoped. It was a little more than eleven months from winter hiring time to Christmas, but all knew that they stood a much better chance of making it back home to friends and loved ones than those who attracted the attention of slave traders. Railroad companies were severe masters, however, and the working lives of slaves owned or hired by railroad companies were harsh. The social mythology of planter paternalism did not permeate railroad camps, despite the labored pronouncements of one southern railroad company that "labor . . . confined to, and growing up with, and on the Road, would create an identity of interest, and feeling between the slaves and the enterprise; the former seeing that on the success of the latter would depend the permanency, and greater comfort of their own situation."[58] Such sentiments were more plausible in the director's office than in the work camp, and while railroads did save money by retaining laborers year after year, enslaved people were motivated by money promised in exchange for overwork rather than affection for the project. The men Fannie Berry witnessed singing "Dis time tomorrow night, / Where will I be? / I'll be gone, gone, gone, / Down to Tennessee" showed no love for the road. Railroad camps gave practical apprenticeships, but there is little evidence that corporate owners or employers were any more interested in policing the personal lives of slaves than tobacconists or other factory owners who paid cash for overwork and boarding out. Industrialists were employers first and foremost.[59]

The stakes for enslaved people working in camps was high. Lewis, Oliver, and Alfred were hired out to work as sawyers on the Richmond and Danville Railroad in Amelia County, in 1849. Among scores of other enslaved men, they took part in a labor culture that was always arduous and usually dangerous. Only one would survive the year. In January, they left the Nottoway County farm of owner Frances Epes for a railroad camp two counties over, in Chesterfield. Nottoway was in the path of the Richmond and Danville Railroad begun in 1847, which by then had progressed about fifty miles southwest of Richmond and was ninety miles northeast of its proposed terminus in Danville. In Chesterfield County, Lewis, Oliver, and Alfred joined a workforce of some forty men that included boys as young as eleven or twelve to men in their late forties, living in temporary encampments called shanties. Railroad workers shared a camp culture with men in other industries, such as the enslaved men who inhabited the shanties housing the hundred-plus slave labor force digging coal in the Chesterfield pits near Midlothian.[60]

Lewis, Oliver, and Alfred spent most of their lengthy workdays on either side of a long, toothy saw. They hewed ties, or sleepers, out of timber cut locally. The ties provided a level base, held the track in place, and kept the rails parallel. Sawing ties was a dangerous business, however. Once measured, a two-man team using a cross-cut saw would cut plane sides out of the cylindrical log so the resulting tie would be about seven inches high and about nine inches wide. The Norfolk and Petersburg road, completed in 1858, used white oak, pine, and cypress. The first and third cuts would be the trickiest since the log's rounded side would face down. Knots from branches or rotted wood complicated the work, and slaves worked outdoors, in the falling snow or blistering sun. Since the saw cut went with the wood grain, skilled ax men could also hew ties. A finished tie was about eight and a half feet long and weighed over three hundred pounds. The tie would sit on a bed of coarse gravel or more often sand, which was the ballast for the railroad bed.[61]

Hewing ties was taxing for Lewis, Oliver, and Alfred, but pneumonia rather than accidents or exhaustion claimed the lives of two of them in the Chesterfield County railroad camp that was their home in 1849. In search of labor, the road's hiring agent had gone to Nottoway County, which was the county with the highest proportion of slaves in the state.[62] Lewis, Oliver, and Alfred's owner, who held twenty-eight slaves in 1850, agreed to take $200 for their hire, so long as the men worked solely in neighboring Amelia County.[63] The Richmond and Danville's hiring agent agreed to return the workers at Christmas, with a new set of clothing, a hat and blanket. Though the company was constructing camps in Amelia County, the railroad had not yet reached there, and the men were set to work sawing lumber into railroad ties across the county line. The owner understood that the work was dangerous and named a physician to attend the men in case of illness, but when the men came down with pneumonia, the railroad's physician treated them instead. Two of the men died. After learning of their deaths, the slaveholder sued the principal owners of the road, Robert Harvey and James Hunter, claiming that they had violated a contract when the workers were sent to Chesterfield to work. A jury found the men liable, but in 1855 Virginia's Supreme Court reversed the circuit court and ordered a new trial.[64]

The issue at stake was whether the railroad had violated a contract and not whether the dangers were foreseeable. Legal remedies for accidents involving the railroads were in short supply, since the law of torts had not caught up with the emerging industry. The case involving the slaves who died from pneumonia turned on whether the railroad had converted them to their own use by working them in Chesterfield County and not Amelia and was thereby liable for damages. Whatever the outcome, it was too late for the two who had died. Others responded to railroad accidents with violence. Joseph Sorrell, a husband, father of five, and laborer from Hanover County whose "valuable cow" was "killed on a railroad" in 1849, retaliated by setting fire to the RFPRR depot on Christmas Eve. The Sorrells owned no real estate, and it is likely that the cow was his biggest moveable asset. When apprehended several months later, the still-furious Sorrell remarked that "if rebuilt," he would "for the sum of $5, cause" the depot to be "burnt" again. He had little hope of winning compensation from the road. When railroad companies lost slave laborers that they owned, such as when Jacob Garry and Robert Millar, slaves of the Norfolk and Petersburg Railroad, were killed in the fall of 1859, their obituaries appeared simply as red ink on the company ledgers. Relatives got no pensions or survivors' benefits.[65]

When they could, railroad companies used gangs of slaves hired together for years at a time. That strategy increased efficiency since a core cadre of experienced men could be augmented by more recent hires whom they would tutor. Fewer green hands meant fewer potential fatalities and quicker, higher-quality work. In 1856 James Hunter of the Richmond and Danville Railroad wrote to Charles B. Fisk, the chief engineer of the Covington and Ohio Railroad, to propose that a gang be used to build substantial parts of the C&O railroad, which was then just in the initial stages of development. From Hanover, Virginia, Hunter planned to "push a negro force upon it which has been in our employment during the last five or six years and all now well used to the business." Whether Fisk took advantage of the offer is unclear, though the veteran workforce had laid beds and built tracks in Tidewater Virginia.[66]

Railroad hiring of the sort Hunter offered Fisk involved a constellation of masters and agents, which rationalized a local hiring market in the same way slave traders rationalized regional slave markets. Hunter directed overseers who drove enslaved people hired from owners. While many slaves brokered their own hiring agreements on the streets of Richmond, agents often contracted for the hire of enslaved railroad workers. The firm of Branch and Company was the biggest in Petersburg. They hired a "boy," Horace, to Francis E. Rives in 1848, for work on the railroad. Negotiations for his labor passed from owner to agent and from agent to contractor. The owner knew that Rives and his Petersburg Railroad had hired Horace, but he had no direct contact with the road. Branch and Company hired Barnett to the Southside Railroad for 1853 for $125. Did he join the gang Fannie Berry witnessed a few years later? Thirty-three year-old Simon was sent to the Southside Railroad as well.

He was owned, along with his mother, an enslaved woman in her sixties, by a Petersburg farmer in his early thirties. Head of a family that included two small children in 1850, Simon's owner likely drew a substantial portion of his income from Simon's hire. Simon was "not hired" in 1853, however. Did he cause trouble for the Southside Railroad or Branch and Company, or did he persuade the owner that his mother needed him back in Petersburg? For some of the enslaved workers, railroad work could be a rough and sometimes adventurous time of learning in which catalogues of collective experience were shared around the evening campfire before sleep silenced tongues. For those who could get under the skin of an overseer or employer, it was punishing work ending with a ticket back to their homes and families. For the feeble or unlucky, it was their last detail.[67]

Shanties inhabited by African American workers were little worse than the temporary camps of white workers, whether Irish or German immigrants. They were crowded, shoddy, hives of disease and discomfort. Workers in shanties were not governed by health and safety regulations, and owners rarely turned up to monitor working conditions. Arriving in South Carolina in the early 1850s, Frederick Law Olmsted wrote, "We came, in the midst of the woods, to the end of the rails. In the vicinity could be seen a small tent, a shanty of loose boards, and a large, subdued fire, around which, upon the ground, there were a considerable number of men, stretched out asleep." That "was the camp of the hands engaged in laying the rails, and who were thus daily extending the distance which the locomotive could run." It was also the temporary terminus of the road. The railroad began again eighty miles away, a distance partly covered by corduroy roads paved with logs. A slave trader and his coffle followed Olmsted off the train near the shanty. "The negro property," he recalled, "which had been brought up in a freight car, was immediately let out on the stoppage of the train. As it stepped on to the platform, its owner asked, 'Are you all here?'" An enslaved man answered in the affirmative. "'Do dysef no harm, for we's all heah,' added another, quoting Saint Peter, in an under tone," Olmsted recalled.[68] The exhausted railroad workers in the nearby shanty seemed to take no notice.

"The railroad hands sleep in miserable shanties along the line," reported abolitionist editor James Redpath, who traveled to the South to see slavery for himself. A North Carolina scene moved him to pity. "Poor fellows!" he exclaimed, "in that God-forsaken section of the earth they seldom see a woman from Christmas to Christmas. If they are married men, they are tantalized by the thought that their wives are performing for rich women of another race those services that would brighten their own gloomy life-pathway." He added, "They may, perhaps—who knows?—have still sadder reflections." That was an understatement. "Their bed is an inclined board—nothing better, softer, or warmer," he reported. "Their covering is a blanket," which many hiring contracts stipulated railroad companies provide. "The fireplaces in these cabins are often so clumsily constructed that all the heat ascends to the chimney, instead of diffusing itself throughout the miserable hut, and warming its more miserable tenants." The November night was "bitterly cold and uncomfortable," and Redpath reported that he "frequently awoke, at all hours, shivering with cold, and found shivering slaves huddled up near the fire." The overseer did not let them quit work "until sunset," Redpath recalled, "and as, after coming to their cabins, they have to cook their ash-cakes, or mush, or dumplings, these huts are by no means remarkable for their cleanly appearance."[69]

Shanties offered little physical comfort to the inhabitants. They had poor sanitation, and daily life, including meals, breaks, and sleep, was regimented according to production demands. Like white workers, enslaved laborers broke up the monotony—when they could—with alcohol bought from local vendors, despite prohibitions from overseers who themselves were typically less than abstemious. In summer, heat and diseases like malaria and yellow fever incapacitated and killed workers. In winter, icy conditions chilled their bones, slowing work, while influenza and pneumonia made corpses out of men. Workers who had not traveled out of the county of their birth before caught diseases from seasoned workers, which were exacerbated by exposure, malnourishment, and the absence of loved ones. Yet despite the awful living conditions, even the dirty and dangerous work on the railroad could be a way of forestalling or avoiding sale. Despicable conditions nevertheless engendered desperate responses.

Railroad work was taxing and often violent, and some slaves refused to work in railroad camps at all.[70] In 1851, a Nelson County, Virginia, hiring agent wrote to a tavern keeper in Augusta County to report on an enslaved man he had hired out "conditionally for one hundred Dollars" to a railroad. The slave had been hired to the tavern keeper, who likely wanted him back. The young man "was anxious to return to" his previous employment, the agent reported, since his current employer "intends to put him on the [rail] Road, and the Boy is not willing to go on the road." The abysmal living conditions were likely more than he could stomach. As a result, the correspondent wrote, "I think you will get him yet." Innkeeping was far less dangerous.[71]

Railroad workers absconded when pressed too hard or when the absence of family became too big a burden to bear. Redpath's proposition that enslaved railroad workers had "still sadder reflections" than their years-long separation from family is confirmed by Peter's ordeal in 1853. Peter was an enslaved man hired to the RPRR who ran off from his work gang and returned to his mother in Caroline County, Virginia. The owner wrote the hiring agent saying he had "endeavored to persuade him to return" to the railroad camp, "which he positively refuses to do, alleging that the overseer of his company hit him with a stick on last Thursday or Friday and threatened to punish him further on Monday, to avoid which he ran away." In response to the violence, Peter "seems determined," his owner reported, "to be sold before he will consent to return." The owner need not have elaborated. If Peter refused to work building the transportation revolution in the upper South, he would be put to work building the cotton revolution in the lower South.[72]

Family considerations were at the heart of Peter's dilemma. In running back to his mother, he illustrated the value of family above some abstract idea of freedom or the money he could possibly earn from overwork. At the hands of an abuser, he acted out of desperation. Despite the fact that the owner considered the mother "a faithful servant" and "on her account," he wrote, he did "not want to separate them," the implication was that of course he would. Peter would have to go back to work or his mother would lose him to a slave trader. If she harbored him, moreover, she might be sold herself. The owner claimed that "if the company can succeed in compelling him to remain with them for the balance of the year," all would be well but warned that "in another effort to escape he would probably not stop in this neighborhood." The railroad contractor would not have had such leverage with a free worker.[73]

Some ran off rather than risking injury. Hudson, who was identified by the fact that he had "the first joint of one of his little fingers . . . cut off during the last year, by one of the rail-road cars" was wanted by a Chesterfield Railroad agent in 1835.[74] Overseers were suspicious of complaints. Olmsted observed a dispute between a North Carolina slaveholder and the slaves whom he hired out to work on a railroad. The slaves' overseer recalled the disputes as "a lesson to me about taming possums, that I ain't agoing to forget in a hurry." Playing possum was common enough that complaints of those forced to work in dangerous living conditions were summarily suspect. Olmsted reported that contractors and overseers "had sometimes been mistaken, and had made men go to work when they afterwards proved to be really ill." One case involved a "sulky" slave who complained of being sick. "He said he couldn't work," the overseer reported, so he "looked at his tongue, and it was right clean." After the inspection, the overseer determined that the slave was suffering from "nothing but damned sulkiness so I paddled him, and made him go to work; but, two days after, he was under ground." In reporting the slave's death, the overseer summed up the loss. "He was a good eight hundred dollar nigger."[75] After realizing that his disbelieving that his slaves were sick had cost him a slave, the slaveholder Olmsted interviewed adopted a policy of giving complaining workers a day off to rest. Better to suffer a ruse than lose valuable property. That was as near as any enslaved workers got to a collective bargaining agreement and shows the high stakes for enslaved workers and how little leverage they had in negotiating with employers who had a limited and temporary interest in the workers they drove.

Some slaveholders understood the risks slaves faced in work camps, even if they had little sympathy. One Virginia slave trader wrote a fellow trader expressing a typical sentiment concerning the dangers that railroad work posed to enslaved workers. "I shall not let my negroes work on the Rail Road any longer than this week," he wrote, "for they don't take any care of them and it is better to feed them and let them do nothing than to have them crippled and not care taken of them." That correspondence took place over a weekend at the start of the Christmas holidays, the customary period when yearly slave hiring contracts expired and new ones were made. The trader penned the letter while on a trip to Alabama to sell other enslaved people he had brought down from Virginia. He was not ambivalent about the outcomes of the projects his slaves had worked on, since he returned from Alabama to Richmond on the railroad and in time to celebrate Christmas with his family. The slaves he had sold did not.[76]

Not all railroad workers were put to work in backbreaking labor. A visitor to Virginia in 1846 traveled on the City Point Railroad and found an African American in charge. "The road was rickety, the engine was rickety, the car was rickety and the *engineer* was rickety—an old man who had no doubt been a slave for seventy years and who served as engineer, conductor and sole manager." That an African American man should find himself in charge of a public conveyance that was also a large and expensive (if "rickety") piece of capital equipment testifies to the skill and ingenuity of black railroad workers. The visitor complimented the engineer's abilities, writing that despite the condition of the "outfit[,] we were only one hour in running the whole distance of twelve miles, notwithstanding the driver had to stop and pull down *bars* whenever they chanced to be up, for in those days the herders used *poles* to prevent their stock trespassing." In the days before cow catchers on locomotives, cowherds and shepherds laid lumber across tracks to prevent damage to their animals grazing nearby. Black engineers on southern roads were rarities but not unheard of, and hierarchies of slaves existed in railroad organizations just as they did in agricultural enterprises. That conductor likely also directed an enslaved fireman or brakeman. In that capacity he was little different from African American drivers on plantations. The following year, the city of Petersburg bought the City Point Railroad and renamed it the Appomattox Railroad. The Southside Railroad gobbled up the Appomattox Railroad in 1854, about the time Fannie Berry recalled hearing the men singing on that road near the Appomattox River west of Petersburg.[77]

Railroad maintenance complemented construction, and the thirty-six enslaved men put to work in Henrico County on the RPRR in 1850 made repairs to the road and shouldered the burden of loading cars, firing the engines, and applying the brakes. Some were company slaves, such as the "two Negro men," valued at $1,500, who were listed among the assets of the company in 1857, along with "locomotive engines and tenders, and snow ploughs, $70,000" and "iron rails, chairs, and spikes." Most were hired. In 1858, creditors reported that the company had paid $2,200 for "Negroe hire due last yr." (The company grossed nearly $157,000 the same year.) That RPRR, whose twenty-four mile track was capitalized at just over $1 million, also owned a tobacco warehouse and stables. Its credit report indicates that the company was "perfectly respon[sible]" in 1851, but that the "Road is [in] v[er]y bad cond[itio]n," Despite the shape of the road, the company was "d[oin]g w[el]l [in] bus[iness]" and "g[oo]d for its contracts."[78]

Slaves hired to the RPRR in the vicinity of Richmond were put to work maintaining the tracks and ties, making sure the roadbed was secure and repairing damage. After word reached the company's creditors that "new rail [was] recently laid down" in the summer of 1854, reports brightened. "D[oin]g well & in g[oo]d reputes" read a report from the winter of 1856. Reports of the firm's financial probity followed through the 1850s. By the summer of 1857, it was "considered" to be in "a prosperous condition. Credit very good." The

RPRR was not atypical. The neighboring RFPRR employed forty-nine enslaved men in two counties by midcentury, whose job it also was to maintain the road. The workforce based in Hanover County numbered twenty-two slaves, all men between twenty-five and forty-five. The RFPRR workforce based at the Richmond railroad depot included twenty-seven enslaved men, aged twenty to ninety. Their work ultimately secured the company's good credit.[79]

In the depots or stations, African Americans and whites worked in proximity to one another once the railroad was operational, yet work was segregated. In 1839, for instance, the Petersburg Railroad force included forty-five African Americans who loaded and unloaded the cars, pumped water, and ported freight from canal boats. They worked alongside ten black brakemen and firemen. Whites included a superintendent, ten engineers, ten carpenters, and four train captains. In 1852, the Virginia Central Railroad employed African Americans all over the road; they worked in depots and water stations and were members of maintenance gangs and a workforce building new track. Of course, wrote one engineer in North Carolina of a mixed workforce, "the negroes in such a case do all the drudgery."[80]

Slaveholders too got a practical education from the railroad. In the first years of railroad construction, many owners did not realize the full ramifications of hiring slaves to a killer of a job and simply sought short-term financial gains. In the 1830s, all American railroads were experimental, and directors tested boosters' claims as to the efficiencies of hiring slaves to construct, maintain, and operate portions of the railroads. In January 1837, the RFPRR paid James Cavanagh and three other slaves fifty cents each to clear snow and an extra dollar for posting a night watch on the road's cars. The following month, the road paid the owners of six slaves twenty-five cents apiece for unloading cars. The company was also experimenting with year-long contracts, such as the $85 it paid to hire Randle, the $90 for Daniel, the $110 for Robert, the $120 for Henry, and the $150 for Smith in 1836. Based on those prices, an owner could expect to make in ten years what a prime field hand was about then selling for in the interstate trade. Like other forms of slave hiring, railroad work could allow owners to earn money off their slaves while they waited for higher market prices from slave traders. Antebellum slave prices in Virginia would peak in 1837 and not reach the same heights for twenty-two years. Owners of Randle, Daniel, Robert, Henry, and Smith may have been waiting for that apex. They could not know future prices, but railroad work would compensate slaveholders for their hesitance in the face of market instability. Owners gambled with their slaves' health, but railroad companies assumed responsibility for feeding and clothing the men and boys they hired in the meantime.[81]

Innovations in hiring gave new contours to slavery, while the high wages railroads paid to slave owners partially compensated owners for the risks to their slave property. Even in the early days of railroad construction, owners had insisted that their property not be put at undue risk. Aaron Marrs discovered that bonds for the RFPRR in 1836 included stipulations that some hired slaves were not to labor "in unhealthy situations," not to work outside the vicinity of the Richmond depot, or "not to work in water." Other Virginia slave hiring contracts explicitly prohibited giving or selling alcohol to slaves, such as canal companies did as incentives to work. In return, owners reaped high wages for the people they put at risk. Corporations protected their own interests. In response to owners' demands, contractors sought to minimize risks for the company and refused to compensate owners for time workers were absent without permission. Enslaved people entered bargains for their labor as well. Some contracts stipulated that slaves receive time off to visit relatives. As time went on, the contracts became more uniform. Enslaved people could expect some customary considerations, such as payment for overwork. That development dampened protests or violent conspiracies since individual interest set worker against worker, undermining solidarity. Marrs contends that as railroad hiring practices became more formalized in the antebellum period, "fairly standard, boilerplate language emerged, with some additional caveats occasionally insisted upon by owners." That was one way in which protoindustrial development advanced along with slavery. Railroads incrementally standardized the terms under which they were willing to hire slaves, making workers more fungible and making it harder for owners to haggle over details.[82]

Slaveholders and enslaved railroad workers were not alone in calculating their odds of survival. The perils of industrial work were well known to insurers, and corporate actuaries assisted slavers in rationalizing a national market for the enslaved when they placed premiums on policies for slaves in dangerous work. Sharon Murphy contends that "all companies charged additional premiums of $0.50 to $2.00 per $100 of insurance for slaves engaged in hazardous occupations such as on steam, canal, pilot, or fishing boats, on railroads, in coal pits or mines, or as engineers or firemen." That could mean a surcharge of between $7.50 and $30 per year on a slave valued at $1,500. Standard life insurance policies for slaves explicitly excluded coverage should the enslaved person be employed in work the company deemed dangerous. The American Life Insurance and Trust Company of Philadelphia insured slaves' lives but stipulated that it would deny payment on claims should the slave "be employed as an Engineer or Fireman in running a Locomotive or Steam Engine, or as an Officer or Brakeman upon a Rail Road, or as an Officer, Hand, or Servant on any Steam or other Vessel, or Raft, or as a Miner of hand in an Coal or other Mine, or in the manufacture or transportation of gunpowder." For a small percentage of the annual hiring fee, owners could insulate themselves from financial losses by insuring slaves in dangerous work. That also gave northern business interests an additional stake in industrial slavery, but it did little for the workers themselves. Instead, once the dangers posed to enslaved people's health were factored out of slaveholders' financial interests, there were fewer incentives to improve health and safety.[83] The risks were real. In 1858, a "negro man" was critically injured working on the South Side Railroad. "He was cutting away an embankment, when the evening train arrived." There was no effort made to stop service during the maintenance. "The negro stood resting upon the handle of his pick, when the jar of the passing train caused the earth to tumble down, burying him beneath it, and throwing his body with so much force upon the handle of the pick as to impale him." Despite the fact that the handle "entered near his stomach, and pierced through emerging from his back," the report continued, "strange to say, his chances of recovery are by no means hopeless."[84]

Railroad work also served to enforce slave discipline and offered slaveholders the option of short-term hiring arrangements, which figured into strategies to punish or otherwise dispose of slaves. Like the threat of sale, the threat of railroad work substituted for overt violence. A planter from Nelson County, Virginia, wrote a Richmond slave trader in 1852 laying out his case for selling a twenty-two year-old man. The planter described the man as "a powerful and efficient hand," but "unfortunately when an infant he was dropped from his nurse's arms and had all his fingers burned off of one hand." The deformity did not leave him helpless, since "with his nubs of fingers and nub of thumb he can pick up any sized pin or needle from a smooth surface, can use a hoe, axe, sledge, shovel, crowbar or any other tool as well as anybody, and he is the last negro I ever expected to sell, particularly as he always up to last February enjoyed a fine character." The incident leading to his sale began with a courtship gone awry. "At that time we gave him our chambermaid as a wife," the slaveholder wrote, "and the week following he broke into my mill and robbed it of half a barrel of flour, which being full fixed on him, his young wife renounced him and he desired to be sold." It is difficult to know the realities concealed within that self-serving assessment. Spurned or else irritated at a slaveholder dictating the course of his affections, the man had sought a desperate way out of the situation. The slaveholder attempted to sell him to a railroad, but the railroad contractor committed to hire him "on trial" for $12.50 per month. After a few months, the contractor returned him, and the man sought to make up with his putative wife. She would not have him. "The girl he claims and is determined to enjoy if possible is a trusty, valuable house servant," the planter continued, "and, if the Law would permit, I would shoot him before he should return to her." Despite his pretense at chivalry, the planter was more interested in disposing of the man than punishing him. The owner offered him for sale in Richmond, a hundred miles to the east, with the endorsement that the man "would make a noble hand in a tobacco factory." In practice, the owner was no paternalist and was simply trying to get rid of a man who could not live up to his expectations. "In buying old slaves," he had counseled a friend in 1849, "we could afford a pretty good price if it was certain they would die as soon as past labor, but the possibility, nay probability of comfortably boarding a superannuated negro 10 to 30 years is appalling." Working them to death, he implied, was more cost effective. Railroad work might have accomplished that. In the meantime, it had offered a temporary way of disposing of the slave he had failed to master.[85]

As in commercial processing and water transportation, railroads held out the opportunity for slaves to earn cash and with it some economic power to defend their interests. Like tobacconists, railroad companies operating in urban areas wrung work from slaves with wages as well as with whips. As a practical matter of compelling bound laborers to operate the roads, companies paid slaves for overwork, giving them an incentive to labor at the brisk pace railroad schedules, directors, and creditors demanded. In the winter of 1845, for instance, the RFPRR paid Captain, Oliver, Carter, William, and Tony between thirty and forty cents for one week of overwork. That was on top of the eighty cents per week the Richmond depot workers received in boarding-out money, which shifted the burden of care from the company to the slaves themselves. Such allowances offered them an extra incentive to economize on food and shelter in the hopes of saving the difference. Oliver and Tony, as well as colleagues Moses, Warner Lindsey, and Roy, earned for themselves more than $50 each in 1845. The same year, twenty-eight enslaved men working on the RFPRR opted for cash payments instead of winter clothing. Twenty-six were paid $7.50 each and two received $9.00 each. Taking cash over clothes indicates that those men prized accumulating property over the risks of exposure and the disease and death resulting from such conditions.[86]

As railroad companies standardized hiring contracts with owners they regularized whether and when they would pay slaves for overwork. The latter was largely an informal set of arrangements, but paying enslaved workers was a way to minimize accidents and increase productivity. It could also discourage sabotage by forced laborers and break up serious plans for rebellion. Virginians recoiling from Gabriel's rebellion of 1800 or the Nat Turner revolt thirty-one years later might have found jarring the way corporations assembled large groups of adult male slaves and drove them to labor with sharp steel implements. But railroad directors were much better social psychologists than the would-be planter paternalists from whom they hired so many slaves. In 1855, directors of the Richmond and Danville Railroad asked the superintendant to "report to the Board from time to time, a list of the names of such hands as may be necessarily employed on extraordinary occasions, for its action, as to the amount that may be awarded to them as a donation for such services." By that time, hiring contractors and road engineers had long known the utility of industrial psychology in the form of offering wages for overwork. The apparent contradiction in paying a hiring fee to an owner and cash wages to his property highlights how market intensification was transforming upper South slavery into a system that simultaneously provided pliable labor to industry and gave bound laborers a stake in the outcomes.[87]

Despite dangers, railroads could work for slaves in more ways than one. An enterprising young G. W. Offley, who was in his mid-twenties, was sent to work on a Maryland railroad. Born enslaved on the Eastern Shore of Maryland in about 1808, he had already demonstrated an aptitude for business before the railroad arrived. He had "learned to make foot mats and horse collars, not of leather but of corn husks; also two kinds of brooms," he reported. "These articles I used to make nights and sell to get money for myself." At sixteen, he recalled, "I commenced taking contracts of wood-chopping, at fifty cents per

cord, and hired slaves to chop for me nights, when the moon shone bright."
Slaves' hiring other slaves was unusual but not unheard of. "We used to catch
oysters and fish nights," he remembered, "and hire other slaves to peddle
them out on Sunday mornings." The resulting networks were critical in permitting those people to maintain family ties. "By this way," Offley explained,
"I have helped some to get their freedom." In his late teens he learned to read,
and in his twenties he began to preach the Gospel. After his stint on the railroad, he then "taught boxing school, and learned to write." Offley did not record his impressions of his Maryland railroad camp in the early 1830s or who
his writing instructors were, but his descriptions of learning to box suggest
the aggressively masculine character of the work and culture. Offley's using
railroad camps as schools was not unique. James Hill, an enslaved man owned
by the Mississippi Central Railroad, "managed to learn the alphabet and the
use of figures" while working in the company's machine shop, much as Frederick Douglass learned the rudiments of writing in a Baltimore shipyard.[88]
Offley's entrepreneurial spirit assisted him well, since he quickly moved on to
managing a hotel in southwestern Delaware, where he traded food for math-
ematics lessons from hungry schoolchildren and from where he escaped to
Hartford, Connecticut, in 1835, on the Underground Railroad.[89]

Offley's was not the only counterstrategy. Railroads gave enslaved people
the opportunity to move about and gather information and in the process
make themselves more valuable to local owners otherwise potentially interested in selling them. An enslaved man from Gordonsville, Virginia, in his
early twenties had become familiar with the railroad. In the 1850s, he was
hired to work in a tobacco factory and traveled to and from that Piedmont
Virginia town along some sixty miles of track. His owner offered him to the
Virginia Central Railroad in the summer of 1861. The owner wrote that he
"would like to hire him to you on the Mail Train, as brakesman, or in any
capacity he may be [used] on that train. You can hire him for 10 per cent
less than you are paying for such hands," the owner added, if "you clothe
him of course. He is perfectly familiar with all the Road from Gordonsville to
Richmond, which I suppose is some recommendation."[90] If hired, the man
who had once been packed off to Richmond to process tobacco would help to
operate the same cars that took him there. If he had family in Gordonsville,
the man might be able to return with news from out of town, and if he had
friends or family in Richmond, he might visit them as well. Helping to operate the road, he would get the opportunity to earn wages, as did an unnamed

"office servant" working for the Orange and Alexandria Railroad in 1861, who received $9 at Christmas.[91]

Notwithstanding the risks they faced and costs they bore, enslaved people viewed railroad mobility strategically, including as a model for their own escape network. They named the safe houses operated to aid fugitive slaves the Underground Railroad and called its agents "conductors," so powerful were the experiences and images of enforced separation associated with the wood, coal, and iron version. The highly articulated terminology of the Underground Railroad became a great invisible parallel to the all-too-visible means by which enslaved people disappeared. Such clandestine networks were just one outcome of workers' discontents and the transportation technology on which they worked. The two sometimes worked in tandem, which is what happened with Washington, who fled from his owner in Taylorsville, Virginia, in 1835. The owner suspected that the twenty-five year-old man had "probably gotten free papers from some free negroes working on the Railroad" that allowed him to make it to a "free State." Had a hand like Offley counterfeited a document attesting to the man's freedom? "There are now a number of Rail-road hands travelling about," the owner contended, and such liberty of movement was unsettling.[92]

In the shadows of relentless modernization, some enslaved people rode the rails away from slavery, though they had to leave families behind in doing so. In 1838, twenty-year-old Frederick Douglass procured a pass from a free black sailor and boarded a train in Baltimore bound for Philadelphia. "The train was moving at a very high rate of speed for that time of railroad travel," Douglass recalled, "but to my anxious mind, it was moving far too slowly." Walter Hawkins would agree. Another enslaved man, he "was up and made for the depot" in his native Washington, D.C., "where he found crowds of people, both white and black, taking their tickets for Baltimore—the whites were being served first." He "stood aside until everyone had been served, and then he stepped boldly to the wicket door to get his, when he was saluted by the ticket-seller with 'Good-morning,' quite a coincidence, as blacks were always expected to salute first." On returning the greeting and requesting a ticket, the clerk asked, " 'Where are you going?' . . . in a short, sharp tone (as if to throw him off his guard), although very good-naturedly." Baltimore was the answer. The ticket agent failed to ask Hawkins to prove he was free, "but the quick reply," according to his biographer, "spoken in a confidential tone, brought the ticket, and Walter handed him the money." Boarding the cars, Hawkins, "took his seat in a dirty one, in which only Negroes were made to travel. Not many minutes after the train started off, having in the same compartment a few Negroes." In order to disguise himself and prevent someone from "more readily recognis[ing] that he was a runaway, or cross-question[ing] him in a manner that might lead him to betray himself, Hawkins played the fool" by pretending he was busy with trifles "until he arrived at Baltimore." Hawkins soon boarded another train for Wilmington, Delaware, and from there another one to Philadelphia, and so on, eventually reaching Canada.[93]

Despite the heroics of slaves such as Douglass or Hawkins, the modernity of slavery in the shape of railroads held little promise of freedom. The solitary souls who escaped on trains with false papers and furtive glances were but single spies compared with the battalions of others crowded in shanties or else packed on cars and taken to the land of cotton. The iron horse was no mystery to those who cut down forests to lay down rails, who cleared snow in winter, and who stoked the engine fires. Enslaved people, perhaps better than anyone else, knew its ramifications for their networks and the increased vulnerabilities it posed for family members.

Epilogue

etween the last decade of the eighteenth century and the onset of civil war, the coastal upper reaches of the southern United States became a slave market society. The ordeals of slaves' networking to protect family members from separation feature as chapters in that history, as the enslaved were put to work in diversified agriculture, processing, and transportation in places where their ancestors had chiefly cultivated tobacco. Enslaved watermen and sailors helped to integrate a national market by ferrying goods to market, while domestic workers toiled in kitchens and parlors and raised the next generation of children. The upper South became more economically diverse as some of the capital generated by selling slaves to distant owners was used to support the intensification of commercial activity. As consequent demand for consumer products rose, so did slaves' productivity, whether they were processing tobacco for a world market or constructing the ships that would take it there. The production and reproduction of African American families with deep roots had significant ramifications for the political economy. Enslaved families bore the costs of laborers sent to the cotton kingdom and those put to work refashioning the landscape nearer to home.

Those who hewed wood for ties and carried water for steam locomotives also bid farewell to their children, who traveled on those same conveyances as goods to market. The advancements in the market that the railroad made possible were embedded within a changing landscape of slavery as slaves who had once driven carts or hilled corn now fired the engines of the upper South's industrial future.

John and Lilly Baptist witnessed the landscape of that historical drama at key moments of its development. Both were born enslaved in Virginia, around 1777, and were still residing in Caroline County when Freedmen's Bureau agents arrived to legalize their marriage in 1866. But for the rare exception, marriages between slaves had no legal status. The Baptists had last been owned by Joseph A. Chandler, physician in his early thirties and owner of nineteen slaves in 1860. But Chandler did not own the Baptists' surviving children, Ellen, 49, Agnes, 45, and Judy, 47. In a time in which the average life expectancy for an American slave was just above thirty, even the Baptists' daughters had lived to be senior citizens.[1]

By the time the Freedmen's Bureau agents interviewed them, John and Lilly Baptist had seen generations brought up and bound away from their corner of the upper South. They were just fourteen when they married in 1791. George Washington was in his first term as president. When that marriage was recognized in law, Abraham Lincoln had already been assassinated. When they took their vows, no American had yet patented a profitable cotton gin or launched a steamboat south of the Potomac River. Florida and the Louisiana territory were claimed by Spain but firmly held by their indigenous owners. The lands that would become the cotton kingdom, from western Georgia to Alabama and Mississippi were owned by the Muskogee-Creeks, Cherokees, Chickasaws, and Choctaws. There were thirteen states then in the United States, and the ink on the Bill of Rights was not yet dry. By 1866, John and Lilly Baptist could look out over the country of their birth and recall generations of their enslaved neighbors carried off to distant lands—friends and kin they had laughed with, worshiped with, and loved—including generations of children who had first seen the sun rise over an old Tidewater landscape of tobacco and wheat and would see it set beneath the new landscape of cotton and sugar.

Since the founding of the federal republic, word had reached the Baptists of nearly every major event, and they had seen signs of corresponding changes in the land. They had been married nine years when Gabriel's rebellion was uncovered in Henrico County, forty miles to the south, and twelve years by the time of the Louisiana Purchase. John Baptist was then working as a farm laborer, and Lilly, born Lilly Timlie, likely toiled in the fields as well. During their prime working years, goods, people, and information moved no faster than the gallop of a horse or a ship at full sail. Like Charles Ball, John Baptist likely drove a wagon loaded with tobacco and corn to a ferry on a river like the Rappahannock or North Anna, which was how it got to market. The Baptists were each about twenty-eight years old when Ball was marched through their native county on his way to the Georgia cotton country, thirty-two when he was captured as a fugitive and lodged in nearby Bowling Green jail, and fifty-three when he was marched through Caroline County to Georgia a second time.

The war in which Ball took part in the meantime was officially about trade and sovereignty, but buried within the rhetoric of national honor was an overriding impulse to expand a slaveholding republic. After British ships disappeared from the Chesapeake, taking many black refugees, the coastal upper South was transformed in part through enslaved people's labors, which helped to integrate local economies through the transportation trades Moses Grandy and those like him had mastered. Following the War of 1812, the United States expanded farther to the west, and Americans conquered the tyranny of distance with canals, roads, and steam power. In doing so they connected the frontier economies of the Tennessee and Mississippi river valleys to their homelands on the Eastern Seaboard. The Baptists witnessed local citizens catch Alabama fever and depart. Many would return, but most white Americans discovered how interconnected their national economy had become during the aftermath of the panic of 1819, when credit froze, production slowed, and workers lost their jobs. Enslaved people had discovered national interconnections already, when they lost members of their families, such as those Francis E. Rives and his partners marched to Mississippi and Alabama the year before the panic. As the cotton kingdom expanded and the tide of commerce rose in ensuing years, its undertow became stronger for every enslaved family living near a port of the domestic slave trade. Those who owned John and Lilly Baptist participated in the new market economy when they bought manufactured clocks (assembled in Richmond) to keep time and manufactured cloth to make clothing. By the time the economy was booming again, in the early 1830s, slaves were becoming more expensive, too. That is when Ball's erstwhile owner appeared on his property as a living nightmare and took him back to Georgia in chains.[2]

Mrs. and Mr. Baptist celebrated forty years of marriage the year the Nat Turner rebellion erupted in southern Virginia, about 100 miles to the South. In the aftermath, panicked southerners sought reprisals and stripped African Americans of most of the few rights and liberties they had secured. In the five years that followed, on the dirt roads converging in Caroline County, from Washington, D.C., and southern Maryland, the Baptists saw more black bodies in chains than ever before, marched soul by soul, southward. They were on the eve of their forty-fifth wedding anniversary when Harriet Jacobs went into hiding in Edenton, 200 miles to the south, while Frederick Douglass worked in a Baltimore shipyard some 110 miles to the north. Their daughters Ellen and Judy were Douglass's age and may have been hired out as well. By the mid 1830s, railroad camps had sprung up in their neighborhood, likely employing relatives, and in the mornings the woods began to ring with hammers and buzz with saws, accompanied by the mournful work songs that ceased only when evening campfires were lit near the shanties. Soon after, coffles of slaves were seen less on roads and more on trains. The couple marked fifty-five years of marriage by the time the United States went to war with Mexico. By then, the Richmond, Fredericksburg, and Potomac Railroad had converted wooden to steel tracks, and Henry "Box" Brown was coming up with the money to pay a saddler to rent his wife and children by working late in a dusty Richmond tobacco factory. Along roads and tracks, men were hanging cables in the skies on poles, and before the decade was out the electromagnetic telegraph flashed communications from Richmond to St. Louis, New York, and Boston.[3]

The Baptists were married nearly sixty years when the United States passed the Fugitive Slave Act. Whatever their owners whispered about abolitionist conspiracies and northern agitation, the Baptists understood that defending slavery meant protecting the prerogatives of men like their owner Chandler to rob black children of mothers and fathers. During that decade their Port Royal neighbor George Fitzhugh won fame for his proslavery apologetics, which obscured the realities to which they had become inured. Thamar and Solomon Bayley had by then passed away and so had Moses Grandy and Charles Ball. But William H. Robinson and London R. Ferebee were still boys forming memories of their parents' dealings with slaveholders and beginning to understand the fragility of their families. In the Baptists' neighborhood, young black men and women, sons and daughters of those who went before, continued to disappear on the larger and more frequent trains. Some were sent south to work in Richmond. Many would not return. In that growing city, Corinna Hinton, Mary Lumpkin, and Ann Davis were forming alliances with slave traders.

In the year they turned eighty-two, after news of John Brown's raid in Harper's Ferry was wired through the electromagnetic telegraph and echoed through the slaves' grapevine version, the Baptists and their neighbors saw increasing unease among their white neighbors. Secession in Virginia and North Carolina soon followed the inauguration of a president whom whites castigated as (and blacks hoped was) an abolitionist. War soon swept into Virginia and hardships followed. Corpses of some young white men returned on the trains soon after that, and many of the Baptists' black neighbors struggled to reach the Union Army, which eventually marched into Caroline County in 1864. John Wilkes Booth was cornered and killed there the following year after assassinating a man who embodied the hesitancy many African Americans felt about the project of Civil War as well as the hopes they had for it.[4] When emancipation finally arrived, on the eve of their seventy-fifth anniversary year, the Baptists had lived in slavery for four score and eight years and had risen and slept every day slavery was sanctioned in Virginia under the federal Constitution.

As changes in the Baptists' homeland can merely suggest, the ordeals of those whose lives are represented here illuminate a history of market intensification and the growth of liberal political economies, which developed for reasons that neither Adam Smith anticipated nor Karl Marx articulated. The economic culture of those enslaved in the upper South was integral to the making of a diverse modern political economy, whose architects embraced invention and ingenuity even as they deployed slaves to shoulder the burdens of its construction, production, and maintenance. Enslaved people had an intensely personal stake in the process. The key to the modes of modernization that made the American South the most robust, dynamic, and profitable slave society in the hemisphere was the African American family. Simultaneously exceptionally strong and incredibly vulnerable, the enslaved family in all its forms was the secret, which even Marx did not discern, hidden at the heart of capitalist development that transformed the upper South into a slave market society, underwrote the agricultural revolutions in the lower South, and sustained the Industrial Revolution in Britain. The ability of enslaved families to reproduce and raise children enabled the living death of the cotton fields, which in turn gave mills in far-off Englands, Old and New, something to spin and weave. The profits of the domestic slave trade, plus the ingenuity of Afri-

can American upper South family members at finding ways and making compromises to save other family members from the slave market is what manned
and womaned and childrened and financed the revival of the coastal upper
South's economies. As their physical burdens mounted, the human costs multiplied. So did counterstrategies.[5]

The interpersonal dynamics surveyed here were markers of that process.
On a personal level, slaves' ordeals followed a similar pattern. Young people
were separated or threatened with separation, which gave rise to strategies
requiring them and their loved ones to reach out to others. Instead of forming a network composed solely of other slaves or within an African American
community, they reached out to those who held the most efficacious means
of preventing further separations or victimization, including slaveholders and
slave traders. That was an irony of the deep contingency of southern history: the commercial redevelopment in which enslaved people took active
part gave some among the enslaved resources that they could exchange for
assistance, and the resulting constellation of bonds refashioned the world of
the enslaved, of slaveholders, and of everyone else. Over time, those arrangements cut through corporate interests and solidarity based on slave status or
racial categorizations. Enslaved networkers also sought nonhuman resources
such as information and cash, which complicates a theory of networks based
on affinal ties or construed solely in terms of interpersonal bonds. Through
the way the enslaved cultivated them, networks exposed contradictions between the dominant familial ideology of nineteenth-century America and the
idols of the marketplace.

Through its ability to interconnect market actors and cast axes of difference as opportunities for alliance, networking also tended to work against
slave rebellions. Following slave uprisings that were arguably pivotal events
in the lives of enslaved people, such as Gabriel's rebellion in 1800, Sancho's
rebellion in 1802, the British invasion of the Chesapeake in 1813–14, and the
Vesey conspiracy in South Carolina in 1822, panicked citizens demanded and
received increased legal protections for their enslaved property. Manumissions became more difficult to procure, whites intensified antiblack violence,
and slave patrols multiplied. Even so, enslaved people like Bayley, Ball, and
Grandy continued to move about their local landscapes, fishing and farming
and even managing other slaves, often out of sight of owners. They did so because they won the confidence of local whites. Following the dissemination of
David Walker's *Appeal* in 1830 and the Nat Turner rebellion of 1831, citizens

of Virginia, North Carolina, and Maryland demanded that greater restrictions be placed on African Americans' movement, independent commerce, literacy, and assembly. They worked to outlaw many forms of associations on which networkers depended. Especially near the border of southeastern Virginia and northeastern North Carolina, white violence against would-be insurrectionists became frenzied. And yet local ties bound together people who looked beyond racial or legal designations of slavery.[6] In Edenton, face-to-face associations among slaves, free people of color, and whites risked white reprisal to help to protect Harriet Jacobs. So long as Douglass brought home cash for his owners, he could roam the streets and ply the shipyards of Baltimore, despite having led an escape attempt and having been called "another Nat Turner" by his captors. Whites terrified of uprisings somehow tolerated slaves working in urban factories buying their own shelter and food and managing their own time outside of work. Following the enactment of the Fugitive Slave Act of 1850, citizens who demanded sweeping federal measures to return slaves who had slipped their chains nevertheless tolerated slave hiring fairs at Christmastime in which enslaved people congregated en masse in Richmond to interview prospective employers. They left it to the architects of the Underground Railroad to construct tracks, staff depots, and ride the rails of the coal and iron version. Fifty years after a skilled, self-hired blacksmith organized a rebellion designed to bring a bloody end to slavery in Virginia, entire camps of military-aged black men sharpened axes, manned saws, and wielded picks, not to the beat of a revolutionary drummer but to the demands of the clock and the commands of a corporation. Cash incentives often worked hand in glove with slaves' networking, which illustrates the unintended consequences of an intensifying market economy. The tenuous possibility of protecting loved ones in that environment tended to make Grandys rather than Gabriels.[7]

Slaveholders talked the game of mastery, whether domination or paternalism, but in the end they were swayed by money. That could lead an enslaved person either to or away from the auction block, and the way it turned out depended on how the cards fell and how one played them. Some of the enslaved, like Bayley, Grandy, and Douglass, hired themselves out, negotiating directly with employers. Ball was able to evade an owner for twenty-one years while he made a life and raised families in southern Maryland. But slaveholders still held most of the winning hands. Owners broke upon slaves' arrangements with violence, often to sell them or their relatives, but the enslaved were not psychologically captivated by them. Enslavers appeared more often as consummately ingenious thieves of their earnings and kidnappers of their children than as protectors. Enslaved people's economic culture was born of experience, not of the scripts that would-be domesticators and ameliorators fashioned largely for themselves. Some slaves like Brown who worked close by an owner nevertheless shouldered the responsibility of buying their own lodging and food, responsibilities they seized as often as were given. The enslaved never conceded the legitimacy of the slave market, even if they spoke the words enslavers wanted to hear. Slave traders peddled a paternalist fantasy that "threatened to collapse at any moment beneath the weight of its own absurdity," while commercial processors wrung more work with wages than with whips. Railroad hiring sent paternalism off the rails since railroaders worked under the supervision of corporations whose overseers had little interest in policing slaves' moral lives and whose labor camps resembled military regiments.[8]

Slaveholders bragged about domesticating an institution they were instead commercializing, but in the process they fashioned an ideology of emotion and sentiment that the enslaved used strategically. The advantages that accrued to enslaved people in domestic service came from emotional appeals that made shrewd use of paternalists' scripts as steps toward building an effective network of protection. That Corinna Hinton, Mary Lumpkin, and Ann Davis were just blocks from the tobacco factory in which Henry "Box" Brown worked also suggests how variable slavery was over the terrain of one city. The different outcomes of their strategies show how protean and fragile both were. Harriet Jacobs's struggles with an owner in Edenton took place in close proximity to where African American mariners not unlike Abel Ferebee worked out of sight of owners for months or years at a time.[9]

Networking and the economic culture to which it gave rise recasts "slave culture" as a historical process rather than as a reshuffling of ancestral legacies. However, the wisdom of ancestors subjected to the Middle Passage survived the journey and was passed down through the generations. African Americans' strategies of gathering wealth in people resembled their African ancestors' core strategy of assembling people within a family idiom of politics. Even if the strategies adopted by African Americans were not a direct consequence of African strategies, the resemblance is striking. For many precolonial African societies, wealth was understood in terms of the productive, reproductive, and security potential that an extended kinship network offered. Even in some of the most intensive slaving polities, such as Dahomey, political leaders incorporated kinship lineages into the ruling line and distributed resources, promising security to allies, clients, and subjects. The classic African strategy in response to intensified slaving was to use the same process of incorporation defensively. In those contexts, slaves were those cut off from lineages and the political organizations they constituted. In a similar register, enslaved Americans practiced a politics of families, neighborhoods, and localities. Networking reconfigured an African strategy of incorporating strangers and even enemies within a family in a very American way; enslaved networkers did not limit ties to other slaves or African Americans. Put another way, the market made strange bedfellows, and slaves' constellations of ties in turn connected their local strategies to the political economy of the nation. Ball's strategies reveal a political consciousness that went well beyond concern for his personal freedom or immediate family as he talked and politicked his way across the southern landscape. Resulting networks reveal more than maps of connections among members of a family, neighborhood, or "community" resisting slavery. Slaves like Ball insisted that citizens recognize their status, as the market for their skills and the goods they produced already did.[10]

Within a hierarchy of values, the enslaved chose family over freedom. Thamar and Solomon Bayley departed for Liberia only after their children had passed away. Charles Ball ran away from Georgia twice and twice sought return to his family in Maryland. Grandy initially returned to his family in North Carolina following manumission, leaving only when the state imposed severe restrictions on free people of color. Peter Robinson returned from California twice to pay his owner installments on his freedom and to see his family. He might have sought passage to St. Catharine's, Ontario, rather than San Francisco. Robinson's son raced back to the Richmond slave trader who had sold him in search of his mother. Harriet Jacobs spent seven years secreted in an attic, watching her children through a small hole until their departure removed the reason for her confinement. Railroad workers sung of the road as a conveyance that carried one away from family. Henry "Box" Brown stayed in Richmond, worked overtime, and emptied his pockets into the hands of his wife's owner until he sold them away. Only then did he hide in a shipping crate and ride the rails to freedom. Some of his enslaved female neighbors turned the tables on their owners by using market identities slavers imposed, "fancy maids," to form domestic relationships instead. Frederick Douglass escaped slavery with plans to reunite with his fiancée after so many members of his family had been sold off and scattered. Family ties were at the center of all of those calculations.

But enslaved Americans faced distinctive challenges conditioned by local possibilities and operated within a severe set of constraints. Bayley did not choose the Methodist Church from among a variety of options for his strategy, any more than Peter Robinson decided that operating a steam tugboat, as opposed to ironwork, would lend him the best chance of keeping his family together. They used the tools in that environment, which illustrates why their local circumstances and the contingencies of historical time and geographic place were critical to their outcomes. They operated within and not against the distinctive political economy of the nineteenth-century upper South. Having agreed to pay for his wife's manumission, Bayley cast about his Delmarva Peninsula for opportunities to earn cash in the first decade of the nineteenth century. Fifty years later, facing a similar prospect, Robinson journeyed thousands of miles to the state of California to raise funds. As some doors closed, others opened. After 1831, Virginians and North Carolinians sought to limit, if not curtail, the type of unsupervised mobility that had allowed slaves like Grandy to ply riverine trades, yet about the time, railroad camps sprung up in which slaves like G. W. Offley could organize his reading and writing lessons. At the same time, perils for the enslaved increased as the market expanded for their children. Railroad hiring was punishing work, to which was added the terror of being employed on the very conveyances that spirited off loved ones.

Slavery ended where it began, and it ended with strategies slaves had honed for generations. The institution that has been historically dated to 1619 when a starving ship's crew sold about twenty Africans at Point Comfort, Virginia, began to unravel in earnest 242 years later at Fort Monroe, situated on the same James River peninsula, when formerly enslaved African Americans presented themselves to the Union army as soldiers of emancipation. In the last half century of slavery in what was by 1861 North America's oldest reproducing slave society, the strategies enslaved people used to keep their families together highlight the commercial centrifuge in which they increasingly found themselves. The enslaved African American residents of Hampton, Virginia, who raced to the Union lines in 1861, and were designated "contraband"

of war, were not fleeing a pre- or antimodern institution held together by the cultural hegemony of would-be planter paternalists. The modernity of slavery was nearly indistinguishable from broader developments in the political economy, including an intensifying market, technological advancement, and increasing economic diversification along with its corollary individual specialization. Some of the first enslaved refugees, like George Scott and William Roscoe Davis, had a broad knowledge of the market and social geography of their corner of the Chesapeake. Scott had fled his owner some years earlier, abetted by both free and enslaved residents of his native Elizabeth City County. He too cultivated a network that reached across color and class lines. Scott had hired himself to white employers and thwarted his owner's repeated attempts to capture him, at one point even confiscating a pistol and bowie knife from the owner in a scuffle. When the Union Army marched down the Virginia Peninsula, Scott became a scout, "a job for which he was well equipped." Roscoe Davis had also cultivated a network of allies. Like Rosy Robinson, his mother was taken from Madagascar, smuggled illegally into Virginia in the 1830s. Raped by a white sailor on the Middle Passage, she gave birth while enslaved in Norfolk. Davis, a first-generation American slave, nevertheless learned to read, write, and eventually preach. Before the war, he was hiring his own time at Old Point Comfort, piloting a pleasure boat in Hampton Roads. The married father of seven was working to win his wife's freedom and secure his own when Virginia secession and the appearance of federal troops settled the issue. Scott and Davis, two of postemancipation Hampton's African American leaders, needed little preparation for the vicissitudes of life after slavery.[11]

John Washington, too, needed little prodding and gathered information that would make him a military asset to the United States even before soldiers arrived in his backyard. He was born in Virginia in 1838. "My first great Sorrow," he wrote, "was caused by seeing one Morning, a number of the 'Plantation Hands,' formed into line, with little Bundles Straped to their backs, Men, Women and children. and all Marched off to be Sold South, away from all that was near and dear to them, Parents, Wives husbands and children; all Separated one from another, perhaps never to meet again on Earth." When he was old enough to learn a trade, his owner separated him from his mother, who remained in Staunton while Washington was sent to Fredericksburg, some one hundred miles to the east, by rail. There he worshiped in the African Baptist Church on Sophia Street, met his future wife, Annie E. Gordon, and was put to work in a factory where he "learned the art of preparing Tobacco for the mill," sometimes earning for himself "$3.00 or 4 extra a week" from overwork. He was tending bar and comanaging the Shakespeare Hotel when the Union Army arrived in April 1862. Unlike those who invaded the Chesapeake some fifty years before, the soldiers who arrived now were countrymen. At breakfast on Good Friday, a Confederate cavalryman burst into the eating saloon warning that the "Yankees" were in nearby Falmouth. Reports of cannon fire punctuated the warning, and Washington recalled that the panicked hotel owner "hurried to his room now came rushing back called me out in the Hall and thrust a roll of Bank notes in my hand and hurriedly told me to pay off all the Servants, and Shut up the house and take charge of every thing," adding "if the Yankees catch Me they will kill me." He had warned Washington that the invaders would "send me to Cuba or cut my hands off or otherwise Maltreat Me." After giving a slave the keys to his hotel, the man then took "off at full speed like the Wind. In less time than it takes me to Write these lines," Washington recalled, "every White Man was out the house. Every Man Servant was out on the house top looking over the River at the Yankees for their glistening bayonets could easily be Seen[.] I could not begin to Express My New born hopes for I felt already like I was certain of my freedom now."[12]

That day, Washington entered the Union lines along with other African Americans, only he had something of immediate value besides his willingness to work. A "large crowd of the Soldiers," he recalled, "gathered around us and asked us all kinds of questions in reference to the Whereabouts of the 'Rebels'[.] I had stuffed my pockets full of Rebel Newspapers and, I distributed them around as far as they would go greatly to the delight of the Men, and by this act Won their good opinions right away." Having immediately demonstrated his utility to the invading army, he assured them that he was "most happy to See them all" and that he "had been looking for them a long time." "All of them seemed to [be] utterly astonished," he recalled. He joined them, working as a scout and cook until he could get his pregnant wife, along with her relatives, to Washington, D.C., and safety. They settled in the nation's capital.[13]

Acknowledgments

his book benefited from an exceptional network. Edward L. Ayers supervised the dissertation from which it developed, emphasizing broad interconnections and the deep roots of historical causation. Though I grew up in a southern place with a slave past, it was not until his colloquium on the nineteenth-century South at the University of Virginia that I learned that the South has an important and distinctive history that transcends region, nation, and hemisphere. His guidance gave vague ideas conceptual coherence and gave wings to my historical imagination. Joseph C. Miller challenged me to examine closely the incremental changes, working misunderstandings, and human strategies—and tragedies—that characterize modern African and Atlantic history. His prompting me to ask questions of American history formulated by Africanists is largely responsible for the book's perspective. Peter S. Onuf guided my understanding of the political economy and intellectual history of British North America and the early United States, always with an eye toward the complex interplay of interests, inheritances, and ideas.

At the National Museum of American History, where a predoctoral fellowship provided the support to launch this project, Pete Daniel and Fath Davis Ruffins offered me pivotal guidance at early stages by encouraging sustained treatment of the conditions under which the enslaved worked and to rethink conventional categories of African American history. This book benefits from two informal mentors as well. Susan E. O'Donovan's consistently insightful suggestions helped to bring critical parts of United States slavery into clear focus. William W. Freehling's encouragement to explore narratives in history and think more critically about causation textures the way I frame historical issues. Cathy Matson and Edward E. Baptist were outstanding guides in the process of making a dissertation into a book and helped to refine and develop important themes. Both read the manuscript for the press and offered invaluable criticism and advice, and together with Bob Brugger they were critical in cutting the weight while increasing the analytical heft of this project. M. J. Devaney gave the final draft a thorough reading and, in addition to making invaluable suggestions regarding meaning and emphasis, saved me from many embarrassing mistakes. The remaining errors are solely my responsibility.

At professional conferences, James F. Brooks, James Bryant, David J. Coles, Melvin Patrick Ely, Steve Deyle, Wayne K. Durrill, Rebecca Fraser, Richard Follett, Ben Marsh, Aaron W. Marrs, James David Miller, Josh Rothman, John Stauffer, Michael Tadman, Brent Tarter, William G. Thomas III, and Peter Wallenstein kindly gave their time and support. Ben Schiller has been a great interlocutor and intellectual provocateur. Other scholars who helped this project along through their kind and helpful correspondence include Michael Chesson, Walter Johnson, Philip J. Schwarz, Leni Sorensen, and Loren Schweninger. Bonnie Martin read and offered feedback on drafts of early chapters, and Phil Troutman has been a true guide through trials of writing and presenting this work, generously sharing much of his own research materials in the process.

I owe many debts to those without whose help and support at the University of Virginia this project would not have been as feasible—or fun. I would like to thank Cindy Aron, Grace Hale, Michael Holt, Heather Warren, Charles McCurdy, Olivier Zunz, Gary W. Gallagher, Brian Balogh, Joseph F. Kett, and Patrick Griffin and fellow students Cheryl Collins, Christa Dierksheide, Martin Ohman, George Van Cleve, Billy Wayson, Brian Murphy, Erik Alexander, David Bridges, Lisa Goff, Bob Jackson, Sarah Maxwell, Vanessa May, Jaime Martinez, Amanda Mushal, Scott Nesbit, Cynthia Nicoletti, Victoria Meyer, Sarah Silkey, Andrew Torget, and Andrew Witmer. I owe Dylan C. Penningroth a special debt for his forbearance in supervising my first attempt at graduate work in history and for critical guidance on aspects of this project. At Arizona State University, I would like to thank all those who have made Tempe a wonderful place to teach, think, research, and write.

Networks involve a complex interplay between human and material resources. This book was no exception. In addition to a Smithsonian Institution predoctoral fellowship, this research was made possible by financial support from the Gilder Lehrman Institute of American History, the Fletcher Jones Foundation at the Huntington Library, and the Joel Williamson Visiting Scholar program at the Southern Historical Collection, University of North Carolina, Chapel Hill. I have also received support from the Virginia Historical Society's Mellon Fellows program, a John Hope Franklin Research Grant from Duke University, a Southern Fund Research Fellowship from the Southern Seminar at the University of Virginia, a Summer Research Travel Grant from the Corcoran Department of History, and two Robert J. Huskey Conference Travel Awards from the University of Virginia. Generous research funds from Arizona State University and a reduction in teaching, thanks to Mark Von Hagen, sped this book to completion. Laura Clark Brown at the Wilson Library of UNC, Chapel Hill, Eleanor A. Mills at the Perkins Library of Duke University, and the outstanding faculty and staff at the Virginia Historical Society, including Nelson Lankford, John McClure, Paige Newman, Frances Pollard, Jeffrey Ruggles, E. Lee Sheppard, and Katherine Wilkins helped the research considerably. I would also like to thank Tony Kent of the Central Rappahannock Heritage Center for his kind help as well.

My family and friends sponsored this project at all stages. For their love and support, I owe a tremendous debt to parents Pat and Roger, who not only sustained my interest in American history from a young age but who also supported that interest through many years of college education and graduate training. Brother Eric and sister-in-law Tiffany have always been enthusiastic about this project, and they opened their home when I visited Washington, D.C., to do research. Ronnie Broadfoot and Nell Carlson graciously welcomed me back to their home on succeeding summer research trips to Boston. Finally, my wife, Margaret, has been a wonderful and loving partner and champion of this project. She and our daughter, Marion, are why I do history.

Notes

Abbreviations

AA	Archive of Americana, Readex
AAS	American Antiquarian Society, Worcester, MA
CRHC	Central Rappahannock Heritage Center, Fredericksburg, VA
DU	Duke University, Durham, NC
HBS	Harvard Business School, Cambridge, MA
HL	Huntington Library, San Marino, CA
LC	Library of Congress, Washington, DC
LVA	Library of Virginia, Richmond
MSA	Maryland State Archives, Annapolis
UNC	University of North Carolina, Chapel Hill
UVA	University of Virginia, Charlottesville
VHS	Virginia Historical Society, Richmond
YU	Manuscripts and Archives, Yale University Library, New Haven, CT

Prologue

1. Historical Census Browser, Geospatial and Statistical Data Center, University of Virginia Library, http://mapserver.lib.virginia.edu, accessed June 1, 2010; Brian Schoen, *The Fragile Fabric of Union: Cotton, Federal Politics, and the Global Origins of the Civil War* (Baltimore: Johns Hopkins University Press, 2009); William E. Weeks, *Building the Continental Empire: American Expansion from the Revolution to the Civil War* (Chicago: Ivan R. Dee, 1996), chaps. 3 and 4; Bradford Perkins, *The Creation of the Republican Empire, 1776–1865* (Cambridge: Cambridge University Press, 1993), chaps. 6 and 8; Daniel Walker Howe, *What Hath God Wrought: The Transformation of America, 1815–1848* (New York: Oxford University Press, 2007), 468 passim. The coastal upper South comprised the Tidewater region of Virginia, the Coastal Plain of North Carolina, Maryland east of the Piedmont, and Delaware. Virginia counties included Accomac (now Accomack), Arlington (and the city of Alexandria), Caroline, Charles City, Chesterfield, Dinwiddie (and the city of Petersburg), Elizabeth City, Essex, Fairfax, Gloucester, Hanover, Henrico (and city of Richmond), Isle of Wight, James City (and the city of Williamsburg), King and Queen, King George, King William, Lancaster, Mathews, Middlesex, Nansemond, New Kent, Norfolk (and the city of Norfolk), Northampton, Northumberland, Prince George, Prince William, Princess Anne, Richmond, Southampton, Spotsylvania, Stafford, Surry, Sussex, Warwick, Westmoreland, and York; Maryland counties included Anne Arundel, Baltimore (and Baltimore city), Calvert, Caroline, Cecil, Charles, Dorchester, Harford,

Howard, Kent, Montgomery, Prince George's, Queen Anne's, Somerset, Saint Mary's, Talbot, and Worcester; and Delaware counties included Kent, New Castle, and Sussex. Eastern North Carolina counties included Beaufort, Bertie, Bladen, Brunswick, Camden, Carteret, Chowan, Columbus, Craven, Currituck, Dauplin, Edgecombe, Gates, Greene, Hertford, Hyde, Jones, Lenoir, Martin, New Hanover, Onslow, Pasquotank, Perquimans, Pitt, Sampson, Tyrrell, Washington, and Wayne.

2. Karen Ordahl Kupperman, *The Jamestown Project* (Cambridge, MA: Harvard University Press, 2007).

3. Claudia Dale Goldin, *Urban Slavery in the American South, 1820–1860: A Quantitative History* (Chicago: University of Chicago Press, 1976); Richard C. Wade, *Slavery in the Cities: The South, 1820–1860* (New York: Oxford University Press, 1964); John W. Blassingame, *The Slave Community: Plantation Life in the Antebellum South* (New York: Oxford University Press, 1972); Frederick Douglass, *Narrative of the Life of Frederick Douglass, an American Slave, Written by Himself* (Boston: Anti-Slavery Office, 1845); Moses Grandy, *Narrative of the Life of Moses Grandy, Late a Slave in the United States of America* (London: Gilpin, 1843), http://docsouth.unc.edu/fpn/grandy/grandy.html, accessed June 1, 2010; Charles Ball, *Slavery in the United States: A Narrative of the Life and Adventures of Charles Ball, a Black Man, Who Lived Forty Years in Maryland, South Carolina and Georgia, as a Slave under Various Masters, and Was One Year in the Navy with Commodore Barney, during the Late War* (New York: John S. Taylor, 1837), http://docsouth.unc.edu/neh/ballslavery/ball.html, accessed June 1, 2010; Henry Box Brown, *Narrative of the Life of Henry Box Brown, Written by Himself* (Manchester, UK: Lee and Glynn, 1851), http://docsouth.unc.edu/neh/brownbox/brownbox.html, accessed June 1, 2010; Fannie Berry to Susie R. C. Byrd, February 26, 1937, in Charles L. Perdue Jr., Thomas E. Barden, and Robert K. Phillips, eds., *Weevils in the Wheat: Interviews with Virginia Ex-Slaves* (Charlottesville: University Press of Virginia, 1976), 30–50.

4. Marie Jenkins Schwartz, *Born in Bondage, Growing up Enslaved in the Antebellum South* (Cambridge, MA: Harvard University Press, 2000), 5 passim; Aliyyah I. Abdur-Rahman, "'The Strangest Freaks of Despotism': Queer Sexuality in Antebellum African American Slave Narratives," *African American Review* 40.2 (2006): 223–37; Brenda E. Stevenson, *Life in Black and White: Family and Community in the Slave South* (New York: Oxford University Press, 1996), 159–61, 208–26, 250–56; Wilma Dunaway, *The African-American Family in Slavery and Emancipation* (Cambridge: Cambridge University Press, 2003), 284–87. I do intend to use the term "family" or else investigate the contents of formerly enslaved people's narratives within an exclusively heterosexual or nuclear set of normative constructions.

5. Jedidiah Morse, *The American Universal Geography; or, A View of the Present State of All the Kingdoms, States, and Colonies in the Known World* (Boston: Lincoln and Edmands, 1819), 571, cited in H. Clay Reed, *Delaware: A History of the First State* (New York: Lewis Historical Publishing Company, 1947), 374; Federal Writers' Project, *Delaware: A Guide to the First State* (New York: Viking Press, 1938), 8; William H. Williams, *Slavery and Freedom in Delaware, 1639–1865* (Wilmington, DE: Scholarly Imprint Resources, 1996), 52–57.

6. Federal Writers' Project, *Maryland: A Guide to the Old Line State* (New York: Oxford University Press, 1940), 13–14.

7. Frederick Douglass, *My Bondage and My Freedom* (New York: Miller, Orton, and Mulligan, 1855), 46–47.

8. Douglass, *Narrative of the Life of Frederick Douglass*, 64.

9. Douglass, *My Bondage and My Freedom*, 34.

10. Alice Jane Lippson and Robert L. Lippson, *Life in the Chesapeake Bay*, 3rd ed. (Baltimore: Johns Hopkins University Press, 2006), 4; James A. Michener, *Chesapeake* (New York: Random House, 1978), 742–44.

11. Federal Writer's Project, *Virginia: A Guide to the Old Dominion* (New York: Oxford University Press, 1956), 10–12, 19; Crandall Shifflett, ed., *John Washington's Civil War: A Slave Narrative* (Baton Rouge: Louisiana State University Press, 2008), xix–xx.

12. Henry Goings, *Rambles of a Runaway from Southern Slavery* (Stratford, Ontario: J. M. Robb, 1869), 9.

13. Harriet Beecher Stowe, *Dred: A Tale of the Great Dismal Swamp*, vol. 2 (Boston: Phillips, Sampson, 1856), 303.

14. Federal Writers' Project, *North Carolina: A Guide to the Old North State* (Chapel Hill: University of North Carolina Press, 1939), 9.

15. William L. Saunders, ed., *The Colonial Records of North Carolina*, 10 vols. (Raleigh: P. M. Hale, 1886–90), 4:443, cited in Alan D. Watson, *Wilmington, North Carolina, to 1861* (Jefferson, NC: McFarland, 2003), 35.

16. Watson, *Wilmington,* 35.

17. David Cecelski, *The Waterman's Song: Slavery and Freedom in Maritime North Carolina* (Chapel Hill: University of North Carolina Press, 2001).

18. Michael Kammen, ed., "Maryland in 1699: A Letter from the Reverend Hugh Jones," *Journal of Southern History* 29.3 (1963): 367–69; Lorena S. Walsh, "Slave Life, Slave Society, and Tobacco Production in the Tidewater Chesapeake," in *Cultivation and Culture: Labor and the Shaping of Slave Life in the Americas*, ed. Ira Berlin and Philip D. Morgan (Charlottesville: University Press of Virginia, 1993), 170–99.

19. Ebeneezer Cook, *The Sot-Weed Factor; or, A Voyage to Maryland* (London: D. Bragg, 1708).

20. Marvin L. Kay and Lorin Lee Cary, *Slavery in North Carolina, 1748–1775* (Chapel Hill: University of North Carolina Press, 1995), 161, 26 passim; Wayne K. Durrill, "Slavery, Kinship, and Dominance: The Black Community at Somerset Place Plantation, 1786–1860," *Slavery and Abolition* 13.2 (1992): 15–16.

21. Lorena S. Walsh, "The Chesapeake Slave Trade: Regional Patterns, African Origins, and Some Implications," *William and Mary Quarterly*, 3rd ser., 58.1 (2001): 139–70; G. Ugo Nwokeji, "African Conceptions of Gender and the Slave Traffic," *William and Mary Quarterly*, 3rd ser., 58.1 (2001): 47–68; Rebecca A. Goetz, "Lurking Indians, Outlying Negroes, and Christian English: Religion and the Construction of Race in the Seventeenth-Century Chesapeake" (PhD diss., Harvard University, 2006); Claude Meillassoux, "The Role of Slavery in the Economic and Social History of Sahelo-Sudanic Africa," in *Forced Migration: The Impact of the Export Slave Trade on African Societies*, ed. J. E. Inikori (London: Hutchinson University Library, 1982), 74–99; Claire C. Robertson and Martin A. Klein, "Women's Importance in African Slave Systems," in *Women and Slavery in Africa*, ed. Claire C. Robertson and Martin A. Klein (Portsmouth, NH: Heinemann, 1997), 3–28; Claude Meillassoux, "Female Slavery," in *Women and Slavery in Africa*, 49–66; John Thornton, *Africa and Africans in the Making of the Atlantic World, 1400–1800*, 2nd ed. (New York: Cambridge University Press, 1998); Suzanne Miers and Igor Kopytoff, "African 'Slavery' as an Institution of Marginality," in *Slavery in Africa: Historical and Anthropological Perspectives*, ed. Suzanne Miers and Igor Kopytoff (Madi-

son: University of Wisconsin Press, 1977), 3–81; William S. McFeely, *Frederick Douglass* (New York: Norton, 1991), chap. 1.

22. Dickson J. Preston, *Young Frederick Douglass: The Maryland Years* (Baltimore: Johns Hopkins University Press, 1980), 3–7; McFeely, *Frederick Douglass*, 5; Douglass, *My Bondage and My Freedom*, 76; Allan Kulikoff, *Tobacco and Slaves: The Development of Southern Cultures in the Chesapeake, 1680–1800* (Chapel Hill: published for the Institute of Early American History and Culture by the University of North Carolina Press, 1986), 352–80.

23. Adam Rothman, *Slave Country: American Expansion and the Origins of the Deep South* (Cambridge, MA: Harvard University Press, 2005), 3; Philip D. Morgan, *Slave Counterpoint: Black Culture in the Eighteenth-Century Chesapeake and Lowcountry* (Chapel Hill: University of North Carolina Press, 1998), 79–95; Lorena Walsh, "Slave Life, Slave Society," 170–99; Kulikoff, *Tobacco and Slaves*; Jennifer L. Morgan, *Laboring Women: Reproduction and Gender in New World Slavery* (Philadelphia: University of Pennsylvania Press, 2004).

24. Edmund S. Morgan, *American Slavery, American Freedom: The Ordeal of Colonial Virginia* (New York: Norton, 1975); Anthony S. Parent Jr., *Foul Means: The Formation of a Slave Society in Virginia, 1660–1740* (Chapel Hill: published for the Omohundro Institute of Early American History and Culture by the University of North Carolina Press, 2003); Kulikoff, *Tobacco and Slaves*, 421; Joyce Appleby, "Thomas Jefferson and the Psychology of Democracy," in *The Revolution of 1800: Democracy, Race, and the New Republic*, ed. James J. Horn, Jan Ellen Lewis, and Peter S. Onuf (Charlottesville: University of Virginia Press, 2002), 155–72.

25. Eva Sheppard Wolf, *Race and Liberty in the New Nation: Emancipation in Virginia from the Revolution to Nat Turner's Rebellion* (Baton Rouge: Louisiana State University Press, 2006); Jessica Millward, "'A Choice Parcel of Country Born': Slave Women and the Transition to Freedom in Revolutionary Maryland" (PhD diss., University of California, Los Angeles, 2003); James Pemberton to Robert Pleasants, August 25, 1790, folder 3, Pleasants Family Papers, mss BR 12–15, Robert Alonzo Brock Collection, HL; Thomas Pleasants, manumissions, November 9, 1781, July 4, 1781, folder 3, Pleasants Family Papers, mss BR 12–15, Robert Alonzo Brock Collection, HL; receipt, advertisement, January 31, 1800, folder 3, Pleasants Family Papers, mss BR 12–15; receipt, sale, January 19, 1821, folder 3, Pleasants Family Papers, mss BR 12–15; David Brion Davis, *Inhuman Bondage: The Rise and Fall of Slavery in the New World* (New York: Oxford University Press, 2006), 226. Receipts survive for the hire of slaves Frank, Sanders, and Sal to Robert Pleasants by their owner Samuel Pleasants in 1772 and 1773; Samuel Pleasants of Philadelphia manumitted some slaves as well, in 1776 (folder 3, Pleasants Family Papers, mss BR 12–15, Robert Alonzo Brock Collection, HL).

26. *Fredericksburg (VA) News*, November 27, 1849; Timothy C. Jacobson and George David Smith, *Cotton's Renaissance: A Study in Market Innovation* (Cambridge: Cambridge University Press, 2001), 55; Dale Tomich and Edward E. Baptist, "A New Census of the Internal Slave Trade: Natchez, Mississippi, 1825–1829," paper presented at the Charting New Courses in the History of Slavery and Emancipation Conference, Long Beach, MS, March 3–6, 2010.

27. Ira Berlin, *Generations of Captivity: A History of African American Slaves* (Cambridge, MA: Harvard University Press, 2003), 161.

28. Thelma Jennings, "'Us Colored Women Had to Go Through A Plenty': Sexual Exploitation of African-American Slave Women," *Journal of Women's History* 1.3 (1990):

45–74; John Brown, *Slave Life in Georgia: A Narrative of the Life, Sufferings, and Escape of John Brown, a Fugitive Slave, Now in England* (London: W. M. Watts, 1855), 2, http://docsouth.unc.edu/neh/jbrown/jbrown.html, accessed June 1, 2010.

29. Walter Johnson, *River of Dark Dreams: Slavery, Capitalism, and Imperialism in the Mississippi Valley's Cotton Kingdom* (Cambridge, MA: Harvard University Press, forthcoming); George M. Fredrickson, *The Black Image in the White Mind: The Debate on Afro-American Character and Destiny, 1817–1914* (New York: Harper and Row, 1971).

30. Phillip D. Troutman, "Slave Trade and Sentiment" (PhD diss., University of Virginia, 2000), app. A, 415–29; Robert H. Gudmestad, *A Troublesome Commerce: The Transformation of the Interstate Slave Trade* (Baton Rouge: Louisiana State University Press, 2003), 17–20; Michael Tadman, *Speculators and Slaves: Masters, Traders, and Slaves in the Old South* (Madison: University of Wisconsin Press, 1996); Steven Deyle, *Carry Me Back: The Domestic Slave Trade in American Life* (New York: Oxford University Press, 2005). Roughly two-thirds of enslaved people's forced migration in the domestic slave trade came at the hands of slave traders.

31. Douglass, *My Bondage and My Freedom*, 69.

32. Troutman, "Slave Trade and Sentiment," app. A, 415–19; Ira Berlin, *Slaves without Masters: The Free Negro in the Antebellum South* (New York: Pantheon, 1974), 29–34, 138–43; Barbara Jeanne Fields, *Slavery and Freedom on the Middle Ground: Maryland in the Nineteenth Century* (New Haven: Yale University Press, 1985), 15–16, 78–84; William W. Freehling, *The Reintegration of American History: Slavery and the Civil War* (New York: Oxford University Press, 2004), 19–20, 182–83. I use Troutman's formula to calculate rates of disappearance of the slave population: on the county level, I take the U.S. census count of aggregate slaves at the beginning of each decade and calculate the rate of natural increase over a decade for an otherwise stable population, then compare that number to the actual number of slaves counted at the end of the decade. In the 1830s to 1850s, perhaps two hundred to five hundred slaves were manumitted annually, most after serving a certain term of years.

33. Historical Census Browser, http://mapserver.lib.virginia.edu, accessed June 1, 2010; for estimates on rates of natural reproduction, see Troutman, "Slave Trade and Sentiment," app. A, 415–19. In Caroline County, Virginia, slaves numbered 10,292 persons in 1790 (59 percent of the total population), reached a high of 10,999 in 1820 (61 percent of the total population), and had settled back to 10,672 (59 percent of the total population) by 1860. Behind those figures, however, lies the social chaos of a slave population that was reproducing at a high rate. Natural increase among enslaved people in the American South as a whole was 27 percent by the 1790s and reached 30.5 percent by the 1820s. In the 1830s, it was 24 percent; in the 1840s, 26.5 percent, and by the 1850s, it had settled to 23.5 percent. During all that time, the slave population of Caroline County fluctuated about 7 percent, which indicates a steady out-migration of enslaved people (Historical Census Browser, http://mapserver.lib.virginia.ed, accessed June 1, 2010; Freedmen's Bureau, *Register of Children of Colored Persons in Caroline County, State of Virginia, Whose Parents Had Ceased to Cohabit on 27th February 1866, Which the Father Recognizes to Be His*, CRHC; Freedmen's Bureau, *Register of Colored Persons of Caroline County, State of Virginia Cohabitating Together as Husband and Wife on 27th February 1866*, CRHC); William Calderhead, "The Role of the Professional Slave Trader in a Slave Economy: Austin Woolfolk, a Case Study," *Civil War History* 23 (September, 1977), 196–98.

34. Brown, *Narrative of the Life of Henry Box Brown*, 2.

35. Troutman, "Slave Trade and Sentiment," 423; William W. Freehling, *Road to Disunion,* vol. 2: *Secessionists Triumphant* (New York: Oxford University Press, 2007), 32–47; Simon Wendt, "Southern Intellectuals and the Defense of Slavery: The Proslavery Thought of George Fitzhugh and Henry Hughes," *Southern Historian* 23 (2002): 56–70; Robert A. Garson, "Proslavery as Political Theory: The Examples of John C. Calhoun and George Fitzhugh," *South Atlantic Quarterly* 84.2 (1985): 197–212.

36. Susan Eva O'Donovan, "Trunk Lines, Land Lines, and Local Exchanges: Operationalizing the Grapevine Telegraph," paper presented at the Gilder Lehrman Center for the Study of Slavery, Resistance, and Abolition, Yale University, December 11, 2006.

37. John W. Blassingame, *Slave Testimony: Two Centuries of Letters, Speeches, Interviews, and Autobiographies* (Baton Rouge: Louisiana State University Press, 1977), 218.

38. Anthony F. C. Wallace, *Long Bitter Trail: Andrew Jackson and the Indians* (New York: Hill and Wang, 1993); Tadman, *Speculators and Slaves,* 141, 170–71; Joan E. Cashin, *A Family Venture: Men and Women on the Southern Frontier* (New York: Oxford University Press, 1991); James David Miller, *South by Southwest: Planter Emigration and Identity in the Slave South* (Charlottesville: University of Virginia Press, 2002).

39. Goings, *Rambles of a Runaway,* 10. On exogamy among slaves in antebellum Virginia, see Herbert Gutman, *The Black Family in Slavery and Freedom, 1750–1925* (New York: Pantheon, 1976), 131–38. Goings's owner Joseph Lawrence Dawson Smith moved his slaves to Lauderdale, Alabama, three hundred miles away in 1824, where he acquired some eighteen hundred acres before his death in 1837 (Margaret Matthews Cowart, *Old Land Records of Lauderdale County, Alabama* [Huntsville, AL: the author, 1996], 197, 201, 202, 208, 209, 213, 258, 259).

40. Ball, *Slavery in the United States,* 36, 86; Douglass, *Narrative of the Life of Frederick Douglass,* 18–19; Henry Stockbridge, "Baltimore in 1846," *Maryland Historical Magazine* 6.1 (1911): 20–34; Dorothy Sterling, ed., *We Are Your Sisters: Black Women in the Nineteenth Century* (New York: Norton, 1985), 58.

41. Cathy Matson, "Introduction to Connection, Contingency, and Class in the Early Republic's Economy," *Journal of the Early Republic* 26.4 (2006): 515–22; Mark M. Smith, *Listening to Nineteenth-Century America* (Chapel Hill: University of North Carolina Press, 2000), chap. 1.

42. Gutman, *Black Family;* Walter Johnson, *Soul by Soul: Life Inside the Antebellum Slave Market* (Cambridge, MA: Harvard University Press, 1999); Walter Johnson, "On Agency," *Journal of Social History* 37.1 (2003): 113–24; Howe, *What Hath God Wrought,* chap. 6.

43. Lois Green Carr, Russell R. Menard, and Lorena S. Walsh, *Robert Cole's World: Agriculture and Society in Early Maryland* (Chapel Hill: published for the Omohundro Institute for Early American History and Culture by the University of North Carolina Press, 1991); Rhys Isaac, *The Transformation of Virginia, 1740–1790* (Chapel Hill: published for the Institute for Early American History and Culture by the University of North Carolina Press, 1982); Kulikoff, *Tobacco and Slaves.*

44. Historical Census Browser, http://mapserver.lib.virginia.edu, accessed June 1, 2010.

45. Seth Rockman, *Scraping By: Wage Labor, Slavery, and Survival in Early Baltimore* (Baltimore: Johns Hopkins University Press, 2009), 234, 240.

46. Edward L. Ayers, *In the Presence of Mine Enemies: War in the Heart of America,*

1859–1863 (New York: Norton, 2003), 3; Edward L. Ayers, *What Caused the Civil War? Reflections on the South and Southern History* (New York: Norton, 2005), chap. 6; Patience Essah, *A House Divided: Slavery and Emancipation in Delaware, 1638–1865* (Charlottesville: University Press of Virginia, 1996), 10, 32–35, 38, 41, 130; Williams, *Slavery and Freedom in Delaware*, 85–92.

47. Gutman, *Black Family*, 197; Sidney W. Mintz and Richard Price, *The Birth of African-American Culture: An Anthropological Perspective* (Boston: Beacon Press, 1992).

CHAPTER ONE: Networkers

1. Solomon Bayley, *Narrative of Some Remarkable Incidents in the Life of Solomon Bayley, Formerly a Slave in the State of Delaware, North America, Written by Himself, and Published for His Benefit, to Which Are Prefixed, a Few Remarks by Robert Hurnard*, 2nd ed. (London: Harvey and Darton, 1825), 48, http://docsouth.unc.edu/neh/bayley/bayley .html, accessed April 15, 2010; Peter T. Dalleo, " 'Persecuted but not forsaken; cut down, but not destroyed': Solomon and Thamar Bayley, Delawarean Emigrants to Liberia," *Delaware History* 31.3 (2006): 141.

2. Historians have followed anthropologists in construing networks among the enslaved as rooted in kinship ties; see Robert Dirks, "Networks, Groups, and Adaptation in an Afro-Caribbean Community," *Man*, n.s., 7.4 (1972): 565–85; John W. Blassingame, *The Slave Community: Plantation Life in the Antebellum South* (New York: Oxford University Press, 1972), 41–42; Herbert Gutman, *The Black Family in Slavery and Freedom, 1750–1925* (New York: Pantheon, 1976), 98, 138, 197; Sidney W. Mintz and Richard Price, *The Birth of African-American Culture: An Anthropological Perspective* (Boston: Beacon Press, 1992), 66; Brenda E. Stevenson, *Life in Black and White: Family and Community in the Slave South* (New York: Oxford University Press, 1996), 170, 209; Wilma A. Dunaway, *The African-American Family in Slavery and Emancipation* (Cambridge: Cambridge University Press, 2003), 259; Wilma A. Dunaway, *Slavery in the American Mountain South* (Cambridge: Cambridge University Press, 2003), 255.

3. Bayley, *Narrative of Some Remarkable Incidents*, v–vii; Dalleo, " 'Persecuted but not forsaken,' " 137–78; Laura F. Edwards, "Status without Rights: African Americans and the Tangled History of Law and Governance in the Nineteenth-Century U.S. South," *American Historical Review* 112.2 (2007): 365–93.

4. Bayley, *Narrative of Some Remarkable Incidents*, 38–39; Patience Essah, *A House Divided: Slavery and Emancipation in Delaware, 1625–1865* (Charlottesville: University Press of Virginia, 1996), 10, 32–35, 38, 41, 130; William H. Williams, *Slavery and Freedom in Delaware, 1639–1865* (Wilmington, DE: Scholarly Imprint Resources, 1996), 85–92; John W. Blassingame, "Using the Testimony of Ex-Slaves," in *The Slave's Narrative*, ed. Charles T. David and Henry Louis Gates Jr. (New York: Oxford University Press, 1985), 78–98. By the dates Bayley gives, his grandmother may have been a great-grandmother.

5. Annamarie Mol and Jessica Mesman, "Neonatal Food and the Politics of Theory: Some Questions on Method," *Social Studies of Science* 26.2 (1996): 419–44; Bruno Latour, *Reassembling the Social: An Introduction to Actor-Network-Theory* (New York: Oxford University Press, 2005); Michel Callon, "Actor-Network Theory: The Market Test," in *Actor Network Theory and After*, ed. John Law and John Hassard (Oxford, UK: Blackwell, 1999), 181–95; John Law, "Notes on the Theory of the Actor-Network: Ordering, Strategy, and Heterogeneity," *Systems Practice* 5.4 (1992): 379–93; Michel Callon and John Law, "On

Interests and Their Transformation: Enrolment and Counter-Enrolment," *Social Studies of Science* 12.4 (1982): 615–25.

6. Susan E. O'Donovan, *Becoming Free in the Cotton South* (Cambridge, MA: Harvard University Press, 2007), chap. 1.

7. In its 1776 constitution, Delaware outlawed new importation of slaves through both the Atlantic and domestic trade. Before the interstate slave trade intensified, the Delaware legislature passed a series of laws restricting slaveholders' property rights in slaves. In 1787, the general assembly forbade sales to the Carolinas, Georgia, and the West Indies. Two years later it forbade sales to Maryland and Virginia and banned slave ships from its ports. Antislavery Quakers in the north of the state and Methodists in the south cooperated to pass those laws. In 1793, Delaware added penalties for kidnapping free persons of color and transporting them across state lines. In the face of behavior such as that of Bayley's owners, in 1797 Delaware strengthened restrictions on slaveholders' property rights by declaring that all slaves sold beyond the state would be automatically freed and the owners levied a fine of £100. Two years later it permitted free people of African descent, under certain circumstances, to give evidence in court. See Helen Tunnicliff Caterall, *Judicial Cases Concerning American Slavery and the Negro*, vol. 4: *Cases from the Courts of New England, the Middle States, and the District of Columbia* (Washington, DC: Carnegie Institution of Washington, 1936), 211–16; Williams, *Slavery and Freedom in Delaware*, 77–98, 144.

8. Bayley, *Narrative of Some Remarkable Incidents*, 39; on a similar gambit to gain legal freedom, see Bruce A. Bender, "Ann Elliott Versus Robert Twilley: Securing a Family's Freedom," *Delaware History* 27.3 (1997): 191–203.

9. Bayley, *Narrative of Some Remarkable Incidents*, 39.

10. Bayley, *Narrative of Some Remarkable Incidents*, 39–40.

11. Leonard Black, *The Life and Sufferings of Leonard Black, a Fugitive from Slavery, Written by Himself* (New Bedford, MA: Benjamin Lindsey, 1847), 7, http://docsouth.unc.edu/neh/black/black.html, accessed August 23, 2007.

12. Bayley, *Narrative of Some Remarkable Incidents*, 18, 25–26.

13. *Federal Gazette and Baltimore (MD) Daily Advertiser*, January 20, 1798, America's Historical Newspapers, Early American Newspapers, ser. 1, 1690–1876, AA, accessed April 27, 2010.

14. Donald Mathews, *Slavery and Methodism* (Princeton: Princeton University Press, 1965), 8–20.

15. Francis Asbury, entry, December 19, 1796, *The Journal and Letters of Francis Asbury*, 3 vols. (London: Epworth Press, 1958), 2:109.

16. Asbury visited Accomack County, Virginia, at least twice in the 1790s, though illness and bad weather interfered with his preaching on both occasions (entry, January 9, 1798, *Journal*, 2:151, 500, 533; Mathews, *Slavery and Methodism*, 23).

17. Mathews, *Slavery and Methodism*, 11.

18. Solomon Bayley to Daniel Cooledge, September 22, 1835, *The Friend* 10 (1836): 102–4, cited in Dalleo, "'Persecuted but not forsaken,'" 139; Bayley, *Narrative of Some Remarkable Incidents*, 18–19; Nathan O. Hatch, *The Democratization of American Christianity* (New Haven: Yale University Press, 1989), 93; Mathews, *Slavery and Methodism*, 22–23.

19. Bayley, *Narrative of Some Remarkable Incidents*, 26.

20. Walter Johnson, *Soul by Soul: Life Inside the Antebellum Slave Market* (Cambridge,

MA: Harvard University Press, 1999), chap. 1; Bayley, *Narrative of Some Remarkable Incidents*, iv.

21. Bayley, *Narrative of Some Remarkable Incidents*, 26–27.

22. Bayley, *Narrative of Some Remarkable Incidents*, 28. "Solomon" and "Tamer" (no surname) obtained a license on December 28, 1798, according to Nora Miller Turman, *Marriage Records of Accomack County, Virginia, 1776–1854, Recorded in Bonds, Licenses and Ministers' Returns* (Bowie, MD: Heritage Books, 1994), 266. This source designates them "FN," or free people of African descent, though that was not necessarily the designation in the original records.

23. Gary B. Nash and Jean R. Soderlund, *Freedom by Degrees: Emancipation in Pennsylvania and Its Aftermath* (New York: Oxford University Press, 1991), chap. 4.

24. That is my calculation. According to census figures, one in two slaves who began the decade enslaved in New York were missing from the nonwhite population by 1830. There were 29,279 free people of color and 10,088 slaves in New York in 1820 and 44,870 free people of color and 75 slaves in 1830. If a natural increase of 28 percent is assumed for both groups, there should have been about 50,000 free people of color living in New York following emancipation, assuming that emigration and immigration were roughly equal. About 5,400—or a little over 50 percent of the number of formerly enslaved people—are missing from the 1830 total for free people of color. That means one in two slaves or former slaves either migrated voluntarily or involuntarily (Geospatial and Statistical Data Center, University of Virginia Library, Historical Census Browser, http://mapserver.lib.virginia.edu/, accessed June 1, 2010). For rates of natural increase, see Philip D. Troutman, "Slave Trade and Sentiment" (PhD diss., University of Virginia, 2000), app. A, 415–19, 423; David Nathaniel Gellman, *Emancipating New York: The Politics of Slavery and Freedom, 1777–1827* (Baton Rouge: Louisiana State University Press, 2006), 202–5.

25. Bayley, *A Narrative of Some Remarkable Incidents*, 2.

26. *Negro Cager v. Philip White*, Court of Common Pleas of Delaware, Sussex, 1 Del. Cas. 181, decided April 1798, Lexis-Nexis Academic, accessed June 5, 2007; Williams, *Slavery and Freedom in Delaware*, 77–98.

27. Bayley, *Narrative of Some Remarkable Incidents*, 2, 18.

28. Walter Johnson, *Soul by Soul*, chap. 4; Bayley, *A Narrative of Some Remarkable Incidents*, 2.

29. For most Americans, personhood in the nineteenth century was like personhood through the ages in societies for which talk of individuals and rights did not exist or was irrelevant to most people (Henry Rosemont Jr. and Roger Ames, *The Chinese Classic of Family Reverence: A Philosophical Translation of the "Xiaojing"* [Honolulu: University of Hawai'i Press, 2009], 11 passim). Freedom was an elastic concept that in the nineteenth-century United States did not so much evoke ideas of Western classical antiquity, for instance, but rather had more purchase in the idiom of political speech, religious discourse, and the realm of ideas concerning republicanism and liberalism (Eric Foner, *The Story of American Freedom* [New York: Norton, 1999]; Orlando Patterson, *Freedom in the Making of Western Culture,* vol. 1 [New York: Basic Books, 1991]).

30. Ellen Hartigan-O'Connor, *The Ties That Buy: Women and Commerce in Revolutionary America* (Philadelphia: University of Pennsylvania Press, 2009), 187.

31. Edward E. Baptist, " 'Stol' and Fetched Here': Enslaved Migration, Ex-Slave Narratives, and Vernacular History," in *New Studies in the History of American Slavery*, ed. Ed-

ward E. Baptist and Stephanie M. H. Camp (Athens: University of Georgia Press, 2006), 243–74; Ira Berlin, *Generations of Captivity: A History of African-American Slaves* (Cambridge, MA: Harvard University Press, 2003), chap. 4; Stephanie Coontz, "Historical Perspectives on Family Studies," *Journal of Marriage and Family* 62.2 (2000): 283–97.

32. Walter Johnson, "On Agency," *Journal of Social History* 37.1 (2003): 113–24; George Yancy, "Historical Varieties of African American Labor: Sites of Agency and Resistance," *Western Journal of Black Studies* 28.2 (2004): 337–53; Mary Jo Maynes, Jennifer L. Pierce, and Barbara Laslett, *Telling Stories: The Use of Personal Narratives in the Social Sciences and History* (Ithaca: Cornell University Press, 2008).

33. Steven Deyle, *Carry Me Back: The Domestic Slave Trade in American Life* (New York: Oxford University Press, 2005), chap. 5.

34. Bayley, *Narrative of Some Remarkable Incidents*, 2, 5.

35. Armistead Wilson, *A Tribute for the Negro: Being a Vindication of the Moral, Intellectual, and Religious Capabilities of the Colored Portion of Mankind; with Particular Reference to the African Race* (Manchester: W. Irwin, 1848), 515, http://docsouth.unc.edu/neh/armistead/armistead.html, accessed January 31, 2008; Bayley, *Narrative of Some Remarkable Incidents*, 6.

36. Bayley, *Narrative of Some Remarkable Incidents*, 7.

37. Bayley, *Narrative of Some Remarkable Incidents*, 18.

38. Bayley, *Narrative of Some Remarkable Incidents*, 18.

39. Bayley, *Narrative of Some Remarkable Incidents*, iv. Dalleo contends that two "likely candidates" were Richard Bassett and George Truitt ("'Persecuted but not forsaken,'" 151). Curiously, an acquaintance many years later wrote that Bayley "was never a good manager of business" (Joseph Bringhurst to Moses Sheppard, February 7, 1832, Moses Sheppard Papers, Friends Historical Library, cited in Dalleo, "'Persecuted but not forsaken,'" 143).

40. Bayley, *Narrative of Some Remarkable Incidents*, iv–v, 40, 44. Bayley does not give the date of the visit to his mother. Leah Bayley was born in February 1800, according to *Narrative of Some Remarkable Incidents*. Dalleo contends she was born free ("'Persecuted but not forsaken,'" 151). Daniel Rogers appears in the census (*Federal Census of 1800*, *Cedar Creek Hundred, Sussex, Delaware*, roll M32-4, p. 300, image 160, www.ancestry.com, accessed January 31, 2008). That record shows a Daniel Rogers whose household corresponds, in age and sex, to the family of Governor Daniel Rogers, who had been governor from September 28, 1797, to January 15, 1799.

41. Bayley, *Narrative of Some Remarkable Incidents*, 28; Darlene Clark Hine, ed., *Black Women in America*, vol. 1 (New York: Oxford University Press, 2005), 198; Wilma Dunaway, *Women, Work, and Family in the Antebellum Mountain South* (Cambridge: Cambridge University Press, 2008), chap. 8; Robert W. Fogel and Stanley Engerman, *Time on the Cross: The Economics of American Negro Slavery* (New York: Norton, 1989 [1974]), 86–89.

42. Bayley, *Narrative of Some Remarkable Incidents*, 28–29; Dalleo, "'Persecuted but not forsaken,'" 15; Barry W. Miles and Moody K. Miles, *Abstracts of the Wills and Administrations of Accomack County, Virginia, 1800–1860* (Bowie, MD: Heritage Books, 2000), viii.

43. A Charles Gardiner appears in the 1820 census for Calvert County, which borders St. Mary's County. He was over forty-five, headed a household of seven that included one free white male sixteen to twenty-six, two females under ten, one female

sixteen to twenty-six. Two members of the household were engaged in commerce. Gardiner owned no slaves (*Federal Census of 1820, Election District 3, Calvert County, Maryland*, rolls M33–40, p. 64, image 64, www.ancestry.com, accessed February 12, 2007).

44. It is unclear what Michael did for Gardiner, but a bill of sale for Michael includes the terms under which Michael could claim his freedom (*Charles L. Gardiner v. Edward Fenwick*, St. Mary's County Court [Equity Papers] 86, Maryland State Archives Special Collections, 4239-27-7, MSA; Bayly E. Marks, "Skilled Blacks in Antebellum St. Mary's County, Maryland," *Journal of Southern History* 53.4 [1987]: 537–64).

45. Bayley, *Narrative of Some Remarkable Incidents*, 29–30; Fogel and Engerman, *Time on the Cross*, 86–89.

46. St. Leger Landon Carter, *Nugae, by Nugator; or, Pieces in Prose and Verse* (Baltimore: Woods and Crane, 1844), 5–6.

47. Deyle, *Carry Me Back*, chap. 4; Bayley, *Narrative of Some Remarkable Incidents*, 29–30.

48. Bayley, *Narrative of Some Remarkable Incidents*, 30–32.

49. Laura F. Edwards, "Enslaved Women and the Law: The Paradoxes of Subordination in the Post-Revolutionary Carolinas," *Slavery and Abolition* 26.2 (2005): 308; Dalleo, "'Persecuted but not forsaken'"; Douglas R. Egerton, "Slaves to the Marketplace: Economic Liberty and Black Rebelliousness in the Atlantic World," *Journal of the Early Republic* 26.4 (2006): 617–39.

50. John Lauritz Larson, *The Market Revolution in America: Liberty, Ambition, and the Eclipse of the Common Good* (New York: Cambridge University Press, 2010), 136–37.

51. No corresponding indenture appears, though they were not infrequent in the county (Gail M. Walczyk, ed., *Accomack Indentures, 1798–1835* [Coram, NY: Publisher's Row, 2002]).

52. Bayley, *Narrative of Some Remarkable Incidents*, 42–46.

53. Essah, *House Divided*, 110.

54. Essah, *House Divided*, chap. 4.

55. Essah, *House Divided*, 121–22.

56. Deyle, *Carry Me Back*, 98–105.

57. Todd A. Herring, "Kidnapped and Sold in Natchez: The Ordeal of Aaron Cooper, a Free Black Man," *Journal of Mississippi History* 60.1 (1998): 341–53; Carol Wilson, *Freedom at Risk: The Kidnapping of Free Blacks in America, 1800–1865* (Lexington: University of Kentucky Press, 1994); *Federal Census of 1820, Camden, Delaware*, roll M33-4, p. 37, image 45, www.ancestry.com, accessed February 29, 2008; Solomon Northup, *Twelve Years a Slave: Narrative of Solomon Northup, a Citizen of New-York, Kidnapped in Washington City in 1841, and Rescued in 1853* (Auburn, NY: Derby and Miller, 1853), http://docsouth.unc.edu/fpn/northup/northup.html, accessed June 1, 2010.

58. *Trenton (NJ) Federalist*, August 4, 1817, America's Historical Newspapers, Early American Newspapers, ser. 1, 1690–1876, AA, accessed May 23, 2007; Susan Eva O'Donovan, "Traded Babies: Enslaved Children in America's Domestic Migration, 1820–60," in *Children in Slavery through the Ages*, ed. Gwyn Campbell, Suzanne Miers, and Joseph C. Miller (Athens: Ohio University Press, 2009), 88–102.

59. Walter Johnson, "Cotton's Dominion: Body, Landscape, and Ecology in the Mississippi Valley," paper presented at the Landscape of Slavery Conference, University of Virginia, March 14, 2008; Calvin Schermerhorn, "Left Behind but Getting Ahead: Antebellum Slavery's Orphans in the Chesapeake, 1820–60," in *Children in Slavery*, 204–24;

Philip J. Schwarz, *Twice Condemned: Slaves and the Criminal Laws of Virginia, 1705–1865* (Baton Rouge: Louisiana State University Press, 1988), 47–59; 200–54; 313–36.

60. Charles Ball, *Slavery in the United States: A Narrative of the Life and Adventures of Charles Ball, a Black Man, Who Lived Forty Years in Maryland, South Carolina and Georgia, as a Slave under Various Masters, and Was One Year in the Navy with Commodore Barney, during the Late War* (New York: John S. Taylor, 1837), 36, http://docsouth.unc.edu/neh/ballslavery/ball.html (accessed June 1, 2010). For a discussion of Ball's voice versus that of his editor, Isaac Fisher, see William L. Andrews, *To Tell a Free Story: The First Century of Afro-American Autobiography, 1760–1865* (Urbana and Chicago: University of Illinois Press, 1986), 81–86; C. Peter Ripley, ed., *The Black Abolitionist Papers*, vol. 3: *The United States, 1830–1846* (Chapel Hill: University of North Carolina Press, 1991), 30.

61. There is debate concerning the authenticity of Charles Ball's narrative and questions about both his identity and the name he uses. Contemporary skeptics and later historians, such as Ulrich Bonnell Phillips, discredited the narrative because of abolitionist involvement in its publication. Recently, scholars have demonstrated its authenticity, though "Ball" may be a pseudonym (J. D. McCord, "Life of a Negro Slave," *Southern Quarterly Review* 28.1 [1853]: 206–27; Ulrich Bonnell Phillips, *Life and Labor in the Old South* [Columbia: University of South Carolina Press, 2007 (1930)], 219; John W. Blassingame, *Slave Testimony: Two Centuries of Letters, Speeches, Interviews, and Autobiographies* [Baton Rouge: Louisiana State University Press, 1977], xxiii–xxvi; Andrews, *To Tell a Free Story*, 62–63; Marion Wilson Starling, *The Slave Narrative: Its Place in American History*, 2nd ed. [Washington, D.C.: Howard University Press, 1988], 106–7; 226–32; John Sekora, "Black Message/White Envelope: Genre, Authenticity, and Authority in the Antebellum Slave Narrative," *Callaloo* 32.3 [1987]: 482–515).

62. Ball, *Slavery in the United States*, 27–28; Samuel Hazard, ed., *Hazard's United States Commercial and Statistical Register*, vol. 5 (Philadelphia: William F. Geddes, 1841), 141; David S. Cecelski, *The Waterman's Song: Slavery and Freedom in Maritime North Carolina* (Chapel Hill: University of North Carolina Press, 2001), chap. 1.

63. Ball, *Slavery in the United States*, 34–35.

64. Ball, *Slavery in the United States*, 33–36.

65. Ball, *Slavery in the United States*, 16–22.

66. Ball, *Slavery in the United States*, 47–48; Susan Eva O'Donovan, "Trunk Lines, Land Lines, and Local Exchanges: Operationalizing the Grapevine Telegraph," paper presented at the Gilder Lehrman Center for the Study of Slavery, Resistance, and Abolition, Yale University, December 11, 2006.

67. Nick Yablon, *Untimely Ruins: An Archaeology of American Urban Modernity, 1819–1919* (Chicago: University of Chicago Press, 2009), 84–85.

68. Ball, *Slavery in the United States*, 48–49, 102; Lacy K. Ford, *Deliver Us from Evil: The Slavery Question in the Old South* (New York: Oxford University Press, 2009), 126–28; David Eltis and David Richardson, "Prices of African Slaves Newly Arrived in the Americas, 1673–1865: New Evidence on Long-Run Trends and Regional Differentials," in *Slavery in the Development of the Americas*, ed. David Eltis, Frank D. Lewis, and Kenneth L. Sokoloff (Cambridge: Cambridge University Press, 2004), 181–218.

69. Douglas C. North, *The Economic Growth of the United States, 1790–1860* (Englewood Cliffs, NJ: Prentice-Hall, 1961), 53.

70. Ball, *Slavery in the United States*, 130–31.

71. Ball, *Slavery in the United States*, 164.

72. *Easton (MD) Republican Star, or, Eastern Shore General Advertiser*, April 16, 1805, America's Historical Newspapers, Early American Newspapers, ser. 1, 1690–1876, AA, accessed April 30, 2010.

73. James A. Rawley with Stephen D. Behrendt, *The Transatlantic Slave Trade: A History, Revised Edition* (Lincoln: University of Nebraska Press, 2005), 279; *Charleston (SC) Daily Advertiser*, July 20, 1804, America's Historical Newspapers, Early American Newspapers, ser. 1, 1690–1876, AA, accessed April 30, 2010; *State Gazette of South Carolina*, January 27, 1791, America's Historical Newspapers, Early American Newspapers, ser. 1, 1690–1876, AA accessed April 30, 2010.

74. Ball, *Slavery in the United States*, 167; Stephanie E. Smallwood, *Saltwater Slavery: A Middle Passage from Africa to American Diaspora* (Cambridge, MA: Harvard University Press, 2007), 189–91.

75. Ball, *Slavery in the United States*, 381; Philip D. Troutman, "Grapevine in the Slave Market: African American Geopolitical Literacy and the 1841 *Creole* Revolt," in *The Chattel Principle: Internal Slave Trade in the Americas*, ed. Walter Johnson (New Haven: Yale University Press, 2004), 203–33; Johnson, *Soul by Soul*, 60- 76; Steven Deyle, "The Irony of Liberty: Origins of the Domestic Slave Trade," *Journal of the Early Republic* 12.1 (1992): 57; Sylviane A. Diouf, *Servants of Allah: African Muslims Enslaved in the Americas* (New York: New York University Press, 1998); John B. Boles, *Black Southerners, 1619–1869* (Lexington: University of Kentucky Press, 1983), 113–16.

76. Ball, *Slavery in the United States*, 345.

77. Ball, *Slavery in the United States*, 387, 389; Susan J. Matt, "You Can't Go Home Again: Homesickness and Nostalgia in U.S. History," *Journal of American History* 94.2 (2007): 478.

78. Ball, *Slavery in the United States*, 423.

79. Ball, *Slavery in the United States*, 425.

80. Marcus Rediker, *The Slave Ship: A Human History* (New York: Viking Press, 2007), 293–94; W. Jeffrey Bolster, *Black Jacks: African American Seaman in the Age of Sail* (Cambridge, MA: Harvard University Press, 1998), chap. 2.

81. Ball, *Slavery in the United States*, 429.

82. Ball, *Slavery in the United States*, 425.

83. Ball, *Slavery in the United States,* 436; Anthony E. Kaye, *Joining Places: Slave Neighborhoods in the Old South* (Chapel Hill: University of North Carolina Press, 2007), chap. 4.

84. Ball, *Slavery in the United States,* 437.

85. Ball, *Slavery in the United States*, 461.

86. *American Beacon and Norfolk (VA) and Portsmouth (VA) Daily Advertiser*, August 25, 1819, America's Historical Newspapers, Early American Newspapers, ser. 1, 1690–1876, AA accessed April 30, 2010.

87. *Washington (DC) Daily National Intelligencer*, June 6, 1814, America's Historical Newspapers, Early American Newspapers, ser. 1, 1690–1876, AA, accessed April 30, 2010.

88. Ball, *Slavery in the United States*, 462–64.

89. Ball, *Slavery in the United States,* 465.

90. Ball, *Slavery in the United States,* 466; Gutman, *Black Family*, 263–67; Drew Gilpin Faust, "Culture, Conflict, and Community: The Meaning of Power on an Ante-Bellum Plantation," *Journal of Social History* 14.1 (1980): 83–98.

91. Ball, *Slavery in the United States,* 467; Walter Johnson, "Clerks All! Or, Slaves with Cash," *Journal of the Early Republic* 26.4 (2006): 648–49.

92. Cecelski, *Waterman's Song,* chap. 3.

93. Ball, *Slavery in the United States,* 469.

94. Christopher T. George, "Mirage of Freedom: African Americans in the War of 1812," *Maryland Historical Magazine* 91.4 (1996): 432; Daniel Walker Howe, *What Hath God Wrought: The Transformation of America, 1815–1848* (New York: Oxford University Press, 2007), 27–29, 100–104, 571–73; Ball, *Slavery in the United States,* 479.

95. Ball, *Slavery in the United States,* 469.

96. Jon Latimer, *1812: War with America* (Cambridge, MA: Harvard University Press, 2007), 251; Cochrane to George Cockburn, July 1, 1814, Cochrane Papers 2346, National Library of Scotland, Edinburgh, cited in George, "Mirage of Freedom," 435.

97. Douglas R. Egerton, *Gabriel's Rebellion: The Virginia Slave Conspiracies of 1800 and 1802* (Chapel Hill: University of North Carolina Press, 1993).

98. James Sidbury, *Ploughshares into Swords: Race, Rebellion, and Identity in Gabriel's Virginia, 1730–1810* (Cambridge: Cambridge University Press, 1997), chaps. 1–3.

99. James Sidbury, "Saint Domingue in Virginia: Ideology, Local Meanings, and Resistance to Slavery, 1790–1800," *Journal of Southern History* 63.3 (1997): 531–52.

100. Egerton, *Gabriel's Rebellion,* pt. 2.

101. Frank A. Cassell, "Slaves of the Chesapeake Bay Area and the War of 1812," *Journal of Negro History* 57.2 (1972): 148.

102. Sara C. Fanning, "The Roots of Early Black Nationalism: Northern African Americans' Invocations of Haiti in the Early Nineteenth Century," *Slavery and Abolition* 28.1 (2007): 61–85; Robin W. Winks, *The Blacks in Canada: A History,* 2nd ed. (Montreal: McGill-Queen's University Press, 1997), chap. 5.

103. For a provocative and compelling counterargument, see John Ashworth, *Slavery, Capitalism, and Politics in the Antebellum Republic,* vol. 1: *Commerce and Compromise, 1820–1850* (Cambridge: Cambridge University Press, 1995).

104. Cassell, "Slaves of the Chesapeake Bay Area," 145.

105. Cassell, "Slaves of the Chesapeake Bay Area," 148–50. Jon Latimer rejects as "baseless" reports that African Americans who fled to the British were later sold to the West Indies (*1812,* 247). Winks likewise notes these reports were false (*Blacks in Canada,* 114). Ball describes a case of a group of African Americans surrendering to the British in the hopes of being freed in Trinidad but notes he never found out what happened to this group after they boarded a ship bound for the West Indies (*Slavery in the United States,* 473).

106. George, "Mirage of Freedom," 426–50; Ball, *Slavery in the United States,* 470.

107. Boston King, "Memoirs of the Life of Boston King, a Black Preacher, Written by Himself, during His Residence at Kingswood School," *Methodist Magazine,* March–June 1798, 105–10, Antislavery Literature Project, Arizona State University, http://antislavery.eserver.org/narratives/boston_king, accessed April 30, 2010; Phyllis R. Blakeley, "Boston King: A Negro Loyalist Who Sought Refuge in Nova Scotia," *Dalhousie Review* 48.3 (1968): 347–56; John N. Grant, "Black Immigrants into Nova Scotia, 1776–1815," *Journal of Negro History* 58.3 (1973): 253–70.

108. Ball, *Slavery in the United States,* 472.

109. Ball, *Slavery in the United States,* 473.

110. Ball, *Slavery in the United States,* 474–76.

111. Ball, *Slavery in the United States*, 467.

112. *Albany (NY) Gazette*, September 9, 1813, America's Historical Newspapers, Early American Newspapers, ser. 1, 1690–1876, AA, accessed April 30, 2010.

113. Latimer, *1812*, 89, 169.

114. Latimer, *1812*, 250–53.

115. Ball, *Slavery in the United States*, 467; Latimer, *1812*, 141, 309–11; George, "Mirage of Freedom," 439; Gerard T. Altoff, *Amongst My Best Men: African Americans and the War of 1812* (Put-in Bay, OH.: Perry Group, 1996), 122–24.

116. Ball, *Slavery in the United States*, 479–80.

117. Altoff, *Amongst My Best Men*, 124–27.

118. Latimer, *1812*, 3–4; Jessica Millward, "'A Choice Parcel of Country Born': Slave Women and the Transition to Freedom in Revolutionary Maryland" (PhD diss., University of California, Los Angeles, 2003).

119. Ball, *Slavery in the United States*, 480.

120. Dylan C. Penningroth, *Claims of Kinfolk: African American Property and Community in the Nineteenth-Century South* (Chapel Hill: University of North Carolina Press, 2002), chap. 2; Betty Wood, *Women's Work, Men's Work: The Informal Slave Economies of Lowcountry Georgia* (Athens: University of Georgia Press, 1995), chap. 8.

121. Ball, *Slavery in the United States*, 480, 513.

122. Ball, *Slavery in the United States*, 481–82; Edward L. Ayers, *Vengeance and Justice: Crime and Punishment in the Nineteenth-Century American South* (New York: Oxford University Press, 1984), 101–5.

123. Ball, *Slavery in the United States*, 481–83; Andrews, *To Tell a Free Story*, 62–63, 85.

124. Howe, *What Hath God Wrought* 345–57; Ball, *Slavery in the United States*, 482–83, 485.

125. Ball, *Slavery in the United States*, 491, 494; Wood, *Women's Work, Men's Work*, 32.

126. Bolster, *Black Jacks*, 191, 200.

127. Ball, *Slavery in the United States*, 510–12; Steven Hahn, *A Nation under Our Feet: Black Political Struggles in the Rural South, from Slavery to the Great Migration* (Cambridge, MA: Harvard University Press, 2003), 53–54; Juliet E. K. Walker, "Racism, Slavery, and Free Enterprise: Black Entrepreneurship in the United States before the Civil War," *Business History Review* 60.3 (1986): 367.

128. Ball, *Slavery in the United States*, 512–13; James Oliver Horton and Lois E. Horton, *Slavery and the Making of America* (New York: Oxford University Press, 2005), 102–3; Emma Jones Lapsansky, "'Since They Got Those Separate Churches': Afro-Americans and Racism in Jacksonian Philadelphia," in *African Americans in Pennsylvania: Shifting Historical Perspectives*, ed. Joe William Trotter and Eric Ledell Smith (University Park: Pennsylvania State University Press, 1997), 93–120; Olaudah Equiano, *The Interesting Narrative of the Life of Olaudah Equiano, or Gustavus Vassa, the African, Written by Himself*, vol. 1 (London: the author, 1789), http://docsouth.unc.edu/neh/equiano1/equiano1 .html, accessed June 1, 2010; Venture Smith, *A Narrative of the Life and Adventures of Venture, a Native of Africa, but Resident above Sixty Years in the United States of America, Related by Himself* (New London [CT]: C. Holt, 1798), http://docsouth.unc.edu/neh/venture/ venture.html, accessed June 3, 2010.

129. Andrews, *To Tell a Free Story*, 82.

130. Ball, *Slavery in the United States*, 514–15; Baptist, "'Stol' and Fetched Here,'" 243–74.

131. Ball, *Slavery in the United States*, 514–17.

132. Edward L. Ayers, *In the Presence of Mine Enemies: War in the Heart of America, 1859–1863* (New York: Norton, 2003), xix–xx, 320, 418.

133. Paul E. Lovejoy, *Transformations in Slavery* (Cambridge: Cambridge University Press, 2000), 47, 68–90, 140–64, 170–74, 182–90, 224–25; Joseph C. Miller, *Way of Death: Merchant Capitalism and the Angolan Slave Trade, 1730–1830* (Madison: University of Wisconsin Press, 1988), 140–68, 232–57; Fogel and Engerman, *Time on the Cross*, 13–37.

134. Dalleo, "'Persecuted but not forsaken,'" 152–68.

135. Eugene Genovese, *Roll, Jordan, Roll: The World the Slaves Made* (New York: Pantheon, 1972), 614; Gregory Brian Durling, "Female Labor, Malingering, and the Abuse of Equipment under Slavery: Evidence from the Marydale Plantation," *Southern Studies: An Interdisciplinary Journal of the South* 5.1–2 (1994): 31–49; A. E. Housman, *The Collected Poems of A. E. Housman* (New York: Henry Holt, 1965), 111; Charles G. Sellers, *The Market Revolution: Jacksonian America, 1815–1846* (New York: Oxford University Press, 1991).

CHAPTER TWO: Watermen

1. Susan Eva O'Donovan, "Traded Babies: Enslaved Children in America's Domestic Migration, 1820–60," in *Children in Slavery through the Ages*, ed. Gwyn Campbell, Suzanne Miers, and Joseph C. Miller (Athens: Ohio University Press, 2009), 88–102; Robert E. Lane, *The Market Experience* (Cambridge: Cambridge University Press, 1991), chap. 11; Gavin Wright, *Slavery and American Economic Development* (Baton Rouge: Louisiana State University Press, 2006).

2. Moses Grandy, *Narrative of the Life of Moses Grandy, Late a Slave in the United States of America* (London: Gilpin, 1843), 7, http://docsouth.unc.edu/fpn/grandy/grandy .html, accessed October 16, 2006; James Sidbury, "Early Slave Narratives and the Culture of the Atlantic Market," in *Empire and Nation: Essays in Honor of Jack P. Greene*, ed. Peter Onuf and Elijah Gould (Baltimore: Johns Hopkins University Press, 2004), 260–74.

3. Federal Writers' Project, *North Carolina: A Guide to the Old North State* (Chapel Hill: University of North Carolina Press, 1939), 12–13; David S. Cecelski, *The Waterman's Song: Slavery and Freedom in Maritime North Carolina* (Chapel Hill: University of North Carolina Press, 2001).

4. Grandy, *Narrative of the Life of Moses Grandy*, 15–16, 46.

5. Grandy, *Narrative of the Life of Moses Grandy*, 15–17; Frederic Bancroft, *Slave-Trading in the Old South* (Columbia: University of South Carolina Press, 1996 [1931]), 93–95.

6. Cecelski, *Waterman's Song*, chap. 1; Michael Tadman, *Speculators and Slaves: Masters, Traders, and Slaves in the Old South* (Madison: University of Wisconsin Press, 1996), 170–71; Grandy, *Narrative of the Life of Moses Grandy*, 9, 14; Robert B. Outland III, *Tapping the Pines: The Naval Stores Industry in the American South* (Baton Rouge: Louisiana State University Press, 2004); Philip D. Troutman, "Grapevine in the Slave Market: African American Geopolitical Literacy and the 1841 *Creole* Revolt," in *The Chattel Principle: Internal Slave Trade in the Americas*, ed. Walter Johnson (New Haven: Yale Univer-

sity Press, 2004), 203–33; Susan Eva O'Donovan, "Trunk Lines, Land Lines, and Local Exchanges: Operationalizing the Grapevine Telegraph," paper presented at the Gilder Lehrman Center for the Study of Slavery, Resistance, and Abolition, Yale University, December 11, 2006.

7. Laura F. Edwards, "Status without Rights: African Americans and the Tangled History of Law and Governance in the Nineteenth-Century U.S. South," *American Historical Review* 112.2 (2007): 365–93.

8. Loren Schweninger, "The Underside of Slavery: The Internal Economy, Self-Hire, and Quasi-Freedom in Virginia, 1780–1865," *Slavery and Abolition* 12.2 (1991): 2–3.

9. McFeely, *Frederick Douglass* (New York: Norton, 1991); John Lauritz Larson, *The Market Revolution in America: Liberty, Ambition, and the Eclipse of the Common Good* (New York: Cambridge University Press, 2010), 2–8; London R. Ferebee, *A Brief History of the Slave Life of Rev. L. R. Ferebee, and the Battles of Life, and Four Years of His Ministerial Life, Written from Memory, to 1882* (Raleigh, NC: Edwards, Broughton, 1882), http://docsouth .unc.edu/fpn/ferebee/ferebee.html, accessed June 1, 2010; Peter B. Hinks, *To Awaken My Afflicted Brethren: David Walker and the Problem of Antebellum Slave Resistance* (University Park: Pennsylvania State University Press, 1997), 137–46; Cecelski, *Waterman's Song,* chap. 5. William H. Robinson notes that his family, including his father, used the name "Cowens," a variant of the name of the family who owned them, Cowan. The family decided much later to adopt the family name Robinson, after Robinson Crusoe, which was a transliteration of Robinson's father's Madagascar family name (*From Log Cabin to the Pulpit; or, Fifteen Years in Slavery*, 3rd ed. (Eau Claire, WI: James H. Tifft, 1913), chap. 25, http://docsouth.unc.edu/fpn/robinson/robinson.html, accessed February 3, 2010.

10. Larson, *The Market Revolution in America*, 76–79; Brian Schoen, *The Fragile Fabric of Union: Cotton, Federal Politics, and the Global Origins of the Civil War* (Baltimore: Johns Hopkins University Press, 2009); C. Knick Harley, "International Competitiveness of the Antebellum American Cotton Textile Industry," *Journal of Economic History* 52.3 (1992): 559–84; Cecelski, *Waterman's Song*, 53.

11. *Baltimore (MD) Patriot and Mercantile Advertiser*, February 12, 1819, 3; David Eltis, "The Volume and Structure of the Transatlantic Slave Trade: A Reassessment," *William and Mary Quarterly*, 3rd ser., 58.1 (2001): 17–46.

12. Tadman, *Speculators and Slaves*, 11–46; Steven Deyle, *Carry Me Back: The Domestic Slave Trade in American Life* (New York: Oxford University Press, 2005), 283–89; Robert H. Gudmestad, *A Troublesome Commerce: The Transformation of the Interstate Slave Trade* (Baton Rouge: Louisiana State University Press, 2003), 19–20; Walter Johnson, *Soul by Soul: Life Inside the Antebellum Slave Market* (Cambridge, MA: Harvard University Press, 1999), 19; Eltis, "Volume and Structure of the Transatlantic Slave Trade," 45; Gavin Wright, *Old South, New South: Revolutions in the Southern Economy Since the Civil War* (New York: Basic Books, 1986), introduction; O'Donovan, "Trunk Lines, Land Lines, and Local Exchanges," 3; Sylviane A. Diouf, *Dreams of Africa in Alabama: The Slave Ship "Clotilda" and the Story of the Last Africans Brought to America* (New York: Oxford University Press, 2006).

13. Edward E. Baptist, *The Half Has Never Been Told: The Migration That Made African America, the United States, and the World* (New York: Basic Books, forthcoming); Reginald Horsman, "Thomas Jefferson and the Ordinance of 1784," *Illinois Historical Journal* 79.2 (1986): 99–112; Walter T. Durham, "The Southwest Territory: Progression Toward Statehood," *Journal of East Tennessee History* 62 (1990): 3–17; David L. Lightner, *Slavery and*

the Commerce Clause: How the Struggle against the Slave Trade Led to the Civil War (New Haven: Yale University Press, 2006), 65; Gudmestad, *A Troublesome Commerce*; Tadman, *Speculators and Slaves*, chap. 2; Deyle, *Carry Me Back*, 6.

14. David Eltis, *Economic Growth and the Ending of the Transatlantic Slave Trade* (New York: Oxford University Press, 1987), chap. 11; Joseph E. Inikori and Stanley L. Engerman, "Introduction: Gainers and Losers in the Atlantic Slave Trade," in *The Atlantic Slave Trade: Effects on Economies, Societies, and Peoples in Africa, the Americas, and Europe*, ed. Joseph E. Inikori and Stanley L. Engerman (Durham: Duke University Press, 1992), 1–21; Robin Blackburn, *The Making of New World Slavery: From the Baroque to the Modern, 1492–1800* (London: Verso, 1996); Adam Rothman, *Slave Country: American Expansion and the Origins of the Deep South* (Cambridge, MA: Harvard University Press, 2005).

15. Tadman, *Speculators and Slaves*, 141, 155, 172–75.

16. Baptist, *The Half Has Never Been Told*; Michael Green, *The Politics of Indian Removal: Creek Government and Society in Crisis* (Lincoln: University of Nebraska Press, 1982); Thomas Fleming, *The Louisiana Purchase* (Hoboken, NJ: Wiley, 2003); Wright, *Old South, New South*, chaps. 2–4; Joseph G. Baldwin, *The Flush Times of Alabama and Mississippi: A Series of Sketches* (New York: Appleton, 1853); Harry L. Watson, *Liberty and Power: The Politics of Jacksonian America* (New York: Hill and Wang, 1990), 155.

17. Dylan C. Penningroth, *The Claims of Kinfolk: African American Property and Community in the Nineteenth-Century South* (Chapel Hill: University of North Carolina Press, 2003), 49 passim; Alan B. Bromberg, "Slavery in the Virginia Tobacco Factories, 1800–1860" (MA thesis, University of Virginia, 1968), 25–26; Harriet Jacobs, *Incidents in the Life of a Slave Girl* (New York: Oxford University Press, 1988), 11; Jean Fagan Yellin, *Harriet Jacobs: A Life* (New York: Basic Books, 2004), chaps. 1–3; John S. Jacobs, "A True Tale of Slavery," in *The Leisure Hour: A Family Journal of Instruction and Recreation*, February 7, 1861, 86, http://docsouth.unc.edu/neh/jjacobs/jjacobs.html, accessed June 1, 2010.

18. Sarah S. Hughes, "Slaves for Hire: The Allocation of Black Labor in Elizabeth City County, Virginia, 1782–1810," *William and Mary Quarterly*, 3rd ser., 35.2 (1978), 260–86; Christopher Phillips, *Freedom's Port: The African American Community of Baltimore, 1790–1860* (Urbana: University of Illinois Press, 1997); W. Jeffrey Bolster, *Black Jacks: African American Seamen in the Age of Sail* (Cambridge, MA: Harvard University Press, 1997); Cecelski, *Waterman's Song*, chap. 1.

19. Melvin Patrick Ely, *Israel on the Appomattox: A Southern Experiment in Black Freedom from 1790s through the Civil War* (New York: Knopf, 2004), 173.

20. Federal Writers' Project, *North Carolina*, 65.

21. Alex Christopher Meekins, *Elizabeth City, North Carolina, and the Civil War: A History of Battle and Occupation* (Charleston, SC: History Press, 2007), 11; Cecelski, *Waterman's Song*.

22. Troutman, "Grapevine in the Slave Market," 205–6.

23. Robert Dirks, "Networks, Groups, and Adaptation in an Afro-Caribbean Community," *Man*, n.s., 7.4 (1972): 565–85; John W. Blassingame, *The Slave Community: Plantation Life in the Antebellum South* (New York: Oxford University Press, 1972), 41–42; Sidney W. Mintz and Richard Price, *The Birth of African-American Culture: An Anthropological Perspective* (Boston: Beacon Press, 1992), 66; Michael Angelo Gomez, *Exchanging Our Country Marks: The Transformation of African Identities in the Colonial and Antebellum South* (Chapel Hill: University of North Carolina Press, 1998), 6. Herbert Gutman argues, for instance, that "the kin network that surrounded" Frederick Douglass "compensated

for [the] disadvantages" of the loss of his mother at an early age (*The Black Family in Slavery and Freedom, 1750–1925* [New York: Pantheon, 1976], 98, 138).

24. *Virginia Chronicle and Norfolk (VA) and Portsmouth (VA) General Advertiser*, December 8, 1792, America's Historical Newspapers, Early American Newspapers, ser. 1, 1690–1876, AA, accessed January 18, 2008; Bolster, *Black Jacks*, chap. 2. Phillip D. Troutman likens the communications network on the Chesapeake to the Internet: local ports acted like servers as people collected and disseminated knowledge and information along the paths of commerce. Enslaved people staffed many of the transportation trades and therefore had Internet-like access to news and information ("Grapevine in the Slave Market," 205–6); Michael J. Jarvis, *In the Eye of All Trade: Bermuda, Bermudians, and the Maritime Atlantic World, 1680–1783* (Chapel Hill: published for the Omohundro Institute of Early American History and Culture University of North Carolina Press, 2010).

25. Grandy, *Narrative of the Life of Moses Grandy*, 14–15; Bolster, *Black Jacks*, chap. 5.

26. *Edenton (NC) Gazette and Commercial Advertiser*, October 17, 1817, July 11, 1814, in Freddie L. Parker, ed., *Stealing a Little Freedom: Advertisements for Slave Runaways in North Carolina, 1791–1840* (New York: Garland Publishing, 1994), 362–63; *Federal Census of 1810, Edenton, North Carolina*, roll M252-39, p. 220, image 401.00, www.ancestry.com, accessed January 29, 2008; Cecelski, *Waterman's Song*, 52–54.

27. Brenda E. Stevenson, *Life in Black and White: Family and Community in the Slave South* (New York: Oxford University Press, 1996), 160; Penningroth, *Claims of Kinfolk*, 43; Henry Goings, *Rambles of a Runaway from Southern Slavery* (Stratford, Ontario: J. M. Robb, 1869), 71–72; Lynda Morgan, *Emancipation in Virginia's Tobacco Belt, 1850–1870* (Athens: University of Georgia Press, 1992); Schweninger, "The Underside of Slavery."

28. Cecelski, *Waterman's Song*, 34; Verene Shepherd and Kathleen E. A. Monteith, "Pen-Keepers and Coffee Farmers in a Sugar-Plantation Society," in *Slavery Without Sugar: Diversity in Caribbean Economy and Society Since the 17th Century*, ed. Verene A. Shepherd (Gainesville: University of Florida Press, 2002), 82–101; Lois Smathers Neal, *Abstracts of Vital Records from Raleigh, North Carolina, Newspapers, 1820–1829*, vol. 2 (Spartanburg, SC: Reprint Company, 1980), 605. Grice's commerce with Havana in 1810 was blamed on an outbreak of yellow fever in Norfolk, Virginia, and Elizabeth City, North Carolina (*Edenton [NC] Gazette*, reprinted in the *New York Columbian*, September 13, 1810). Grice was listed as master of the *Commerce* in "Evening Post Marine List" (*New-York Evening Post*, October 18, 1802). By the 1820s, he was shipping coffee, linens, logwood, and passengers between Aux Cayes, now Les Cayes, Haiti, and the port of New York City ("Maritime List," *New-York Evening Post*, June 13, 1821). He served as magistrate for Elizabeth City in 1802 after a slave uprising in Camden, Currituck, and Pasquotank counties, taking testimony of witnesses ("More About the Negroes," reprinted from an unnamed Norfolk, Virginia, newspaper in the *New-York Herald*, June 2, 1802, America's Historical Newspapers, Early American Newspapers, ser. 1, 1690–1876, AA, accessed February 12, 2007).

29. Grandy, *Narrative of the Life of Moses Grandy*, 17.

30. Cecelski, *Waterman's Song*, 47; "Obituaries," *Richmond (VA) Enquirer*, August 8, 1823, America's Historical Newspapers, Early American Newspapers, ser. 1, 1690–1876, AA, accessed February 12, 2007; Neal, *Abstracts of Vital Records,* 513. Grice was at least forty-five in 1810, Muse was about thirty-nine, and Grandy was twenty-four. Grice

owned twenty-eight slaves, Muse forty-two, and Grandy four (*Federal Census of 1810, Pasquotank County, North Carolina*, roll M252-41, p. 901, image 378.00, www.ancestry .com, accessed January 29, 2007).

31. That Trewitt may have been a Truitt of Snowhill, Worcester County, Maryland, who captained ships carrying cargoes from the port of Havana to New York and Baltimore (*New York Commercial Advertiser*, December 16, 1805, *Baltimore [MD] North American and Mercantile Daily Advertiser*, May 10, 1808, and *New York Columbian*, May 22, 1810, America's Historical Newspapers, Early American Newspapers, ser. 1, 1690–1876, AA, accessed February 12, 2007). Newspapers also reported the death in 1825 of "Myers F. Truet, a native of Philadelphia, but for many years a resident of Tyrrel County," who died in Edenton.

32. Neal, *Abstracts of Vital Records*, 709; Grandy, *Narrative of the Life of Moses Grandy*, 22–23. William T. Muse, whom Grandy identified as "Mews" in the narrative, owned some forty-one slaves in 1810, three of whom were hired out in Chowan County (*Federal Census of 1810, Pasquotank County, North Carolina*, roll M252-41, p. 915, image 392.00, www.ancestry.com, accessed January 29, 2007; *Federal Census of 1810, Captain Creecy's District, Chowan, North Carolina*, roll M252-39, p. 225, image 411.00, www.an cestry.com, accessed January 29, 2007).

33. Cecelski, *Waterman's Song*, 32; Grandy, *Narrative of the Life of Moses Grandy*, 11; Kemp P. Battle, *History of the University of North Carolina*, vol. 1: *From Its Beginning to the Death of President Swain, 1789–1868* (Raleigh, NC: Edwards and Broughton, 1907), 280, http://docsouth.unc.edu/nc/battle1/battle1.html, accessed March 6, 2007; "Appointment of Revenue Officers," *City of Washington (DC) Gazette*, March 24, 1821, America's Historical Newspapers, Early American Newspapers, ser. 1, 1690–1876, AA, accessed January 24, 2007; Neal, *Abstracts of Vital Records*, 621.

34. Cecelski, *Waterman's Song*, 47; Outland, *Tapping the Pines*, chaps. 2–3.

35. Harriet Beecher Stowe, *Dred: A Tale of the Great Dismal Swamp*, vol. 2 (Boston: Phillips, Sampson, 1856), 303.

36. Grandy, *Narrative of the Life of Moses Grandy*, 25.

37. Grandy, *Narrative of the Life of Moses Grandy*, 27; Mark M. Smith, "Old South Time in Comparative Perspective," *American Historical Review* 101.5 (1996): 1463.

38. Grandy, *Narrative of the Life of Moses Grandy*, 32–33; Cecelski, *Waterman's Song*, 52.

39. Cecelski, *Waterman's Song*, 52; Grandy, *Narrative of the Life of Moses Grandy*, 32–35; Neal, *Abstracts of Vital Records*, 621.

40. Cecelski, *Waterman's Song*, 53–54; Grandy, *Narrative of the Life of Moses Grandy*, 42; W. Jeffrey Bolster, "'To Feel Like a Man': Black Seamen in the Northern States, 1800–1860," *Journal of American History* 76.4 (1990): 1183.

41. *Federal Census of 1840, Suffolk County, Massachusetts*, roll M704-429, p. 198, image 871, www.ancestry.com, accessed September 17, 2010; Grandy, *Narrative of the Life of Moses Grandy*, 7, 16, 46–48, 50–51.

42. Hughes, "Slaves for Hire," 283; Barbara Jeanne Fields, *Slavery and Freedom on the Middle Ground: Maryland in the Nineteenth Century* (New Haven: Yale University Press, 1985), 27–28. Some 40 percent of taxpayers hired slaves in the mixed farming and maritime county of Elizabeth City, Virginia, in the mid–1780s.

43. Frederick Douglass, *Narrative of the Life of Frederick Douglass, an American Slave, Written by Himself* (Boston: Anti-Slavery Office, 1845), 2, http://docsouth.unc.edu/neh/ douglass/douglass.html, accessed January 24, 2007; Johnson, *Soul by Soul*, chap. 1.

44. Dylan C. Penningroth, "My People, My People: The Dynamics of Community in Southern Slavery," in *New Studies in the History of American Slavery*, ed. Edward E. Baptist and Stephanie M. H. Camp (Athens: University of Georgia Press, 2006), 169; Thomas C. Buchanan, "The Slave Mississippi: African-American Steamboat Workers, Networks of Resistance, and the Commercial World of the Western Rivers, 1811–1880" (PhD diss., Carnegie Mellon University, 1998).

45. Schweninger, "The Underside of Slavery"; Stevenson, *Life in Black and White*, 160; Midori Takagi, *"Rearing Wolves to Our Own Destruction": Slavery in Richmond, Virginia, 1782–1865* (Charlottesville: University Press of Virginia, 1999), 37, 147 passim; Morgan, *Emancipation in Virginia's Tobacco Belt*; Jonathan D. Martin, *Divided Mastery: Slave Hiring in the American South* (Cambridge, MA: Harvard University Press, 2004), 81.

46. Frederick Douglass, *My Bondage and My Freedom* (New York: Miller, Orton, and Mulligan, 1855), 447–48; *Baltimore (MD) Patriot and Mercantile Advertiser*, November 17, 1815, 3; Charles Keenan, *Baltimore Directory for 1822 and 1823* (Baltimore: R. J. Matchett, 1822), 306, www.archive.org/details/baltimoredirecto1822keen, accessed May 1, 2010.

47. McFeely, *Frederick Douglass*, 28, 30–31.

48. T. Stephen Whitman, *The Price of Freedom: Slavery and Manumission in Baltimore and Early National Maryland* (Lexington: University of Kentucky Press, 1997), chap. 3; Douglass, *My Bondage and My Freedom*, 141.

49. McFeely, *Frederick Douglass*, 30–31, 37–39.

50. Douglass, *My Bondage and My Freedom*, 156–57; McFeely, *Frederick Douglass*, 33–36; Caleb Bingham, ed., *Columbian Orator* (Middlebury, VT: William Slade, 1816), i; Daneen Wardrop, " 'While I am Writing': Webster's 1825 *Spelling Book*, the Ell, and Frederick Douglass's Positioning of Language," *African American Review* 32.4 (1998): 649–60; Lisa A. Sisco, " 'Writing in the Spaces Left': Literacy as a Process of Becoming in the Narratives of Frederick Douglass," *American Transcendental Quarterly* 9.3 (1995): 195–227; Daniel J. Royer, "The Process of Literacy as Communal Involvement in the Narratives of Frederick Douglass," *African American Review* 28.3 (1994): 363–74.

51. Historical Census Browser, Geospatial and Statistical Data Center, University of Virginia Library, http://mapserver.lib.virginia.edu, accessed May 1, 2010.

52. Douglass, *My Bondage and My Freedom*, 167.

53. Waldo E. Martin Jr., *The Mind of Frederick Douglass* (Chapel Hill: University of North Carolina Press, 1986), 20.

54. Douglass, *My Bondage and My Freedom*, 200.

55. Douglass, *My Bondage and My Freedom*, 238; Frederick Douglass, *Life and Times of Frederick Douglass* (Boston: De Wolfe and Fiske, 1892), 140, 175, http://docsouth.unc.edu/neh/dougl92/dougl92.html, accessed June 16, 2007.

56. Douglass, *Narrative of the Life of Frederick Douglass*, 98–99; Ulrich Bonnell Phillips, *Life and Labor in the Old South* (Columbia: University of South Carolina Press, 2007 [1930]), 177; Robert W. Fogel and Stanley Engerman, *Time on the Cross: The Economics of American Negro Slavery* (New York: Norton, 1989 [1974]), chap. 3.

57. Douglass, *Narrative of the Life of Frederick Douglass*, 98–99; Fionnghuala Sweeney, *Frederick Douglass and the Atlantic World* (Liverpool, UK: Liverpool University Press, 2007), chap. 3.

58. Barbara E. Wallace, " 'Fair Daughters of Africa': African American Women in Baltimore, 1790–1860" (PhD diss., University of California, Los Angeles, 2001); McFeely, *Frederick Douglass*, 65–68.

59. John Thomas Scharf, *History of Baltimore City and County, from the Earliest Period to the Present Day* (Philadelphia: Louis H. Everts, 1881), 293.

60. Dickson J. Preston, *Frederick Douglass: The Maryland Years* (Baltimore: Johns Hopkins University Press, 1980), 146; McFeely, *Frederick Douglass*, 63; Robin Law, ed., *From Slave Trade to "Legitimate" Commerce: The Commercial Transition in Nineteenth-Century West Africa* (Cambridge: Cambridge University Press, 1995); Herbert S. Klein, *The Atlantic Slave Trade* (Cambridge: Cambridge University Press, 1999), chap. 8.

61. Douglass, *My Bondage and My Freedom*, 146; Douglass, *Narrative of the Life of Frederick Douglass*, 33; Herman Melville, *Moby-Dick* (New York: Knopf, 1991), 132; Joseph C. Dorsey, *Slave Traffic in the Age of Abolition: Rico, West Africa, and the Non-Hispanic Caribbean, 1815–1859* (Gainesville: University of Florida Press, 2003).

62. Douglass, *My Bondage and My Freedom*, 349; Eric Foner, *Free Labor, Free Soil, Free Men* (New York: Oxford University Press, 1970); Seth Rockman, *Scraping By: Wage Labor, Slavery, and Survival in Early Baltimore* (Baltimore: Johns Hopkins University Press, 2009), chaps. 5 and 8.

63. Rockman, *Scraping By*, 133.

64. Rockman, *Scraping By*, 246.

65. Ferebee, *A Brief History*, 6–7.

66. Olly Whitehurst lived with Sally Whitehurst, sixty, and Peter, twenty-one, a farmer. Whitehurst owned $500 worth of real estate (*Federal Census of 1850, Indian Ridge, Currituck County, North Carolina*, roll M432-627, p. 184, image 370, www.ancestry.com, accessed October 16, 2006; Ferebee, *A Brief History*, 6–7).

67. Meekins, *Elizabeth City*, 15, 87; *Elizabeth City (NC) Democratic Pioneer*, October 18, 1859, cited in "Historic Elizabeth City: The Architectural Heritage of Elizabeth City, North Carolina," www.historicelizabethcity.org/text/1.3.1.html, accessed March 18, 2010.

68. David Brion Davis and Sidney Mintz, *The Boisterous Sea of Liberty: A Documentary History of America from Discovery Through the Civil War* (New York: Oxford University Press, 1998); Eric Foner, *The Story of American Freedom* (New York: Norton, 1998).

69. Clement Eaton, "Slave-Hiring in the Upper South: A Step Toward Freedom," *Mississippi Valley Historical Review* 46.4 (1960): 669; Douglas R. Egerton, "Markets without a Market Revolution: Southern Planters and Capitalism," *Journal of the Early Republic* 16.2 (1996): 207–22; Ted Maris-Wolf, "Self-Enslavement in Virginia, 1854–1864," paper presented at the Charting New Courses in the History of Slavery and Emancipation Conference, Gulfport, Mississippi, March 3–6, 2010. The 1850 and 1860 censuses list an Enoch Ferebee, a farmer, whose estate grew substantially in the decade of the 1850s. In 1850, twenty-eight year-old Enoch Ferebee lived in Currituck County, North Carolina, listed his occupation as "farmer," and claimed to own $2,000 worth of real estate and twelve slaves. He is listed on the same census sheet as Sally and Peter Whitehurst and on the same slave schedule in which Sally Whitehurst was listed as owning four slaves, including a black female aged thirty and a black male aged eight. In 1860, thirty-nine year-old E. D. Ferebee of Currituck County, North Carolina, owned $6,000 worth of real estate and $15,000 worth of personal property, including twenty-three slaves. London Ferebee was born in 1849; he reported that his mother Chloe died in 1859, after twenty-two years of marriage to his father. If Abel had married in his early twenties, in 1837, he would have been in his mid-forties by 1860 (*Federal Census of 1850, Indian Ridge, Currituck, North Carolina*, roll M432-627, p. 184B, image 374, www.ancestry.com, accessed

October 16, 2006; *Federal Census of 1850, Slave Schedule, Indian Ridge, Currituck County, North Carolina*, M432-651, p. 1, image 1, www.ancestry.com, accessed September 17, 2010; *Federal Census of 1860, Indian Ridge, Currituck County, North Carolina*, roll M653-895, p. 267, image 5, www.ancestry.com, accessed October 16, 2006; *Federal Census of 1860, Slave Schedule, Indian Ridge, Currituck County, North Carolina*, p. 3, image 3, www.ancestry.com, accessed October 16, 2006).

70. Martin, *Divided Mastery*, chaps. 3 and 5; Cecelski, *Waterman's Song*, 27, 71, 137–38.

71. Gutman, *Black Family*, 129, 132–33.

72. Grandy, *Narrative of the Life of Moses Grandy*, 46, 50; Eric Anthony Sheppard, *Ancestor's Call* (Elkridge, MD: Tech-Rep Associates, 2003), 118–19. Moses Grandy was living in Boston's second ward; three males ten to twenty-four are listed, along with one male twenty-four to thirty-five and one female twenty-six to fifty-five (*Federal Census of 1840, Suffolk County, Massachusetts*, roll M704-429, p. 198, image 871, www.ancestry.com, accessed September 17, 2010).

73. Wayne K. Durrill, "Slavery, Kinship, and Dominance: The Black Community at Somerset Place Plantation, 1786–1860," *Slavery and Abolition* 13.2 (1992): 15–16; Stevenson, *Life in Black and White*, 170, 209; Wilma A. Dunaway, *The African-American Family in Slavery and Emancipation* (Cambridge: Cambridge University Press, 2003), 259; Wilma A. Dunaway, *Slavery in the American Mountain South* (Cambridge: Cambridge University Press, 2003), 255.

74. Robinson, *From Log Cabin to the Pulpit*, 158; Robert Francis Engs, *Freedom's First Generation: Black Hampton, Virginia, 1861–1890* (New York: Fordham University Press, 2004), chap. 1.

75. Robinson, *From Log Cabin to the Pulpit*, 11, 47; Alan D. Watson, *Wilmington, North Carolina, to 1861* (Jefferson, NC: McFarland, 2003), 218.

76. Watson, *Wilmington*, 204; California Department of Insurance, slave-era insurance registry, www.insurance.ca.gov/0100-consumers/0300-public-programs/0200-slavery-era-insur, accessed May 15, 2010.

77. Robinson, *From Log Cabin to the Pulpit*, 11–12. The majority of the population of New Hanover County, North Carolina, was African American. In 1850, slaves accounted for over 48 percent of the population and free people of color 5 percent. In 1850, slaves made up 46 percent of the population and free people of color 4 percent (Historical Census Browser, University of Virginia, Geospatial and Statistical Data Center, http://mapserver.lib.virginia.edu, accessed February 12, 2010).

78. Robinson, *From Log Cabin to the Pulpit*, 11, 26; Bolster, *Black Jacks*; Jeff Forrett, "Slaves, Poor Whites, and the Underground Economy of the Rural Carolinas," *Journal of Southern History* 70.4 (2004): 783–824.

79. Robinson, *From Log Cabin to the Pulpit*, 26.

80. Robinson, *From Log Cabin to Pulpit*, 13; David S. Cecelski, "The Shores of Freedom: The Maritime Underground Railroad in North Carolina, 1800–1861," *North Carolina Historical Review* 71.2 (1994): 174–206; Cecelski, *Waterman's Song*, 123–27.

81. Mark S. Granovetter, "The Strength of Weak Ties," *American Journal of Sociology* 78.6 (1973): 1360–80. My thanks to Douglas Bristol for this reference.

82. Mark S. Granovetter, "The Strength of Weak Ties: A Network Theory Revisited," in *Sociological Theory*, vol. 1, ed. Randall Collins (San Francisco: Jossey-Bass, 1983), 201–33.

83. Terry Alford, *Prince among Slaves: The True Story of an African Prince Sold into Slavery in the American South* (New York: Harcourt Brace Jovanovich, 1977).

84. Robinson, *From Log Cabin to the Pulpit*, 13.

85. J. S. Holliday, *The Rush for Riches: The Gold Fever and the Making of California* (Berkeley: University of California Press, 1999); Daniel Walker Howe, *What Hath God Wrought: The Transformation of America, 1815–1848* (New York: Oxford University Press, 2007), chap. 20.

86. Leonard L. Richards, *The California Gold Rush and the Coming of the Civil War* (New York: Knopf, 2007), 73–78.

87. Quinard Taylor, "Urban Black Labor in the West, 1849–1949: Reconceptualizing the Image of a Region," in *The African American Urban Experience: Perspectives from the Colonial Period to the Present*, ed. Joe William Trotter, Earl Lewis, and Tera W. Hunter (New York: Palgrave Macmillan, 2004), 101.

88. Greg Gaar and Ryder W. Miller, *San Francisco: A Natural History* (Charleston, SC: Arcadia Publishing, 2006); Gray A. Brechin, *Imperial San Francisco: Urban Power, Earthly Ruin* (Berkeley: University of California Press, 2006); "Marine Intelligence," *New York Times*, March 15, 1858.

89. "Internal Improvements," *Debow's Review* 14.4 (1853): 407–13, Making of America, http://name.umdl.umich.edu/acg1336.1-14.004, accessed February 10, 2010; John Haskell Kemble, "Pacific Mail Service between Panama and San Francisco, 1849–1851," *Pacific Historical Review* 2.4 (1933): 405–17; John Haskell Kemble, "The Genesis of the Pacific Mail Steamship Company," *California Historical Society Quarterly* 13.4 (1934): 386–406.

90. Robinson, *From Log Cabin to the Pulpit*, 17. African Americans had served on whaling ships in the Pacific since at least the 1820s (Martha S. Putney, *Black Sailors: Afro-American Merchant Seamen and Whalemen Prior to the Civil War* [Westport, CT: Greenwood, 1987], 46).

91. Hinks, *To Awaken My Afflicted Brethren*, 137–46; Douglass, *My Bondage and My Freedom*, 338.

92. Robinson, *From Log Cabin to the Pulpit*, 14–16.

93. Douglass, *My Bondage and My Freedom*, 448.

CHAPTER THREE: Domestics

1. George Fitzhugh, "Slavery Justified," in *Sociology for the South* (Richmond, VA: A. Morris, 1854), 245–46, http://docsouth.unc.edu/southlit/fitzhughsoc/fitzhugh.html, accessed June 1, 2010.

2. William H. Robinson, *From Log Cabin to the Pulpit; or, Fifteen Years in Slavery*, 3rd ed. (Eau Claire, WI: James H. Tifft, 1913), 25, http://docsouth.unc.edu/fpn/robinson/robinson.html, accessed February 3, 2010.

3. Robinson, *From Log Cabin to the Pulpit*, 35–39; David S. Cecelski, *The Waterman's Song: Slavery and Freedom in Maritime North Carolina* (Chapel Hill: University of North Carolina Press, 2001), 123–38.

4. Robinson, *From Log Cabin to the Pulpit*, 42–44; Philip D. Troutman, "Grapevine in the Slave Market: African American Geopolitical Literacy and the 1841 *Creole* Revolt," in *The Chattel Principle: Internal Slave Trade in the Americas*, ed. Walter Johnson (New Haven: Yale University Press, 2004), 203–33; Walter Johnson, *Soul by Soul: Life Inside the Antebellum Slave Market* (Cambridge, MA: Harvard University Press, 1999), 167.

5. Historical Census Browser, Geospatial and Statistical Data Center, University of Virginia Library, http://mapserver.lib.virginia.edu, accessed May 1, 2010.

6. Frederick Law Olmsted, *A Journey in the Seaboard Slave States, with Remarks on Their Economy* (New York: Dix and Edwards, 1856), 19, http://docsouth.unc.edu/nc/olm sted/olmsted.html, accessed March 19, 2010.

7. Robinson, *From Log Cabin to the Pulpit*, 45.

8. Robinson, *From Log Cabin to the Pulpit*, 45–46; Johnson, *Soul by Soul*, chap. 4; Olmsted, *A Journey in the Seaboard Slave States*, 375.

9. Robinson, *From Log Cabin to the Pulpit*, 46; Steven Deyle, *Carry Me Back: The Domestic Slave Trade in American Life* (New York: Oxford University Press, 2005), chap. 8.

10. Robinson, *From Log Cabin to the Pulpit*, 46–47; Walter Johnson, "The Future Store," in *The Chattel Principle*, 1–31; Roberta Sassatelli, *Consumer Culture: History, Theory, and Politics* (London: SAGE, 2007), chap. 1.

11. Robinson, *From Log Cabin to the Pulpit*, 47; W. Eugene Ferslew, *Second Annual Directory for the City of Richmond: To Which Is Added a Business Directory for 1860* (Richmond, VA: Ferslew, 1860), www.mdgorman.com/Written_Accounts/1860%20Business %20Directory.htm, accessed June 1, 2010.

12. The desperate tactic of enlisting those responsible for dislocations was not altogether unusual. A young South Carolina railroad worker "bought by the company," an official recorded, "desired to be sold as he wished to accompany his mother who had been bought by a person about to leave the state." The matter was referred to the president of the South Carolina Canal and Railroad Company (entry, November 16, 1835, minute book, board of directors, 1835–41, South Carolina Canal and Rail Road Company, Ms84–149, Norfolk Southern Historical Collection, Norfolk, VA). Thanks to Aaron Marrs for this reference.

13. Robinson, *From Log Cabin to the Pulpit*, 59, 69.

14. Robinson, *From Log Cabin to the Pulpit*, 74.

15. Robinson, *From Log Cabin to the Pulpit*, 75.

16. Robinson, *From Log Cabin to the Pulpit*, 76.

17. Robinson, *From Log Cabin to the Pulpit*, 98–113.

18. Phillip D. Troutman, "Correspondences in Black and White: Sentiment and the Slave Market Revolution," in *New Studies in the History of American Slavery*, ed. Edward E. Baptist and Stephanie M. H. Camp (Athens: University of Georgia Press, 2006), 214.

19. For two opposing views, see William Link, *Roots of Secession: Slavery and Politics in Antebellum Virginia* (Chapel Hill: University of North Carolina Press, 2004), and Takagi, *"Rearing Wolves to Our Own Destruction": Slavery in Richmond, Virginia, 1782–1865* (Charlottesville: University Press of Virginia, 1999).

20. John T. Thornton to Lewis Hill, January 15, 1842, Lewis Hill Papers, mss BR 92, Robert Alonzo Brock Collection, HL.

21. R. V. Tiffey to R. H. Dickinson, February 7, 1847, R. H. Dickinson and Brothers, correspondence, 1846, U.S. Slavery Collection, box 1, folder 2, AAS; "Girl Susan," February 23, 1847, R. H. Dickinson and Brothers, daybook, 1846–49, U.S. Slavery Collection, folio volume, AAS.

22. William Spotswood Fontaine to Hill and Dabney, May 1, 1840, December 16, 1840, Robert Hill, correspondence and documents, 1778–1857, mss BR 41, Robert Alonzo Brock Collection, HL.

23. Elisha Berry held thirty-three slaves in 1840; the census information includes women and children who conform to the ages of Eliza, Randall, and Emily (*Federal Census of 1840, Prince George's County, Maryland*, roll M704-169, p. 10, image 27, www .ancestry.com, accessed March 10, 2007).

24. Helen W. Brown, *Index of Marriage Licenses, Prince George's County, Maryland, 1776–1886* (Baltimore: Genealogical Publishing Company, 1995), 207; Annette Gordon-Reed, *The Hemingses of Monticello: An American Family* (New York: Norton, 2008), 106.

25. Solomon Northup, *Twelve Years a Slave: Narrative of Solomon Northup, a Citizen of New-York, Kidnapped in Washington City in 1841, and Rescued in 1853* (Auburn [NY]: Derby and Miller, 1853), 54, http://docsouth.unc.edu/fpn/northup/northup.html, accessed March 10, 2007; William W. Freehling, *The Road to Disunion*, vol. 2: *Secessionists Triumphant, 1854–1861* (New York: Oxford University Press, 2007), 222–27.

26. Northup, *Twelve Years a Slave*, 54. The trader in question was James Burch, identified in the census as a resident of Washington, D.C., and owner of seven slaves in 1840. The 1850 census does not identify an occupation or approximate value of his estate but does list him as the owner of three slaves (*Federal Census for 1840, Washington, District of Columbia*, roll M740-35, p. 38, image 78, www.ancestry.com, accessed March 16, 2007; *Federal Census for 1850, Ward 1, Washington, District of Columbia*, roll M432-56, p. 31, image 68, www.ancestry.com, accessed March 16, 2007; *Federal Census for 1850, Slave Schedule, Ward 1, District of Columbia*, M432-57, p. 1, image 1, www.ancestry .com, accessed March 16, 2007).

27. Northup contends that this was slave trader Theophilus Freeman's intention (*Twelve Years a Slave*, 87).

28. That was Peter Compton, owner of five slaves in 1840 (*Federal Census of 1840, Rapides Parish, Louisiana*, roll M740-128, p. 195, image 401, www.ancestry.com, accessed March 16, 2007).

29. Northup, *Twelve Years a Slave*, 159.

30. Deborah Gray White, *Ar'n't I A Woman?: Female Slaves in the Plantation South*, 2nd ed. (New York: Norton, 1999); Elizabeth Fox-Genovese, *Within the Plantation Household: Black and White Women of the Old South* (Chapel Hill: University of North Carolina Press, 1988); Stephanie M. H. Camp, *Closer to Freedom: Enslaved Women and Everyday Resistance in the Plantation South* (Chapel Hill: University of North Carolina Press, 2004).

31. B. S. Herndon to Lewis Hill, December 31, 1853, Lewis Hill Papers, mss BR 41, Robert Alonzo Brock Collection, HL.

32. Robert Russell, *North America: Its Agriculture and Climate, Containing Observations on the Agriculture and Climate of Canada, the United States, and the Island of Cuba* (Edinburgh: A. and C. Black, 1857), 151.

33. Russell, *North America*, 151; Ulrich Bonnell Phillips Papers, ms 397, folder 266, box 28, YU; Schweninger, "The Underside of Slavery." Thanks to Susan E. O'Donovan for a copy of the document from the Phillips Papers.

34. Seth Rockman, *Scraping By: Wage Labor, Slavery, and Survival in Early Baltimore* (Baltimore: Johns Hopkins University Press, 2009), 41.

35. *Richmond (VA) Enquirer*, July 9, 1830, America's Historical Newspapers, Early American Newspapers, ser. 1, 1690–1876, AA, accessed April 30, 2010; Ferslew, *Second Annual Directory*, 21. Another authority contends that Omohundro's third wife Corinna was Corinna Clark, b. 1823. Malvern Hill Omohundro, The Omohundro Genealogical

Record: *The Omohundros and Allied Families in America* (Staunton, VA: McClure Printing Company, 1951), 472.

36. Suzanne G. Schnittman, "Slavery in Virginia's Urban Tobacco Industry" (PhD diss., University of Rochester, 1986), 132–37.

37. William Wells Brown, *Clotel; or, The President's Daughter: A Narrative of Slave Life in the United States* (London: Partridge and Oakey, 1853). Brown had witnessed the slave market firsthand as a young man when, not unlike Robinson, he was put to work as a slave trader's assistant. Entries showing Silas Omohundro buying or selling slaves at R. H. Dickinson's auction include, for example, April 1, 1846, April 24, 1846, June 29, 1846, July 28, 1846, January 27, 1847, March 31, 1847, March 23, 1847, May 1, 1847, May 31, 1847, June 9, 1847, June 15, 1847, July 5, 1847, July 23, 1847, September 1, 1847, January 10, 1849, and March 3, 1849 (R. H. Dickinson and Brothers, daybook, 1846–49, U.S. Slavery Collection, folio volume, AAS; market and general account book, 1858–64, folder 5, Silas Omohundro Business and Estate Records, 1842–82, accession 29642, LVA).

38. George Fitzhugh, "Southern Thought," *De Bow's Review* 28.4 (1857): 347.

39. Deyley, *Carry Me Back*, 126–27.

40. Isaac Franklin to Rice Ballard, January 1, 1834, Rice C. Ballard Papers, Wilson Library, UNC.

41. James Franklin to Rice Ballard, May 13, 1832, and Isaac Franklin to Rice Ballard, November 1, 1833, Rice C. Ballard Papers, Wilson Library, UNC.

42. Robert H. Gudmestad, "The Richmond Slave Market, 1840–1860" (MA thesis, University of Richmond, 1993), 107.

43. Edward E. Baptist, "'Cuffy,' 'Fancy Maids,' and 'One-Eyed Men': Rape, Commodification, and the Domestic Slave Trade in the United States," *American Historical Review* 106.5 (2001), 1619–50; Ethan Allen Andrews, *Slavery and the Domestic Slave-Trade in the United States* (Boston: Light and Stearns, 1836), 166.

44. Accounts of Silas and R. H. Omohundro's slave trade, 1857–64, mss 4122, Small Library Special Collections, UVA; Tadman, *Speculators and Slaves*, 125.

45. James C. Scott, *Weapons of the Weak: Everyday Forms of Peasant Resistance* (New Haven: Yale University Press, 1985).

46. Farmers Bank of Virginia with Silas Omohundro, 1847–59, folder 2, Silas Omohundro Business and Estate Records, 1842–82, accession 29642, LVA; market and general account book, 1858–64, folder 5, Silas Omohundro Business and Estate Records, 1842–82, accession 29642, LVA; Laura F. Edwards, "Status without Rights: African Americans and the Tangled History of Law and Governance in the Nineteenth-Century U.S. South." *The American Historical Review* 112.2 (2007): 365–93.

47. Clement M. Husbands, *The Law of Married Women in Pennsylvania, with a View of the Law of Trusts in that State* (Philadelphia: T. and J. W. Johnson, 1878), 7.

48. Philip D. Troutman, "Slave Trade and Sentiment" (PhD diss., University of Virginia, 2000), 105–6.

49. Scott, *Weapons of the Weak*.

50. Laura F. Edwards, "Enslaved Women and the Law: Paradoxes of Subordination in the Post-Revolutionary Carolinas," *Slavery and Abolition* 26.2 (2005): 307; market and account book, 1858–64, folder 5, Silas Omohundro Business and Estate Records, 1842–82, accession 29642, LVA.

51. *Cooper, Executor v. Omohundro*, 86 U.S. 65, 22 L. Ed. 47, 19 Wall. 65 (1873), LexisNexis Academic, accessed June 5, 2010.

52. Troutman, "Slave Trade and Sentiment," 112; Husbands, *Law of Married Women in Pennsylvania*, 7

53. Will book 2, Richmond City Circuit Court, 228, LVA.

54. Will book 2, Richmond City Circuit Court, 228, LVA; *Federal Census of 1870, Jefferson Ward, Richmond, Virginia*, roll M593-1653, p. 488, image 340, www.ancestry.com, accessed December 12, 2006; money paid out and received, misc. reel 1315, boarding charges, 1851–64, Silas Omohundro Business and Estate Records, 1842–82, accession 29642, LVA.

55. Johnson, *Soul by Soul*, chap. 4.

56. Charles Emory Stevens, *Anthony Burns: A History* (Boston: Jewett , 1856), 189–90, http://docsouth.unc.edu/neh/stevens/stevens.html, accessed December 11, 2006; Troutman, "Grapevine in the Slave Market," 211; Matthew R. Laird, *Preliminary Archaeological Investigation of the Lumpkin's Jail Site (44HE1053), Richmond, Virginia* (Williamsburg, VA: James River Institute for Archaeology, 2006).

57. African Baptist Church, Richmond, minutes, 1841–59, bk. 1, misc. reel 494, LVA. Thanks to Philip Schwarz for this research.

58. Stevens, *Anthony Burns*, 192–93.

59. Gordon S. Barker, "Secession and Slavery as a Positive Good: The Impact of the Anthony Burns Drama in Boston and Virginia," *Virginia Magazine of History and Biography*, 118.2 (2010): 137–73; Troutman, "Slave Trade and Sentiment," 106; Stevens, *Anthony Burns: A History*, 193. Michael Chesson writes that "some of the best families in the city were involved in the trade, often as silent partners in a firm. Firms listed as commission merchants, etc., had extensive business in the trade; not just those listed specifically as Negro traders" (email to author, December 17, 2006). Robert Lumpkin, aged fifty-four in 1860, was estimated to own some $20,000 worth of personal property and $6,845 worth of real property (*Federal Census for 1860, Ward 1, Richmond, Virginia*, roll M653-1352, p. 144, image 147, www.ancestry.com accessed, January 17, 2007).

60. Stevens, *Anthony Burns*, 191; Abigail Tucker, "Devil's Half Acre," *Smithsonian* 39.12 (2009): 20–22.

61. Tucker, "Devil's Half Acre," 22.

62. Baptist, " 'Cuffy,' 'Fancy Maids,' and 'One-Eyed Men.' "

63. *Federal Census for 1880, Wards 20 and 21, Philadelphia, Pennsylvania*, roll T9-1180, enumeration district 417, p. 457.1000, image 0361, www.ancestry.com, accessed July 24, 2008; *Davis v. Crouch*, 94 U.S. 514, 24 L. Ed. 281 (1876), http://bulk.resource.org/courts.gov/c/US/94/94.US.514.html, accessed July 24, 2008.

64. *Federal Census for 1850, Richmond, Virginia*, roll M432-951, p. 399, image 325, www.ancestry.com, accessed July 24, 2008.

65. *Federal Census for 1860, Ward 1, Richmond, Virginia*, roll M653-1352, p. 132, image 135, www.ancestry.com, accessed July 24, 2008; *Federal Census for 1860, Slave Schedule, Ward 1, Richmond, Virginia*, M653-1392, p. 44, image 44, www.ancestry.com, accessed July 24, 2008.

66. *Federal Census for 1860, Ward 1, Richmond, Virginia*, roll M653-1352, p. 132, image 135; *Federal Census for 1860, Slave Schedule, Ward 1, Richmond, Virginia*, M653-1392, p. 44, image 44, www.ancestry.com, accessed July 24, 2008.

67. Will of Hector Davis, executed March 21, 1859, cited in *Davis v. Crouch*.

68. *Daily Richmond (VA) Enquirer*, October 9, 1862; *Richmond (VA) Enquirer*, March 30,

1863, America's Historical Newspapers, Early American Newspapers, ser. 1, 1690–1876, AA, accessed July 25, 2008; Ferslew, *Second Annual Directory*, 2.

69. Audubon Davis, obituary, *New York Times*, March 16, 1885; *Federal Census of 1900, Ward 37, Philadelphia, Pennsylvania*, roll T623-1478, enumeration district 497, p. 8B, image 361, www.ancestry.com, accessed July 25, 2008. In this census record, Ann Davis was listed as a mother of five with two children still alive; it is indicated that she could read and write.

70. David Walker, *David Walker's Appeal, in Four Articles, Together with a Preamble, to the Coloured Citizens of the World, but in Particular, and Very Expressly, to those of the United States of America, Written in Boston, State of Massachusetts, September 28, 1829* (Boston: by the author, 1830), http://docsouth.unc.edu/nc/walker/walker.html, accessed July 25, 2008.

71. Walker, *Appeal*, 28; Thomas Jefferson, *Notes on the State of Virginia* (Philadelphia: Prichard and Hall, 1788), xiv, xviii, http://docsouth.unc.edu/southlit/jefferson/jeffer son.html, accessed July 25, 2008.

72. *New-Hampshire Patriot and State Gazette*, September 14, 1829, America's Historical Newspapers, Early American Newspapers, ser. 1, 1690–1876, AA, accessed May 12, 2007; Walker, *Appeal*, 28.

73. Walker, *Appeal*, 30.

74. Walker, *Appeal*, 29–30; Henry Mayer, *All On Fire: William Lloyd Garrison and the Abolition of Slavery* (New York: Norton, 1998), chap. 6; Peter B. Hinks, *To Awaken My Afflicted Brethren: David Walker and the Problem of Antebellum Slave Resistance* (University Park: Pennsylvania State University Press, 1997), 137–39; 239. Strains of Walker's lines of thinking are evident in Stanley Elkins, *Slavery: A Problem in American Intellectual and Institutional Life* (Chicago: University of Chicago Press, 1959).

75. In a forthcoming book on the Turner revolt, Wayne K. Durrill argues that the rebellions of 1830–32 were related and coordinated and that after them many conspirators who were not killed were sold off to the lower South, where they rebelled again.

76. Margaret Washington, "'From motives of delicacy': Sexuality and Morality in the Narratives of Sojourner Truth and Harriet Jacobs," *Journal of African American History* 92.1 (2007): 57–73.

77. Harriet Jacobs, *Incidents in the Life of a Slave Girl, Written by Herself*, ed. L. Maria Child (Boston: published for the author, 1861), 63, http://docsouth.unc.edu/fpn/jacobs/jacobs.html, accessed March 15, 2010.

78. Jean Fagan Yellin, *Harriet Jacobs: A Life* (New York: Basic Books, 2005), 24; Jacobs, *Incidents*, 31.

79. Yellin, *Harriet Jacobs*, 17.

80. Yellin, *Harriet Jacobs*, 28–29.

81. Yellin, *Harriet Jacobs*, 30, 39–40; Jacobs, *Incidents*, 126, 129–30.

82. Yellin, *Harriet Jacobs*, 26; Jacobs, *Incidents*, 86, 129–30.

83. Allen Parker, *Recollections of Slavery Times* (Worcester, MA: Charles W. Burbank, 1895), 58, http://docsouth.unc.edu/neh/parker/parker.html, accessed June 1, 2010; Yellin, *Harriet Jacobs*, chap. 3, 279n.

84. Frederick Douglass, *Narrative of the Life of Frederick Douglass, an American Slave, Written by Himself* (Boston: Anti-Slavery Office, 1845), 2–4, http://docsouth.unc.edu/neh/douglass/douglass.html, accessed February 1, 2008.

85. Jacobs, *Incidents*, 129–30; Yellin, *Harriet Jacobs*, 33–35.

86. "D. In Edenton, at the house of Mrs. E. Horniblow, on the 30th [August, 1810] on his way home, Mr. John B. Hunter, of Williamstown," in Lois Smathers Neal, *Abstracts of Vital Records from Raleigh, North Carolina Newspapers, 1799–1819*, vol. 1 (Spartanburg, SC: Reprint Company, 1979), 254.

87. Freddie L. Parker, *Running for Freedom: Slave Runaways in North Carolina, 1775–1840* (New York: Garland, 1993); Jacobs, *Incidents*, 11–14.

88. Yellin, *Harriet Jacobs*, 9–12.

89. Shipping news, *Norfolk (VA) American Beacon*, March 24, 1817, December 15, 1817, April 23, 1818, November 7, 1815, May 24, 1816, America's Historical Newspapers, Early American Newspapers, ser. 1, 1690–1876, AA, accessed January 17, 2008.

90. The canal company faced its own labor problems, advertising a reward for the recapture of Joe, Dempsey, March, and Willoughby in 1818. The four enslaved men, between twenty-three and thirty years of age, had absconded that spring. All had been bought from different owners in Camden and Currituck counties and were property of the canal company (*Edenton [NC] Gazette and Commercial Advertiser*, May 12, 1818, cited in Freddie L. Parker, *Stealing a Little Freedom: Advertisements for Slave Runaways in North Carolina, 1791–1840* [New York: Garland, 1991], 365).

91. *Edenton (NC) Gazette*, April 22, 1830, cited in Yellin, *Harriet Jacobs*, 33.

92. *Edenton (NC) Gazette and North Carolina Advertiser*, October 15, 1811, cited in Parker, *Stealing a Little Freedom*, 356–57.

93. *Edenton (NC) Gazette*, January 14, 1812, cited in Parker, *Stealing a Little Freedom*, 359.

94. Yellin, *Harriet Jacobs*, 12–14. Blount's brother Lemuel Hoskins married into the Norcom family of Chowan County, North Carolina. Blount was also likely related to Sawyer through Mary Bonner Blount, who married James Iredell Tredwell in 1827; the marriage bond had been drawn up by Sawyer (Lois Smathers Neal, *Abstracts of Vital Records from Raleigh, North Carolina Newspapers, 1820–1829*, vol. 2 [Spartanburg, SC: Reprint Company, 1980], 707; Lucy Nita Bonner Neblock, *The Bonner Legacy: A History of Some of the Bonners* [Oak Grove, MO: A and L Computing, 1999], 41; "Queries and Answers," *North Carolina Historical and Genealogical Register* 1.3 [1900]: 460–61; "Notes and Queries," *North Carolina Historical and Genealogical Register* 2.3 [1901]: 312–13; *Federal Census for 1830, Edenton, North Carolina*, roll M19-119, pp. 335–337, images 29–35, www.ancestry.com, accessed September 18, 2010).

95. Jacobs, *Incidents*, 160–66.

96. Yellin, *Harriet Jacobs*, 55–60.

97. Georgia Kreiger, "Playing Dead: Harriet Jacobs's Survival Strategy in Incidents in the Life of a Slave Girl," *African American Review* 42.3/4 (2008): 607–21.

98. Jacobs, *Incidents*, 170; Yellin, *Harriet Jacobs*, 45–48; Cecelski, *Waterman's Song*, 135. Seamen faced severe penalties for aiding fugitives (Bolster, *Black Jacks: African American Seamen in the Age of Sail* [Cambridge, MA: Harvard University Press, 1997], 212–13).

99. Jacobs, *Incidents*, 172; Yellin, *Harriet Jacobs*, 54–55; Herbert Dale Pegg, *The Whig Party in North Carolina* (Chapel Hill, NC: Colonial Press, 1968), 87–95.

100. Yellin, *Harriet Jacobs*, 60; Jacobs, *Incidents*, 172.

101. Laura F. Edwards, "Status without Rights," 365–93.

102. Jacobs, *Incidents*, 193.

103. Yellin, *Harriet Jacobs*, chap. 5.

104. Tucker, "Devil's Half Acre," 22.

105. Jacobs, *Incidents*, 193.

106. John W. Blassingame, *The Slave Community: Plantation Life in the Antebellum South*, rev. ed. (New York: Oxford University Press, 1979); White, *Aren't I A Woman?*, chap. 4; Ben Schiller, "Learning Their Letters: Critical Literacy, Epistolary Culture, and Slavery in the Antebellum South," *Southern Quarterly* 45.3 (2008): 11–29.

CHAPTER FOUR: Makers

1. *Richmond (VA) Enquirer*, August 29, 1804, America's Historical Newspapers, Early American Newspapers, ser. 1, 1690–1876, AA, accessed April 29, 2010; J. B. Taylor, *Biography of Elder Lott Cary, Late Missionary to Africa* (Baltimore: Armstrong and Berry, 1837), 13, http://docsouth.unc.edu/neh/taylor/taylor.html (accessed March 21, 2007).

2. Walter Johnson, *Soul by Soul: Life Inside the Antebellum Slave Market* (Cambridge, MA: Harvard University Press, 1999), 242n7; Charles B. Dew, *Ironmaker to the Confederacy: Joseph R. Anderson and the Tredegar Iron Works* (Richmond: Library of Virginia, 1999); Robert Starobin, *Industrial Slavery in the Old South* (New York: Oxford University Press, 1970); Robert Starobin, "The Economics of Industrial Slavery in the Old South," *Business History Review* 44.2 (1970): 131–74; Robert L. Lewis, *Coal, Iron, and Slaves: Industrial Slavery in Maryland and Virginia, 1715–1865* (Westport, CT: Greenwood Press, 1979); Richard C. Wade, *Slavery in the Cities: The South, 1820–1860* (New York: Oxford University Press, 1964); entries, December 20, 1849 (Silas Omohundro), December 28, 1849 (Hope H. Slatter), R. H. Dickinson and Brothers, daybook, 1846–49, U.S. Slavery Collection, folio volume, AAS.

3. Leni Sorensen, "Absconded: Fugitives in the Daybook of the Richmond Police Guard, 1834–1844" (PhD diss., College of William and Mary, 2005), 39; accounts, 1830–64, Taliaferro Papers, sec. 2, mss 1 T 1438 a 6–10, VHS. Martha was hired to George Steel, who was listed as a "clerk" in the 1850 census (*Federal Census of 1850, Richmond, Virginia*, roll M432-951, p. 348, image 223, www.ancestry.com, accessed March 19, 2007). The 1850–51 Richmond city directory has the following entry: "STEEL, GEORGE, bookkeeper, with James C. Crane & Son" (William L. Montague, *Montague's Richmond Directory* [Richmond, VA: William L. Montague, 1850–51], 103).

4. Robert W. Fogel and Stanley L. Engerman, *Time on the Cross: The Economics of Negro Slavery* (New York: Norton, 1989 [1974]), 56; Sarah S. Hughes, "Slaves for Hire: The Allocation of Black Labor in Elizabeth City County, Virginia, 1782–1810," *William and Mary Quarterly*, 3rd ser., 35.2 (1978): 264, 283.

5. Gregg D. Kimball, *American City, Southern Place: A Cultural History of Antebellum Richmond* (Athens: University of Georgia Press, 2000), 28–29; accounts, 1830–64, Taliaferro Papers, sec. 2, mss 1 T 1438 a 6–10, VHS. Mary Ann was hired out to painter Frederick Smith who lived about seven blocks from Miles's employment, on Broad Street between Fifth and Sixth streets (*Montague's Richmond Directory*, 215).

6. Accounts, 1830–64, Taliaferro Papers, sec. 2, mss 1 T 1438 a 6–10, VHS.

7. Warner T. Taliaferro was estimated to own $31,000 worth of real estate in 1850 and 136 slaves housed locally; 87, or 64 percent, of these slaves were located in Gloucester County. Only twenty-one, or 16 percent, were over twenty years of age and only five, or about 4 percent, were over thirty. No slave on Taliaferro's Gloucester County

plantations was over thirty-eight years of age in 1850. Through P. M. Tabb, Taliaferro hired out nineteen men, fifteen women, and eighteen children for the year 1845; most women were hired out with their children and two children were hired out separately, but in all it seems that Taliaferro was subordinating family ties to the hiring market since all of the men worked in tobacco or other industries, and only Miles and Martha's marriage is mentioned. In 1860, his real estate was worth $33,750 and personal property $100,200 (*Federal Census of 1850, Gloucester County, Virginia*, roll M432-946, p. 87, image 174, www.ancestry.com, accessed March 16, 2007; *Federal Census of 1860, Gloucester County, Virginia*, roll M653-1347, p. 754, image 407, www.ancestry.com, accessed March 16, 2007; *Federal Census of 1850, Slave Schedule, Gloucester County, Virginia*, roll M653-987, pp. 51–52, images 51–52, www.ancestry.com, accessed March 16, 2007; accounts, 1830–64, Taliaferro Papers, sec. 2, mss 1 T 1438 a 6–10, VHS).

8. Midori Takagi, *"Rearing Wolves to Our Own Destruction": Slavery in Richmond, Virginia, 1782–1865* (Charlottesville: University Press of Virginia, 1999), 49; Suzanne G. Schnittman, "Black Workers in Antebellum Richmond," in *Race, Class, and Community in Southern Labor History*, ed. Gary M. Funk and Merl E. Reed (Tuscaloosa: University of Alabama Press, 1994), 83.

9. Samuel Cottrell is listed at 118 Main Street in 1850 and J. H. Colquitt at 82 Main Street (Montague, *Montague's Richmond Directory*, 67).

10. Henry Box Brown, *Narrative of the Life of Henry Box Brown, Written by Himself* (Manchester, UK: Lee and Glynn, 1851), 37, http://docsouth.unc.edu/neh/brownbox/ brownbox.html, accessed June 7, 2009; Jeffrey Ruggles, *The Unboxing of Henry Brown* (Richmond: Library of Virginia, 2003), 6–16.

11. Ulrich Bonnell Phillips, *Life and Labor in the Old South* (Columbia: University of South Carolina Press, 2007 [1930]), 177.

12. Brown, *Narrative*, 37.

13. Charles F. Irons, *The Origins of Proslavery Christianity: White and Black Evangelicals in the Colonial and Antebellum Virginia* (Chapel Hill: University of North Carolina Press, 2008); John Ernest, "Traumatic Theology in the 'Narrative of the Life of Henry Box Brown, Written by Himself,'" *African American Review* 41.1 (2007): 19–31.

14. Charles Stearns, *Narrative of Henry Box Brown, Who Escaped from Slavery* (Boston: Brown and Stearns, 1849), 37–40, http://docsouth.unc.edu/neh/boxbrown/boxbrown .html, accessed May 3, 2007.

15. Stearns, *Narrative*, 38, 48; John T. O'Brien, "Factory, Church, and Community: Blacks in Antebellum Richmond," *Journal of Southern History* 44.4 (1978): 509–36.

16. Luther Porter Jackson, *Free Negro Labor and Property Holding in Virginia, 1830–1860* (New York: Appleton-Century, 1942), 50–69; Frederic Bancroft, *Slave-Trading in the Old South* (Baltimore: J. H. Furst, 1931), 145; Joseph Clarke Robert, *The Tobacco Kingdom: Plantation, Market, and Factory in Virginia and North Carolina, 1800–1860* (Durham: Duke University Press, 1938); Alan B. Bromberg, "Slavery in the Virginia Tobacco Factories, 1800–1860" (MA thesis, University of Virginia, 1968); Suzanne G. Schnittman, "Slavery in Virginia's Urban Tobacco Industry" (PhD diss., University of Rochester, 1986).

17. Ira Berlin, *Generations of Captivity: A History of African-American Slaves* (Cambridge, MA: Harvard University Press, 2003), 30; Robert William Fogel, *Without Consent or Contract: The Rise and Fall of American Slavery*, vol. 1 (New York: Norton, 1989), 114–53; Rhys Isaac, *The Transformation of Virginia, 1740–1790* (Chapel Hill: published for the Institute of Early American History and Culture by the University of North Carolina

Press, 1982), 308–57; G. Ugo Nwokeji, "African Conceptions of Gender and the Slave Traffic," *William and Mary Quarterly,* 3rd ser., 58.1 (2001), 47–68.

18. Moses Grandy, *Narrative of the Life of Moses Grandy, Late a Slave in the United States of America* (London: Gilpin, 1843), 16, http://docsouth.unc.edu/fpn/grandy/grandy.html, accessed October 16, 2006; Joseph E. Inikori, "Slavery and the Revolution in Cotton Textile Production in England," in *The Atlantic Slave Trade: Effects on Economies, Societies, and People in Africa, the Americas, and Europe,* ed. Joseph E. Inikori and Stanley L. Engerman (Durham: Duke University Press, 1992), 145–82; Ronald Bailey, "The Slave(ry) Trade and the Development of Capitalism in the United States: The Textile Industry in New England," in *The Atlantic Slave Trade,* 205–46.

19. Charles G. Sellers, *The Market Revolution: Jacksonian America, 1815–1846* (New York: Oxford University Press, 1991), chaps. 4 and 13; Barbara Jeanne Fields, *Slavery and Freedom on the Middle Ground: Maryland in the Nineteenth Century* (New Haven: Yale University Press, 1985), 55–57; John Majewski, *A House Dividing: Economic Development in Pennsylvania and Virginia before the Civil War* (New York: Cambridge University Press, 2000); Christopher Clark, "Slavery and Development in a Dual Economy: The South and the Market Revolution," in *The Market Revolution in America,* ed. Melvyn Stokes and Stephen Conway (Charlottesville: University Press of Virginia, 1996), 43–73.

20. Suzanne Miers and Igor Kopytoff, eds., *Slavery in Africa: Historical and Anthropological Perspectives* (Madison: University of Wisconsin Press, 1977); Kathleen J. Higgins, *"Licentious Liberty" in a Brazilian Gold-Mining Region: Slavery, Gender, and Social Control in Eighteenth-Century Sabará, Minas Gerais* (University Park: Pennsylvania State University Press, 1999).

21. Dylan C. Penningroth, *The Claims of Kinfolk: African American Property and Community in the Nineteenth-Century South* (Chapel Hill: University of North Carolina Press, 2003), 43.

22. Herbert Gutman, *The Black Family in Slavery and Freedom, 1750–1925* (New York: Pantheon, 1976); Mary P. Ryan, *Cradle of the Middle Class: The Family in Oneida, New York, 1790–1865* (New York: Cambridge University Press, 1981). Although *Cradle of the Middle Class* is a study of a northern community, the changes Ryan describes came about as a consequence of the same market intensification that southerners were experiencing.

23. Schnittman, "Slavery in Virginia's Urban Tobacco Industry," 103; Lynda Morgan, *Emancipation in Virginia's Tobacco Belt, 1850–1870* (Athens: University of Georgia Press, 1992); Loren Schweninger, "The Underside of Slavery: The Internal Economy, Self-Hire, and Quasi-Freedom in Virginia, 1780–1865," *Slavery and Abolition* 12.2 (1991): 1–22; Christopher Phillips, *Freedom's Port: The African American Community of Baltimore, 1790–1860* (Urbana: University of Illinois Press, 1997).

24. Petition of John Mayo Jr., William Gathright, Hobson Owen, et al. to the Virginia General Assembly, Henrico County, June 8, 1782, Legislative Records, LVA; Schweninger, "The Underside of Slavery," 2–3; Hughes, "Slaves for Hire," 285. Hughes found that by 1810, 82.5 percent of farm owners used hired slave labor; so did 65 percent of tenants and 81 percent of households in the port village of Hampton ("Slaves for Hire," 260–86).

25. Jack Temple Kirby, *Mockingbird Song: Ecological Landscapes of the South* (Chapel Hill: University of North Carolina Press, 2006), 83. Tobacco manufacturers appear in the 1819 Richmond city directory (John Maddox, *The Richmond City Directory, Register and Almanac for the Year 1819* [Richmond: John Maddox, 1819], 34).

26. Nick Yablon, *Untimely Ruins: An Archaeology of American Urban Modernity, 1819–1919* (Chicago: University of Chicago Press, 2009), 87.

27. William Segar Archer to William Ransom Johnson, March 9, 1828, folder 24, Pegram-Johnson Correspondence, mss BR 98, Robert Alonzo Brock Collection, HL.

28. James Hagarty to Benjamin F. Harris, January 19, 1820, Papers of the Gerry and Coles Families, 1783–1825, HM 58205, HL; Curwen and Hagarty to Henry Clark, December 28, 1822, Papers of the Gerry and Coles Families, 1783–1825, HM 58205, HL.

29. Allan Kulikoff, *Tobacco and Slaves: The Development of Southern Cultures in the Chesapeake, 1680–1800* (Chapel Hill: published for the Institute of Early American History and Culture by the University of North Carolina Press, 1986), 358–71; Morgan, *Emancipation in Virginia's Tobacco Belt*; Bonnie L. Martin, " 'To Have and To Hold' Human Collateral: Mortgaging Slaves to Build Virginia and South Carolina" (PhD diss., Southern Methodist University, 2006).

30. J. B. Taylor, *Biography of Elder Lott Cary, Late Missionary to Africa* (Baltimore: Armstrong and Berry), 9–16; John Saillant, ed., " 'Circular Addressed to the Colored Brethren and Friends in America': An Unpublished Essay by Lott Cary, Sent from Liberia to Virginia, 1827," *Virginia Magazine of History and Biography* 104.4 (1996): 481–504.

31. Schnittman, "Slavery in Virginia's Urban Tobacco Industry," 115; Takagi, *"Rearing Wolves to Our Own Destruction,"* 24; Douglas Walter Bristol Jr., *Knights of the Razor: Black Barbers in Slavery and Freedom* (Baltimore: Johns Hopkins University Press, 2009), chap. 4; Historical Census Browser, Geospatial and Statistical Institute, University of Virginia, http://mapserver.lib.virginia.edu, accessed June 18, 2007.

32. Elna C. Green, *This Business of Relief: Confronting Poverty in a Southern City, 1740–1940* (Athens: University of Georgia Press, 2003), 42.

33. Robert H. Gudmestad, "The Richmond Slave Market, 1840–1860" (MA thesis, University of Richmond, 1993), 73; Rodney D. Green, "Quantitative Sources for Studying Urban Industrial Slavery in the Antebellum U.S. South," *Immigrants and Minorities* 5.3 (1986): 305–16.

34. *Richmond (VA) Enquirer*, September 14, 1832, America's Historical Newspapers, Early American Newspapers, ser. 1, 1690–1876, AA, accessed June 25, 2007; Todd L. Savitt, *Medicine and Slavery: The Diseases and Health Care of Blacks in Antebellum Virginia* (Champagne: University of Illinois Press, 1978), 80–82.

35. *Baltimore (MD) Sun*, August 19, 1850, America's Historical Newspapers, Early American Newspapers, ser. 1, 1690–1876, AA, accessed June 25, 2007.

36. Frederick Law Olmstead, letter to the *New-York Daily Times*, March 30, 1853, in Charles E. Beveridge and Charles Capen McLaughlin, eds., *The Papers of Frederick Law Olmstead*, vol. 2: *Slavery and the South, 1852–1857* (Baltimore: Johns Hopkins University Press, 1977), 119. On slavery and clock time, see Mark M. Smith, *Mastered by the Clock: Time, Slavery, and Freedom in the American South* (Chapel Hill: University of North Carolina Press, 1997), chap. 5.

37. Stearns, *Narrative*, 41–42; Ruggles, *Unboxing*, 10; Robert, *Tobacco Kingdom*, 197.

38. Peter J. Rachleff, *Black Labor in the South: Richmond, Virginia, 1865–1890* (Philadelphia: Temple University Press, 1984), 6–7; Ruggles, *Unboxing*, 2–11; Nannie Mae Tilley, *The Bright-Tobacco Industry, 1860–1929* (Chapel Hill: University of North Carolina Press, 1948), 159.

39. Charles Dickens, *American Notes* (New York: Modern Library, 1996), 149–50.

40. Dickens, *American Notes*, 150–51.

41. Dickens, *American Notes*, 161–62.

42. Dickens, *American Notes*, 165, 171.

43. Dickens, *American Notes*, 158.

44. Schnittman, "Slavery in Virginia's Urban Tobacco Industry," 142.

45. Thomas P. Jones, *An Address on the Progress of Manufactures and Internal Improvement* (Philadelphia: Judah Dobson, 1827), 11, cited in Seth Rockman, "The Unfree Origins of American Capitalism," in *The Economy of Early America: Historical Perspectives and New Directions*, ed. Cathy D. Matson (University Park: Pennsylvania State University Press, 2006), 360n81; Takagi, *"Rearing Wolves to our Own Destruction,"* 82–84; Adam Smith, *Wealth of Nations*, 2 vols. (New York: Classic House Books, 2009), vol. 2, bk. 4, chaps. 7 and 9; Nicholas Onuf and Peter Onuf, *Nations, Markets, and War: Modern History and the American Civil War* (Charlottesville: University of Virginia Press, 2006), chap. 4; James T. Kloppenberg, "The Virtues of Liberalism: Christianity, Republicanism, and Ethics in Early American Political Discourse," *Journal of American History* 74.1 (1987): 9–33; Cedric J. Robinson, "Capitalism, Slavery, and Bourgeois Historiography," *History Workshop* 23.1 (1987): 122–40.

46. Daybook of the Richmond Police Guard, 1834–41, mss 1481, Small Library Special Collections, UVA.

47. Accounts, 1830–64, Taliaferro Papers, sec. 2, mss 1 T 1438 a 6–10, VHS; daybook of the Richmond Police Guard, 1834–41, mss 1481, Small Library Special Collections, UVA.

48. Takagi, *"Rearing Wolves to our Own Destruction,"* 28–29.

49. Frederick Douglass, *My Bondage and My Freedom* (New York: Miller, Orton, and Mulligan, 1855), 268.

50. Angela M. Hornsby-Gutting, "Manning the Region: New Approaches to Gender in the South," *Journal of Southern History* 75.3 (2009): 663–73; Aliyyah I. Abdur-Rahman, "'The Strangest Freaks of Despotism': Queer Sexuality in Antebellum African American Slave Narratives," *African American Review* 40.2 (2006): 223–37; Siobhan B. Somerville, *Queering the Color Line: Race and the Invention of Homosexuality in American Culture* (Durham: Duke University Press, 2000).

51. Takagi, *"Rearing Wolves to our Own Destruction,"* 29; Ira Berlin and Herbert Gutman, "Natives and Immigrants, Free Men and Slaves: Urban Workingmen in the Antebellum American South," *American Historical Review* 88.5 (1983): 1186.

52. Robert Russell, *North America: Its Agriculture and Climate, Containing Observations on the Agriculture and Climate of Canada, the United States, and the Island of Cuba* (Edinburgh: A. and C. Black, 1857), 152.

53. Catherine Cooper Hopley, *Life in the South from the Commencement of the War, Being a Social History of Those Who Took Part in the Battles, from a Personal Acquaintance with Them in Their Own Homes, from the Spring of 1860 to August 1862* (New York: Da Capo Press, 1974 [1863]), 153; Alexander Mackay, *The Western World; or, Travels in the United States in 1846–47: Exhibiting Them in Their Latest Development, Social, Political and Industrial; Including a Chapter on California* (Philadelphia: Lea and Blanchard, 1849), 285.

54. John W. Blassingame, "Using the Testimony of Ex-Slaves," in *The Slave's Narrative*, ed. Charles T. David and Henry Louis Gates Jr. (New York: Oxford University Press, 1985), 78–98.

55. Phillips, *Life and Labor in the Old South*, 177.

56. Noah Davis, *A Narrative of the Life of Rev. Noah Davis, a Colored Man, Written by*

Himself, at the Age of Fifty-Four (Baltimore: J. F. Weishampel Jr., 1859), 54–59, http://docsouth.unc.edu/neh/davisn/davis.html, accessed March 16, 2007.

57. J. G. Miller to Browning, Moore, and Company, April 25, 1860, Papers of the Cornelius Chase Family, box 6, folder 5, Manuscripts Division, LC.

58. George M. Dillard to R. H. Dickinson and Company, February 5, 1856, Papers of the Cornelius Chase Family, box 6, folder 6, Manuscripts Division, LC.

59. D. J. Southerland to R. H. Dickinson, December 29, 1861, Papers of the Cornelius Chase Family, box 6, folder 6, Manuscripts Division, LC; *Richmond (VA) Whig*, January 12, 1841; *Richmond (VA) Enquirer*, January 27, 1857. January sales suggest that the enslaved people's hiring arrangements were not to be renewed or that their owners thought they would bring more money at hiring time.

60. John Taylor Jr. to Lewis Hill, January 1, 1842, Lewis Hill Papers, mss BR 92, Robert Alonzo Brock Collection, HL.

61. Elizabeth Keckley, *Behind the Scenes; or, Thirty years a Slave, and Four Years in the White House* (New York: G. W. Carleton, 1868), 24–25, http://docsouth.unc.edu/neh/keckley/keckley.html, accessed March 16, 2007.

62. Brown, *Narrative*, 38–39.

63. William L. Montague, *The Richmond Directory and Business Advertiser, for 1852* (Baltimore: J. W. Woods, 1852), 20.

64. Brown, *Narrative*, 38–42; Phillips, *Life and Labor in the Old South*, 177. Brown's version contains a more detailed account of the episode than Stearns's 1849 biography.

65. Montague, *Montague's Richmond Directory*, 60.

66. Brown, *Narrative*, 38–45.

67. R. G. Dun Collection, Virginia, vol. 43, Baker Business Library, HBS.

68. Brown, *Narrative*, 42–45.

69. Brown, *Narrative*, 42–45.

70. Phillips, *Life and Labor in the Old South*, 177.

71. Schnittman, "Slavery in Virginia's Urban Tobacco Industry," 27.

72. Sarah N. Roth, " 'How a Slave was Made a Man': Negotiating Black Violence and Masculinity in Antebellum Slave Narratives," *Slavery and Abolition* 28.2 (2007): 255–75.

73. Ruggles, *Unboxing*, 22–27; Marcus Wood, " 'All Right!': The Narrative of Henry Box Brown as a Test Case for the Racial Prescription of Rhetoric and Semiotics," *Proceedings of the American Antiquarian Society* 107.1 (1997): 65–104; John Ernest, "Outside the Box: Henry Box Brown and the Politics of Antislavery Agency," *Arizona Quarterly* 63.4 (2007): 1–24.

74. *Smith v. Commonwealth*, 47 Va. 696, 6 Gratt. 696 (1849), Lexis-Nexis Academic, accessed June 22, 2007; "Horrible Death," *Columbia Daily South Carolinian*, October 3, 1856. Thanks to Amanda Mushal for this reference.

75. Ruggles, *Unboxing*, 21–22; African Baptist Church, Richmond, minutes, 1841–59, bk. 1, misc. reel 494, LVA. Thanks to Philip Schwarz for this research.

76. Willie Lee Rose, *Slavery and Freedom*, ed. William W. Freehling (New York: Oxford University Press, 1982), 35; Orlando Patterson: *Slavery and Social Death: A Comparative Study* (Cambridge, MA: Harvard University Press, 1982); Joseph A. Schumpeter, *Capitalism, Socialism, and Democracy* (New York: Harper Brothers, 1942), 82–85. Not all scholars agree with the proposition that slavery and commercial processing enterprises were mutually reinforcing; see Rodney D. Green, "Black Tobacco Factory Workers and Social

Conflict in Antebellum Richmond: Were Slavery and Urban Industry Really Compatible?" *Slavery and Abolition* 8.2 (1987): 183–203.

CHAPTER FIVE: Railroaders

1. George Rogers Taylor, *The Transportation Revolution, 1815–1860*, vol. 4: *The Economic History of the United States* (New York: Harper and Brothers, 1951); William G. Thomas III, *Jupiter's Bow: Railroads, the Civil War and the Roots of Modern America* (New Haven: Yale University Press, forthcoming); Aaron Marrs, *Railroads in the Old South: Pursuing Progress in a Slave Society* (Baltimore: Johns Hopkins University Press, 2009), 62.

2. Sharon Ann Murphy, "Securing Human Property: Slavery, Life Insurance, and Industrialization in the Upper South," *Journal of the Early Republic* 25.4 (2005): 615–52; Edward W. Phifer, "Slavery in a Microcosm: Burke County, North Carolina," *Journal of Southern History* 28.2 (1962): 144–46, 157, 165; Todd L. Savitt, *Race and Medicine in Nineteenth- and Early Twentieth-Century America* (Kent: Kent State University Press, 2006), 89–101.

3. *Richmond (VA) Enquirer*, October 13, 1835, America's Historical Newspapers, Early American Newspapers, ser. 1, 1690–1876, AA, accessed June 22, 2007; Garrett Ward Shelton and C. William Hill Jr., *The Liberal Republicanism of John Taylor of Caroline* (Madison: Fairleigh Dickinson University Press, 2008), 69–88; Laura Croghan Camoie, *Irons in the Fire: The Business History of the Tayloe Family and Virginia's Gentry, 1700–1860* (Charlottesville: University of Virginia Press, 2007).

4. Edwin Archer Randolph, *The Life of Rev. John Jasper, Pastor of Sixth Mt. Zion Baptist Church, Richmond, Va., from His Birth to the Present Time, with His Theory on the Rotation of the Sun* (Richmond, VA: R. T. Hill, 1884), 5–6, http://docsouth.unc.edu/neh/jasper/jasper.html, accessed October 27, 2007.

5. *Richmond (VA) Enquirer*, April 4, 1837, America's Historical Newspapers, Early American Newspapers, ser. 1, 1690–1876, AA, accessed June 22, 2007.

6. *Richmond (VA) Enquirer*, January 12, 1832; *Baltimore (MD) Patriot*, January 14, 1829, America's Historical Newspapers, Early American Newspapers, ser. 1, 1690–1876, AA, accessed June 22, 2007.

7. *Baltimore (MD) Patriot*, March 1, 1826, cited in Seth Rockman, *Scraping By: Wage Labor, Slavery, and Survival in Early Baltimore* (Baltimore: Johns Hopkins University Press, 2009), 72.

8. Barbara Jeanne Fields, *Slavery and Freedom on the Middle Ground: Maryland in the Nineteenth Century* (New Haven: Yale University Press, 1985), 44–45; Rockman, *Scraping By*, 28–43, 72, 242–45; Ulrich Bonnell Phillips, *Life and Labor in the Old South* (Columbia: University of South Carolina Press, 2007 [1930]), 177.

9. Robert J. Brugger, *Maryland, a Middle Temperament: 1634–1980* (Baltimore: Johns Hopkins University Press, 1988), chap. 5; Marrs, *Railroads in the Old South*, chap. 1; John A. Munroe, *History of Delaware* (Newark: University of Delaware Press, 1979), 96–129; Phifer, "Slavery in Microcosm," 137–65; Henry V. Poor, *History of the Railroads and Canals of the United States*, vol. 1 (New York: J. H. Schultz, 1860), 562–68, 572–601; business ledger, Francis Everod Rives Papers, 1817–48, Perkins Library, DU.

10. Business ledger, Francis Everod Rives Papers, 1817–48, Perkins Library, DU; Phillips, *Life and Labor in the Old South*, 177.

11. Frederick Law Olmsted, *A Journey in the Seaboard Slave States, with Remarks on*

Their Economy (New York: Dix and Edwards, 1856), 194–96, http://docsouth.unc.edu/nc/olmsted/olmsted.html, accessed October 9, 2007; Michael Tadman, *Speculators and Slaves: Masters, Traders, and Slaves in the Old South* (Madison: University of Wisconsin Press, 1996), 196–98.

12. Melvin Patrick Ely, *Israel on the Appomattox: A Southern Experiment in Black Freedom from 1790s through the Civil War* (New York: Knopf, 2004), 151–81.

13. *Richmond (VA) Enquirer*, January 28, 1834, cited in Joseph Clarke Robert, *The Tobacco Kingdom: Plantation, Market, and Factory in Virginia and North Carolina, 1800–1860* (Durham: Duke University Press, 1938), 65.

14. Olmsted, *A Journey in the Seaboard Slave States*, 364–65.

15. John Thomas Scharf, *The Chronicles of Baltimore, Being a Complete History of "Baltimore Town" and Baltimore City from the Earliest Period to the Present Time* (Baltimore: Turnbull Brothers, 1874), 433–34.

16. J. C. Webster, *Last of the Pioneers; or, Old Times in East Tenn., Being the Life and Reminiscences of Pharaoh Jackson Chesney (Aged 120 Years)* (Knoxville, TN: S. B. Newman, 1902), 74–75, http://docsouth.unc.edu/neh/webster/menu.html, accessed October 9, 2007; John Lauritz Larson, *The Market Revolution in America: Liberty, Ambition, and the Eclipse of the Common Good* (New York: Cambridge University Press, 2010), 84.

17. *State v. Francis E. Rives*, 27 N.C. 297, 5 Ired. L. 297 (1844), Lexis-Nexis Academic, www.lexis-nexis.com, accessed October 9, 2007. In 1850, Rives owned thirteen slaves, aged less than a year to fifty-nine, though none were between ten and twenty-five (*Federal Census of 1850, Slave Schedule, Petersburg, Virginia*, roll M432-986, p. 283, image 29, www.ancestry.com, accessed October 9, 2007).

18. Webster, *Last of the Pioneers*, 74–75.

19. Richmond and Petersburg Railroad, annual report, 1857, Virginia and Tennessee Railroad, annual report, 1860, Railroad Annual Reports, 1856–60, Board of Public Works, LVA; Robert S. Starobin, "The Economics of Industrial Slavery in the Old South," *Business History Review* 44.2 (1970): 131–74; Charles B. Dew, *Bond of Iron: Master and Slave at Buffalo Forge* (New York: Norton, 1994); Charles B. Dew, *Ironmaker to the Confederacy: Joseph R. Anderson and the Tredegar Iron Works* (Richmond: Library of Virginia, 1999).

20. James A. Ward, "A New Look at Antebellum Southern Railroad Development," *Journal of Southern History* 39.3 (1973): 409–20; Marrs, *Railroads in the Old South*, table 2; Federal Writers' Project, *Delaware: A Guide to the First State* (New York: Viking Press, 1938), 74–76. Maryland railroad workers, like the ones in Delaware, were largely recent immigrants from Europe. There was a large pool of recent immigrants in Baltimore, for instance: 36,000 foreign-born residents, or 21 percent of the population of 170,000 by 1850 (Brugger, *Maryland, a Middle Temperament*, 270).

21. Chauncey Mitchell Depew, ed., *1795–1895: One Hundred Years of American Commerce*, vol. 1 (New York: D. O. Haynes, 1895), chap. 19; Charles W. Turner, "Railroad Service to Virginia Farmers, 1828–1860," *Agricultural History* 22.4 (1948): 239–48; Marrs, *Railroads in the Old South*, table 2.

22. Marshall Wingfield, *A History of Caroline County, Virginia* (Baltimore: Regional Publishing, 1969 [1924]), 34–35; Fannie Berry to Susie R. C. Byrd, February 26, 1937, in Charles L. Perdue, Jr., Thomas E. Barden, and Robert K. Phillips, eds., *Weevils in the Wheat: Interviews with Virginia Ex-Slaves* (Charlottesville: University Press of Virginia, 1976), 39; Ely, *Israel on the Appomattox*, 365–407.

23. Fannie Berry to Susie R. C. Byrd, February 26, 1937, 39.

24. Turner, "Railroad Service to Virginia Farmers"; Kenneth W. Noe, *Southwest Virginia's Railroad: Modernization and the Sectional Crisis* (Urbana: University of Illinois Press, 1994), 82–83; Marrs, *Railroads in the Old South*, 154–55. The *Richmond (VA) Daily Dispatch*, January 2, 1860, contains a petition from twenty citizens advocating the slave trade.

25. James W. C. Pennington, *A Narrative of Events of the Life of J. H. Banks, an Escaped Slave, from the Cotton State, Alabama, in America* (Liverpool, UK: M. Rourke, 1861), 46–49, http://docsouth.unc.edu/neh/penning/penning.html, accessed March 5, 2008.

26. Pennington, *A Narrative of Events of the Life of J. H. Banks,* 48–49; Aaron W. Marrs, "The Iron Horse Turns South: A History of Antebellum Southern Railroads" (PhD diss., University of South Carolina, 2006), 106–7; Nicholas Guyatt, "'The Outskirts of Our Happiness': Race and the Lure of Colonization in the Early Republic," *Journal of American History* 95.4 (2009): 986–1011.

27. Accounts of Silas and R. H. Omohundro's slave trade, 1857–64, mss 4122, Small Library Special Collections, UVA.

28. Olmstead, *A Journey in the Seaboard Slave States,* 308, 375.

29. Edmund Taylor to Lewis Hill, June 20, 1853, Lewis Hill Papers, mss BR 92, Robert Alonzo Brock Collection, HL.

30. Daniel Walker Howe, *What Hath God Wrought: The Transformation of America, 1815–1848* (New York: Oxford University Press, 2007), 1.

31. Thomas Williams to R. H. Dickinson and Brothers, August 19, 1848, R. H. Dickinson and Brothers, correspondence, box 1, folder 5, U.S. Slavery Collection, AAS.

32. Frederick Law Olmsted, letter to the *New-York Daily Times,* April 5, 1853, in Charles E. Beveridge and Charles Capen McLaughlin, eds., *The Papers of Frederick Law Olmsted,* vol. 2: *Slavery and the South, 1852–1857* (Baltimore: Johns Hopkins University Press, 1977), 122; Stephanie M. H. Camp, *Closer to Freedom: Enslaved Women and Everyday Resistance in the Plantation South* (Chapel Hill: University of North Carolina Press, 2004), 60–92; W. Jeffrey Bolster, *Black Jacks: African American Seamen in the Age of Sail* (Cambridge, MA: Harvard University Press, 1998). For a compelling discussion of how technology is embedded in modern capitalist political economies, see Richard Stivers, *The Illusion of Freedom and Equality* (Albany: State University of New York Press, 2008).

33. Parr and Farrish to Betts and Gregory, March 30, 1860, box 7, folder 4, Papers of the Cornelius Chase Family, Manuscripts Division, LC.

34. Thomas Williams to R. H. Dickinson and Brothers, May 26, 1847, R. H. Dickinson and Brothers, correspondence, box 1, folder 5, AAS.

35. Unsigned telegraph to Browning, Moore and Company, June 20, 1860, box 6, folder 5, Papers of the Cornelius Chase Family, Manuscripts Division, LC.

36. W. F. Askew to Dickinson, Hill and Company, February 19, 1856, box 6, folder 6, Papers of the Cornelius Chase Family, Manuscripts Division, LC.

37. S. C. Woodroof to Moore and Dawson, September 2, 1860, box 6, folder 10, Papers of the Cornelius Chase Family, Manuscripts Division, LC.

38. T. H. Lipscomb to Moore and Dawson, August 28, 1860, August 30, 1860, September 18, 1860, box 6, folder 10, Papers of the Cornelius Chase Family, Manuscripts Division, LC; Johnson, *Soul by Soul: Life Inside the Antebellum Slave Market* (Cambridge, MA: Harvard University Press, 1999), chap. 6.

39. George Fitzhugh, *Sociology for the South* (Richmond, VA: A. Morris, 1854), 51.

40. Henry David Thoreau, *Walden* (New York: Harper and Row, 1963), 119, 120, emphases in original.

41. Ralph Waldo Emerson, *Selected Essays, Lectures, and Poems* (New York: Random House, 1990), 325.

42. Olmstead, *Journey in the Seaboard Slave States*, 303.

43. Marrs, *Railroads in the Old South*, 57–61.

44. Eleanor Little Eanes, "The Negro in Greensville County," in *Historical and Biographical Sketches of Greensville County, Virginia, 1650–1967*, ed. Douglas Summers Brown (Emporia, VA: Riparian Woman's Club, 1968), 128–29.

45. Rockman, *Scraping By*, 30–31; Historical Census Browser, Geospatial and Statistical Center, University of Virginia, http://mapserver.lib.virginia.edu, accessed March 4, 2008; bond for Armistead, January 6, 1836, folder 8, box 2, Richmond, Fredericksburg, and Potomac Railroad, VHS, cited in Marrs, *Railroads in the Old South*, 73; Charles W. Hildreth, "Railroads out of Pensacola, 1833–1883," *Florida Historical Quarterly* 37.3 (1959): 403; W. J. Rorabaugh, *The Alcoholic Republic: An American Tradition* (New York: Oxford University Press, 1979), chap. 5. In 1851 a Baltimore newspaper reported on a riot involving Irish railroad workers in Marion County, Virginia (now West Virginia), which is one county over from the Pennsylvania border in north-central West Virginia (*Baltimore [MD] Sun*, March 24, 1851, America's Historical Newspapers, Early American Newspapers, ser. 1, 1690–1876, AA, accessed June 22, 2007).

46. *Amherst (NH) Farmers' Cabinet*, November 6, 1856, America's Historical Newspapers, Early American Newspapers, ser. 1, 1690–1876, AA, accessed April 29, 2010.

47. Central Railroad of Georgia Reports, cited in Marrs, "The Iron Horse Turns South," 114.

48. "Slave Labor on Railroads," *Columbia Daily South Carolinian*, December 2, 1856, Nineteenth-Century U.S. Newspapers, Gale Cengage Learning, accessed June 22, 2007.

49. American Life Insurance and Trust Company, policy no. 5152, March 16, 1860, mss2 M9922 a 1, VHS.

50. Claudius Crozet to Charles B. Fisk, April 13, 1855, Covington and Ohio Railroad, Virginia Railroads Collection, 1828–94, ms BR 194, Robert Alonzo Brock Collection, HL.

51. Robert F. Hunter and Edwin L. Dooley Jr., *Claudius Crozet: French Engineer in America, 1790–1864* (Charlottesville: University Press of Virginia, 1989), 157, cited in Marrs, *Railroads in the Old South*, 81.

52. Henry Hayes Lockwood to G. F. Watson, December 31, 1862, Orange and Alexandria Railroad, 1851–72, Virginia Railroads Collection, 1828–94, ms BR 189, Robert Alonzo Brock Collection, HL; Brooks Miles Barnes and William G. Thomas III, "The Countryside Transformed: The Railroad and the Eastern Shore of Virginia, 1870–1935," Virginia Center for Digital History, University of Virginia, www2.vcdh.virginia.edu/eshore/index.php, accessed June 2, 2010.

53. *Federal Census of 1850, Slave Schedule, New Hanover County, North Carolina*, roll M432-683, n.p., images 18–21, www.ancestry.com, accessed September 24, 2010; Fannie Berry to Susie R. C. Byrd, February 26, 1937, 39; Marrs, *Railroads in the Old South*, 71.

54. Brenda E. Stevenson, *Life in Black and White: Family and Community in the Slave South* (New York: Oxford University Press, 1996), 223–24.

55. Marrs, *Railroads in the Old South*, 55–56.

56. *Richmond (VA) Enquirer*, October 25, 1836, America's Historical Newspapers, Early American Newspapers, ser. 1, 1690–1876, AA, accessed April 30, 2010.

57. Not all railroad companies hired men exclusively. An Atlanta, Georgia newspaper ran an ad for the Southwestern Railroad, which reads in part: "THE SOUTHWESTERN R.R. CO. wishes to hire for the year of 1853 to work on the repairs of their road, sixty able bodied negro fellows and twelve women. They will be fed, clothed, and have necessary medical attention when sick— Wages paid quarterly at the Company's office, Macon" (*Atlanta [GA] Intelligencer*, November 26, 1852, Urich Bonnell Phillips Papers, series 15, box 27, folder 250, YU. Thanks to Susan E. O'Donovan for this research).

58. *Fourth Annual Report of the President and Directors to the Stockholders of the Louisville, Cincinnati and Charleston Rail-Road Company, September, 1840* (Charleston, SC: A. E. Miller, 1840), 19, cited in Marrs, "The Iron Horse Turns South," 120–21.

59. Fannie Berry to Susie R. C. Byrd, February 26, 1937, 39.

60. Chesterfield's upper section was home to a mining labor camp of 1 woman, twenty-four, and 113 men, ages eleven to fifty-eight, overseen by A. F. D. Gifford, a miner about forty-one years old (*Federal Census of 1850, Upper Chesterfield County, Virginia*, roll M432-940, p. 107, image 214, www.ancestry.com, accessed June 22, 2007; *Federal Census of 1850, Slave Schedule, Upper Chesterfield County, Virginia*, roll M432-985, pp. 641–45, images 52–54, www.ancestry.com, accessed June 22, 2007).

61. Norfolk and Petersburg Railroad, annual report, 1859, Railroad Annual Reports, 1856–60, Board of Public Works, LVA.

62. Nottoway County's population was 71 percent enslaved in 1850 and 73 percent enslaved on the eve of the Civil War. The next highest was neighboring Amelia County, with 70 percent and 71 percent respectively (Historical Census Browser Geospatial and Statistical Data Center, University of Virginia, http://mapserver.lib.virginia.edu, accessed June 27, 2007).

63. Frances Epes was listed as a farmer by occupation who owned $9,000 worth of real estate (*Federal Census of 1850, Nottoway County, Virginia*, roll M432-965, p. 367, image 186, www.ancestry.com, accessed June 22, 2007; *Federal Census of 1850, Slave Schedule, Nottoway County*, roll M432-991, p. 643, image 59, www.ancestry.com, accessed June 22, 2007). On the culture of railroad and coal workers, see Scott Reynolds Nelson, *Steel Drivin' Man: John Henry, the Untold Story of an American Legend* (Oxford: Oxford University Press, 2006), 79–81.

64. *Harvey et al. v. Epes*, 53 Va.153, 12 Gratt. 153 (1855), Lexis-Nexis Academic, accessed June 22, 2007.

65. "Arrest of a Supposed Incendiary," *Baltimore (MD) Sun*, September 16, 1850, America's Historical Newspapers, Early American Newspapers, ser. 1, 1690–1876, AA, accessed June 25, 2007; *Federal Census of 1850, West District, Hanover County, Virginia*, roll M432-949, p. 375, image 168 (Joseph Sorrell), www.ancestry.com, accessed June 25, 2007; Norfolk and Petersburg Railroad, annual report, 1859, Railroad Annual Reports, 1856–60, Board of Public Works, LVA; Barbara Young Welke, *Recasting American Liberty: Gender, Race, Law, and the Railroad Revolution, 1865–1920* (New York: Cambridge University Press, 2001).

66. James Hunter to Charles B. Fisk, April 25, 1856, mss BR 194, Covington and Ohio Railroad, Virginia Railroads Collection, 1828–94, Robert Alonzo Rock Collection, HL. Hunter, a forty-year-old who gave his occupation in 1860 as a farmer, was a native

of Pennsylvania (*Federal Census of 1860, Fairfax, Virginia*, roll M653-1343, p. 797, image 217 [South Orange and Alexandria Railroad], www.ancestry.com, accessed June 27, 2007).

67. Branch and Company, auction and hiring records, mss3 B7327 a FA1, VHS; *Federal Census of 1850, Petersburg, Virginia*, roll M432-941, p. 384, image 339, www.ancestry.com, accessed October 10, 2007; Martin, *Divided Mastery*, chaps. 2–3.

68. Olmstead, *A Journey in the Seaboard Slave States*, 377; Marrs, "The Iron Horse Turns South," 143–44.

69. James Redpath, *The Roving Editor; or, Talks with Slaves in the Southern States* (New York: A. B. Burdick, 1859), 138.

70. The *Louisiana Courier* reported on May 25, 1840: "On the evening of Saturday last about 9 o'clock, a dispute occurred between two negroes belonging to the Ponchartrain Railroad Company—one of them struck the other on the right side of the head in such a severe manner, as to cause death in a few minutes. The perpetrator of the crime has been arrested, and will be tried before the Parish Court" (Urich Bonnell Phillips Papers, series 15, box 25, folder 114, YU; thanks to Susan E. O'Donovan for this research).

71. John W. Dickinson to Matthew Bryan, January 4, 1851, Urich Bonnell Phillips Papers, folder 145, YU.

72. William H. Fitzhugh to Lewis Hill 26 May 1853, Lewis Hill Papers, mss BR 92, Robert Alonzo Brock Collection, HL.

73. William H Fitzhugh to Lewis Hill 26 May 1853, Lewis Hill Papers, mss BR 92, Robert Alonzo Brock Collection, HL.

74. *Richmond (VA) Enquirer*, January 17, 1835, America's Historical Newspapers, Early American Newspapers, ser. 1, 1690–1876, AA, accessed April 29, 2010.

75. Olmstead, *A Journey in the Seaboard Slave States*, 188–90.

76. A T[?] Rux[?] to E. H. Stokes, December 18, 1861, box 6, folder 13, Papers of the Cornelius Chase Family, Manuscripts Division, LC.

77. Ezra Michener, *Autobiographical Notes from the Life and Letters of Ezra Michener, M.D.* (Philadelphia: Friends' Book Association, 1893), 57; Marrs, *Railroads in the Old South*, 58; *Federal Census of 1850, Slave Schedule, Petersburg, Virginia*, roll M432-986, p. 245, image 10 (Appomattox Railroad), www.ancestry.com, accessed June 25, 2007.

78. Richmond and Petersburg Railroad, annual report, 1857, Railroad Annual Reports, 1856–60, Board of Public Works, LVA; R. G. Dun and Company, Virginia, vol. 43, HBS.

79. R. G. Dun and Company, Virginia, vol. 43, HBS; Richmond and Petersburg Railroad, annual report,1857, Railroad Annual Reports, 1856–60, Board of Public Works, LVA; *Federal Census of 1850, Slave Schedule, Henrico County, Virginia*, roll M432-988, p. 601, image 82 (Richmond and Petersburg Railroad), www.ancestry.com, accessed June 25, 2007; *Federal Census of 1850, Slave Schedule, Hanover County, Virginia*, roll M432-988, p. 82, image 82 (Richmond, Fredericksburg, and Potomac Railroad), www.ancestry.com, accessed June 25, 2007; *Federal Census of 1850, Slave Schedule, Louisa County, Virginia*, roll M432-989, p. 81, image 82 (Virginia Central Railroad), www.ancestry.com, accessed June 25, 2007; *Federal Census of 1850, Slave Schedule, Henrico County, Virginia*, roll M432-988, p. 629, image 96 (Richmond, Fredericksburg, and Potomac Railroad), www.ancestry.com, accessed June 25, 2007.

80. John McRae to J. L. Gregg, February 6, 1851, John McRae letterbook, 5, Wiscon-

sin Historical Society, Madison, cited in Marrs, "The Iron Horse Turns South," 140; *Federal Census of 1850, Slave Schedule, Henrico County, Virginia*, roll M432-988, p. 601, image 82, (Richmond and Petersburg Railroad), www.ancestry.com, accessed June 25, 2008; *Federal Census of 1850, Slave Schedule, Hanover County, Virginia*, roll M432-988, p. 82, image 82 (Richmond, Fredericksburg, and Potomac Railroad), www.ancestry.com, accessed June 25, 2008; *Federal Census of 1850, Slave Schedule, Louisa County, Virginia*, roll M432-989, p. 81, image 82 (Virginia Central Railroad), www.ancestry.com, accessed June 25, 2008; *Federal Census of 1850, Slave Schedule, Henrico County, Virginia*, roll M432-988, p. 629, image 96 (Richmond, Fredericksburg, and Potomac Railroad), www.ancestry.com, accessed June 25, 2008; *Federal Census of 1850, Slave Schedule, Petersburg, Virginia*, roll M432-986, p. 245, image 10 (Appomattox Railroad), www.ancestry.com, accessed June 25, 2008.

81. Marrs, *Railroads in the Old South*, 76–77.

82. Bond for Nat and Sam, January 2, 1836, bond for Ben, Lewis, and Braxton, January 6, 1836, folder 8, box 2, Richmond, Fredericksburg, and Potomac Railroad, VHS, cited in Marrs, *Railroads in the Old South*, 62–63, 73; Midori Takagi, *"Rearing Wolves to Our Own Destruction": Slavery in Richmond, Virginia, 1782–1865* (Charlottesville: University Press of Virginia, 1999), 49.

83. Sharon Ann Murphy, "Security in an Uncertain World: Life Insurance and the Emergence of Modern America" (PhD diss., University of Virginia, 2005), 323–85, 360–61; American Life Insurance and Trust Company, policy no. 5152, March 16, 1860, mss2 M9922 a 1, VHS.

84. *Pittsfield (MA) Sun*, April 1, 1858, America's Historical Newspapers, Early American Newspapers, ser. 1, 1690–1876, AA, accessed April 29, 2010.

85. William Massie to Christopher T. Estis, March 16, 1849, Urich Bonnell Phillips Papers, ms 397, box 42, YU; William Massie to M. H. Hart, June 21, 1852, Urich Bonnell Phillips Papers, series 17, box 42, YU. William Massie (1795–1862) was a wealthy planter and slaveholder who owned $100,000 worth of real estate in 1850 and over 100 slaves (*Federal Census of 1850, Slave Schedule, Nelson County, Virginia*, roll M432-990, pp. 1007–11, images 35–37, www.ancestry.com, accessed June 28, 2007; *Federal Census of 1850, Nelson County, Virginia*, roll M432-963, p. 256 image 74, www.ancestry.com, accessed June 28, 2007).

86. Marrs, *Railroads in the Old South*, 79–80; Rockman, *Scraping By*, chap. 7.

87. Richmond and Danville Railroad, minute book, November 13, 1855, cited in Marrs, "The Iron Horse Turns South," 154.

88. George P. Rawick, ed., *The American Slave: A Composite Autobiography,* supplement, ser. 1, vol. 8: *Mississippi Narratives*, pt. 3 (Westport, CT: Greenwood, 1977), 1015, cited in Marrs, *Railroads in the Old South*, 59; Frederick Douglass, *My Bondage and My Freedom* (New York: Miller, Orton, and Mulligan, 1855), 169–72.

89. G. W. Offley, *A Narrative of the Life and Labors of the Rev. G. W. Offley, a Colored Man, Local Preacher and Missionary* (Hartford, CT, 1859), 7–12, http://docsouth.unc.edu/neh/offley/offley.html, accessed October 27, 2007; John W. Blassingame, "Using the Testimony of Ex-Slaves," in *The Slave's Narrative*, ed. Charles T. David and Henry Louis Gates Jr. (New York: Oxford University Press, 1985), 78–98.

90. O. H. P. Terrell to H. G. Whitcomb, September 21, 1861, Virginia Central Railroad, 1859–67, Virginia Railroads Collection, 1828–94, mss BR 200, Robert Alonzo Brock Collection, HL.

91. Receipt, Orange and Alexandria Railroad, December 26, 1861, Orange and Alexandria Railroad, 1851–72, Virginia Railroads Collection, 1828–94, mss BR 193, Robert Alonzo Brock Collection, HL.

92. *Richmond (VA) Enquirer*, November 13, 1835, America's Historical Newspapers, Early American Newspapers, ser. 1, 1690–1876, AA, accessed April 30, 2010.

93. Brown, *Narrative of Henry Box Brown, Written by Himself* (Manchester, UK: Lee and Glynn, 1851); Frederick Douglass, *Life and Times of Frederick Douglass* (Hartford, CT: Park, 1881), 199, http://docsouth.unc.edu/neh/douglasslife/douglass.html (accessed October 27, 2007); S. J. Celestine Edwards, *From Slavery to a Bishopric; or, The Life of Bishop Walter Hawkins of the British Methodist Episcopal Church Canada* (London: Kensit, 1891), 56–57, http://docsouth.unc.edu/neh/edwardsc/edwards.html, accessed October 27, 2007.

Epilogue

1. Freedmen's Bureau, *Register of Colored Persons of Caroline County, State of Virginia Cohabitating Together as Husband and Wife on 27th February 1866*, CRHC; *Federal Census of 1860, Slave Schedule, Caroline County, Virginia*, roll M653-1388, p. 104, image 105, www.ancestry.com, accessed June 7, 2007; *Federal Census of 1860, Caroline County, Virginia*, roll M653-1339, p. 731, image 161, www.ancestry.com, accessed June 7, 2007; Herbert S. Klein, *A Population History of the United States* (Cambridge: Cambridge University Press, 2004), 83.

2. Jon Latimer, *1812: War with America* (Cambridge, MA: Harvard University Press, 2007), chaps. 2–3 and 18; Joseph T. Rainer, "The 'Sharper' Image: Yankee Peddlers, Southern Consumers, and the Market Revolution," in *Cultural Change and the Market Revolution in America, 1789–1860*, ed. Scott C. Martin (Lanham, MD: Rowman and Littlefield, 2004), 90–92; Thomas Dionysius Clark and John D. W. Guice, *The Old Southwest, 1795–1830: Frontiers in Conflict* (Norman: University of Oklahoma Press, 1996); Joan Cashin, *A Family Venture: Men and Women on the Southern Frontier* (New York: Oxford, 1991).

3. Marshall Wingfield, *A History of Caroline County, Virginia* (Baltimore: Regional Publishing, 1969 [1924]), 34–35.

4. Drew Gilpin Faust, *The Republic of Suffering: Death and the Civil War* (New York: Knopf, 2008), 91–92, 154–56.

5. Karl Marx, *Capital: A Critique of Political Economy*, vol. 1, trans. Ben Fowkes (London: Penguin, 1992), pts. 5, 6, and 8; Adam Smith, *Wealth of Nations*, 2 vols. (New York: Classic House Books, 2009), vol. 2, bk. 4, chaps. 7 and 9; Steven Deyle, *Carry Me Back: The Domestic Slave Trade in American Life* (New York: Oxford University Press, 2005), 291–96.

6. Melvin Patrick Ely, *Israel on the Appomattox: A Southern Experiment in Black Freedom from 1790s through the Civil War* (New York: Knopf, 2004), 175–85.

7. Frederick Douglass, *My Bondage and My Freedom* (New York: Miller, Orton, and Mulligan, 1855), 200.

8. Walter Johnson, *Soul by Soul: Life Inside the Antebellum Slave Market* (Cambridge, MA: Harvard University Press, 1999), 109.

9. Edward E. Baptist, " 'Cuffy,' 'Fancy Maids,' and 'One-Eyed Men:' Rape, Commodification, and the Domestic Slave Trade in the United States," *American Historical Review*

106.5 (2001): 1619–50; William W. Freehling, *The Road to Disunion*, vol. 2: *Secessionists Triumphant, 1854–1861* (New York: Oxford University Press, 2007), chaps. 3–5.

10. Suzanne Miers and Igor Kopytoff, *Slavery in Africa: Historical and Anthropological Perspectives* (Madison: University of Wisconsin Press, 1977), 39, 60 passim; Harold K. Schneider, "People as Wealth in Turu Society," *Southwest Journal of Anthropology* 24.4 (1968): 375–95; Kristin Mann, *Slavery and the Birth of an African City: Lagos, 1760–1900* (Bloomington: Indiana University Press, 2007), introduction; Jane I. Guyer, "Wealth in People and Self-Realization in Equatorial Africa," *Man*, n.s., 28.2 (1993): 244, 259; Paul E. Lovejoy, *Transformations in Slavery: A History of Slavery in Africa* (Cambridge: Cambridge University Press, 2000), 9; Joseph C. Miller, *Way of Death: Merchant Capitalism and the Angolan Slave Trade, 1730–1830* (Madison: University of Wisconsin Press, 1988), 43, 47, 50; Joseph C. Miller, "A Theme in Variations: A Historical Schema of Slaving in the Atlantic and Indian Ocean Regions," in *The Structure of Slavery in Indian Ocean African and Asia*, ed. Gwyn Campbell (London: Frank Cass, 2004), 190; Edna G. Bay, *Wives of the Leopard: Gender, Politics, and Culture in the Kingdom of Dahomey* (Charlottesville: University Press of Virginia, 1998); Michael Angelo Gomez, *Exchanging our Country Marks: The Transformation of African Identities in the Colonial and Antebellum South* (Chapel Hill: University of North Carolina Press, 1998), 6; Alex Callinicos, "Marxism and Politics," in *What is Politics? The Activity and Its Study*, ed. Adrian Leftwich (Cambridge, UK: Polity Press, 2004), 59; Steven Hahn, *A Nation under Our Feet: Black Political Struggles in the Rural South, from Slavery to the Great Migration* (Cambridge, MA: Harvard University Press, 2003), 53–54 passim; Susan E. O'Donovan, "Trunk Lines, Land Lines, and Local Exchanges: Operationalizing the Grapevine Telegraph," paper presented at the Gilder Lehrman Center for the Study of Slavery, Resistance, and Abolition, Yale University, December 11, 2006; James Oakes, "The Political Significance of Slave Resistance," *History Workshop Journal* 22.1 (1986): 89–107; Walter Johnson: "On Agency," *Journal of Social History* 37.1 (2003): 113–24; Anthony E. Kaye, *Joining Places: Slave Neighborhoods in the Old South* (Chapel Hill: University of North Carolina Press, 2007), chap. 8. In places where land was plentiful, labor was scarce, and groups were vulnerable to slaving, a key strategy for providing security and developing resources was to assemble people into productive political groups. The most successful were those who turned around and raided for slaves as a defensive strategy in order to protect their clients and allies, but the underlying idea that human resources were of paramount importance could not have been lost on African Americans.

11. Robert Francis Engs, *Freedom's First Generation: Black Hampton, Virginia, 1861–1890* (New York: Fordham University Press, 2004), 11.

12. Crandall Schifflett, ed., *John Washington's Civil War: A Slave Narrative* (Baton Rouge: Louisiana State University Press, 2008), 10–11, 27–30, 39, 44–49.

13. Schifflett, ed., *John Washington's Civil War*, 44–49, 71–79.

Essay on Sources

Primary Sources

This book reexamines the development of the Chesapeake and coastal North Carolina over several decades from the points of view of the enslaved. Evidence comes largely from the formerly enslaved who published their narratives or told their stories to interviewers or amanuenses. In addition to relying on biographers' accounts and scholarship supporting their authenticity, I use contemporary records to confirm their reliability as primary sources. Often, names of owners or associates appeared in the federal census or contemporary newspapers. Using published slave narratives is risky, not the least because most published before 1865 were written with abolitionists' sponsorship. Subjects this book investigates in detail include Charles Ball, Solomon Bayley, Henry "Box" Brown, Frederick Douglass, London R. Ferebee, Moses Grandy, Harriet Jacobs, and William H. Robinson; it seeks to give readers of slave narratives a context for the stories they tell by linking the historical circumstances of authors.

Conventional readings of slave narratives, which are shaped by their abolitionist sponsors, map the struggle for freedom on flight to the north, obscuring the motivation to preserve families and keep them in place by struggling against a dynamic institution's powerful pull to the south. Through archival sources such as business records, newspapers, correspondence, and government documents, I have pieced together lives of the enslaved that illuminate surprising aspects of this history, aspects that do not fit into standard categories of analysis and to which the lives of Corinna Hinton Omohundro Davidson, Mary Lumpkin, and Ann Davis bear witness. To access other articulate witnesses among the formerly enslaved, I also use published primary sources such as John W. Blassingame, *Slave Testimony: Two Centuries of Letters, Speeches, Interviews, and Autobiographies* (Baton Rouge: Louisiana State University Press, 1977), Charles L. Perdue Jr., Thomas E. Barden, and Robert K. Phillips, eds., *Weevils in the Wheat: Interviews with Virginia Ex-Slaves* (Charlottesville: University Press of Virginia, 1976), and George P. Rawick, ed., *The American Slave: A Composite Autobiography* (Westport, CT: Greenwood Press, 1972–79).

This project would have been much more difficult to undertake without the full online text access to scores of relevant slave narratives and biographies provided by the Documenting the American South project at the University of North Carolina (UNC). I use several slave narratives digitized by UNC, including Charles Ball, *Slavery in the United States: A Narrative of the Life and Adventures of Charles Ball, a Black Man, Who Lived Forty Years in Maryland, South Carolina and Georgia, as a Slave Under Various Masters, and Was One Year in the Navy with Commodore Barney, during the Late War* (New York: John S. Taylor, 1837), Solomon Bayley, *Narrative of Some Remarkable Incidents in the Life of Solo-*

mon Bayley, Formerly a Slave in the State of Delaware, North America, Written by Himself, and Published for His Benefit, to Which Are Prefixed, a Few Remarks by Robert Hurnard, 2nd ed. (London: Harvey and Darton, 1825), Henry Box Brown, *Narrative of the Life of Henry Box Brown, Written by Himself* (Manchester, UK: Lee and Glynn, 1851), Noah Davis, *A Narrative of the Life of Rev. Noah Davis, a Colored Man, Written by Himself, at the Age of Fifty-Four* (Baltimore: J. F. Weishampel Jr., 1859), Frederick Douglass, *Narrative of the Life of Frederick Douglass, an American Slave, Written by Himself* (Boston: Anti-Slavery Office, 1845), Frederick Douglass, *My Bondage and My Freedom* (New York: Miller, Orton, and Mulligan, 1855), London R. Ferebee, *A Brief History of the Slave Life of Rev. L. R. Ferebee, and the Battles of Life, and Four Years of His Ministerial Life, Written from Memory, to 1882* (Raleigh, NC: Edwards, Broughton, 1882), Moses Grandy, *Narrative of the Life of Moses Grandy, Late a Slave in the United States of America* (London: Gilpin, 1843), Solomon Northup, *Twelve Years a Slave: Narrative of Solomon Northup, a Citizen of New-York, Kidnapped in Washington City in 1841, and Rescued in 1853.* (Auburn [NY]: Derby and Miller, 1853), Harriet Jacobs, *Incidents in the Life of a Slave Girl, Written by Herself*, ed. L. Maria Child (Boston: published for the author, 1861), James W. C. Pennington, *A Narrative of Events of the Life of J. H. Banks, an Escaped Slave, from the Cotton State, Alabama, in America* (Liverpool, UK: M. Rourke, 1861), William H. Robinson, *From Log Cabin to the Pulpit; or, Fifteen Years in Slavery*, 3rd ed. (Eau Claire, WI: James H. Tifft, 1913), Charles Stearns, *Narrative of Henry Box Brown, Who Escaped from Slavery* (Boston: Brown and Stearns, 1849), and J. B. Taylor, *Biography of Elder Lott Cary, Late Missionary to Africa* (Baltimore: Armstrong and Berry, 1837). My goal in using slave narratives or, as Paul Lovejoy more accurately calls them, freedom narratives, is to mine them for the quotidian details that reveal how enslaved people developed strategies to defend family members or else incorporate allies, patrons, and other resources into their networks.

The second group of primary sources includes records of slavers and the records of those who traded with them, such as business records, including banking, insurance, and credit records, and correspondence. This group of records sheds light on the culture of market actors, whether they be railroad companies, slave traders, hiring agents, or the enslaved interviewed by government agents or owned by railroads, for example. Correspondence and business records complement the perspectives of formerly enslaved authors and their abolitionist editors, often corroborating accounts and revealing the conditions under which the enslaved made their choices. Important collections include: U.S. Slavery Collection, American Antiquarian Society; Francis Everod Rives Papers, Duke University; the R. G. Dun and Company Collection, Harvard Business School; Robert Alonzo Brock Collection, Huntington Library; Papers of the Cornelius Chase Family, Manuscripts Division, Library of Congress; Silas Omohundro Papers, Library of Virginia; Bureau of Refugees, Freedmen, and Abandoned Lands Cohabitation Registers, Library of Virginia; railroad annual reports, 1856–60, Library of Virginia; St. Mary's County Court (Equity Papers), Maryland State Archives; daybook of the Richmond Police Guard, Small Library Special Collections, University of Virginia; accounts of Silas and R. H. Omohundro's slave trade, 1857–64, Small Library Special Collections, University of Virginia; account books, P. M. Tabb and Son, American Life Insurance Agency and Trust Company records, Virginia Historical Society; Dickinson, Hill, and Company accounts, Virginia Historical Society; Bureau of Refugees, Freedmen, and Abandoned Lands, Cohabitation Register for Caroline County, 1866, Central Rappahannock Heritage Center, Fredericksburg, Virginia. Susan O'Donovan graciously turned over her notes from the Ulrich Bonnell Phillips Papers at Yale University, which proved to be quite helpful.

The third and final important group of primary materials comes from online databases. For more than two decades, scholars have debated how computers and digital archives should influence historical research and writing. Recently, digital archives have provided historians with dazzling possibilities in the data that they make available and also powerful new tools for research. For this book, digital archives of newspapers turned up information that was able to shed light on slave narratives, for instance. Evidence of enslaved people's history is notoriously difficult to find since most did not leave a manuscript trail. This project might have involved hundreds of additional hours searching through microfilm reels were it not for online census and other data such as marriage and military records. The Library of Congress's American Memory website makes available thousands of documents relevant to this subject, including ex-slave testimony, recordings, and photographs. Court cases, which often include rich testimony, are available online as well through Lexis-Nexis. Other digital resources that have been particularly useful are America's Historical Newspapers, Early American Newspapers, Series 1, 1690–1876, Archive of Americana, published by Readex, a division of NewsBank; Ancestry.com; and the Historical Census Browser, Geospatial and Statistical Center, University of Virginia.

Secondary Sources

Recent scholarship on the United States domestic slave trade has placed markets for and movements of enslaved Americans at the center of the history of North American slavery rather than on the peripheries. Guiding my approach to the subject are Walter Johnson, *Soul by Soul: Life Inside the Antebellum Slave Market* (Cambridge, MA: Harvard University Press, 1999), Phillip D. Troutman, "Slave Trade and Sentiment" (PhD diss., University of Virginia, 2000), and a pair of articles, Edward E. Baptist, " 'Stol' and Fetched Here': Enslaved Migration: Ex-Slave Narratives, and Vernacular History," in *New Studies in the History of American Slavery*, ed. Edward E. Baptist and Stephanie M. H. Camp (Athens: University of Georgia Press, 2006), 243–74, and Laura F. Edwards, "Status without Rights: African Americans and the Tangled History of Law and Governance in the Nineteenth-Century U.S. South," *American Historical Review* 112.2 (2007): 365–93. Johnson, Troutman, Baptist, and Edwards investigate slavery starting with the enslaved.

I draw on Ira Berlin's magisterial syntheses, *Generations of Captivity: A History of African-American Slaves* (Cambridge, MA: Harvard University Press, 2003) and *Many Thousands Gone: The First Two Centuries of Slavery in North America* (Cambridge, MA: Harvard University Press, 1998), for periodization. Steven Deyle's comprehensive book on the domestic slave trade, *Carry Me Back: The Domestic Slave Trade in American Life* (New York: Oxford University Press, 2005), supplies many of the critical details and contexts.

Viewing the upper and lower South as distinct and complementary, Robert H. Gudmestad, *A Troublesome Commerce: The Transformation of the Interstate Slave Trade* (Baton Rouge: Louisiana State University Press, 2003), and James David Miller, *South by Southwest: Planter Emigration and Identity in the Slave South* (Charlottesville: University of Virginia Press, 2002), are instructive guides to the meanings of movements of slaves and slaveholders within the American South. Michael Tadman, *Speculators and Slaves:*

Masters, Traders, and Slaves in the Old South (Madison: University of Wisconsin Press, 1989), is an indispensable guide to the business of slave trading and the effects on enslaved families. Scholarship on slave hiring and slavery in specialized enterprises that informs this book's analyses include: Jonathan D. Martin, *Divided Mastery: Slave Hiring in the American South* (Cambridge, MA: Harvard University Press, 2004), Charles B. Dew, *Bond of Iron: Master and Slave at Buffalo Forge* (New York: Norton, 1994), Midori Takagi, *"Rearing Wolves to Our Own Destruction": Slavery in Richmond, Virginia, 1782–1865* (Charlottesville: University Press of Virginia, 1999), and Susanne G. Schnittman, "Slavery in Virginia's Urban Tobacco Industry, 1840–1860" (PhD diss., University of Rochester, 1987). Dew forges a richly textured and compelling narrative of the economic culture of slavery in central Virginia's ironworks. Takagi shrewdly investigates the working culture of slaves in Richmond's commercial processing industry, and Schnittman gives life to slave labor culture in tobacco factories.

My guides to the ins and outs of the railroad and maritime industries are: Aaron Marrs, *Railroads in the Old South: Pursuing Progress in a Slave Society* (Baltimore: Johns Hopkins University Press, 2009), and David S. Cecelski, *The Waterman's Song: Slavery and Freedom in Maritime North Carolina* (Chapel Hill: University of North Carolina Press, 2001). Marrs's stellar study of southern railroad development shapes my analysis of enslaved people working on the railroad, and Cecelski's careful investigation of enslaved boatmen makes sense of the commercial enterprises in which slaves took part in northeastern North Carolina. Jeffrey Bolster, *Black Jacks: African American Seamen in the Age of Sail* (Cambridge, MA: Harvard University Press, 1998), presents a muscular and memorable portrait of African Americans in one of the few occupations in which their talents were integral and recognized by contemporaries.

Scholarship on enslaved families has been of primary importance. Dylan C. Penningroth, *Claims of Kinfolk: African American Property and Community in the Nineteenth-Century South* (Chapel Hill: University of North Carolina Press, 2002), in many ways shapes this book's analysis of enslaved people's family life and culture. Penningroth's "My People, My People: The Dynamics of Community in Southern Slavery," in *New Studies in the History of American Slavery*, exposes interconnections between enslaved people's market participation and the law. Herbert Gutman, *The Black Family in Slavery and Freedom, 1750–1925* (New York: Pantheon, 1976), is still foundational. Brenda E. Stevenson, *Life in Black and White: Family and Community in the Slave South* (New York: Oxford University Press, 1996), illuminates the intricate, unexpected interconnections among enslaved families within a single county, and these connections indicate broader patterns of African American life in the coastal upper South. Stephanie M. H. Camp, *Closer to Freedom: Enslaved Women and Everyday Resistance in the Plantation South* (Chapel Hill: University of North Carolina Press, 2004), and Jennifer L. Morgan, *Laboring Women: Reproduction and Gender in New World Slavery* (Philadelphia: University of Pennsylvania Press, 2004), offer illuminating perspectives and persuasive arguments concerning African American women's connections, culture, and reproduction.

Useful counterpoints to the coastal upper South are Wilma A. Dunaway's related studies, *The African American Family in Slavery and Emancipation* (Cambridge: Cambridge University Press, 2003) and *Slavery in the American Mountain South* (Cambridge: Cambridge University Press, 2003). Dunaway's work on the structure of enslaved families informs the arguments in this book. Annette Gordon-Reed, *The Hemingses of Monticello: An American Family* (New York: Norton, 2008), and Joshua D. Rothman, *Notorious in the*

Neighborhood: Sex and Families Across the Color Line in Virginia (Chapel Hill: University of North Carolina Press, 2003), are essential to a critical understanding of family life in a slave society. Marie Jenkins Schwartz, *Born in Bondage: Growing Up Enslaved in the Antebellum South* (Cambridge, MA: Harvard University Press, 2000), and Wilma King, *Stolen Childhood: Slave Youth in Nineteenth-Century America* (Bloomington: Indiana University Press, 1995), ground my contentions regarding children in slavery. Sharla Fett, *Working Cures: Healing, Health, and Power on Southern Slave Plantations* (Chapel Hill: University of North Carolina Press, 2002), reveals that the enslaved viewed healing and health in very different ways than did slaveholders. Her thesis suggests the broader mutual misunderstandings at the heart of antebellum southern society.

Two other works, Barbara Jeanne Fields, *Slavery and Freedom on the Middle Ground: Maryland in the Nineteenth Century* (New Haven: Yale University Press, 1985), and Deborah Gray White's classic, *Ar'n't I A Woman? Female Slaves in the Plantation South*, 2nd ed. (New York: Norton, 1999), pose significant challenges to the arguments this book advances. In the process of learning that there is much to argue with in these books, I have discovered that it is nearly impossible to stand on the shoulders of giants without at some point standing on their toes. Sterling Stuckey, *Slave Culture: Nationalist Theory and the Foundations of Black America* (New York: Oxford University Press, 1987), has guided my thinking on slave culture as interplay between historical process and cultural heritage. As a study in the racial dimensions of culture in antebellum Virginia, Melvin Patrick Ely, *Israel on the Appomattox: A Southern Experiment in Black Freedom from 1790s through the Civil War* (New York: Knopf, 2004), has been exceedingly helpful. Sorting out the limits of what enslaved people could do under the constraints of violence, law, and their historically contingent circumstances proves less difficult than it initially seems it might under the guidance of James C. Scott, *Weapons of the Weak: Everyday Forms of Peasant Resistance* (New Haven: Yale University Press, 1985), and Walter Johnson, "On Agency," *Journal of Social History* 37.1 (2003): 113–24.

On gender and labor in the transition from slavery to emancipation, two superb books shape this study: Lynda Morgan, *Emancipation in Virginia's Tobacco Belt, 1850–1870* (Athens: University of Georgia Press, 1992), and Susan E. O'Donovan, *Becoming Free in the Cotton South* (Cambridge, MA: Harvard University Press, 2007). O'Donovan's brilliant investigation at the intersection of gender and postwar economics is a model of scholarship. A pair of articles to which I have returned many times are Wayne K. Durrill, "Routine of Seasons: Labour Regimes and Social Ritual in an Antebellum Plantation Community," *Slavery and Abolition* 16.2 (1995): 161–87, and Wayne K. Durrill, "Slavery, Kinship, and Dominance: The Black Community at Somerset Place Plantation, 1786–1860," *Slavery and Abolition* 13.2 (1992): 1–19. Durrill details the agricultural rhythms of a particular plantation and tracks family life across time, showing exceptional sensitivity to the points of view of those enslaved in northeastern North Carolina. Jessica Millward, "'A Choice Parcel of Country Born': Slave Women and the Transition to Freedom in Revolutionary Maryland" (PhD diss., University of California, Los Angeles, 2003), is compelling as well.

Works that have supplied the broader contexts for slavery and slaving in North America include Robin Blackburn, *The Making of New World Slavery: From the Baroque to the Modern, 1492–1800* (London: Verso, 1996), and David Eltis, *Economic Growth and the Ending of the Transatlantic Slave Trade* (New York: Oxford University Press, 1987). Ira Berlin and Philip D. Morgan, eds., *Cultivation and Culture: Labor and the Shaping of Black Life in the Americas* (Charlottesville: University Press of Virginia, 1993), especially Lorena S. Walsh's article, "Slave Life, Slave Society, and Tobacco Production in the Tidewater Chesapeake, 1620–1820," 170–99, has provided critical contexts, as has Stephanie E. Smallwood, *Saltwater Slavery: A Middle Passage from Africa to American Diaspora* (Cambridge, MA: Harvard University Press, 2007).

Two critical books on the importance of slavery in the formative experience of British North America are Edmund S. Morgan, *American Slavery, American Freedom: The Ordeal of Colonial Virginia* (New York: Norton, 1975), and Anthony S. Parent Jr., *Foul Means: The Formation of a Slave Society in Virginia, 1660–1740* (Chapel Hill: published for the Omohundro Institute of Early American History and Culture by the University of North Carolina Press, 2003). Influential books on the contexts that locate enslaved people on the social and political landscape, which inform my thinking about the place of slavery in United States history, include Robert William Fogel, *Without Consent or Contract: The Rise and Fall of American Slavery*, vol. 1 (New York: Norton, 1989), Robert W. Fogel and Stanley Engerman, *Time on the Cross: The Economics of American Negro Slavery* (New York: Norton, 1989 [1974]), Melvyn Stokes and Stephen Conway, eds., *The Market Revolution in America* (Charlottesville: University Press of Virginia, 1996), and Philip J. Schwarz, *Twice Condemned: Slaves and the Criminal Laws of Virginia, 1705–1865* (Baton Rouge: Louisiana State University Press, 1988).

Gavin Wright, *Slavery and American Economic Development* (Baton Rouge: Louisiana State University Press, 2006), guides my framing of economic issues regarding slavery and offers a compelling counterpoint to my argument. On the political economy of cotton production and commerce, I found two books in particular very enlightening. Brian Schoen, *The Fragile Fabric of Union: Cotton, Federal Politics, and the Global Origins of the Civil War* (Baltimore: Johns Hopkins University Press, 2009), is a work of excellent scholarship and elegant writing, and Timothy C. Jacobson and George David Smith, *Cotton's Renaissance: A Study in Market Innovation* (Cambridge: Cambridge University Press, 2001), is a fine history. John Lauritz Larson, *The Market Revolution in America: Liberty, Ambition, and the Eclipse of the Common Good* (New York: Cambridge University Press, 2010), admirably responds to Charles G. Sellers's classic, *The Market Revolution: Jacksonian America, 1815–1846* (New York: Oxford University Press, 1991).

The following four books on the United States political economy during this period are particularly instructive: Daniel Walker Howe, *What Hath God Wrought: The Transformation of America, 1815–1848* (New York: Oxford University Press, 2007), John Ashworth, *Slavery, Capitalism, and Politics in the Antebellum Republic*, vol. 1: *Commerce and Compromise, 1820–1850* (Cambridge: Cambridge University Press, 1995), Nicholas Onuf and Peter S. Onuf, *Nations, Markets, and War: Modern History and the American Civil War.* (Charlottesville: University of Virginia Press, 2006), and Adam Rothman, *Slave Country: American Expansion and the Origins of the Deep South* (Cambridge, MA: Harvard University Press, 2005). Howe provides a richly textured account of the political, social, and economic history of a critical period in United States history. Ashworth advances an elegant thesis, and Rothman offers a persuasive explanation regarding the formation of the lower South. Seth Rockman, *Scraping By: Wage Labor, Slavery, and Survival in Early Baltimore* (Baltimore: Johns Hopkins University Press, 2009), is an outstanding work of political economy and labor history of ordinary people, which explains as much about the United States generally as it does about its corner of that republic.

With regard to politics, I am indebted to William W. Freehling's account of the many "Souths" within the slave South. His *Road to Disunion*, vol. 1: *Secessionists at Bay, 1776–1854* (New York: Oxford University Press, 1990), and *The Road to Disunion*, vol. 2: *Secessionists Triumphant, 1854–1861* (New York: Oxford University Press, 2007), carry forward a political narrative in a convincing manner and also demonstrate the connections between contingent events as well as their larger ramifications. Laura F. Edwards's analysis in both "Status without Rights" and her excellent "Enslaved Women and the Law: Paradoxes of Subordination in the post-Revolutionary Carolinas," *Slavery and Abolition* 26.2 (2005): 305–23, of slaves' legal status versus their civic standing shapes my understanding of the issue. A classic work, Ulrich Bonnell Phillips, *Life and Labor in the Old South* (Columbia: University of South Carolina Press, 2007 [1930]), proves a useful guide, even though I reject his characterizations of the enslaved. Steven Hahn, *A Nation under Our Feet: Black Political Struggles in the Rural South, from Slavery to the Great Migration* (Cambridge, MA: Harvard University Press, 2003), and Susan E. O'Donovan, "Trunk Lines, Land Lines, and Local Exchanges: Operationalizing the Grapevine Telegraph," unpublished paper presented at the Gilder Lehrman Center for the Study of Slavery, Resistance, and Abolition, Yale University, December 11, 2006, has directed my thinking about the politics of African Americans in slavery and beyond.

State and local histories bolster much of the analysis here. A pair of books on Delaware is essential for understanding this small state with big resonances: Patience Essah, *A House Divided: Slavery and Emancipation in Delaware, 1625–1865* (Charlottesville: University Press of Virginia, 1996), and William H. Williams, *Slavery and Freedom in Delaware, 1639–1865* (Wilmington, DE: Scholarly Imprint Resources, 1996). William Link, *Roots of Secession: Slavery and Politics in Antebellum Virginia* (Chapel Hill: University of North Carolina Press, 2003), advances a seductive argument in a provocative analysis of the connections between enslaved people's agency and political changes. John Majewski, *A House Dividing: Economic Development in Pennsylvania and Virginia before the Civil War* (New York: Cambridge University Press, 2000), provides useful comparisons of related but differently oriented industrial developments. An essential guide to Richmond before the Civil War is Gregg D. Kimball, *American City, Southern Place: A Cultural History of Antebellum Richmond* (Athens: University of Georgia Press, 2000). A quite informative pair of books on coastal North Carolina cities are very helpful to accessing local complexities: Alex Christopher Meekins, *Elizabeth City, North Carolina, and the Civil War: A History of Battle and Occupation* (Charleston, SC: History Press, 2007), and Alan D. Watson, *Wilmington, North Carolina, to 1861* (Jefferson, NC: McFarland, 2003).

Proponents of actor-network theory help to conceptualize the ties that bound people to other people and to resources and in the process make sense of such abstractions as the market. Bruno Latour, *Reassembling the Social: An Introduction to Actor-Network-Theory* (New York: Oxford University Press, 2005), is edifying. My analysis of the enslaved as market actors benefits from essays in John Law and John Hassard, eds., *Actor Network Theory and After* (Oxford: Blackwell, 1999). Quirky but provocative, Annamarie Mol and Jessica Mesman, "Neonatal Food and the Politics of Theory: Some Questions on Method," *Social Studies of Science* 26.2 (1996): 419–44, offers a way to think about networks and alliances or axes of difference therein. According to anthropologists and historians working on enslaved families, networks were kinship ties. John W. Blassingame, *The Slave Community: Plantation Life in the Antebellum South* (New York: Oxford University Press, 1972), Herbert Gutman, *The Black Family in Slavery and Freedom, 1750–1925* (New York: Pantheon Books, 1976), and Sidney W. Mintz and Richard Price, *The Birth of African-American Culture: An Anthropological Perspective* (Boston: Beacon Press, 1992), construe networks as kinship networks. Anthony E. Kaye, *Joining Places: Slave Neighborhoods in the Old South* (Chapel Hill: University of North Carolina Press, 2007), provides insights into how to conceptualize associations in terms of neighborhoods that account for associations, alliances, and animosities across lines of race, class, and gender.

My analyses of economic culture and society in early America are informed by Ellen Hartigan-O'Connor, *The Ties That Buy: Women and Commerce in Revolutionary America* (Philadelphia: University of Pennsylvania Press, 2009). On kidnapping, Carol Wilson, *Freedom at Risk: The Kidnapping of Free Blacks in America, 1800–1865* (Lexington: University of Kentucky Press, 1994), is insightful. Edward L. Ayers, *Vengeance and Justice: Crime and Punishment in the Nineteenth-Century American South* (New York: Oxford University Press, 1984), remains an authority on the subject. Race is a supple and dynamic historical concept. Douglas R. Egerton, *Gabriel's Rebellion: The Virginia Slave Conspiracies of 1800 and 1802* (Chapel Hill: University of North Carolina Press, 1993), and James Sidbury, *Ploughshares into Swords: Race, Rebellion, and Identity in Gabriel's Virginia, 1730–1810* (Cambridge: Cambridge University Press, 1997), undergird my arguments concerning historical issues of race in Virginia. Eva Sheppard Wolf, *Race and Liberty in the New Nation: Emancipation in Virginia from the Revolution to Nat Turner's Rebellion* (Baton Rouge: Louisiana State University Press, 2006), complements Egerton's and Sidbury's focus on rebellions. In thinking about race as a category of analysis, David Brion Davis, *Inhuman Bondage: The Rise and Fall of Slavery in the New World* (New York: Oxford University Press, 2006), and George M. Fredrickson, *The Black Image in the White Mind: The Debate on Afro-American Character and Destiny, 1817–1914* (New York: Harper and Row, 1971), are essential, as is Anthony Parent's discussion of the historical complexities in *Foul Means.*

On slave narratives, I have found the following books indispensable. William L. Andrews, *To Tell a Free Story: The First Century of Afro-American Autobiography, 1760–1865* (Urbana and Chicago: University of Illinois Press, 1986), and William L. Andrews, ed., *North Carolina Slave Narratives: The Lives of Moses Roper, Lunsford Lane, Moses Grandy, and Thomas H. Jones* (Chapel Hill: University of North Carolina Press, 2003). The classic work on slave narratives, Marion Wilson Starling, *The Slave Narrative: Its Place in American History*, 2nd ed. (Washington, DC: Howard University Press, 1988), is also a useful work. In addition, I rely on several extraordinary biographies, including William S. McFeely, *Frederick Douglass* (New York: Norton, 1991), Jean Fagan Yellin, *Harriet Jacobs: A Life* (New York: Basic Books, 2004), and Jeffrey Ruggles, *The Unboxing of Henry Brown* (Richmond: Library of Virginia, 2003).

Scholarship on which I rely that has not yet been published, whose authors were kind enough to share with me, include Edward E. Baptist's book on forced migration and its central place within the early United States political economy, Walter Johnson's book on slavery in the cotton industry in the Mississippi Valley, William G. Thomas III's book on railroads and the Civil War, and Wayne K. Durrill's book on Nat Turner's rebellion. Historians are better at explaining the past than predicting the future, but all four will be important books.

Writing history is a challenge, but there are some excellent models that balance narrative interest with analytical heft. Joseph C. Miller, *Way of Death: Merchant Capitalism and the Angolan Slave Trade, 1730–1830* (Madison: University of Wisconsin Press, 1988), details the incremental, awful, and unintended consequences of the rise of eighteenth-century merchant capitalism in the Atlantic world in the grim shape of the south Atlantic slave trade. Other models for writing included Johnson, *Soul by Soul*, Penningroth, *The Claims of Kinfolk*, and Rhys Isaac, *The Transformation of Virginia, 1740–1790* (Chapel Hill: published for the Institute of Early American History and Culture by the University of North Carolina Press, 1982). Isaac peers into the front parlors, back bedrooms, slave quarters, churches, and fields of eighteenth-century Virginia with an anthropologist's eye, taking in small details and revealing their larger social importance. Attempting to detail the everyday experiences of African Americans, I model Baptist, " 'Stol' and Fetched Here.' " For how to think about the relationship between digital scholarship and history, I draw on William G. Thomas III and Edward L. Ayers, "An Overview: The Differences Slavery Made: A Close Analysis of Two American Communities," *American Historical Review* 108.5 (2003): 1299–1307. The inspiration for this book's style is Edward L. Ayers's *In the Presence of Mine Enemies: The Civil War in the Heart of America, 1859–1863* (New York: Norton, 2003). Tracing networks among enslaved people through time entails both undertaking the kind of detective work that Isaac displays in *The Transformation of Virginia* and engaging with the subtle and exhilarating new ways of thinking about the interconnectedness of historical actors exemplified in *In the Presence of Mine Enemies*.

Index